Pianos and Politics in China

Pianos and Politics in China

Middle-Class Ambitions
and the Struggle
over Western Music

Richard Curt Kraus

New York   Oxford
OXFORD UNIVERSITY PRESS
1989

Oxford University Press

Oxford   New York   Toronto
Delhi   Bombay   Calcutta   Madras   Karachi
Petaling Jaya   Singapore   Hong Kong   Tokyo
Nairobi   Dar es Salaam   Cape Town
Melbourne   Auckland

and associated companies in
Berlin   Ibadan

Published by Oxford University Press, Inc.,
200 Madison Avenue, New York, New York 10016

Oxford is a registered trademark of Oxford University Press

Library of Congress Cataloging-in-Publication Data
Kraus, Richard Curt.
Pianos and politics in China.
Includes index.
1. Music—20th century—China—Political aspects.
2. Music and state—China. 3. China—Cultural policy.
4. Musicians—China—Bibliography. I. Title.
ML336.5.K72   1989   780'.951   88-25251
ISBN 0-19-505836-4

9 8 7 6 5 4 3 2 1

Printed in the United States of America

This song is dedicated to my parents,
Joe W. and Betsy C. Kraus

Preface

During China's Cultural Revolution, the piano was likened to a coffin, in which notes rattled about like the bones of the bourgeoisie. This harsh assessment of an instrument which has been one of the proud carriers of Western musical culture has been attributed to Mao Zedong's widow, Jiang Qing. In fact, Jiang had a soft spot in her heart for pianos, which she helped save from Red Guard destruction, although she felt no affection for the music written for the piano by European composers. The piano became the object of hostile attention because it is *the* Western musical instrument, only tentatively rooted in a society busily rejecting Western influence. Moreover, the piano makes a poor fit with Chinese culture, even compared to, say, the violin, oil painting, or ball-room dancing. The piano is industrial; it rose to prominence with Europe's bourgeoisie. Possessing a remarkable facility for harmony, and with its tonal intervals permanently fixed to the Western twelve-note chromatic scale, it incorporates a non-Chinese aesthetic. But most important, the piano's social base in China was weak and vulnerable. Those who owned and played the piano were urban, prosperous, intellectual, and removed from China's traditional culture.

Two decades later, many of these same factors have turned the piano and other Western musical instruments into emblems of modernization. Western music is flourishing; Beijing has opened China's first modern concert hall, and winners of international music prizes are hailed for contributing to China's international prestige. A 1986 film, *The Fascinating Village Band,* featured peasants who purchase trumpets and trombones; newly prosperous from Deng Xiaoping's economic reforms, they use European music to demonstrate their acquisition of modern culture.

This book is not just about pianos, but about the Chinese people who enjoy playing and listening to pianos, clarinets, violas, accordions, and all the other instruments that make up Western musical culture. Because China's reception of European culture has been volatile, the minority community of lovers of Western music often has been embattled. This book explores not only their story, but also the broader issue of China's participation in an international culture born in Europe, the home of its former oppressors.

Western music's first point of vulnerability is its foreignness in a century of China's rebellion against foreign domination. The vigorous broom of Chinese nationalism has swept roughly over the music of Beethoven and Debussy; many have viewed these examples of Western art as dirt left behind by cultural imperialism, to be cleansed for the sake of China's autonomy and dignity. The ways in which Chinese enthusiasts for European music have responded to this challenge and survived is an important part of the story which follows.

The second weight bearing against the West's music is social. The sounds of Chopin and Tchaikovsky are alien to the peasant majority of China's population, while the minority which embraces such music has often been object of suspicion and hostility in China's revolutionary century. Our Western music does not simply float acrosss China to all ears alike, but instead is especially beloved by the members of the urban middle class. By examining the music of that class, we can better understand the ambiguities of middle-class China. Alien yet patriotic, revolutionary yet elitist, this class continues to be alternately admired and resented in China today.

Western music is marginal to Chinese culture, yet it is closely connected to the center of China's politics by the issues it raises, and by the personal and institutional connections on which it rests. These complex relationships have varied with the changing power of the urban middle class. Because the status of its urban and middle-class patrons has varied so greatly, Western culture has had a highly unstable reception in China. The careers of individual artists are inevitably buffeted by these political waves, but offer a vantage from which to view the complex interaction of culture and politics in modern China.

I have made the abstractions of cultural conflict more concrete by organizing this book around the lives of four important Chinese musicians whose careers embody the contradictions of Western culture and Chinese politics. First is the composer Xian Xinghai. Before his death in Moscow in 1945, he studied at the Paris Conservatory, wrote movie music in Shanghai, and joined the Communist Party in Yan'an. His short but eventful career provides a useful starting point for discussing the place of Western music in China before the Communist victory in 1949.

The other three, Fou Ts'ong, Yin Chengzong, and Liu Shikun, are the great virtuoso pianists to emerge in the People's Republic of China. They are contemporaries, each winning international fame between 1955 and 1962, whose careers have intersected at many points. The Chinese value international prizes as evidence that Asia's musicians can master the art of the West. Each of these pianists has enjoyed eminence in China for his European successes, but each has also endured political opprobrium. While their musical successes have been similar, their notorieties have been distinctive, reflecting their different ways of relating to China's politics. Fou Ts'ong defected in 1959, then returned to China after a twenty-year exile in Europe. Yin Chengzong embraced the radical politics of the Cultural Revolution, only to be purged after the death of Mao Zedong and then to renew his career in the United States. Liu Shikun married the daughter of Ye Jianying, one of the founders of the Red Army, and China's head of state after the Cultural Revolution. His musical career rose and fell along with Ye's political fate. Ye is now dead, and Liu recently languished in jail, charged with corruption.

These four biographies are set amidst topical chapters in which I develop three major themes. First, I place China's cultural conflicts in an international perspective; disputes over Third World pianos cannot be understood without reference to China's place at the farthest edge of an expanding Western international order. What is the political significance of Chinese speaking the so-called "international language" of European music? Europe's nineteenth century bourgeoisie enjoyed music as an art, but also used its symbols for social and political purposes. China's weaker middle class attempted to repeat this process, but with very different effects. China's experience forces a reconsideration of the comfortable old saw that music is the international language. On the contrary, music typically is a highly national form of expression. The international-language myth arises only from the perspective of powerful nations, whose often well-intentioned citizens need to prettify their cultural influence over weaker peoples. If music were indeed so international, Americans should be able to hear Chinese opera as easily as the people of Shanghai can now hear Beethoven. The cultural sharing that takes place is most frequently on Western terms, as the stronger partner of the relationship.

Second, although China's cosmopolitan and modernizing musical leadership has often been overwhelmed by the recurring political demand for cultural populism, there has nonetheless been a steady Westernization of Chinese music. Cosmopolitan musical leaders seek to minimize the impact of traditional Chinese musical practices, arguing that modern music, like modern science, must meet international standards. Populist politians often seek to encourage musicians to develop a distinctive Chinese music, minimizing the impact of the West, yet they remain suspicious of remnants from China's ''feudal'' culture. Even the Cultural Revolution continued the Westernizing trend; despite its ban on European composers, political leaders such as Jiang Qing promoted Western instruments, harmony, and choral singing.

Third, much recent scholarly and journalistic writing on China's intellectuals presents these cultural cosmopolitans simply as passive victims of political repression. I offer a more subtly shaded image of China's middle-class intellectuals, showing their energy and ambition as well as their vulnerability. These sophisticates are politically important beyond their numbers, and have been both honored and humiliated in the previous generation's political turbulence. Their skills make them important for China's industrialization, but their elitism and hostility toward China's native arts breeds resentment toward the urban middle class in a nation which is still strongly influenced by the Communists' populist revolution. The fate of Brahms and Berlioz in China is tied directly to the political position of this Western-oriented elite.

Music is a disembodied and transitory art. Although much of the music I discuss has been recorded, many pieces have not been available to me. Even when I can listen to a recording or look at a score, the social experience which makes this music politically interesting is lost. I have compensated for this loss by turning to the written record. In addition to ordinary difficulties presented by Chinese political sources, I have been faced with the hyperbolic language of press agents and music critics. The talents of currently favored musicians (dead or alive) are routinely exaggerated, while musicians in disgrace are either ignored or discussed in vicious terms, forcing me to read between a larger number of lines than usual, even for the study of Chinese politics.

Interviews with current and former residents of the People's Republic of China have helped me make sense of the written record. Unlike Americans, who sometimes cannot easily imagine that this has been a serious research project, Chinese immediately grasp the links between the worlds of politics and art. Their love of gossip about both has been one of the pleasures of my research. I have altered the identity of many of these informants in order to protect them and their families against possible embarrassment or harassment.

I am a political scientist, not a musicologist; I am interested less in the character of the music I discuss than in the controversies which surround it. Nevertheless, readers are entitled to my biases about the Chinese musical world I analyze. Is this music any good? This book's three pianists are certainly great, and often have been so acclaimed by Chinese and non-Chinese critics. But what about all the Yellow River Cantatas and Long March Symphonies that have been written and performed in China as its composers seek to add their voices to those of Haydn and Liszt? There are still very few Chinese compositions that sound remarkable to Western ears. Many surely are no less boring or silly than much Western music of recent decades. Even much of our own beloved classical tradition is also disappointing sometimes. It is unfair to compare modern Chinese music only to Mozart and Brahms, forgetting both failed contemporary experiments and such historical embarrassments as our ghastly and mostly forgotten tradition of battle music (Beethoven's *Wellington's Victory* is the leading survival). In addition, the best of our music is often wedded to texts every bit as horrible as those used by China's composers. Schubert, for instance, freely set bad poetry along with his songs of Goethe and Heine. And both Schubert (in *Rosamunde*) and Carl Maria von Weber (in *Euryanthe*) collaborated with the absurd dramatist Helmine von Chezy, whose texts are as silly as any ode to the Great Leap Forward. Whatever one thinks of China joining international concert life, no one ought sneer because China has yet to produce a Schubert, Stravinsky, or Messiaen. Few countries have, and we seem to have run short of such talents in the West today.

I have used *pinyin* romanization throughout the book, except when individuals are known by other forms (Fou Ts'ong, Ma Sitson, Chou

Wen-chung). I have changed other romanizations in some quotations for the sake of consistency. Unless otherwise noted, all translations are my own.

Many individuals and institutions have helped me as I have worked on this book. Research materials, advice, and answers to my questions flowed kindly from David Bachman, Elizabeth Bernard, Marc Blecher, Caitriona Bolster, Francoise Calin, Arif Dirlik, Lowell Dittmer, John Dolfin, Joe Esherick, George Fencl, Ellen Judd, Hee-jin Kim, Steve Kohl, Kung Wen-kai, Ellen Johnston Laing, Jane Larson, Wendy Larson, Lee Wei-chin, Mao Yu-run, Maurice Meisner, Liang Mingyue, Colin Mackerras, Barry Naughton, Stan Rosen, Mark Russell, Sherwin Simmons, Dorothy Solinger, Jonathan Spence, Robert Trotter, Reeve Vanneman, Janet Wasko, Isabel Wong, Lynn White, Xu Luo, Ye Wa, and Michael and Jeanine Zenge. I have been assisted as well by several individuals in China who would prefer that their conversations remain private, and whose identities I have sometimes concealed with psuedonyms. Yin Chengzong graciously agreed to answer my questions about his career on several occasions. The Universities Service Centre of Hong Kong, and its director, John Dolfin, provided me with both desk space and stimulation, as it has countless others. My colleagues in political science and Asian studies at the University of Oregon humored me in many ways. Joe Esherick, Sue Glover, Ellen Johnston Laing, Colin Mackerras, and Barry Naughton offered detailed suggestions for improving my prose and my arguments. My wife, Mary Erbaugh, did this in addition to tolerating cheerfully the constant intrusion of my musical and political obsessions into her own life. Parts of this book were tried out in talks at Columbia University and Duke University. I thank Edwin Winckler and Arif Dirlik for making this possible. In Washington, Robert Teng and Mi Chu Wiens of the Asian Division of the Library of Congress helped me find essential materials. The Conservatoire Nationale Supérieur de Musique provided important information. Generous grants and fellowships from the National Endowment for the Humanities, the Fulbright-Hayes Faculty Research Abroad Program, and the University of Oregon sustained my research. Time for writing the book was provided by a grant from the Joint Committee on Chinese Studies of the American Council of Learned Societies and the Social Science Research Council, financed in part by the Ford Foundation, the Andrew W. Mellon Foundation, and the National Endowment for the Humanities. None of these

people or organizations should be blamed for factual errors remaining
in this book. Nor should I, for that matter. I have done the best I can,
but the Chinese government often treats its policies on the arts as if
they are military secrets; this has forced me to rely more than I would
have wished on gossip and sometimes-speculative Hong Kong sources.
But the refrain of art's bond to politics resounds clearly enough through
any lingering inaccuracies.

Eugene, Oregon   R. C. K.
March 1989

Contents

Pianos and Politics in China

1

Cosmopolitan Culture at Capitalism's Periphery

Western music spread to the rest of the world as Europe's power grew in the aftermath of the twin revolutions of capitalism and industrialization. China lies far at the outreaches of Europe's influence, yet even the Celestial Empire began to adopt Western music.[1] But however attractive the sounds of our culture may be, the Chinese did not adopt them for aesthetic reasons alone. Soldiers, merchants, and missionaries brought European music along with them as they fought, sold, and preached their way through the Orient. They encountered a native Chinese music very different in its assumptions, and also an emerging Chinese middle class that adopted aspects of European culture both as an emblem of its own modernity and as a key to transforming its weak and impoverished nation.

The Origins of Western Music in China

Europe's early diplomatic missions to China included musicians to awe the Chinese with their ceremony. Among the ninety-five members of the notorious embassy of the British Lord Macartney in 1793–1794 were five German musicians, who played two violins, a viola, a violoncello, a bassoon, two basset-horns, a clarinet, a German flute, and a fife, supplied by the pioneer musicologist, Charles Burney.[2] This seems a sweetly harmonious ensemble, but as the Chinese came to know less friendly and better armed expeditions, they learned also the martial sounds of trumpets and drums in a military band. By the 1880s, Beijing residents were familiar with the band maintained by Robert Hart, the Irishman imposed upon the Chinese to head their customs service.[3] Indeed, by the time the Qing dynasty collapsed in 1911, the warlord armies that salvaged pieces of its authority all had brass bands, just as their officers copied the gaudy uniforms of the imperialist armies.[4]

Christian missionaries had once been more important than soldiers and diplomats in introducing Western music to China. The Jesuit Matteo Ricci, determined to win China to Christianity by converting its leaders, patiently hauled a primitive harpsichord across China from 1583 until he was allowed to present it to the emperor in 1601. Ricci also brought along a harpsichordist to train four of the emperor's eunuch musicians. Ricci and the eunuchs composed eight songs in Chinese for the entertainment and edification of the emperor.[5] Other Jesuits followed Ricci's example in using music to charm the mandarins into tasting Christianity; Grimaldi and Pereira presented both a harpsichord and an organ to the Kangxi emperor, which he asked them to play for him in 1679.[6]

Western music was spread more widely after Britain humiliated China in the Opium War in 1839. The subsequent series of unjust treaties forced China to open its cities to Westerners so that they might sell addictive drugs and preach the Christian religion, in addition to engaging in more ordinary commercial activities. Thousands of missionaries came to China with pianos for thumping out hymns to save heathen souls. Among these heathen was Hong Xiuquan, leader of the Taiping Rebellion. Prefiguring the revolutionary uses of Westernized music in the twentieth century, Hong adopted the Protestant hymn "Old Hundred" as an anthem for his "Heavenly Kingdom."[7]

The Western merchants who first came to China were notable more for their interest in profit than in art. By European standards they formed a rough crowd, and only slowly felt the need to add music to their expatriate communities.[8] At first this meant more bands; in 1879 a municipal public band was started in Shanghai by a German professor and six other European musicians. By 1907 the band had become the Shanghai Municipal Symphony Orchestra.[9] The increasingly respectable Western community also imported pianos as its members attempted to recreate in the treaty ports the comforts of European bourgeois culture. Somerset Maugham visited one remarkable residence, which he dubbed "My Lady's Parlour": an English expatriate had moved into a Beijing temple, remaking it in European style, with her silver-framed pictures of the Princess of Schleswig-Holstein and the Queen of Sweden set proudly atop her grand piano.[10]

Despite growing Chinese interest, European music was still centered around the emigré population. In 1917 the Shanghai orchestra hired an Italian conductor, Mario Paci, who led the small Western musical community for the next four decades.[11] Paci's orchestra included many White Russian and Italian musicians, but no Chinese until the 1930s; its audience was mostly white, although the players' salaries came from taxes levied against Chinese households by the imperialist municipal government.[12] Even when a few Chinese musicians were added to the orchestra, their pay was lower and they had no social interaction with the European musicians.[13]

The Russian revolution sent thousands of White Russians in flight to China. In musical matters, at least, the Russians were demonstrably less racist than most of the Treaty Port Caucasians. While the most impoverished of this group scandalized other Europeans by working as bodyguards and prostitutes for the Chinese, others supported themselves as musicians. White Russian jazz bands played in Shanghai, Harbin, and Qingdao.[14] More classically minded players gave piano or violin lessons to young bourgeois Chinese. When the Shanghai Conservatory was established in the 1920s, several Russians joined its faculty. And two young Russian composers, Aaron Avshalomov and Alexander Tcherepnin, demonstrated unusual interest in Chinese music and musicians.

Alexander Tcherepnin came to China from Paris in 1934 as a consultant to the Ministry of Education.[15] Tcherepnin lived in Shanghai and Beijing until 1937, bringing unprecedented enthusiasm to the promotion of European music among the Chinese, although he insisted that Chinese musicians avoid slavishly copying the West. He urged his students to learn to use local color by writing with the indigenous pentatonic (five-tone) scale, and to adapt Western techniques for their own culture. Tcherepnin encouraged young Chinese musicians to listen to music of China's peasants, rather than go abroad to study in conservatories.[16] In 1934 he donated a prize for the best short piano piece "with Chinese characteristics." The winner was He Luting, who wrote a ditty called "The Cowherd's Flute." The young composer (who identified himself as Rodin Ho) later became a revolutionary and, after Liberation, president of the Shanghai Conservatory; he and his music will concern us in future pages.[17] Tcherepnin showed his zeal for Chinese music by learning to play the *pipa* (a Chinese lute) and attending the Chinese opera. He began publishing a series of piano pieces by young Asian composers in Tokyo in 1935; "The Cowherd's Flute" was the first in the series. Not only did he perform the prize-winning piano pieces, he insisted that the programs for his recitals be printed in Chinese as well as English, despite his manager's insistence that ninety percent of his audiences would be Europeans, and that the few Chinese present would be able to read English.[18]

Caucasians also formed the audiences for the concerts of such famous performers as Fritz Kreisler, Efram Zimbalist, Artur Rubinstein, Feodor Chaliapin, and John MacCormack.[19] Rubinstein played unhappily to non-Chinese audiences in Shanghai, Beijing, Tianjin, and Hong Kong, until someone hastily arranged a recital for university students in Guangzhou.[20] But such an event only underscored the normal segregation of musical life. The major exception was the music of the missionaries, which ranged from primitive hymns in outlying missions to performances of Handel's *Messiah* and Brahms' *German Requiem* in Beijing, Haydn's *Creation* in Nanjing, and Bach's B-minor Mass in Shanghai.[21]

Later in the 1930s, Europe's musical presence in Shanghai was enlivened by the addition of eighteen thousand European Jewish refugees. A large number were professional and amateur musicians, and a surprisingly rich concert life began under very adverse conditions, including a chamber orchestra in the city's Hongkew ghetto. Most of this musical activity was for the Jewish community, but some overflowed into the Chinese city. The refugees had a radio station which played music from its library of ten thousand records and broadcast weekly live concerts. Ten refugee musicians joined the Shanghai Municipal Orchestra, while others became professors at the conservatory and St. John's University.[22]

Education in Western music developed slowly.[23] There was a short-lived music school in Beijing in 1922, but the Shanghai Conservatory was not begun until 1927. In contrast, schools for Western painting were relatively widespread: one was established in Shanghai in 1912. By 1929 such cities as Chengdu, Xiamen, Suzhou, and Wuchang all had Western-style art academies, and thousands of students were learning European perspective, figure painting, and oils.[24]

Chinese education in the new music seemed especially backward compared with more systematic efforts in Japan.

> [T]he 1869 request of the Satsuma domain that William Fenton, band leader of the British Tenth Marine Battalion, train thirty men in band music was motivated primarily by a desire to complete their military table of organization rather than any great fascination with the music as such. The national military ministries followed suit in 1871. . . .[25]

Japanese schools taught Western music by 1882, and a Western conservatory was established in 1885. "A generation later, official Japanese school music books contained about the same material as the American: Mendelssohn songs and 'The British Grenadiers'—all with Japanese words—as well as 'Home, Sweet Home' and 'The Last Rose of Summer.' "[26] When Nie Er, the Chinese composer and revolutionary, heard Rubinstein play a concerto in Tokyo in 1935, he wrote in his diary "admirable, admirable!", so impressed was he that the orchestra had only one European member.[27] It was only during World War II, in Chongqing, that an orchestra of Chinese musicians could be formed.[28]

The war with Japan seriously disrupted the emigré musical community, but Western music continued, although indirectly, under Japanese auspices. The new invaders promoted the music of Jiang Wenye, a protégé of Tcherepnin who had been born in the Japanese colony of Taiwan in 1910.[29] With Japanese training, Jiang was installed by the puppet government as professor at Beijing Normal University. Jiang's ballet about Yang Guifei, *The Perfumed Concubine,* was performed in both Beijing and Tokyo, as was his orchestral *Music of the Confucian Temple*. When Japanese officials banned the broadcast of music written by Americans and Britons, Jiang's opportunities increased. He enjoyed publication, performance, and recording by Japan's leading orchestra (now the NHK). Jiang was fond of Stravinsky and Bartók, whom he viewed as examples of art leaving the West's rationality in favor of a more Eastern approach. He was optimistic that an "Oriental renaissance" would begin at the conclusion of war.[30]

Despite the ethnic segregation of semicolonial concert life, a Chinese audience for Western music began to emerge in the first half of the century and has since grown considerably, if erratically. Who are these Chinese who learned to play pianos and enjoy Beethoven symphonies? That hackneyed but invaluable phrase "the rising middle class" suggests an answer, but in China the middle class did not rise, or at least it failed to rise to a position of dominance before it was repressed by revolution and radical Maoism. Still, after the agents of Western imperialism, the great social carrier of Europe's culture in China was the urban middle class.

Chinese aficionados of European music are almost exclusively interested in a fairly narrow range of pieces from the Western repertory. They like the composers of the first Viennese school: Mozart, Beethoven, and Schubert; also Brahms and such eastern Europeans as Tchaikovsky and Chopin. Neither baroque nor renaissance music is popular, nor is there much interest in such established twentieth-century composers as Stravinsky or Bartók. Western opera is only rarely performed, nor is there much interest in chamber music. Religious works are unappealing, as their Christian origins seem more strident and proselytizing in Asia than in their homeland. The Chinese, then, accept as Western classical music the symphonic warhorses of the nineteenth century, and of course, the romantic literature for piano. Why should music representing the most bourgeois phase of the history of European culture find an audience in China? This affinity may partly be explained by the simple fact that first the European expatriates and then the Japanese invaders all loved the bourgeois classics, and these were the examples of Western music which the Chinese heard. But there is a subtler explanation as well. The artistic preferences of the Chinese middle class flow also from the social implications which are embedded within this musical culture. Before continuing to discuss the Chinese middle class and its musical enthusiasms we must first consider the social and political context which gave rise to the Western classics.

Middle-Class Music in Europe

In 1921, the sociologist Max Weber, in a little known study, offered some still-useful ways of looking at the history of Western music.[31] Weber was concerned with the place of music in the process which he saw as the rationalization of Western society. He discussed harmony, polyphony, tonality, and, in his concluding chapter, the history of musical instruments, where he makes some interesting comments about the social history of the piano.

Around 1700 Bartolomeo di Francesco Cristofori (1655–1731), harpsichord maker for Prince Ferdinand de Medici of Florence, invented the piano.[32] Unlike the contemporary violins of Stradivari and Guarneri, Cristofori's piano was not immediately exploited. Carl Philipp Emanuel Bach was an early enthusiast, introducing the piano to his employer, Frederick the Great, in 1746. Frederick bought several for his court, and played one for Johann Sebastian Bach the following year.[33] But the elder Bach, like other baroque musicians, did not care for the piano; indeed, nearly a century passed after Cristofori's invention before the piano became a popular instrument, and then only after it had been rediscovered and improved by instrument-makers in Germany and England.

Max Weber's explanation for this delay is that Italy was insufficiently bourgeois. The middle-class home of northern Europe eventually provided a place for the piano that was lacking in Italy, which was too fond of *a cappella* singing and opera.

> It is the peculiar nature of the piano to be a middle-class instrument. . . . It is no accident that the representatives of pianistic culture are Nordic peoples, climatically house-bound and home-centered in contrast to the South. In Southern Europe the cultivation of middle-class home comforts was restricted by climatic and historical factors. The piano was invented there but did not diffuse quickly as in the North. Nor did it rise to an equivalent position as a significant piece of middle-class furniture.
>
> The unshakable modern position of the piano rests upon the universality of its usefulness for domestic appropriation of almost all treasures of music literature, upon the immeasurable fullness of its own literature and finally on its quality as a universal accompanying and schooling instrument.[34]

In this setting, the emergence of a mass market for pianos encouraged the technical improvements which made it a more satisfactory instrument. Let us take Weber's cue, and look at the music of Europe's middle class as it rose in power and status between the French Revolution and the middle of the nineteenth century.

Patronage

Although there were some notable exceptions, such as Handel's popular theatrical works in London, most classical music before the French Revolution was a luxury, obtainable only by the wealthy, who were most often titled and employed both composers and players for their exclusive entertainment. The replacement of feudal patronage by a commercial market in music is symbolized neatly by Haydn, who wore livery most of his career as provider of house music for the Esterházy family, only to become Haydn the entrepreneur in the 1790s, when he went to London to write symphonies by contract for Salomon's public concerts. The transition was in fact much more gradual, and Mozart, Beethoven, Carl Maria von Weber, and others wrote for both court and bourgeoisie.[35] The breakdown of the patronage system freed musicians from aristocratic domination. "The musician no longer sold himself without reserve to a lord: he would sell his labor to a number of clients, who were rich enough to pay for the entertainment, but not rich enough to have it to themselves."[36] Sometimes the difference can easily be heard. Although Mozart composed both operas in 1791, *The Magic Flute,* with its plot of freemasonry and nonsense written in German for a popular audience, sounds different from *The Clemency of Titus,* which praises royalty with noble melodies sung in Italian and composed for the Austrian Emperor Joseph II. More often, it is difficult to determine whether one of Beethoven's works is more "bourgeois" than another, although it is easy to see why *Fidelio* was a middle-class crowd-pleaser.

Especially after the Napoleonic wars, the increasing prosperity of Europe's middle class (and the decline of much of the old aristocracy) stimulated the development of a musical market, in which musicisns signed commercial contracts with publishers or impresarios who arranged public concerts. Concert societies "hired large halls and the musicians played for payment to ever-increasing audiences. This led to the creation of a free market for musical products, corresponding to the literary market with its newspapers, periodicals and publishers."[37] With rising standards of living, stable prices, economic growth, and peace, there was a European boom in both instrument sales and music publishing. New techniques in manufacture and marketing allowed these two industries to feed each other quite efficiently.[38]

The market for John Broadwood's pioneering English piano firm around the turn of the eighteenth century extended to Beethoven in Vienna, but it "derived less from the quality of musical life than from the affluence and social ambitions of a prosperous middle class. It was essentially a matter of income and spending power which was greater, more widespread, and growing faster in Britain than anywhere else."[39] This new middle-class audience came to listen to music for its own sake, for the first time "unrelated to any other purpose, such as had hitherto been the case in church, at the dance, at civic festivities or even in the social framework of court concerts.[40]

Content

The content of the new music was middle class in several ways. Most obvious was explicit mockery of the aristocracy, as in the various popular operatic settings of the Figaro plays of Beaumarchais: *The Barber of Seville* by Paisiello or Rossini, and *The Marriage of Figaro* by Mozart. Such satire meant that the censorship of librettos and song texts was a normal part of musical life, especially in reactionary Hapsburg Vienna. There even so apolitical a musician as Franz Schubert often collided with the censors, and was once arrested with a group of young intellectuals who would today be described as dissidents.[41]

A subtler bourgeois influence was the growth of program music in late–eighteenth-century Vienna, where

> Thousands of well-to-do middle-class simpletons, many with no particular acuteness of hearing, were now ambitious to own instruments and to attend concerts and operas; they found it much easier and much more entertaining to recognize something that was supposed to sound like a croaking frog than to savor the delights of a well-woven three-voice counterpart.[42]

Similar considerations led to the replacement of classicism by romantic style. Arnold Hauser argues that musical romanticism's concern for dramatic expression is explained by the composer's new dependence on a relatively ignorant and inattentive audience, which "had to be roused and captivated by more effective means than those to which the older public had responded." Composers for the middle class "developed the musical composition into a series of constantly renewed impulses, and worked it up from one expressive intensity to another." The need to win the middle-class audience "again and again" as customers led to "the concentration, the forcing and piling up of effects . . . which conditioned that loaded style struggling constantly to intensify the expressiveness of the composition, which typifies the music of the nineteenth century."[43] In such an environment, the piano was a perfect instrument. It could produce gradations in sound level, giving it access to the expression of romantic "feeling" which the harshly brilliant harpsichord of the aristocracy, incapable of dynamic variation, could not attain.

Technique

The new techniques for the middle class were not only expressive, they were loud. The evolution of the piano in the early nineteenth century is a progression of ever-stronger and louder instruments, with more and more keys. In part this was dictated by the need to keep up with increasingly demanding virtuosos. Liszt played so violently that he learned to perform with a spare piano in reserve. Heinrich Heine described the virtuoso in Paris in 1844: "He is here, the Attila, the scourge of God, for all Erard's pianos, which trembled at the news of his coming and now writhe, bleed and wail under his hands."[44]

New manufacturing techniques combined with aesthetic changes to produce a new music for the European middle class. The piano's dynamism was sustained by over two hundred strings, arranged over a frame bearing several tons of tension, leading eventually to steel frames. The manufacture of the industrial piano required the technical capacity to draw wire to a tensile strength of over two hundred pounds.[45]

> The much tauter strings of the new iron-framed pianos made available not only a grander dynamic range, but sonorities which carried farther and lasted longer, and could be graded more suggestively with the pedal— by half-pedaling, for example, where a mere touch of dampers to strings can suppress higher and softer notes while lower and louder notes still resound.[46]

Berlioz described the musical impact of the new technique in a characteristically embellished letter to Liszt in 1841:

> You can confidently say, adapting Louis XIV: "I am the orchestra! I am the chorus and the conductor as well. My piano sings, broods, flashes, thunders. It rivals the keenest bows in swiftness; it has its own brazen harmonies and can conjure on the evening air its veiled enchantment of

insubstantial chords and fairy melodies, just as the orchestra can and without all the paraphernalia. I need no theatre, no special scenery, no vast construction of tiers and ramps. I don't have to wear myself out taking interminable rehearsals. I don't require a hundred musicians or even twenty—I don't require any at all. I don't even require any music. A large room with a grand piano in it, and I have a great audience at my command.''[47]

Greater volume was also necessary because the intimacy of aristocratic homes had given way to new concert halls which had to be filled with sound sufficient for holders of inexpensive seats to be able to enjoy the performance. Moreover, the piano was forced to compete in concertos with ever-larger and louder orchestras, as string players began adapting their instruments for greater volume, with wire strings, new bridges and bows (for easier production of chords and a more massive sound), violin chinrests and cello endpins (to permit heavier bowing), and the use of extensive vibrato (to carry the sound farther). Wind instruments were redesigned with new materials and additional keys in order to produce a sound that was both louder and more homogeneous. Completely new instruments were invented as the bourgeoisie experimented with its orchestra. Some were accepted, such as the tuba. Others, such as the accordion or the numerous inventions of Adolphe Saxe, were not easily welcomed into the palace of bourgeois music. As they joined the movement for a smoother, more consistently blended tone for the romantic orchestra, drummers began to strike their kettledrums with sticks softer than those of the previous century that had produced clearer and harsher sounds. Players had less performance freedom as regularized notation controlled ornamentation and instrumentation. And the rise of the conductor brought discipline to the symphony orchestra, which came to resemble a musical factory with its own specialized division of labor.[48]

Even the human voice was reformed for the middle-class audience. The French Revolution's blows against feudalism closed the era of the *castrati,* whose brilliant soprano voices had made them the superstars of the eighteenth-century opera.[49] The subsequent need to override the noisier orchestras and to fill larger opera houses with sound led to a new style of singing with the music of Rossini and Meyerbeer, which demanded that its singers produce tones from the chest rather than the head.

Music as Social Marker

The European bourgeoisie was keenly aware of the subtle role of the arts in separating classes as well as in oiling the passage of individuals from one to another. The European middle class of early industrialization used music aggressively, as it employed other social symbols to expropriate the cultural pretensions of the old aristocracy, and to raise itself above the working class. Arthur Loesser described Mozart's Vienna concerts of the 1780s. "Music was a good social alpenstock; if some on the higher trails of the ascent seized it, many, many times that number sought to employ its pleasant help up the lower slopes."[50] The Austrian high nobility took up the piano with Mozart in the 1780s, followed soon by the high bourgeoisie. Then, in a chain reaction through the next decade, merchants, manufacturers, lawyers, physicians, professors, and bureaucrats all joined the rush to own pianos.[51] As the instrument descended through the social hierarchy to the increasingly prosperous middle class, the market expanded, encouraging innovation in manufacturing techniques.

Weber's description of the piano as "a significant piece of middle class furniture" captures its social equivalence to the automobile, personal computer, compact disc player, or other status commodity in late twentieth-century America. Even unplayed, the piano demonstrated the good taste and social position of its owner; played, it made (sometimes) beautiful music.

The piano enabled the middle-class family to use music as a focus for its home life. In its youth, as now, the piano was predominantly a musical instrument for women.[52] While most of the celebrated virtuosos were male, the armies of piano students were young women, given lessons as an aid to feminine decorum. After all, once a middle-class family owned a piano, who was to play it? Even a marginally musical daughter could demonstrate to the world that the family was one of quality. And pianistic talents enhanced the marriage prospects of a young woman, revealing discipline as well as refinement.

The growing middle class sparked such a boom in music and in pianos that by 1824, Stendahl, who wanted a world full of great singers, expressed concern for the "wearisome prolixity of adequate pianists," especially young ladies studying between the ages of nine and twelve. Stendahl predicted that supply and demand would assure that piano playing would be "out of date by 1840."[53] Stendahl was mistaken. In Vienna in 1800, five percent of the households owned pianos. In Paris in 1845, it was twenty percent, and by the end of the century, with declining costs of manufacture, "every family that considered itself above the 'working class' level owned one, or aimed to own one and to let its daughters learn to play it a little."[54]

Outside the home, Europe's middle class found concerts to be an arena for affirming and improving social position, especially when opera and politics were still closed to them, and middle-class charities did not yet exist. Between 1826 and 1846 concerts increased over three hundred percent in London, nearly five hundred percent in Paris, and almost fifty percent in Vienna (which had a head start).[55] As the century progressed, all of the great capitals build new classically-inspired music palaces where middle-class patrons might celebrate the democracy of the concert hall.[56]

But the middle class did not only look at the aristocracy which still glittered above it, however diminished its actual power. Music was also important in maintaining the border with the working class below. Music was held to uplift laborers, but this was music of a less refined sort, especially that performed by choirs and bands. The revolutionary French state had laid foundations for a new kind of popular music. The National Guard and the mass army of the 1790s had musical ensembles which spread music education among their working-class members, with a marked impact on amateur music after the end of the Napoleonic wars.[57] Charles Dickens wrote in 1850 that "music has of late years been gradually descending from the higher to the humbler classes," praising two iron foundries for establishing bands, which offered "a rational and refined amusement for classes whose leisure time would otherwise probably have been less creditably spent than in learning or listening to music."[58]

Many workers were also drawn to choruses, which required no formal musical training. These sometimes had a political edge, with dissent from artisan members quelled by a leadership drawn from their social betters. Choruses were in fact banned in Vienna until the 1840s.[59] The distinction between singers who could read musical notation and those who could not was an important social as well as musical gap. According to an 1876 German folksong collection: "The singer who is trained to read music looks down with a sympathetic smile on the 'common sing-along' of the people."[60]

China's Own Music

Europe's middle-class music arrived in a nation which already pos-
sessed an ancient and richly complex musical culture of its own.[61]
China has instruments three thousand years old, sufficiently ancient
that no one now knows what kind of music they made. The two-
thousand-year-old *qin* (a kind of zither) is still played, even if the
music it originally played is lost. China's size and population also
assure enormous diversity within this musical tradition, so that easy
generalizations are suspect. But its contrast to European music is sharp
enough.

The Sound of Chinese Music

Chinese music has a distinctive sound, just as the materials, techniques, and traditions of Chinese painting give it a special look. Immediately obvious to the Western ear are gongs, cymbals, clappers,
and the characteristic texture of plucked lutes and zithers. Bass and
tenor sounds are lacking, as is the distinctive bright ring of brass instruments.[62] The music is often pentatonic, but sometimes it also uses
a seven-tone scale or even microtones. Chinese singing voices are high
and nasal in contrast to those of European vocal traditions.

China's music stresses treble parts because it lacks the sophisticated
harmony and polyphony of European music. Nor is there rhythmic
complexity to compare with that of African music; most music is in
simple duple meter. Instead Chinese music has elaborated a very subtle sense of timbre (or tonal color) unknown to Western tradition. For
instance, The *qin,* the ancient zither of China, is a subtle and quiet
instrument for which "there are very great possibilities of modifying
the colouring of one and the same tone."

> In order to understand and appreciate this music, the ear must learn to
> distinguish subtle nuances: the same note, produced on a different string,
> has a different colour; the same string, when pulled by the forefinger or
> the middle finger of the right hand, has a different timbre. The tech-
> nique by which these variations in timbre are effected is extremely com-
> plicated: of the vibrato alone there exist no less than 26 varieties.[63]

Van Gulik describes a finger technique for one of the types of vibrato, the *yin,* a vibrato that imitates "A cold cicada bemoaning the

coming of autumn.'' There are more than ten permutations of this one vibrato.

> There is the *changyin,* a drawn-out vibrato, that should recall "the cry of a dove announcing rain"; the *xiyin,* a thin vibrato, that should make one think of "confidential whispering"; the *yuyin,* swinging vibrato, that should evoke the image of "fallen blossoms floating down with the stream", etc. Remarkable is the *dingyin*—the vacillating movement of the finger should be so subtle as to be hardly noticeable. Some handbooks say that one should not move the finger at all, but let the timbre be influenced by the pulsation of the blood in the fingertip, pressing the string down on the board a little more fully and heavily than usual.[64]

The Chinese-American composer, Chou Wen-chung, considers timbre as important as pitch: a Chinese melody played on the piano remains incomplete because it is deprived of sufficient variation in timbre.[65]

China's Opera

The only Chinese music of which most Westerners have any impression is opera. I have little to say about the politics of opera in this book, in part because it has been so thoroughly analyzed by Mackerras, but also because it is considered by the Chinese to occupy a artistic and intellectual category quite separate from music.[66] In the West, the relationship between opera's music and its drama is problematic. In recent decades, stage directors have become increasingly important, and singers who act well are held in high regard. But dull actors with glorious voices can still enjoy professional success; our opera is ultimately a musical, rather than a literary art. In contrast, Chinese opera is firmly anchored in the world of literature. New operas are created by dramatists, not musicians. The music is important, but is in the hands of the performers, who use considerable improvisational flexibility in singing a traditional set of tunes.

Although opera is organized into its own bureaucratic sphere, it exercises considerable influence over the world of music. The accompanying instruments of the opera orchestra are also used in popular Chinese music. There are more than three hundred varieties of regional opera in China. Beijing opera is the most famous of these in the West, but it is in fact one of the newest, conventionally being dated from 1790, and grew in national popularity as European imperialism was gnawing away at Chinese sovereignty in the nineteenth century.

Program Music

Abstract music is rare in China. Instead, most Chinese music bears titles descriptive of its content. The greatest number are psychological titles, in which the music sets a mood, such as the tranquillity of "Autumn Moonlight Over the Serene Lake." There are descriptive titles for music that illustrates a story, as in the famous *pipa* piece, "Ambushed from All Sides," which describes a 202 B.C. victory of Liu Bang, founder of the Han Dynasty, with marching troops, clashing weapons, and battle cries. And there is music imitating the sounds of nature, such as "Night Rain on the Banana Leaves." [67]

Typical of the last is *Meihua sannong* [Three Variations on the Plum Blossom], which, in one version, has ten parts: [68]

1. Evening moon over the mountains.
2. First variation: Calling the moon. The tones penetrate into the wide mist.
3. Second variation: Entering the clouds. The tones penetrate into the clouds.
4. The blue bird calls the soul.
5. Third variation: Trying to pass the Heng river. The tones imitate a long-drawn sigh.
6. Tones of a jade
7. Plaques of jade hit by a cool breeze.
8. Tones of an iron flute.
9. Plum blossoms dancing in the wind.
10. Infinite longing.

The prominence of program music reflects the preeminence of literature among the arts of China. Because much music had no notation, titles became useful mnemonic devices for performers. The titles often do not have a very close relationship to the music (the *pipa* piece "Moonlight over the Spring River" was formerly called "Flute and Drum in the Setting Sun"), but this seems less important than meeting the popular expectation that music bear a title. [69]

Music is Not Property

The great tradition of European classical music honors the composer of genius, who creates and then owns an original work of art. China's music does not reflect the inspiration and emotion of a single musician. Instead, Chinese music is typically rearranged and altered from preexisting sources. Although there are several traditions of notation, much music has been transmitted orally, or by a combination of notation and the instruction of a master performer.[70] From a Western point of view, this makes authorship difficult to establish; from a Chinese perspective, the question is irrelevant. This lack of obsession for the sacred text of the inspired composer reflects premodern China's distance from the individualism generated by centuries of capitalist development. Because music is not property, it does not matter who owns it, nor has there been a fetish of novelty and pride for innovation. Music has much in common with Chinese conventions in painting, where emulation of the style of a past master was accorded high prestige unimaginable in the more individualistic West.[71]

Music and Social Class

Most Chinese music can fairly be called "poor man's music"; popular instruments are simple, inexpensive, and accessible to ordinary people.[72] Before the development of a national communications system, popular music had considerable regional variation. Popular music was also most often performed by spare-time musicians, rather than by well-trained professionals. This gave Chinese music considerable flexibility, but also a tradition of low performance standards when judged by the professional criteria that emerged in this century.[73]

In contrast, the literati enjoyed a national musical culture of the upper class, similar to their shared patronage of the same literature or painting.[74] The musical emblem of the Chinese elite was the *qin*, a seven-stringed zither. Confucius himself is imagined as a *qin* player, and the best instruments are old ones. The instruments were expensive, as were lessons for playing it. Moreover, its complex system of notation required sophisticated literacy. If these factors were not sufficient to preserve the *qin* for gentlemen, rules were drawn up which forbade certain classes of people from playing the *qin*, such as actors, singing-girls, merchants, and foreigners.[75] Most Chinese never even heard the exclusive music of the *qin,* although its name was familiar from references in popular storytelling and opera.[76] Many wealthy Chinese who could not play the *qin* would hang one on the wall as a badge of status, not unlike later bourgeois displays of elegant but un-played pianos.

The music of the *qin* is quiet and complex, with literary titles allud-ing to mandarin culture. The *qin* player aspired to the Confucian goal of inner cultivation, to reach a refined state of mind that could not easily be shared with another.[77] The *qin* was thus not an instrument for public performance but rather for the private musings of the learned amateur. Indeed, *qin* culture developed the ideal of music so intimate and so refined that it was soundless.

> The ideal state of mind is achieved by inducing its activity level below normal or ambient levels, not by exciting it to higher levels of activity and then permitting it to return to the normal or ambient after a perfor-mance "climax." The voice of the *qin* is literally below ambient sound levels; one must be unusually quiet and attentive to hear it and engage in appreciation of its music. The history of keyboard instruments in the West is one of technical advances toward greater volume, from the panteleon and clavichord to the "forte-piano" of Mozart's day to the electric piano of today. In the history of the *qin,* the opposite seems to have occurred, with large, multiple-string instruments evolving toward an ideal of small, sparsely stringed, and even stringless ones.[78]

Foreign Influence

Until the anti-imperialist revolution of this century, China has usually been open to foreign music. By the Tang Dynasty in the seventh cen-tury the emperor maintained ten orchestras: two played Chinese music, but the others specialized in the music of Xiliang, Indo-China, Korea, Kucha, Bokhara, Kashgar, Samarkand, and Turfan.[79] Many instru-ments regarded as traditionally Chinese were borrowed from abroad, such as the erhu, a two-stringed fiddle imported from northwestern nomads in the thirteenth century, and the lute-like *pipa,* which was brought from the Middle East in the Han Dynasty.[80]

Yet after fifteen hundred years, Confucian purists still regarded the *pipa* as a "barbarian" instrument, and there were brief reactions against foreign music, such as an unsuccessful imperial order of 592 to restore music to its Chinese essence.[81] Still, in the end, the Qing Dynasty

Court entertained guests with "bodies of barbarian music"—ensembles which played Mongolian, Tibetan, Korean, Moslem, Burmese, and Vietnamese musics, suggesting an openness toward the music of other cultures that the West does not know.[82]

Music, Power, and Confucian Cosmology

China's artistic tradition firmly linked music to statecraft. The Confucian elite may have favored a very personal vision of music for its members, but it also regarded popular and ceremonial music as a public matter. Indeed, Confucian ideology maintained that only in periods of decay did music come to be regarded primarily as a source of personal pleasure.[83] Although the European classics were often written in praise of some monarch or other, this practice fell off sharply as the aristocracy was replaced by the nineteenth-century bourgeoisie, so that Europe's exported romantic music said little about public affairs.

Confucian political philosophy was concerned with recovering an ancient golden age, lost to the present because people had strayed from their original goodness. Confucian music theory had the same obsession. The lost music of the golden age regulated the relations among people and between people and nature. Once, after hearing the ancient and perfect music of *Shao*, Confucius was so affected that he lost his desire to eat meat for three months.

Bad music was believed to harm its hearers and their society. The classic negative example was the salacious music of "The Mulberry Grove above the Pu River," whose tones were those "of a state facing extinction. The administration was dissolute, and the people wandered about haplessly. They vilified their superiors and behaved with such selfish abandon that nothing could save the situation." The composer, coerced into writing these potent airs by King Zhou of Shang, drowned himself in despair after completing his commission.[84]

Hoping to restore rituals lost in the anti-Confucian Qin Dynasty, the emperor Han Wudi set up the first music bureau in 112 B.C., with a staff of eight hundred. These music officials provided ceremonial music so that court rituals might be in accord with heaven. They collected popular songs in order to assess the feelings of the people, following the role ascribed to Confucius as the editor of the *Shijing* [Book of Odes]. They also provided music for educating and civilizing the emperor's subjects, especially barbarians and the young.[85]

The perfect music of the past had been established by the legendary Yellow Emperor, who ordered his chief musician to fix a standard pitch.[86] He made a set of twelve pipes from the best bamboo and tuned them according to the songs of the male and female phoenix.[87] But the original pitches were lost, and subsequent music became less accurate, with baleful social consequences. The musical goal of the Confucian state was to rediscover the Yellow Emperor's original pitch relationships, in order to restore harmony to human affairs.

A recurring feature of imperial politics, then, was the organization of efforts to find the "yellow-bell" pitch, the lowest in the series of twelve tones, and the one upon which all other intonation depended.[88] When the yellow bell was not set properly, the legal system, crop cycle, water supply, and public virtue all suffered.

> The accuracy of the pitches was debated passionately at court. The yellow-bell pitch, being the pitch on which the other eleven were ultimately based, had to be accurate or the entire system failed. At least since the beginning of the Han, scholars were not assured of the accuracy of the yellow-bell pitch, and it became symbolic of what was lost from China's classical age. Tuners were lost through neglect during the tumultuous years of the late Zhou. Detailed and reliable instructions were destroyed by the Qin. Various efforts were made to recover the correct standard, but a sense prevailed that the situation was getting worse.[89]

Elaborate efforts were devised to rediscover the yellow bell's natural essense using pinwheels and fans. Scholars measured the movement of ashes placed in twelve pitchpipes which had been embedded in the ground, reasoning that the ashes would be moved by the cosmic tide to reveal the correct yellow bell pitch.[90] The loser of one third-century court battle over how to cast a bell properly was made to work as a groom in the imperial stables.

Confucian officials doggedly pursued the correct music over two millennia, making at least thirty-five pitch reforms between the late Zhou period (third century B.C.) and the fall of the Qing Dynasty in 1911.[91] One concerned mandarin was Kong Shangren (1648–1718), a lineal descendent of Confucius of the sixty-fourth generation. Kong, a dramatist and waterworks official, is best remembered as the author of the *Peach Blossom Fan*. He searched for the correct musical ritual throughout his life, writing *Theory of Pitch in Classical Music* and *Ceremonial Music of the Confucian Shrine*. Kong wrote sadly about his endeavors:

Music theory is profound and abstruse, hardly capable of being understood by erratic or vulgar minds. I have long studied my family's teachings and was fortunate to have used the official ritual vessels which they have preserved, only a tenth of which have survived. For the past twenty years, I have conducted careful research on them and used it [*sic*] in ceremonies in Qufu and in the Imperial Palace in Peking. Yet I fear that over time, error has compounded error so that the original methods and intentions have been lost.[92]

The Musical Culture of China's Urban Middle Class

Instead of embracing Confucian melancholy about music of the past, China's middle class happily turned to European sounds as the music of the future. The piano, our emblematic musical instrument, was called the *gangqin,* or the steel *qin,* even though it is in many ways antithetical to China's traditional art. The piano embraces equal temperament, which is at odds with Chinese tuning practices. The pentatonic tendencies in Chinese music are not honored in the twenty-four possible keys within its octaves, and the construction of the keyboard encourages harmonic experimentation unfamiliar in Chinese tradition. The piano repertory abounds in sonatas, variations, and other nonprogrammatic forms that are foreign to the evocative tradition of China's instrumental music. The piano's machine-drawn wires are under two hundred pounds of pressure, and can only be constructed in modern factories, with an elaborate division of labor. The piano is an instrument for virtuoso display, leaving little room for the understated amateur ideal of Confucian art. A piano is expensive, well beyond the means of most Chinese families, and it is the quintessential musical instrument of the Western bourgeoisie. Of course, the attraction lies in the antithesis: because the piano embodies qualities opposite to China's own music, it has been seen by modernizers as the proper vehicle for musical progress.

European music did not immediately dominate China, but rather joined "the great variety of musics, all living side by side, affecting each others' sound and performance context," which is characteristic of third-world nations.[93] China's own musical traditions continued to change alongside the new foreign element, much as they did when Chinese imported central Asian sounds in the Tang dynasty. The *sizhu* (silk and bamboo) music of Jiangnan is an example of a "traditional" music that was consolidated only in this century. The unorthodox combination of native instruments into new ensembles around Shanghai may suggest indirect foreign influence, but more clearly shows the continued vitality of China's own music.[94] It is important to remember that China's music is alive, and continues to attract listeners, although over the century they have declined among urban middle-class citizens.

The Composition of the Middle Class

The makeup of the Chinese middle class has varied over time. It began with a native bourgeoisie. Capitalism grew in China along the coast and up the great Yangzi River, in the so-called treaty ports that Western and Japanese imperialists forced open to their trade.[95] Alongside imperialist firms grew Chinese capitalist enterprises in such cities as Tianjin, Guangzhou, Wuhan, Xiamen, and above all, Shanghai. Chinese capitalists initially began as compradores, middlemen between China and the culturally and linguistically ignorant imperialist merchants, but by the early twentieth century they had become a force of their own, however minuscule they seemed in contrast to the massive peasantry of the interior. This old bourgeoisie was legally ended in the 1956 collectivization of industry and commerce, although former property owners continued to draw interest payments from government bonds, and their influence continues to be disproportionate to their numbers.

Intellectuals form a second section of the urban middle class. However ambiguous the category of intellectual in a modern industrial society, it "takes on a clear-cut meaning when applied to the elite in China." There it simply distinguishes the educated from the uneducated masses, with "higher" and "lower" intellectuals indicating the amount of one's formal education.[96] Many of China's higher intellectuals (often defined as college graduates) have bourgeois origins, which led to enormous grief after the Communists came to power. Since Liberation, most of these intellectuals have been state employees. It is important to bear in mind that they form a very small group. In 1956 there were only one hundred thousand higher intellectuals out of a population of over six hundred million.[97] In 1982, higher intellectuals had grown to over 4.5 million out of a population of a billion, still a tiny percentage of the population.

A third group of the urban middle class is drawn from the new

Communist officialdom. Formally these are state officials, like most higher intellectuals. But their social origins are typically distinct. The Communist Party's protracted revolution left little time for formal education, yet many of these officials love art, or crave the "bourgeois" respectability which artistic interests convey. The interaction of this group with their former enemies in the bourgeoisie has been complex. Western students of China understandably have been fascinated by this conflict, but have thereby often ignored the post-Mao tendency of the Communist bureaucracy "to acquire class roots . . . by fostering the interest it shared with the middle class."[98]

The "urban middle class" is not a class, but a status group, sharing the symbols of culture. Using the concept of an urban "middle class" permits a more nuanced treatment of all three groups; it directs attention to areas of agreement, or at least disputation over shared symbols, instead of focusing solely on the open conflict between intellectuals and the Communist Party. "Urban middle class" is thus a composite social identity, embracing distinct and often antagonistic social groups. Shared culture masks many of these social rifts even as it defines the set of symbols which each middle class group seeks to use, and delimits a special set of political issues. Even in Europe, however, the unity of the nineteenth-century "middle class" is also questionable.[99]

Status Competition

Even nonmusical members of the urban middle class are interested in Western music as a source of prestige. The trappings of Western culture are a status symbol for many wealthy Chinese, who would hire brass bands for funerals or purchase pianos for their children, inviting their friends to admire the new instrument's dignified bulk and capacity for noise.

The prestige of the piano came not only from its presence in emigré homes, but from its status in high bourgeois European consciousness. Loesser describes a mental ambience of comforting softness:

> By its presence, the piano betokened the self-satisfaction with which the well-to-do of the later century regarded themselves. It expressed their sense of progress achieved and maintained, their comfortable equation of moral with financial superiority, their tolerant disdain of laborers and "backward" peoples, their certainty of the exact location of "woman's place," and their general sense of security. "God's in his Heaven, Dinner's at seven, All's right with the world" was the silent

counterpoint to much of the piano's music, and even to the piano's silence. The piano was safe, safe as the Bank of England; and both institutions seemed somehow vaguely related.[100]

How could the elite in semicolonial China not want to partake of such feelings of reassuring ease? The rage for Western culture was so great by the 1920s that even Pu Yi, the deposed emperor, whiled away his hours with piano lessons in Tianjin, albeit without great success. According to the former emperor's Australian tutor, he liked "simple duets in which he plays the top part with both hands together while somebody goes thump in the bass."[101]

Cosmopolitans in Culture

Many of the Communist Party's leaders came from China's interior, and regarded urban China as decadent and foreign. Marie-Claude Bergere argues effectively that their opinion, sometimes unthinkingly assumed by Western students of China, is inaccurate and unjust. The "other China," as she describes Shanghai, was very Chinese, not just a foreign pimple on the great body of peasant China.[102] Shanghai's relative integration into the world economy established "a modern Chinese tradition."

> This tradition expresses a fundamental requirement: that of a development which is at once national and open to the rest of the world. It marks a deep rupture with the Sinocentrism and the politics of a rural and bureaucratic state. This more or less complete integration into world civilization characterizes every manifestation of life in Shanghai.[103]

If the treaty ports were centers of imperialist domination, they were also centers of modern Chinese thinking. The great anomaly of Shanghai was that it supported Chinese intellectuals of the first rank, yet was economically and politically dominated by a mentally loutish Western community. Shanghai became the literary capital of modern China with the vital activity of such writers as Lu Xun, Guo Moruo, Xu Zhimo, and Mao Dun. The segregation of the Chinese and foreign communities, with potential humiliations awaiting any Chinese, assured that the city's cosmopolitan intellectuals would be nationalist as well.[104]

Especially after the May Fourth (1919) movement, an influential current among urban intellectuals catered for the first time to an urban and middle-class audience with a radical iconoclasm toward Chinese culture. Confucian culture and political authority seemed so intimately connected as to be inseparable, so that rejecting the old politics also meant rejecting traditional art.[105]

As the new middle class and its intellectuals blamed China's feudal traditions for impeding economic and political progress and for perpetuating China's international weakness, interest in Western and Japanese culture rose accordingly. According to Bonnie McDougall,

> On the whole, Chinese writers at this time regarded Western literature as superior to their own classical and folk tradition. A collective admission on this scale is remarkable, especially when applied to crucial questions of social identity, yet it was possible for the Chinese to sustain their tremendous enthusiasm for Western literature without falling into a crippling sense of inferiority.[106]

Jospeh Levenson described the rise of this cosmopolitan attitude in a study of European plays translated for the Chinese stage. Like the mandarins they were replacing, the new cosmopolitans delighted in their own sophistication. But instead of serving as guardians to China's rich civilization, they saw themselves as pioneers who prodded China into modern world culture.[107] Similar attitudes toward music emerged, which cosmopolitan intellectuals regarded "as not only an alternative but a categorically superior one to their own." Modern schools rejected Chinese music as feudal and backward.[108]

The cosmopolitan program to modernize music may be understood most simply as the introduction of reforms which parallel those of Europe in the late eighteenth and nineteenth centuries. The parallels are suggestive, not precise. Much that we now take for granted in our high musical tradition comes from the rapid innovation and experimentation of the years between Mozart and Wagner, as the middle class supplanted the aristocracy as the major influence in music. This great project of musical reform is being repeated in China in our century, for some of the same reasons: premodern forms of elite patronage have been replaced by a growing new urban middle-class audience. Thus it is not surprising that many of the European reforms have direct Chinese counterparts, such as they busy redesign of traditional musical instruments: nylon and metal replace the silk strings of the *pipa,* to which new frets are added for ease of transposition. And as in Europe, music has emerged as a separate sphere of public artistic activity, not tied to religious, dramatic, or ceremonial concerns. China's own musical tradition has been enriched for centuries by free borrowing from other cultures, but the contemporary changes are unprecedented in scope.

Treaty-port musicians were as iconoclastic and cosmopolitan in their tastes and their aesthetic program as were the more famous writers of the May Fourth era. Unlike erhus, pianos were "scientific," and could help bring down the remnants of feudal culture the way trumpets flattened the walls of Jericho. The optimistic presumption of unbroken progress entertained by the musicians of the middle class seems quite Victorian.

Late Industrialization

China's industrialization and the growth of its urban middle class is "late." Art and literature produced for the middle class during Europe's industrialization were already in the international cultural inventory before the Chinese middle class even began to take shape. As this class began to find its own identity early in the twentieth century, it adapted the norms and values already embedded within European art. Not only did Balzac, Chopin, and Dickens provide fine entertainment, but they also spread middle-class values. The piano thus preceded its "natural" social basis to China, but was quickly taken up as soon as a modern middle class began to appear.

Chinese cosmopolitans rejected the music of the old upper class and of popular tradition, choosing instead a ready-made foreign art. There is some irony in Chinese who, rejecting the feudal *qin* and peasant tunes, enjoy Haydn's minuets or Schubert's laendler, perhaps oblivious to the reflected sounds of European peasant dances. Similarly, Chinese cosmopolitans rejected Beijing opera as feudal, although it was a newer (but not more "modern"?) art form than the symphonies of Mozart.

One major difference between China's experience and the European precedent is China's semicolonial status, which lasted until 1949. The West did not modernize its culture under external political pressure. For many Chinese musicians, direct emulation of the West has been a clear goal. More commonly, musicians have rejected "complete Westernization," yet have insisted on defining modernity in terms of features basic to Western music, such as the increased use of harmony, or choral singing. The modernization of music cannot easily be separated from questions of cultural imperialism, which often makes Chinese discussions of these issues ambiguous. Is ''modern'' music Western, or is it a scientific music for all people, including Chinese?

A related difference appears in the political context for musical reform. Europe's middle class built its concert halls and invented its saxophones alongside a broader decline of state patronage of the arts. China had no bourgeois revolution, and like its industrialization, musical reform has been state directed, rather than commercial. This is not only harmonious with traditional Chinese notions of the relationship of art to power, but it also reflects the need of Third World nations to strengthen their own state power in order to deal effectively with powerful foreign rivals. China's middle class has sometimes been deeply disappointed in the results of state-led reforms in the arts, but few have advocated that the state abandon its role as chief impresario.

Populism Against Cosmopolitanism

Although both musical and political leaders have agreed since early in this century that China's musical tradition is outdated and too closely bound to a feudal society, populist political forces resist the cosmopolitan embrace of Western art. An elitist, cosmopolitan, modernizing musical leadership finds itself in frequent tension with a recurring demand for cultural populism. Modernizing musical leaders seek to minimize the impact of traditional Chinese musical practices, arguing that modern music must be accepted internationally, like modern science. Politicians often encourage musicians to develop China's musical heritage, minimizing the impact of the West. The elitist modernizers have been successful over the long run, but at great cost to individual musicians who are forced to react to political demands for cultural populism.

The populists have been centered in the Communist Party, especially after its mass recruitment of peasant leaders during its two decades of revolutionary struggle. One of the ironies of modern Chinese politics is that the Confucian marriage of music to statecraft has endured, with the revolutionary Communist Party as its vehicle. Revolutionary Communists and Confucians both believe that art can induce political change, a view at odds with the tradition of bourgeois music in the West. This is an issue that puts the cosmopolitans on the spot.

If music aids statecraft, and if art can empower, then what class of people should be trusted with music? Once asked, this question is likely to be answered to the disadvantage of the urban middle class.

Music as Metaphor and Commodity

The International Language

Nettl has described "the intensive imposition of Western music and musical thought upon the rest of the world" as the most important event in the last century of music history.[109] Modern China's reception of Western classical music cannot be understood as an intrinsic fascination with the melodies, harmonies, and rhythms of Tchaikovsky and Brahms. However appealing our music may be, if its diffusion reflected a simple aesthetic choice, it would not have been delayed until the spread of Western political, military, and economic power across the globe. Despite the historical association of cultural exchange with power politics, the global dissemination of European music has given rise to one of the enduring pieties of the modern age, the metaphor of music as a "universal language," a kind of aesthetic Esperanto that transcends petty national differences, uniting all humankind in an airy realm of spiritual beauty.[110] The metaphor holds out the illusion that music is a bridge across the dark and dangerous waters of politics.

But music not only transcends social differences, it can also accentuate them, serving as a symbol to be loved or hated. Recall the patriotic banning of Wagner in the United States during World War I, and the imprisonment and deportation of Karl Muck, the Swiss-born but German-speaking conductor of the Boston Symphony.[111] Or think of the German purge of music by the Jews Mendelssohn and Bruch in the 1930s, or the repeatedly unsuccessful efforts to include Wagner on the programs of the Israel Philharmonic.[112]

Our Western denial of music's association with conflict is extreme. Even as we sing anthems for our nations and fight songs for our sports teams, we want to believe in music's higher spirituality. Theodor Adorno argued that music is the special art of the European bourgeoisie, and that it is ideological, a form of sonic false consciousness.[113] Politically naive assumptions about music persist because, like all ideologies, someone finds them useful. The international language metaphor, for instance, enables China's cosmopolitans to minimize their discomfiting alienation from Chinese society, even as it permits Westerners to focus on something more pleasant than the imperialist structure by which our music traveled to Shanghai and Beijing. But torn from its original time and place, music assumes new social functions, even in the West. When the symbols, gestures, and traditions of European music are transplanted to China, their significance must be altered in ways both petty and profound.

Politically naive approaches to culture persist also because most social scientists ignore the arts, regarding them as trivial or derivative, reflecting such "real" factors as steel production, birth rates, and election results. Others are reluctant to look dispassionately at questions of artistic taste, which Pierre Bourdieu calls "the area par excellence of the denial of the social."

> The denial of lower, coarse, vulgar, venal, servile—in a word, natural—enjoyment, which constitutes the sacred sphere of culture, implies an affirmation of the superiority of those who can be satisfied with the sublimated, refined, disinterested, gratuitous, distinguished pleasures forever closed to the profane. That is why art and cultural consumption are predisposed, consciously and deliberately or not, to fulfil a social function of legitimating social differences.[114]

Much writing on the politics of culture is insufficiently complex because it is politically naive. Materialism may sometimes be a vulgar way of looking at art, but it is never inappropriate when seeking to understand art's political and social context. This means looking at the institutions through which culture is created and transmitted, as well as the artists' own political interests. While this sounds straightforward, it is not the normal way of relating the arts to politics. More common is a tendency toward idealistic twaddle, treating the artist as a creature far above the political world, which exists only to malign and distort true beauty. Consider, for example, the view of Boris Schwarz, author of an invaluable study of *Music and Musical Life in Soviet Russia 1917–1970.*

> Attempts to control music through censorship and autocratic rules have been made since antiquity. The Council of Trent regulated church music in the sixteenth century. Puritan England persecuted music and musicians. The French Revolution censored an opera because the word "liberty" was not used conspicuously. Imperial Vienna interfered with Bee-

thoven's *Lenore*. The Tsarist regime forbade Rimsky-Korsakov's opera *Le Coq d'Or* because it pictured an autocrat as a fool. Shostokovich's *Lady Macbeth of Mtsensk* was branded as "chaos instead of music." The list could be prolonged ad infinitum. But music won out in every case because its spirit is free and unfettered, its meaning implicit, not explicit. "A Symphony to Man's pure and noble spirit," this is how Prokofiev described his own Fifth Symphony.[115]

By placing art solely *against* politics, treating it as the innocent victim of a hateful world of conflict, we misconstrue the circumstances under which art survives and flourishes, unless we believe in magic. The relationship of art and the state is not all collision, but also includes large doses of cooperation. To pretend otherwise is either naive or dissembling, and does little to help us understand the real political world of the artist.

It is easier to believe in the apparent separation of music from politics in the West, where most musicians appear to have apolitical careers. It is exceptional when Western musicians take public positions on political issues, such as Artur Rubinstein's refusal to play in Germany, Pablo Casals' opposition to Franco, or Leonard Bernstein's enthusiasm for the Black Panthers. The Chinese tradition, however, assumes that culture occupies a central place in political and social affairs. Twentieth-century Chinese thought elaborates the premodern conviction that writers and artists are graced with power and responsibility despite their limited material resources. In the Chinese vision, power is validated by cultural prowess. The conventional Western dichotomy of artist and politician makes little sense when considering the passionate commitment with which both Confucian ministers and modern Central Committee members paint landscapes and write poetry. The musicians of modern China have made their careers under the assumption that power and art are closely wedded, and thus their careers are politically more complex than any in the contemporary West.

Musical Orientalia

If music is an international language, this tongue must have a history. But when one looks at the growth of an international exchange in sounds between Europe and Asia, one finds a pattern of increasing Asian subordination.

European and Asian musics coexisted on a much more equal basis before improvements in military technology permitted Europe to dominate the politics of Asia. Indeed, equal temperament, one of the foundations of modern European music, was discovered in China by Zhu Caiyu in 1584. Although Zhu's *New Account of the Science of the Pitch-pipes* was not adopted in China, its theory of pitch relationships was borrowed by Europeans in the sixteenth century; its regularized approximations of pitch later would permit the piano to participate in eighteenth- and nineteenth-century European ensemble music.[116] In 1777, Pere Amiot returned from China with a *sheng*, which stimulated European instrument makers to experiment with the "use of the free reed principle," ultimately giving rise to the accordion.[117] It is probably not fair to blame the Chinese for the accordion,[118] but the episode certainly reflects a rough equality between China and Europe in the exchange of musical values.

For most of the eighteenth century, Europeans imagined China to be the wise and "flowery Empire of Cathay" which appeared in their stylish chinoiserie:

> a land of poetry and graciousness, a spacious garden of azaleas, paeonies, and chrysanthemums, where the most serious business in life is to drink tea in a latticed pavilion, beside a silent lake, beneath a weeping willow; to listen to the music of piping and tinkling instruments, and to dance, to dance for ever, among the porcelain pagodas.[119]

By the time pianos and equal temperament were established in Europe, the early romantics were curious about the music of Asia, though mostly as an exotic titillation. Among its samples of chinoiserie, the Macartney embassy returned to England with a Chinese boatmen's song, harmonized into a novelty for clavichord or piano, to be played as good middle-class citizens drank their Chinese tea.[120] In Vienna, Giacomo Casanova proposed to the music-loving Emperor Joseph II that he organize a "Chinese *fiesta*" for the amusement of the capital.[121] Carl Maria von Weber based part of his incidental music to *Turandot*, and one of his four-hand pieces (the one later used by Hindemith in his *Symphonic Metamorphoses on Themes by Carl Maria von Weber*) upon an allegedly Chinese pentatonic theme found in Rousseau's musical dictionary.[122]

Such examples of musical chinoiserie appeared in a Europe still charmed by a confection of drums, cymbals, and triangles called "Janissary music," presumed to imitate the military bands of Europe's old enemies, the Turks. The Allegretto of Haydn's Symphony No. 100 and the Rondo alla Turca of Mozart's Piano Sonata K. 331 are only the most famous examples of Janissary music. In 1810 the Stein piano company manufactured a "Giraffe" piano which included a special pedal that caused mallets to strike a bell and to hit the soundboard from rear, imitating a bass drum.[123] The Turk was also a stock figure on the operatic stage, often ludicrous, as in Mozart's *Abduction from the Seraglio,* but sometimes noble, as in Rossini's *Mohammed II.*

Turkey returned the musical compliment. Composer Gaetano Donizetti's elder brother, Giuseppe, was hired as chief of music to the Ottoman armies in 1828. Before his death in 1856, he introduced European scales, notation, and harmony, receiving as honors the title of "Donizetti Pasha," and permission to enter the harem as singing master. When Liszt performed in Constantinople in 1847, "Donizetti Pasha" served as his companion when the virtuoso met Sultan Agdul Medjid. The composer of *Lucia di Lammermoor* wrote a "Gran Marcia Militare Imperiale" for this Sultan, and was rewarded with membership in the Turkish Order of Thourat.[124]

But these crossings of Eastern and Western music were not politically innocent. The citizens of an increasingly powerful Europe were ever more inclined to view the East as a sinister region where static and unchangeable despotisms ruled over corruptly sensual kingdoms of evil and weakness.

> The more fully the Orient fell under the sway of the Europeans powers, the deeper it came to be sublimated in the imagination, in literature, painting, music, and fashion. The *Arabian Nights* appeared in Europe at a time that coincided with Turkish defeat. "Turkish Rondos" were incorporated into European music when the Ottomans had ceased being a real threat to Europe's stability. And after Napoleon's conquest of Egypt, turbans were all the rage in the West. A shift in attitude had become strikingly visible by the nineteenth century; an ignorant awe had become a familiar contempt.[125]

The publication of "Chopsticks" in Glasgow in 1877 may mark the high point of European self-satisfaction and condescension.[126] This durable piano piece offers as an image of Chinese culture an obnoxious ditty, falsely harmonized, written in an uncharacteristic triple time, and easily mastered—like the Orient itself—by children and beginners.[127] "Chopsticks" was poor preparation for understanding the real music of China. When the recording pioneer F. W. Gaisberg visited China in 1903, he made 325 recordings of Chinese music in order to create a market for Western phonographs. He confessed, however, that

> the differences between the tunes of any two records were too slight for me to detect. On one occasion a dirty beggar was singing a lamentation and a visitor (Capt. Daniels of the SS. *Chuzan*) asked our *comprador* if it wasn't a love song. The reply was, "No, he is singing about his grandmother."[128]

The inability of Westerners even to begin to understand Chinese music underscores the fact that the allegedly international language of music speaks only with a European accent. Three decades later, when Hollywood made a movie of Pearl Buck's *The Good Earth*, Metro-Goldwyn-Mayer's Irving Thalberg negotiated, unsuccessfully, with Arnold Schoenberg for suitably "Chinese" background music.[129]

No less absurdly but considerably more viciously, lovable Eddie Cantor used the language of music to promote understanding of China in a Florentz Ziegfield show, *Kid Boots*, where he sang in mock Chinese melody:

> I've got a wonderful mother, But of late she's not the same.
> Things were O.K. until the day Ma learned a new Chinese game.
> China you're poison to me, You broke up my whole family:
> Since Ma is playing Mah Jong, Pa wants all the "Chinks" hung.
> We get rice chop suey each night, Chinese cooking you should see how
> Pa is looking.
> Ma wears a kimona. She yells "Pung" and "Chow."
> Ma left dishes in the sink, Pa went out and killed a "Chink."
> Ma plays Mah Jong now.[130]

The exchange of musics had become one-sided; China imported Western music while Westerners mocked China's. Mei Lan-fang, the great Beijing opera star, toured the United States in 1929, but as an oddity, much like a pachyderm in the circus. As no one had informed the United States immigration officials that music transcended national borders, Mei and his entire opera company were arrested as illegal immigrants when they arrived in Seattle.[131]

An International Market in the Machines of Music

Music is also a commodity, one which has assumed several forms since the rise of capitalism. Today, the capture of sounds on records, tapes, disks, and films is the leading form of musical property. For the nineteenth century the chief musical commodity was, of course, the piano. The history of its production shows a movement from West to East, as the international division of labor has shifted the factories for early capitalist products from center to periphery.

By the middle of the nineteenth century, piano manufacturing, the clearest industrial manifestation of the spread of middle class music, was big business. Only twelve London factories employed more than three hundred workers; one was Broadwood, a piano-maker. In 1850 annual world piano output was fifty thousand, priced at the annual income of a clerk or school teacher. By 1900 output was five hundred thousand, and the cost had dropped to three months of the income of clerk or school teacher.[132] Such rapid expansion began to saturate the middle class with pianos. As domestic sales became more difficult, the piano industry turned to the classic capitalist solutions for overproduction: a search for foreign markets, destruction of stock, and planned obsolescence.

One early market was North America. George Astor, an English piano-maker, used his younger brother as his New York agent at the turn of the nineteenth century. John Jacob Astor supported himself by selling his brother's pianos and other instruments until he turned to furs.[133] Turkish interest in pianos was spurred by the Crimean War, which brought British and French warships, bank loans, and cultural influence to Istanbul. During the war, "grand pianos with especially shortened legs were exported to Turkish harems, allowing the player to recline elegantly on cushions while still being able to reach the keyboard."[134]

But foreign sales stimulated foreign competition. U.S. manufacturers such as Henry Steinway (Heinrich Steinweg) took advantage of advanced German technology. Europeans were chauvinistic about the quality of American pianos, and were thus shocked when, at the 1867 Paris exposition, the top awards were given to Steinway of New York and Chickering of Boston.[135] The Americans made the piano a stronger instrument, as they had to overcome the problems of shipping their instruments "over a vast country on a crude transportation network.''[136] Both of these factors made U.S. instruments well suited to compete in an increasingly world market.

Another solution to overproduction was to destroy unwanted inventory. The 1904 Convention of American Piano Manufacturers resolved to condemn to the flames all of their ''outdated'' models. A public conflagration of pianos was staged, followed by a ''banquet at which elegies were spoken to the memory of old pianos, and fiery speeches delivered to the Glory of Progress.''[137]

The music industry also introduced new pianos to replace old ones, especially with new technology to make the piano accessible to the marginally musical customer, resulting in the player piano. At the turn of century the player piano was introduced to undermine the durability of the piano, in a successful effort to persuade households to buy a second piano, or to upgrade an aging instrument. In the United States, by 1919 more player pianos were sold than real ones, and at significantly higher prices.[138]

But even the marvel of the piano without a pianist could not keep the industry afloat. The trendy clientele for the player piano was stolen by the still more modern phonograph and radio, and the automobile became a more potent status symbol for the bourgeois family. The Great Depression, of course, struck hard at a luxury item that a decreasing number of people wanted to play. Between 1910 (the high tide of piano production) and 1935, piano production fell from 370,000 to 61,000 in the United States, from 120,000 to 4,000 in Germany, and from 75,000 to 55,000 in Britain.[139] When prosperity returned after World War II, manufacturers tried to meet the shortage by removing player mechanisms from old instruments and slimming their cases to rehabilitate them into conventional pianos.[140] But by this time, the world piano market was changing again, with production moving to Asia.

Gaisberg's turn-of-the-century efforts to sell phonographs and recordings to China had not been notably successful; there were sales in the treaty ports, and a bigger market among overseas Chinese.[141] The piano was still the modern musical commodity of choice for Asia. The first major purchase of pianos by Asian customers was from Knabe of Baltimore in 1879, which exported instruments to the Japanese public schools. The previous year—a mere decade after the Meiji Restoration—a Japanese-built piano was exhibited (and mostly ignored) at the Paris International Exposition. By the turn of the century, Japanese used their own pianos for schools, not Western ones. By 1916 Japan was itself exporting instruments at $25 apiece to China, India, Thailand, and Australia.[142]

Pianos are heavy and expensive to transport, yet there was little Third World manufacture before World War II. Outside of Europe and North America, prewar piano production was limited to five Japanese manufacturers, two Indian, one Brazilian, and three Chinese. The Chinese firms were apparently all colonial enterprises. One, the Lazaro company of Shanghai, began in 1896 and employed sixty Chinese workers by 1909. The Shanghai Piano Company and the Morrison Company of Hong Kong began operations in the 1920s.[143]

Since World War II, piano production has dropped sharply in Western Europe and North America. The United States has eighteen million people capable of playing its stock of thirty million pianos, ninety percent of which are not regularly used.[144] Still reeling from the rise of the guitar as the standard issue instrument for American youth, piano manufacturers are now struggling against a new assault from Asian makers of electronic keyboards.[145] Piano-making is still a relatively labor-intensive industry, so Germany and the United States maintain their leadership only in the most expensive instruments. Steinway remains the international standard, but the proud name of America's second maker, Baldwin, was recently befouled by late capitalist high jinks, as it was turned into a shell for a flashy but quickly bankrupt financial conglomerate.[146] United States piano manufacturers declined from 160 in the 1920s to 4 in the 1980s; seventy percent of pianos sold in the United States are now made in Asia.[147]

This middle-class commodity has moved to the lands where the middle class is still growing. Japanese production increased tenfold between 1953 and 1963, and Japan became the world's top producer in 1969. The Soviet Union also increased its production tenfold between 1953 and 1970. As with Japan, "the demand for pianos reflects improved living standards, an insatiable thirst for music which is stimulated by consistent education, and perhaps by 'Victorian' patterns of social aspiration."[148] The rising power in pianos is South Korea, which now threatens Japanese leadership in pianos as it erodes its advantages in automobile production; South Korea passed Japan in piano exports in 1986.[149]

China acquired self-sufficiency in piano-making during the Great Leap Forward, when in 1960 its steel industry first made piano wire.[150]

Recently, China has become the newest exporter of pianos, seeking to undersell Korean instruments. The Guangzhou Piano Factory, with a thousand workers, proudly exports its instruments to Italy, its largest customer. By selling inexpensive instruments in the land of Cristofori, the Chinese have brought the history of this middle-class commodity full circle.

At one level, this is merely offshore production by low-wage nations for sale to richer ones. Only twenty percent of the instruments from the Guangzhou Piano Factory will be sold to Chinese cosmopolitans. Yet these instruments will be played by Asians like Zubin Mehta, Seiji Ozawa, and Kyung-hua Chung, who will participate fully in the global culture of European classical music.

2

The Ambiguous Legacy of Composer Xian Xinghai

One of the most famous composers of our century is Chinese. His name is Xian Xinghai, and he is virtually unknown outside his own country. Xian, who died in 1945, was trained in the Western classical tradition at the Paris Conservatory, yet he was also a Communist who believed that music's function is to arouse people to revolutionary activism. Xian wrote the first Chinese symphony, yet he was also Yan'an's leading musical cadre, the composer of revolutionary marches and the *Yellow River Cantata.*[1] Xian attracts interest merely by the juxtaposition of such cultural antitheses in a single career. But his story is more than a curiosity. Xian's life as a Western-style musician had to be negotiated through China's profound ambivalence toward Western culture, which shaped both Xian's opportunities and his art. Xian embodied all the contradictions that have enveloped Western music in the People's Republic that honors him, and his life prefigures the parameters for conflicts about Western culture since 1949.

Western Music at the Margins of Chinese Culture

Xian Xinghai began life at the margin of a decaying Confucian social order. The year of his birth, 1905, saw the abolition of the imperial civil service examination that had helped maintain a centralized Confucian orthodoxy over Chinese thought for centuries.[2] By 1911 the political institutions of the old order were overthrown in revolution. In the absence of a strong central political and moral authority, foreign cultural influence spread rapidly throughout China.

Xian's marginality was multilayered, beginning with his birth into a family of boat people—hereditary residents of the waters of southern China who were never fully admitted into the Confucian system. Popular belief held the boat people to be descended from traitors to an emperor of the Song dynasty, who exiled them to live forever on the waters.[3] Boat people, like criminals and actors, were formally excluded from the imperial examination system, and thus were ineligible for bureaucratic careers. The poverty of the boat people was extreme; their women were often forced into prostitution, and all were treated with disdain by even the poorest land-dwellers.

The Xian family was escaping its lowly status; Xian's grandfather had settled on land, and Xian's father had wed a tough-minded peasant, Huang Suying. Yet fishing and water transport remained the family occupation; Xian was born on a boat in the Pearl River one bright night, inspiring his name, Xinghai ("Stars and Sea"). Huang Suying was widowed before Xian's birth, forcing her to take refuge with her father in Macao, Portugal's Chinese colony. Young Xian began life amidst sails, nets, and tales of far-off lands, as his grandfather made his living fishing at sea. When the old man died in 1911, Huang Suying took the young Xian to the English colony of Singapore, where some of her husband's relatives had emigrated, thereby following a traditional course of Cantonese in crisis to seek their fortunes in the "South Seas."

Thus Xian was marginal to Chinese culture in three important ways: he was a boat person, he had no father, and he was an Overseas Chinese. To this list he would later add Christianity and Communism, albeit on different occasions. Xian's mother was determined that her son should overcome these handicaps; she worked as a servant in order to pay for her son's education in Singapore. This schooling was varied, beginning with four years of traditional Chinese training in the classics, then a year of colonial education in an English-run primary school, followed by two years in a modern primary school run by a branch of Guangzhou's Lingnan University, an American missionary institution. In this last school, Huang Suying worked as a laundress, while Xian had his first exposure to Western music, singing hymns and taking lessons on a piano in the school auditorium. In her determination to aid Xian's education, Huang Suying resembles the great Confucian model, the mother of Mencius, who moved her home three times in order to find an environment in which her son's talents might be nurtured.

In 1918 the Singapore school principal arranged for Xian to return to China to attend a secondary school attached to Lignan University in Guangzhou; later Xian attended Lingnan itself, a center for modern education in southern China.[4] It was in the Westernized environment of Lingnan that Xian's passion for music blossomed. Xian began to study with Lingnan's American violin teacher, and to teach himself to play the clarinet as well. A controversial American philosophy teacher was even more important in introducing Xian to the world of Western art, talking to him after class of Beethoven, Bach, Picasso, Matisse, and modern Western thought.[5]

Xian's poverty forced him to take an assortment of odd jobs, including musical gigs which earned him the nickname of "Clarinet King of South China." He also played in Lingnan's brass band, a Westernized ensemble of thirty young Chinese playing Western instruments ranging from piccolo to tuba. An even more mixed cultural flavor is captured in a photograph of the Lingnan orchestra: half of the sixteen young musicians wear traditional long robes, but violinist Xian sports a necktie; he stands behind the band's woman saxophonist—an emancipated jazz-age touch.[6]

Xian's classmates elected him one of the leaders of their Young Men's Christian Association, a point concealed by most of his biographers.[7] His Lingnan friends were also a Western-oriented crowd and included Situ Qiao, who later studied in Paris and New York, returning to China to become well known in the highly Westernized art of oil painting.[8]

For most of his educational career, Xian was enrolled in elite institutions filled with children of China's most prosperous families. At Lingnan, his mother worked as a servant at the university to contribute to his tuition, while Xian took on odd jobs. In addition to musical performances, Xian worked as a typist, a teacher in a worker's night school, and, in 1923, as a part-time conductor of Lingnan High School's brass band. Western music may have seemed to Xian to offer a career which promised upward mobility. Music was an art that was not tied to the prejudices of traditional Chinese society, and must have seemed both modern and liberating to a poor, stigmatized but talented young man. Musical pioneers such as Xiao Youmei and Zhao Yuanren suggested the possibility of participating in the creation of a new Chinese music that would replace feudalism with modernity, just as the stars of the May Fourth Movement were doing in fiction and poetry.[9]

Xian's increasing seriousness about music led him northward in the autumn of 1925 to enroll in Beijing University's music school, which had been started three years earlier by Xiao Youmei, recently returned from music studies in Leipzig. Xian studied violin with an emigré Russian, supporting himself by working as an assistant in Beijing University's library, as had the young Mao Zedong not many years before. But the music school was closed by warlords in the following year, whereupon Xian returned to Guangzhou. There he gave music lessons and led the band at Lingnan Middle School until graduation from Lingnan University in 1928. He also spent considerable time with the YMCA, including organizing its annual Christmas concert.[10]

Xian enrolled in Shanghai's newly established National Conservatory. Xiao Youmei, who had been head of the former music program at Beijing University, brought Xian along with others of his Beijing students to form the new school's first class of twenty-seven members.[11] There Xian remained for a year an a half, studying violin and piano. He was soon joined by his mother, fleeing the political disorders in Guangzhou.

Xian began a serious political commitment in Shanghai. His own poverty and the disdain accorded boat people may have inclined him to political radicalism. In Shanghai his political consciousness was encouraged by participation in a literary and artistic group known as the Southern Society (*Nanguoshe*). Tian Han, a writer of Chinese operas and an impresario for the left (and later a major cultural official in the People's Republic) had founded the Southern Society in 1925 in order to radicalize literature, opera, film, and music.[12] The Southern Society's productions criticized arranged marriages and other feudal practices, and Xian took part both as violinst and narrator.[13]

How did Xian reconcile his political radicalism with a musical taste that was not only elitist, but foreign as well? This tension had not yet become a critical one for Chinese intellectuals. In the eyes of the May Fourth generation of reformers, foreign culture was modern culture, a weapon against the oppressive feudal weight of China's own arts. With many other young urban intellectuals, Xian's political radicalism included a profoundly iconoclastic stance toward China's national culture.[14] Xian received a letter from his mother describing the killing of his "uncle" Huang in the defeat of the Guangzhou Commune. His response was a gesture from European romanticism: Xian took out his violin and played Massenet's "Elegie."[15]

To this cosmopolitan outlook Xian added an elitist sense of mission that he was destined to bring music to China's masses. He wrote an article for the Shanghai Conservatory's journal in 1929 advocating music for the common people as a way of strengthening China, posing the problem of why there had been no Chinese Beethoven, Schubert, or Wagner. Beethovens would come forth, argued Xian, when there was more music; a China where everyone could sing, dance, and play music would produce musical geniuses easily enough. Yet the elite of musicians must devote their souls to this goal: "We must do things that ordinary people cannot achieve, moreover we must endure suffering which ordinary people cannot endure."[16] More conventional voices were also advocating musical education as a basis for national reform. During the 1920s Wang Guangqi introduced the German music education system to China with explicitly political goals.[17]

When Xian organized student opposition to a tuition increase, his political activism resulted in his expulsion from the Shanghai Conservatory. Frustrated in his musical education (there was no other conservatory in China), and convinced that the West's musical path was China's necessary future, Xian decided to go to Europe and study Western music at its source. Xian traveled to Singapore as a stowaway on a British ship in October 1929; there, friends and relatives helped him purchase a steamer ticket to France in January, 1930.[18]

The Paris Conservatory

Between the two world wars, Paris was the mecca to which composers traveled either to demonstrate their modernism or to learn it. Stravinsky and Prokofiev both came to Paris in the wake of the Russian Revolution, as a whole generation of Americans such as Aaron Copland, Walter Piston, and Virgil Thomson came to learn to write music in the new style with Nadia Boulanger. Heitor Villa-Lobos came to Paris from Brazil, traditionally Francophile in culture. But Xian showed little interest in *avant-garde* developments. Perhaps he found the impressionist school of Debussy to show a happy resemblance to China's tradition of programmatic music. In Paris, Xian was helped by another former Lingnan student, the violinist Ma Sicong (Ma Sitson). Ma introduced Xian to his violin teacher, Paul Oberdoeffer, a professor at the Paris Conservatory.[19]

Xian arrived in a Europe with growing interest in the musical exotica of Africa, Asia, and Latin America. Unlike the decorous sounds of "Chopsticks" or the amusing oddity of Janissary music, the Third World had become a source of strange and sometimes savage musical practices that progressive European composers could use to shock the conservative musical establishment. The consolidation of Western political domination meant that the music of non-European peoples would be presented as primitive (for Africa) or overcivilized (for Asia). Such music required the hand of a modern European composer to turn it into vigorous art. Every rising composer had to have a Third World piece. Igor Stravinsky's *Song of the Nightingale,* set in imperial China, was benign enough, but Bela Bartók's ballet *The Miraculous Mandarin* (which was first performed in 1925), was nastily racist. Bartók's music luridly described an oversexed Chinese mugging victim, who refuses to die from his wounds until physically satisfied by the woman who had lured him to his beating. Francis Poulenc was inspired by the music he heard at the Paris Colonial Exposition of 1931 to include a sweetly "Balinese" section in his Concerto for Two Pianos of 1932, as he had written a "processional for the Cremation of a Mandarin" in 1917, and the sniggeringly racist "Rapsodie Negre" (sung to nonsense poetry by the "Liberian poet Makoko Kangourou") which had launched his career. Darius Milhaud used his experience in Brazil and Harlem for a series of compositions inspired by jazz and other "native" music. The taint of racism extended throughout Europe; Soviet diplomacy courted China, yet in Moscow, Reinhold Gliere's ballet, *The Red Poppy,* presented "a parody of the Chinese revolution, in which heroic Russians came to the aid of primitive yellow people with the demeanor of insects."[20]

Although Europe's composers found the Third World to be a rich source of inspiration, they were less interested in having real colonial and semicolonial subjects come to Paris. Xian was understandably proud when he became the first Asian admitted into the Paris Conservatory's composition class. There he steeped himself in the established traditions of Western musical culture rather than in exploring the exuberant musical rebellion that now captures our attention. At the conservatory

Xian's teacher was Paul Dukas, whom Xian proudly identifies as "one of the world's three great musicians."[21] Another illustrious name was his teacher Vincent D'Indy, himself a pupil of Franck, and composer of *Symphony on a French Mountain Air* and other pieces that formed an important part of the musical repertory of the period.

Xian's own compositions attempted to use some Asian "color" in the established style of his impressionist professors.[22] He enjoyed the success of hearing his work in public performances, including at least one radio broadcast where his work was introduced by Prokofiev. Yet we know nothing about Xian's impressions of Prokofiev and other younger and more iconoclastic Parisian composers whose music he encountered, such as Arthur Honegger, Darius Milhaud, Francis Poulenc, or Olivier Messiaen (also a D'Indy student, with whom Xian overlapped one year at the conservatory). But Xian was exhilarated by being in a leading shrine of European music after years of attempting to master Western music under China's unfavorable conditions. Under the spell of treading the same ground as Debussy, Gounod, Chopin and Saint-Saëns, he had little interest in joining or even acknowledging the rebellion against this musical tradition then taking place around him.

Xian's personal life in Paris was no easier than it had been in China. He was still desperately poor, working at odd jobs to support himself. He waited on tables, gave manicures in barbershops, cared for children, answered telephones, copied music, and even played his violin as a street musician. Xian's poverty made him unpopular with other Chinese students in Paris, most of whom were supported by their wealthy families, and who had little time for such a drudge as Xian. He was hurt by this treatment, especially when the others considered his street-playing damaging to China's national honor. For a while Xian found refuge in the home of a sculptor who aided impoverished artists.[23] Xian repeatedly and unsuccessfully sought financial support from the Chinese government; his poverty led him even to think of moving to Germany to study military music, because there was a possibility that he might find financial aid for such a practical project.[24]

Xian's professors at the conservatory took note of his poverty. Oberdoeffer charged no tuition for violin lessons, and Paul Dukas added clothes and money to the encouragement he gave his only Asian pupil. Xian was awarded a prize for the piece he wrote to gain entry to the conservatory's advanced composition class. When asked what prize he wanted, he specified a ticket entitling him to meals at the conservatory.[25]

Unlike most Chinese students in Paris, Xian maintained contacts with the Chinese guest-workers then in France, playing the "Internationale" on his violin at one meeting in an initial effort to unite his art and his politics.[26] At another workers' meeting he was deeply affected by newsreels full of humiliating scenes of China's poverty: floods, starving refugees, rickshaw pullers, and the violent political repression of 1927. His experience was similar to that of Lu Xun, who was a student in a Japanese medical school when he was enraged by slides of the beheading of a Chinese prisoner, and by the maddening passivity of the Chinese crowd at the execution.

Xian's personal poverty and his emotional distress at the China's fate inspired his work, in the great romantic tradition. He wrote a song, "Wind,"

> just when my life seemed most hopeless. I was living in a small and shabby room at the top of a seven-story house; the room's doors and windows were all broken. Paris is always colder than South China, and on that winter night there was also a raging wind. I had no blanket and could not get to sleep. The only thing to do was to light the lamp and start writing. The wind blew fiercely into the room and the kerosene lantern (I could not turn on the electric light) blew out again and again. I became very depressed, and as I listened, shivering, to the freezing wind shake the walls and roar through the windows, my heart beat fiercely along with the wind. All of the bitterness, cruelty, pain, and misfortune of life in our homeland surged forth. I could not control my own feelings, but took advantage of the wind to write out my emotions and complete this composition.[27]

Despite the personal kindnesses of the conservatory faculty, many of Xian's other European experiences were also radicalizing, underscoring the disjuncture between Westerners and their art. Xian attended the 1931 colonial exposition, but found it considerably less charming than Poulenc did. A journey to Britain was marred when customs officials denied him entry, making him wait for hours until the Chinese embassy would vouch for his student status. Xian returned to China in the summer of 1935 without graduating from the conservatory.[28] The pain of his European years caused him to view colonial Hong Kong with fresh repugnance. On the long voyage home, Xian wrote more music, anticipating his still ill-defined future as a Chinese composer.

Shanghai and the National Salvation Song Movement

When Xian returned to Shanghai in the summer of 1935, he received some press attention for his European successes but found little employment for his talents. He tried to arrange for a public performance of his works. The Shanghai Symphony Orchestra was normally closed to Chinese; before going to Paris, Xian had applied for a post as clarinetist in 1929, but was rejected. After his return, however, he appealed to Mario Paci, the orchestra's conductor and a graduate of the Paris Conservatory. Paci agreed to invite Xian to conduct a concert of Beethoven's Eighth Symphony and some of his own works. But the project was aborted in rehearsal, when some of the European orchestra's musicians refused to play under the baton of a Chinese, especially when a violinist on the faculty of the Shanghai Conservatory described Xian's expulsion a few years before.[29] Paci canceled the concert, leaving Xian embittered by the contrast between the orchestra's "noblest" music and the racism of Shanghai's Europeans, who "were not willing to allow a weak people to have its day."[30]

Xian found some musical encouragement from two Russians, Alexander Tcherepnin and the composer Aaron Avsholomov, a Shanghai resident whose opinion Xian valued to the end of his life.[31] Xian began to give violin lessons, and busied himself by beginning to write the first Chinese symphony. But the students were few and no one had commissioned the symphony. Xian, now thirty years old, was forced to depend again on his mother's servant's wages for his daily needs.[32]

Rather unusually, financial salvation came from the forces of the left, as Xian became the central figure in China's "national salvation song movement." Xian resumed his old ties with members of the Southern Society, setting words of Tian Han to music. Tian was happy to re-encounter Xian, because Nie Er, the composer in his group of leftist artists, had recently drowned at a Japanese beach. Despite some political risk (Nie had fled to Japan to avoid arrest, and Tian Han himself had just been released from prison), Xian took Nie's place.

Nie Er (1912–1935) was the wonderful pseudonym of Nie Shouxin. "Er" means "ear" in Chinese, while the character for the surname

"Nie" consists of three symbols for ear (Nie also used the Western-ized pseudonym "George Njal"). Like Xian, Nie was a marginal fig-ure in traditional Chinese society: his invalid father was a Kunming physician, and he was raised by his mother, who belonged to the *Dai* minority. He acted in movies, played the violin, and began his com-posing career with a march and waltz for harmonica. Nie died at the age of twenty-three, and wrote only some thirty pieces of music. The best known of these is the "March of the Volunteers," China's na-tional anthem. Tian Han's words exhorted young Chinese:

> Arise all you who refuse to be slaves.
> With our flesh and blood, let us build our new Great Wall!

This song was heard in a 1935 movie, *Children of the Storm*, which spread it throughout the nation. Nie's music was revolutionary in China for describing ordinary working people such as stevedores and news-paper vendors, rather than traditionally grandiose subjects.[33]

The political climate in China at the end of 1935 was highly charged: in Beijing, student demonstrations on December 9 demanded that Chiang Kaishek resist Japanese aggression. In a radical departure for Xian's art, Tian Han put him to work on a "Battle Song:"

> Our hearts are war drums, our throats are bugles!

Some musicians ridiculed Xian for writing such political songs, but the change gave Xian a place of his own in the Chinese art world.[34]

These "mass songs" that Xian, Nie, and other leftist composers created were musically simple but politically important. They created a musical genre that is still prominent in China today.[35] They are usu-ally sung either without accompaniment, or with piano, accordion, or (in elaborate settings) band. Musical sophisticates may add simple chords, but the accompaniment often merely doubles the melody. Most are in major keys, they are written with a limited vocal range, and there is no modulation within the songs. The tunes are repeated stroph-ically for different verses. Those written in the 1930s typically had marchlike rhythms.

These songs were not intended to be great music; they were music for mobilization: their quick rhythms, easy range, easily enunciated and highly political lyrics were initially designed to inspire political courage and to aid mass demonstrations. By singing together, young Chinese would build a shared consciousness. The marchlike beat would help them advance on a demonstration target in unity and with resolve. Western models for this music are common: in Paris, Xian had been struck by the sound and sight of a crowd of marchers singing the "Marseillaise" on Bastille Day.[36]

Sometimes these songs had a very specific purpose. Zhang Hanhui, a Communist drama worker and composer in Xi'an, wrote "On the Banks of the Songhua River" around the time of the Xi'an Incident in 1936, when Chiang Kaishek was kidnapped by Manchurian troops in order to inspire more forceful resistance to Japanese aggression. Zhang Hanhui taught his song to homesick Manchurian troops and their potential allies in order to fuel anti-Japanese sentiment: "My home is on the banks of the Songhua River, there are my compatriots, there are my old and feeble mom and dad!" His sentimental lyrics brought tears to lonely Manchurian eyes and helped create a climate favorable to the second united front between the Guomindang and the Communist Party.[37]

Xian tried to find inspiration in the music of oppressed people, recalling the fishing songs he heard as a child. But he also practiced a kind of working-class musicology which the Communist Party has not celebrated. He once accompanied a Southern Society friend to visit singing girls in Nanjing, sitting at the side and recording their tunes while his friend socialized in their company.[38]

Xian's "Battle Song" and his "Song of National Salvation" were recorded and sold very successfully by Shanghai's Baidai Record Company. This British-owned firm hired Xian to write more of these popular songs, as it had hired Nie Er in 1934.[39] But the Guomindang confiscated the recording master of "Battle Song" in order to stop production of a recording that called attention to the government's failure to resist the Japanese.[40] Xian was unwilling to compose other kinds of popular music, and so he resigned when his employer refused to record more political songs.[41]

Again following the example of Nie Er, Xian joined the film business. With the backing of Tian Han, he became head of the music department of the New China Film Company, where he enjoyed a high income and access to a glamorous crowd.[42] The Chinese film industry of the 1930s was complex, accommodating for a while a community of committed leftist artists who appreciated the potential of movies for propaganda work. Not all of the movies they made were explicitly political; one of the movies to which Xian contributed music, for instance, was a horror film entitled *Song at Midnight*. Others, such as *Youth on the March*, were more explicit in their messages.[43]

Political repression slowed the national salvation movement. The New China Film Company turned from politics to costume dramas and sexy comedies, leading Xian to resign in order to continue political work as the war with Japan intensified. Xian grumbled of his boss in the classic manner of artists everywhere: "He thought that he could completely purchase my creative will with one hundred and fifty *yuan* monthly salary."[44] He continued to write occasional movie music, which paid as much per song as he had earned per month at the record company. In addition, he composed incidental music for plays by the celebrated dramatist, Cao Yu.[45] Under increasing censorship, he spent more time bringing music to ordinary Chinese, giving violin instruction to poor students and leading choruses of workers.[46] These consciousness-raising ensembles were sometimes large, such as the four thousand workers, students, and shop clerks who met in June 1936 for a "Song-singing Meeting" under the auspices of the "Mountain and Sea Work-Study League" of Shanghai.[47]

The Nationalist Party begrudgingly agreed to cooperate with the Communists after the Xi'an Incident of December 12, 1936, when unhappy troops from Manchuria kidnapped Chiang Kaishek, threatening to kill him if he did not offer greater resistance to the Japanese. After the Japanese attact upon Shanghai in July 1937, Xian toured the interior with a propaganda team organized by underground Communist Party workers. The team gave concerts and organized "Great Song Demonstrations" in Suzhou, Nanjing, Kaifeng, and Luoyang. Its members visited coal mines, factories, shops, villages, and schools, leaving behind newly organized choruses and at least partially trained music cadres to continue propaganda work through music.

In Wuhan, Xian tried working for the government. In April 1938, he joined the Third Office of the Military Affairs Commission's Political Department in Wuhan. Zhou Enlai had become deputy director of the Political Department in an effort to forest United Front politics against the Japanese. In the Third Office, Guo Moruo headed an impressive band of propaganda workers (including Tian Han), whose enthusiasm always exceeded what the Guomindang would tolerate.

Xian was in charge of musical propaganda, including composing and disseminating his songs. Xian organized "singing teams"—political choruses of committed young people. Xian married a member of one of these teams in July 1938: Qian Yunling, a teacher and the daughter of a Wuhan social scientist. Her team met twice weekly under Xian's direction to learn national salvation songs, conducting, composition and the rudiments of musical knowledge. Afterwards members dispersed to set up new singing teams themselves, and to carry out resistance propaganda on the streets.[48]

A high point of Xian's musico-political activism came in July 1938, when hundreds of thousands of marchers carried torches and sang his songs, including a chorus of nearly a hundred thousand singers on two hundred boats in the Yangzi River. Xian had become the Busby Berkely of the Chinese Left.[49] But the Guomindang authorities disbanded the teams, and even struck the words "national salvation" from the printed program for one singing demonstration.[50]

By the end of 1938 Xian had written almost four hundred songs bearing such titles as "Protect Marco Polo Bridge," "National Salvation Demonstration Song," "The March 8th Women's' Day Song," "Song of War of Resistance to Japan," "To the Enemy's Rear," and "In the Taihang Mountains."[51] Xian also tried his hand at larger musical forms, but only specific political occasions, such as a cantata to commemorate the death of Gorky.

This musical activity was certainly unlike anything Xian had studied at the Paris Conservatory, and he was a long way from composing the great Chinese symphony, which remained incomplete while he was busy with politics. Nevertheless this was rooted firmly in another Western musical tradition: the hyms of the Christian missionaries. The sounds of hearty Christian fellowship can be heard in Xian's militant "To the Enemy's Rear," and the four-square rhythms of the "Battle Song of Resistance Against Japan," reverberate with overtones of the salvation of heathen souls. Xian Xinghai's YMCA orgins are carefully concealed in most publications about the life of this most venerated of composers in the People's Republic. Yet the linkage between songs for the salvation of the nation and those for the salvation of souls was apparent to Xian's contemporaries. W. H. Auden and Christopher Isherwood report hearing Chinese parishioners at a Church of Canada mission in rural Henan singing as a hynm Nie Er's "March of the Volunteers," retrofitted with Christian vocabulary, although Tian Han's chorus of "Arise! Arise!" is happily suited for both political and religious use.[52]

Even the methods for spreading group singing were taken directly from the Christian missionaries, who had their own reasons for developing effective techniques for spreading messages. The missionaries introduced a simplified musical notation (*jianpu*) that is easy to teach and print. This notation represents musical notes though a system of numbers (for pitch), dots (for octaves), and lines (for note length). It is still widely used in the People's Republic of China, where the system is said to have Japanese origins.[53]

In both the revolutionary song movement and in his collegiate work with the Young Men's Christian Association, Xian worked among educated young people from high schools and colleges who liked to sing and had been exposed to Western music in the treaty ports.[54] Despite Xian's desire to extend the movement to include more workers, shop clerks, and peasants, these groups (especially the peasants) were less familiar with group singing than urban intellectuals. The music of the national salvation movement could not transcend the social obstacles that impeded united front politics in the 1930s.

Later, in Yan'an, Xian criticized his work from this period, saying that his understanding of workers was inadequate,

> and my compositions were still shallow and insubstantial. But they were far richer than my Paris compositions. Even the style of my Paris works was uncertain. It had only the style of the impressionist school plus a little Chinese flavor. What made me especially happy was that my composition had found a path, absorbing the feelings of the oppressed. I became confident how to apply my strengths of the problem of our native land's peril. I felt that my compositions had progressed a step; they began to be bound up with practical struggle.[55]

Yan'an as a City of Song

Xian was increasingly unhappy in Wuhan. Although he was well paid, he found the atmosphere in the Third Office to be lazy, while the Guomindang was undoing his work by disbanding the singing teams and censoring his songs. When Xian was invited to head the music department of the Lu Xun Arts Academy in the Communists' capital of Yan'an in 1938, he accepted after satisfying himself that his needs for artistic freedom would not be compromised.[56] Although like many leftist intellectuals Xian was not a Communist, he had been working closely with Party members since his return to China. He had little hesitation in working directly with the organization that took most seriously the use of music to promote radical change.

Even in 1938 Yan'an was shrouded in legend. This small city in northern Shaanxi became the capital of the Communist revolution when Mao and his troops arrived in 1936 at the conclusion of the Long March from the Jiangxi Soviet. Yan'an was an improverished cultural backwater, and several people advised Xian not to go. But he was not alone in moving to Yan'an. The Party was recruiting angry young Chinese intellectuals to bring their cosmopolitan skills to the boondocks, to join in fighting the Japanese with a vigor that the Guomindang could not match. Yan'an was under Guomindang blockade, so Xian's move was not simple. In November 1938, Xian and his new wife rode from the city of Xi'an through the Guomindang inspection point disguised as an Overseas Chinese merchant couple.[57]

The Communist Party had used the arts politically before Yan'an, although on a more limited basis.[58] Early in the 1920s the radical organizer Peng Pai wrote revolutionary songs in folksong style in order to mobilize the Guangdong peasantry. When the Communist Party established its Soviet government in Jiangxi in 1928, the Red Army similarly taught peasants new revolutionary words to traditional folksongs, in addition to singing the "Internationale" and Soviet marches. The Jiangxi Soviet's model country, Xingguo, had a "Blue Blouse Troupe," which staged recruiting drives, entertained prisoners, and even "sang songs at the front during battle, both to encourage Red Army soldiers and to urge enemy soldiers to desert."[59] But innovation was difficult in the Jiangxi Soviet; there were few professional artists, and limited familiarity with local art forms. The Party had only two or three musicians, none of whom knew how to compose.[60] Qu Qiubai advised Party cultural workers to simply to put new words to old tunes because these "were often better than what could be composed new and that, since they were already familiar to the peasants, they could be learned easily and spread rapidly."[61]

Thus when the Communist made Yan'an their capital at the end of the long march, they were eager to tap the new anti-Japanese and revolutionary enthusiasm of young intellectuals to improve their propaganda work. One should not exaggerate the importance of culture in Yan'an; the revolutionary and anti-imperialist war was the Party's highest priority. Yet culture was a part of the strategy for winning that war;

the amount of artistic activity is striking, given Yan'an paucity of resources.

One of Xian's close associates was Zheng Lucheng (1918–1976), a composer of Korean nationality, who in 1963 reminisced about Yan'an:

> Everyone sang then, morale was very high. At first we sang Red Army songs, like "The Three Main Rules of Discipline and the Eight Points of Attention," and we also had local folk songs. Later, the songs of Nie Er, Xian Xinghai, and Lu Ji also became popular, like "In the Taihang Mountains." This revolutionary and expressive song was very stirring; as soon as you began singing, people would be moved endlessly. . . . Resist-Japan University had nearly ten thousand students, divided into a great many companies, each one of which had a conductor. Whenever major reports were made, there were gathered on the field from five to six thousand up to ten thousand people. We learned songs for half an hour or an hour before we began: this group would sing, then that group would sing, all very enthusiastically. First, some groups would choose female teams to sing, followed then by singing contests on all sides. Yan'an is a small place, between the mountain and the river. When ten thousand people sang at once, the earth seemed to move and the mountain shake. We sang before class, we sang before eating, and whole units sang on the march. Students sang, cadres sang, ordinary people sang. There was solo singing, ensemble singing, and choral singing. Yan'an was not only the sacred place of the revolution, it also became a true city of song.[62]

There are three reasons for this effort to build a Vienna in rural Shaanxi. One is the traditional Chinese propensity to view the arts as an intimate aspect of political and social life. Especially as Mao Zedong gradually increased his power within the Party by systematically signifying Marxism, he raised the status of culture and ideological work above the priorities set by European Marxism. Second, the urban intellecturals who abandoned Shanghai and other cities for a life of rural revolution counted singing as a type of modernity. As revolution was modern, revolutionaries would naturally sing. A third reason flows directly from the poverty of Yan'an. Art can be cheap, especially the kinds of mass mobilizing activities for which Yan'an became famous. In the absence of television, radio, and record players, music was an inexpensive way to boost moral and build a sense of community. The Party's leaders were convinced that cultural activity could make a critical difference in the struggle against both the Japanese and the Guomindang, much as a grateful Napoleon felt when he allegedly said to Roger de Lisle, composer of the "Marseillaise," "You have saved the need for many cannon with your music."

To accomplish this, the Party in 1938 established an arts academy, named after Lu Xun (1881–1936), the great leftist writer whose death was still being mourned. Literature and drama were its most important components, but there was also much music, far out of proportion to the number of musicians, who were as scarce in Yan'an as they were throughout China. The Lu Xun Arts Academy had over 50 faculty members and 100 research and professional staff, graduating 685 cultural cadres between 1938 and 1945.[63] Yan'an's other training schools, for military and Party personnel, were much larger.

The Lu Xun Arts Academy, housed in a former Christian church, was one of six cadre training schools in Yan'an.[64] Xian's job was similar to his responsibilities in Wuhan, except that he had fewer resources but more political support and encouragement. The academy trained cultural cadres who were to go out and raise consciousness for the revolution. Xian taught these young cadres how to compose songs and to organize and conduct choral groups. He also supervised the academy's own choir, in addition to musical responsibilities at three of Yan'an's other schools, the Anti-Japanese Military and Political College, the Chinese Women's College, and the North Shaanxi Public School.[65]

In Yan'an, Xian shared the austere life of China's revolutionary base. He lived in a cave, he worked in the fields, and he wore shoes which he made himself of straw and cotton.[66] Nonetheless, Xian said he enjoyed a better living in Yan'an than Paris, even if it was poorer than Wuhan or Shanghai. Yet Xian stood out in several respects. He held an important cultural post and thus received better treatment than most people. The academy personnel enjoyed better food than others, for instance.[67] Among all the newly arrived urban intellectuals, Xian's working class origins must have been an asset, as workers were rare in rural northern China. But the Cantonese which helped disguise his entry to Yan'an had a negative side, as Xian spoke Mandarin very poorly, even for a Cantonese.[68]

Xian was not only the head of Yan'an's "conservatory," he was also its composer-in-residence. His music was genuinely popular, and soon after his arrival he began to receive requests for special songs. A

"Youth Training Class Song" was followed by anthems which Xian provided specifically for various schools, training classes, work units, and military detachments.[69]

Xian found the new stimuli of Yan'an a congenial atmosphere for composing. In his year and a half there, he wrote four cantatas, two operas, and "probably five or six hundred songs."[70] Although much of this music was written very quickly, Xian began to mix Western and Chinese elements in new ways, especially in the bigger pieces, such as a *Production Cantata* (to spur output in opposition to the Guomindang blockade), and in an opera (*geju*), Song of the Soldiers' Advance. These words consciously mixed Western composition techniques with Chinese instruments and national spirit.[71]

The use of Chinese instruments was more than an esthetic whim. Yan'an was so poor that it had no piano until Chen Yi (later to become China's foreign minister) sent one from the New Fourth Army, but it apparently did not arrive until after Xian's departure.[72] Other than a handful of such easily portable items as violins and accordions, there were no Western instruments in Yan'an, leading Xian to assemble available Chinese instruments to discover if he could use them to compensate for the lack of pianos, oboes, and violas.

Xian's famous *Yellow River Cantata*, celebrated for its combination of Chinese and Western instruments, and its "rich national color," was born amidst the discipline of scarcity, as was much of Yan'an culture.[73] Little in Xian's past training encouraged him to accept the instruments which he now embraced in his makeshift orchestra: a guitar, an *erhu* (two-stringed fiddle), a *dizi* (bamboo flute), native drums, bugles, a bass *huchin* (another fiddle) fashioned from an oil drum, and a new percussion instrument made of a enameled vat filled with spoons.[74] If a full orchestra of European instruments had been available, Xian would have sacrificed his experiments in local color; he in fact wanted no fewer than twelve trumpets, twelve trombones, and six horns for his orchestra.[75] While working on the cantata, Xian wrote: "I am just now researching the characteristics of Chinese musical instruments, and am thinking of using their strong points to make up for the current lack of Western instruments."[76]

The *Yellow River Cantata* carried Xian's propaganda songs of the national salvation movement to a new and grander level. It celebrates China's land and people, and the guerrilla war against Japan. Its lyrics are somewhat classical in style, as befit even Communist art before

Mao's 1942 "Talks at the Yan'an Forum." But the music still took
as its great slogan, "Protect the Yellow River!" The movements of
the cantata are introduced by a narrator, speaking dramatically over an
instrumental introduction:

> Friend! Have you been to the Yellow River? Have you crossed the
> Yellow River? Do you still recall the boatmen on the river, and how
> they risk their lives struggling against the terrifying waves? If you have
> forgotten, then listen!

A chorus of rowing and laughing boatmen follows, then a peasant
woman's lament, and a hymn to China's physical majesty, as well as
musical references ranging from ancient Chinese tunes to Nie Er's
"March of the Volunteers." There had never been anything like it. In
Wong's view,

> It is by far the most convincing synthesis of Western and Chinese music
> idioms. In a single work it unites such diverse techniques and elements
> as, for example, the Chinese folk antiphonal singing style called *duikou
> chang*, the Chinese fisherman's work song called *haozi*, traditional
> Chinese percussive patterns and instrumentation, Hugo Wolf's declam-
> atory recitative style (adapted to the Chinese language), the traditional
> Western contrapuntal technique of choral writing, and, finally, the at-
> mospheric orchestral effects of the French Impressionistic school.[77]

The Lu Xun Arts Academy was an important center of evening entertainment in Yan'an and many of the Party's most important leaders
attended its concerts and plays. Mao Zedong attended the first performance of the *Yellow River Cantata* on April 13, 1939, and although
the singing and playing was reportedly scrappy, he indicated his enthusiasm by sending a bottle of ink and a Parker fountain pen to the
composer.[78]

The cantata was immediately popular, and was often performed on
ceremonial occasions, such as the May 11, 1939 concert to commemorate the first birthday of the Lu Xun Arts Academy, or in July of the
same year to celebrate Zhou Enlai's return to Yan'an. Zhou wrote an
inscription for Xian, which certainly would have puzzled Dukas and
D'Indy at the Paris Conservatory: "Roar for the War of Resistance,
Set to music the cry of the masses!"[79] Xian's cantata was also performed in Guomindang-controlled Kumming, Chengdu, and Chongqing, as well as by the musicians of China's allies in New York,
Moscow, and London.[80]

Xian's musical triumph was followed by his admission into the Communist Party. Xian had been a leftist since the 1920s, but often, like many urban intellectuals, he placed struggle against imperialism before domestic issues, and was unsophisticated about Marxism. But his path from nationalism to socialism was common among young intellectuals of his time. He began studying Marx and Lenin in earnest after his arrival in Yan'an. At first he reacted to political life in the Communist capital by thinking there were too many meetings, but later he defended their importance in working out problems.[81] Xian's letter of application for Party membership speaks of the Party's ability to help him reach his goal of creating a new Chinese music for the masses, colored with the spirit of the nation, but also appeals for more Party support for music comparable with that for literature, the art which dominated Yan'an.[82] Xian's cheerful radicalism is suggested by his inscription on a student's copy of the Soviet textbook, *Short History of the Communist Party of the Soviet Union (Bolshevik):*

> You sing, I sing, everyone sings. We must sing for victory in the War of Resistance against Japan, we must sing for the future of the new China. Now that you have this *History of the Communist Party*, you can sing even better songs.[83]

One evening in May 1940, Xian and his wife were invited to dinner at the home of Mao Zedong. Chinese sources do not indicate how frequently the Xians socialized with the Chairman and his young wife, Jiang Qing, but this occasion was special: a farewell dinner. A group of Soviet film-makers had been in China to make a documentary to be called *The Eighth Route Army and the People*. On the instructions of the Central Committee, Xian went to Moscow to compose music appropriate to the film.[84] Although this assignment meant leaving his wife and young daughter behind, it also offered an opportunity to work on his music under calmer conditions. But neither Xian nor Mao realized that the journey would last for five years, that Xian would never return to China, and that the Yan'an musical life which he had nurtured would undergo a radical change in his absence.

Populist Versus Cosmopolitan Revolutionaries

When intellectuals like Xian came to Yan'an, they were welcomed for their activism, their skills, and their revolutionary attitudes. But the longer the Communists remained in Yan'an, the greater the tension between the iconoclastic and cosmopolitan culture of the urban intellectuals and the very traditional folk culture of the peasants in the Shen-Gan-Ning Border Region. Modernized, eurocentric culture had little appeal to the often illiterate peasants who formed the Communists' social base. Yet these were the people whose energies the arts of Yan'an were to unleash, whose sons had to be mobilized into the Eighth Route Army.

Xian Xinghai's ambivalent attitude was typical of urban intellectuals in Yan'an. Even before coming to the Communist capital, he had railed against those musicians who plagiarized and copied Western music.

> I am an Eastern composer, I want to compose music with the color of the Eastern nationalities, that the broad masses of the people will enjoy, and to offer my own strength for the liberation of my nation's peoples and the liberation of the oppressed peoples of the East.[85]

The spirit of national resistance against the Japanese, and the political need to win over the peasants of northern China encouraged a concern with native culture. Xian often stopped on roadside to record local folk songs, filling more than seven books of folk music, an activity that would have shocked his conservative professors at the Paris Conservatory.[86] And he arranged for the Academy's Folk Song Research Association to transcribe the local songs brought to Yan'an by youth from all of China. But still he regarded songs as basis for the music of backward peoples. China, he said, was somewhat more progressive than the Eskimos, American Indians, Africans, and Australian aborigines, but still had not escaped the "stage of song music." Traditional music should be improved by adding the harmony and counterpoint that he had studied in Europe. And even though he was willing to explore peasant instruments for *The Yellow River Cantata*, he still wanted to make them modern. He planned a textbook of music theory for his Yan'an students, to include a chapter on "How to Improve and Create Chinese Musical Instruments."[87]

In the beginning, the cosmopolitan artists were willing to make a bow toward local culture. But as the cosmpolitans who studied scientific socialism and read Marx castigated "the idiocy of rural life," they also stiffened their antipathy toward peasant superstition and feudal custom. Indeed, in the early 1940s Yan'an's cultural leaders were worried about raising the standards of their revolutionary art, and relatively less concerned abut popularizing it or providing public entertainment for the Yan'an community.[88]

Qu Qiubai had mocked the cosmpolitan impulse among China's intellectuals before the Party came to Yan'an.

> The cadres of revolutionary literature are captives of the bourgeois May Fourth cultural movement. The majority of them are standing on the other side of a Great Wall—they do not have a common language with the Chinese working people, and to the middle and lower ranks of the people they are almost "foreigners." They live in "their own country of intellectual youth" and in the stationery stores of the Europeanized gentry.[89]

The politicians who led the Communist Party were sophisticates but not cosmopolitans. Seeking a way to break down this "great wall" that the intellectuals brought from Shanghai to Yan'an, Mao Zedong, in his famous "Talks at the Yan'an Forum on Literature and Art," advocated a culture that was both populist and nationalist (but not cosmopolitan), a culture that would address the needs of the peasants whose support the Party must arouse for victory.

The "Yan'an Forum" of 1942 was part of a broader rectification of the Party, a process which resulted in greater emphasis upon the populist mass line, in further adaptations of Marxist theory to fit Chinese conditions, and in the consolidation of Mao Zedong's position as chief leader of the Communist Party.[90] Mao spoke twice in May to the Party's cultural workers, advocating strenuous efforts to identify with ordinary peasants.[91] If the artists themselves were urban intellectuals, then they must try to cease being outsiders, to "submerge themselves in the ordinary life of the countryside in order to become different people in the course of living altered lives."[92] Mao denounced art for art's sake, and insisted that "all culture or literature and art belongs to a definite class and party, and has a definite political line."[93]

Mao's "Talks at the Yan'an Forum" remains a fundamental text in China's cultural politics. In 1942, it led to a disciplining of the artistic forces which Mao commanded in Yan'an. In music, the first fruit of the Yan'an forum was the politicized adaptation of the northern Chinese dances, songs, and variety acts known as *yangge*. *Yangge* are traditionally performed by peasant amateurs at New Year. It is often described as a rice-planting song, but while *yangge* can mean "rice sprout" in some areas, in others it does not.[94] The Lu Xun Arts Academy

Propaganda Troupe first reformed the *yangge* for political use in the 1943 Spring Festival. This initial effort still seemed to have a Western flavor, as the orchestra added seven violins and a cello to native flutes, gongs, cymbals, and drums. Indeed, it was only after the Yan'an Forum that music students were required to study folksong and local opera. Before the Forum, they had performed a "Viennese Rhapsody," dressed formally in ties and tails.[95] Traditional *yangge* often had a comic eroticism that the music workers now removed as they reshaped this native art to include mass-mobilizing political messages about such issues as literacy, women's rights, and fighting the Japanese. The *yangge* were adaptable to local customs and easy to teach, making them symbols of the Party during this period. Three slogans ruled *yangge* productions: "short and snappy," "self-composed and self-performed," and "real people and real events."[96] Such music was popular as well as politically sound. By late 1944 there were almost a thousand *yangge* troupes.[97]

The other famous musical response to the Yan'an Forum was *The White-Haired Girl,* a 1945 opera which rivals *The Yellow River Cantata* as a milestone in the creation of a new Chinese music. This opera (not to be confused with the glitzier ballet of the same title composed under Jiang Qing's supervision in the 1960s) was based on the northern Chinese legend of Yang Xier, a young peasant woman who flees after being raped by a bullying landlord, Huang Shiren. In hiding, her hair turns white, leading villagers to mistake her for a spirit. The Communist army captures the spirit, who then appears before a mass meeting and dramatically denounces her oppressor. *The White-Haired Girl* became very popular for its portrayal of an oppression easily understood by peasants.

> In the first performance, as the Eighth Route Army caught the landlord and the chorus sang "Hack Huang Shiren to a thousand pieces!" the audience was roused to such anger that it demanded Huang's execution. The landlord had to be hastily ushered offstage. Another time, a soldier in the audience raised his gun to kill the landlord to avenge his own family. Fortunately he was restrained in time. In the end, the script had to be altered to include a proclamation of the execution of Huang Shiren.[98]

The White-Haired Girl was written collectively by several members of the Lu Xun Arts Academy. The principal composer was Ma Ke, a former chemistry student who have been trained by Xian in Yan'an.

Working with five other composers, Ma set the text of He Jingzhi and Ding Yi to a music that was based closely on peasant singing styles, yet with a Westernized flavor that sets it apart from traditional Chinese opera.[99] In accord with Yan'an populism, Ma Ke rejected "China's 'orthodox faction' of musicians," for whom "only Western music is pure music." Such musicians claimed that only the styles of Wagner or Puccini were appropriate for opera, even when the subject was Chinese. Ma insisted that the rich experiences of the Chinese people could not be expressed "in the musical language of the West's previous generation." But neither could traditional Chinese opera be a guide. According to Ma, Chinese opera remained the highest art of feudal society, despite modern reforms to make it more attractive to the urban petty bourgeoisie. Instead, one had to turn for inspiration to the music of the peasants, "the art of society's oppressed masses." Ma and his fellow composers worked with peasant musicians to find raw melodic material in their folk songs, then worked at "raising them to become opera music" by fashioning them into arias and adding choral music, an overture, and other Western forms and orchestrating them with mixed Sino-European instrumentation.[100]

Return to Europe

In Moscow, Xian was unaware of Yan'an's populist trend in music. War in China—and soon in the Soviet Union also—made communication impossible. For the next five years, Xian worked without supervision by the Chinese Communist Party. While he did nothing that would embarrass the Party, his work took a very different course than developments in Yan'an. After the rigors of Yan'an under blockade, Xian enjoyed returning to Europe and the rich concert life of Moscow.[101] He had time for study (of Russian, as well as music), and he met prominent Soviet composers, such as Reinhold Gliere and Dmitri Kabelevsky.[102] Although there is no record, one imagines that he resumed contact with Prokofiev, who had returned to the Soviet Union in 1933.

Freed from the constant demand to compose occasional pieces for the revolution, the pleasures of Soviet music inspired him to complete his long-postponed symphony, which he called the *National Liberation Symphony* and dedicated to "The Central Committee of the Great

Chinese Communist Party and its Glorious Leader Comrade Mao Zedong.'' Xian had completed a full piano score in 1937, but had only
been able to work on the orchestration intermittently because of political work and a shortage of music paper in Yan'an. The four-movement
symphony is clearly a nationalist work, celebrating China's scenery
and history, inspired by Chinese dances, and with a finale entitled
''Establish New Democratic China''[103] He also rescored *The Yellow
River Cantata* for conventional symphony orchestra, using five-line
notation, so it could be performed in Europe and the United States.[104]

Away from China, it is clear that Xian regarded this symphony as
his serious work. He dismissed the hundreds of revolutionary songs
rather abruptly: ''Although they had no special artistic value, they have
already fulfilled my responsibility to the people!''[105] This comment
makes it easier to understand Xian's eagerness to help his student Li
Huanzhi with an instrumental quintet at Yan'an. Amidst all the political music, the quintet was so unusual that Xian could not contain his
enthusiasm.[106]

The German invasion of June 1941 made Xian's presence in the
Soviet Union a burden on his hosts, who postponed completion of the
China documentary.[107] He left Moscow to return to China in Septem-
ber 1941, but could proceed no further than Outer Mongolia. The
Guomindang refused reentry to Xian and other Communists. Xian pe-
titioned unsuccessfully for a year, during which he worked in Ulan
Bator. There he practiced the skills that he had learned in Yan'an,
training Mongol musicians, and leading a chorus and band at the Chinese
Workers Club. In addition, he studied Mongol folk music, using it as
the basis for some new instrumental compositions.[108]

Despairing of gaining Guomindang permission to enter to China,
Xian returned to the Soviet Union in November 1942.[109] But instead
of the battlefield of embattled Moscow, Xian went to the Kazakh Republic, where he spent a year in Alma-Ata. Again, he used his skills
in mass cultural work, helping to establish a network of musical institutions in northern Kazakh. He also completed his Second Symphony
The Sacred Battle, commemorating the Soviet struggle against fas-
cism, and dedicated to Stalin and the Soviet Red Army. This symphony includes musical representations of fascist tanks and bombs,
and of the four allies: the Soviet Union, China, Britain, and the United
States. An Andante is supposed to depict mutual aid treaties between
the Soviet Union and the United States and Britain.[110]

Xian's works away from China were certainly more serious than his revolutionary songs. They include a "tone painting," *Chinese Life*, with representations of boat people on the river, peasants in the fields, youthful coolies, and a night in a village. As his final work Xian wrote a *Chinese Rhapsody* based on folk melodies from around China, including the *yangge* of northern Shaanxi, as well as songs from Shanxi and Guangdong.[111]

Xian's health deteriorated. After three months of pneumonia he was moved to a Moscow hospital in spring of 1945. Under wartime conditions Xian had been unable to contact Yan'an since 1941; Guo Moruo was in Moscow and took word back to Yan'an of Xian's illness.[112] Xian was also suffering from peritonitis, as well as heart and liver disease. Cheered by Japan's defeat, he remained optimistic of his chances for recovery, asking Gliere for music paper and, on his deathbed, writing a "thirty-five year plan" for future composition. He died on October 30, 1945 at 40 years of age, and was buried outside Moscow. There his ashes remained until 1983, when they were put in Beijing's Babaoshan Cemetery.[113] Two weeks after his death there was a memorial service in Yan'an, for which Mao contributed an inscription: "Grieve the People's Musician Comrade Xian Xinghai!"[114]

The Legacy of Xian Xinghai

When news of Xian's death reached Yan'an, a minor cult was born. Xian Xinghai would be the "people's musician." By stressing the revolutionary uses to which Xian put his Paris training, the eminently bourgeois musical art of the West could be given a home in the new China. But the two sides of Xian—Communist and impressionist, cosmopolitan symphonist serving a peasant revolution—have adhered to each other with difficulty.

For the middle class of China's cities, Xian became a romantic figure. By 1947 Xian Xinghai was the model for a character in a popular movie, *Eight Thousand Li of Clouds and Moon*. In one scene, the Xian-figure is seen extending half his body out of a window, playing the violin with all his heart.[115] Although the film was not an Asian *Amadeus*, Xian Xinghai's legend has reached a comparable status for the cosmopolitans of China's urban middle class. His vigorous spirit, life of struggle, and early death placed him in the most romantic tra-

dition of Chopin, Schubert, Weber, and Mozart. Xian's life weighed
more heavily than his mostly unperformed compositions in making
him the first genuine Chinese composer. As the cosmopolitans viewed
him, Xian was not the "people's musician" of Mao Zedong, but a
romantic symbol of China's determination to achieve world recognition in what cosmopolitan Chinese regard as international culture. For
less sophisticated members of China's middle class, Xian and Nie Er
are vaguely blended together into one great Western-style composer of
the Left, dead in youth and venerated by the Party.[116]

For professional musicians, however, Xian is far more important
than dreamy romanticism about art. He represents an entire generation
of Chinese musicians who have struggled with the relationship between cosmopolitan musical culture and the concrete demands of China's revolution. Nie Er wrote in his diary, on February 7, 1932: "How
to make revolutionary music?' I spent the whole day thinking about
this question, but in the end did not think of a concrete plan."[117] Xian
came closer to an answer, suggesting a way of linking "modern"
musical art from Europe to revolutionary demands for new techniques
of mobilizing the masses. In Beijing there is a small shrine for Xian
in the form of a memorial room in the Chinese Music Research Institute, containing the piano he played in Shanghai and furniture he used
in Outer Mongolia.[118] Xian is held up as a model for professional,
Westernized musicians because of his studies at the Paris Conservatory, and for his skill at writing the politicized music that the times
demanded.

Xian was also the patron or fellow worker of many musicians who
have become members of the Chinese musical establishment. Many
studied within him in Yan'an or Wuhan, and many others of this generation of musical leadership feel a bond with him. The fact that Xian,
after the age of six, spent one half of his life abroad, sets him apart.
But in other ways he is representative of an entire cohort of musicians
who came of age before the establishment of the People's Republic.
Most are from eastern and southern China, the areas of greatest Western penetration. Thirty-eight Chinese composers born before 1920 have
biographies in *Yinyue Xinshang Shouce* [Handbook of Music Appre-
ciation]; thirteen are from the lower Yangzi region (Jiangsu, Zhejiang,
Shanghai) and six are from Guangdong (including Macao).[119] Although the biographies give scanty information about social background, they cite the petty bourgeois occupations held by many of

these musicians before joining the revolution, which continue the pre-
cident began by Xian with his office work in the film and record business. Nie Er was a shop clerk selling piece goods and tobacco before
he joined a record company. Composer Mai Xin (1915–1947) was a
clerk for an insurance company before he participated in the new music movement.[120]

The Xian Xinghai cult in music resembles the Lu Xun cult in literature.[121] Xian was a leading figure of the revolutionary era, safely
dead. His status as patron saint of his art has been sustained by his
Yan'an students and colleagues who have built their subsequent careers in the cultural bureaucracy in part on their ties to Xian, who
showed how to combine his two great loves; bourgeois music and
socialist revolution.

Xian's official legacy stresses populism at the expense of cosmo-
politan interests. In his short Chinese career, Xian had constantly bent
Western art to the needs of Chinese politics, and he did so joyfully.
Since Xian was dead, his legacy could be bent still further with im-
punity. Here is Ma Ke, Xian's disciple and biographer, composer of
The White-Haired Girl, and leading member of the musical establish-
ment after 1949 as vice-director of the Institute of Chinese Traditional
Music and director of the Chinese Opera Theater:

> His most important lesson to us is: we must not write music for music's
> sake; the only way to develop music successfully is to make it serve
> the revolution. Virtually all his works deal with the life of the masses,
> using forms loved by the masses; hence they combine a popular style
> with a revolutionary content. [Xian] studied traditional Chinese music
> seriously, although he was not a traditionalist who clung to the past;
> and at the same time he also absorbed and adapted the useful elements
> of Western music to develop Chinese music. In this way he succeeded
> in making his music both modern and revolutionary.[122]

Neither the Paris Conservatory student not the Moscow symphonist is
discernible in this image. Departing even further from Xian as admirer
of Dukas and D'Indy, during the Cultural Revolution his widow described her husband so that he resembled Lei Feng, the Maoist hero
of self-abnegation, as she bragged about his modesty, his charity to
the needy, his generosity in helping others to complete their tasks, and
his love for the masses and Chairman Mao.[123]

Xian's populism was real, and is easily heard in his still-popular

Yellow River Cantata and revolutionary songs. But the compositions that he regarded most highly are infrequently played. For all the talk about Xian as the composer of the first Chinese symphony, for instance, it is astonishing that his *National Liberation Symphony* was first performed only in 1985.[124] When, on his deathbed, Xian assigned opus numbers to his important works, he excluded his hundreds of revolutionary songs, returning at the end to favor cantatas, symphonic music, piano suites, and other conventional forms of European musical culture. But these works were sealed, preventing not only performance but study.[125]

Until 1980 important facts about Xian's life were not readily accessible. His Christian background, his ties to Ma Sitson (Ma Sicong) his Moscow catalog of compositions, his American teachers at Lingnan, and his ties to the Russians Avsholomov and Tcherepnin in Shanghai were all concealed. His failure to graduate from the Paris Conservatory is still unacknowledged in China. In 1962 a two-volume collection of materials of Xian was published but not given public distribution: instead, access was restricted as if it contained military secrets. This is now changing; the first book in a multivolume set of Xian's works was published for open distribution in December 1986 in Guangdong, and there is talk of making available preliberation recordings on which Xian sings his own and other works.[126]

Xian's populism has been exaggerated and his cosmopolitan side diminished for political reasons. Revolution, sweeping over the arts in twentieth-century China, forced a choice: music could be modern because it resembled Europe's, or it could be modern because it served the revolution. The politics of Chinese music has allowed a degree of cohesion between these two conceptions of modernity. Although they sometimes coincide, they can also diverge. When elitism prevails (as in the Hundred Flowers or the Deng Xiaoping reform period), musicians are asked to make Western forms Chinese, or to show Chinese mastery of "international" musical technique. When populism is dominant (as at Yan'an or in the Cultural Revolution), the musician's task is to adopt national forms into modern music that serves the revolution.

Because Xian is linked to both cosmopolitan and populist musical cultures in China, his image has been used to obscure the tensions between them in death, as in life. The Xian Xinghai cult is unusual in that it has endured, like Lu Xun's, despite the changes in China's political climate. Xian was honored by the radicals of the Cultural Revolution and he is now honored by their elitist successors. Musicians know how cosmopolitan Xian was. Party cultural leaders emphasize his populism in order to encourage Xian's musical descendants to continue his political as well as his musical heritage. Yet China's "music workers" have found his sainted image useful for their own purpose of protecting the entire enterprise of Western classical music. At the same time, the Left's simplification of Xian Xinghai's complexity has caused many Western-style musicians to sneer privately at his memory today.[127]

The cosmopolitans began by regarding modern European music as beyond politics. European musical culture offered freedom from the oppressive Confucian concern with music's political impact. But that concern was never far beneath the surface, as in reformer Liang Qiqiao's fear that China's lethargic music was to blame for military weakness.[128] Revolution and foreign invasion forced modern urban intellectuals to apply their music explicitly to political purposes. Xian did not consciously adopt Confucian musical precepts, but his politicized career was in harmony with a traditional Chinese union of art and statecraft. The political crisis masked the tensions between populist and cosmopolitan by forcing the two to join in political action. After the Japanese were defeated and the revolution consolidated, China's leaders found it harder to combine cosmopolitan and populist impulses without turning to compulsion.

3

The Defector: Fou Ts'ong

The first internationally celebrated pianist of the People's Republic was Fou Ts'ong, whose family is a model of modernizing cosmopolitanism. Fou's father was the noted translator and essayist, Fu Lei. In 1956 the twenty-three-year-old Fou Ts'ong (Fu Cong)[1] was already among China's most celebrated musicians, and his proud father was a leading member of Shanghai literary life. Yet ten years later this prominent family of bourgeois intellectuals, seemingly well integrated into the new regime, had been destroyed. Fou Ts'ong was in exile, having refused to return to China from his studies in Warsaw, and his parents had become two of the most notorious suicides of the Cultural Revolution. Fu Lei subsequently has been posthumously rehabilitated, and his son has returned to China as an honored musician. Many Chinese take the personal tragedy of the Fou family as emblematic of the fate of China's urban intellectuals.

A Rebellious Prodigy

The Fu family was too prominent and too prosperous to be typical of urban intellectuals. But at their moment of success, they were exemplary of what this class could aspire to in the new China. In recent years, partly because of the family's tragic history and partly because of the renewed influence of their class, the Fus have become a posthumous model for upright behavior, principled integrity, and child-rearing. The principal text by which their model is transmitted is a volume of letters written by Fu Lei to Fou Ts'ong in his years abroad. This book offers a glimpse into the emotional life of a leading Chinese intellectual family through a period of great change. It describes an extraordinary relationship between father and son, one which shaped both Fou Ts'ong's career and Fu Lei's destruction.

Fu Lei was born in 1908 in a village near Shanghai.[2] Like his contemporary, Xian Xinghai, he was raised by a strong-willed mother after his father's death. They also both studied in France, although Fu Lei's father had been a wealthy landlord, making Fu one of the prosperous Chinese students who disdained the likes of Xian, playing he violin on the streets of Paris.[3] Fu returned to China to join the faculty of Shanghai Arts University.[4] Unlike Xian, but more typical of Shanghai's urban intelligentsia, Fu Lei did not join the revolution.

The Significance of Jean-Christophe

Fu Lei's translations of French literature were an important conduit of European culture into China. Fu translated fourteen novels of Balzac, and was especially renowned for his Chinese version of Romain Rolland's *Jean-Christophe*.[5] The Chinese cosmopolitans' vision of European culture often lags by several years or decades behind what is actually stylish in Europe. Xian Xinghai's enthusiasm for Dukas and D'Indy and disinterest in Stravinsky or Schoenberg is one example. Another is the Chinese fondness for Romain Rolland, the French novelist who lived between 1866 and 1944.[6]

Rolland's reputation has faded considerably since he won the Nobel prize for literature in 1915. He was best known for *Jean-Christophe*, a novel in ten volumes which presented the story of Jean-Christophe Krafft, an imaginary master composer.[7] This massive and sentimental novel describes a Beethoven-like figure, a visionary artist at odds with a vulgar and hostile society. The book is full of what was once highly regarded as lofty idealism, but which seems gushy and mock-heroic by the more ironic tastes of the late-twentieth-century West. In France, old socialists and starry-eyed adolescents still read *Jean-Christophe*, and it is still popular in China, where Rolland's highly romantic conception of the artist has been an influential image of Western musical art.

Jean-Christophe is a sensitive genius in an unappreciative world.

Although he enjoys artistic triumph in the end, his life is one of cease-less struggle. It is clear throughout the book that only a sensitive and cultivated elite is capable of understanding true music, while ordinary people are attracted to the gaudy show of the moment. In the course of this saga, Jean-Christophe must overcome small-minded artistic fac-tions, cultural conservatives who are unwilling to make way for prog-ress, and above all, the divisive force of nationalism. After an encoun-ter with German militarism, Jean-Christophe is forced to leave his mother behind and flee his native Rhineland to begin a new musical career in Paris.

Rolland does not represent music as a product of society, but rather as an ether which floats above it, awaiting the appreciation of the talented few.

> Music, serene music, how sweet in thy moony light to eyes wearied of the harsh brilliance of this world's sun! The soul that has lived and turned away from the common horse-pond, where, as they drink, men stir up the mud with their feet, nestles to thy bosom, and from thy breasts is suckled with the clear running water of dreams.[8]

This is a long way from Yan'an and the *Yellow River Cantata*. Music for Rolland is a transcendant art, rising above class and nation.

Rolland's dedication appealed to China's cosmopolitans: "To the Free spirits—of all nations—who suffer, fight, and will prevail." The theme of embattled culture spoke to the urban middle-class Chinese who often despaired of modernizing an uncomprehending feudal China. Shanghai's Commercial Press published Fu Lei's translation of *Jean-Christophe* in 1937; twenty years later it was reprinted by People's Literature Publishing House.

Jean-Christophe's success made Fu Lei an important literaty figure, and was also financially rewarding. According to Red Guard accounts, Fu Lei earned 33,880 *yuan* (approximately $17,000) in royalties from *Jean-Christophe*, ranking him as the sixteenth most highly paid on a (possibly incomplete) list of Chinese authors. This sum is well below that of Ba Jin (229,624 *yuan*), Mao Dun (182,266 *yuan*), or Ding Ling (70,248 *yuan*), but comparable to royalties earned by such popular novels as Yang Mo's *Song of Youth* (43,400 *yuan*) or Zhou Libo's *The Hurricane* (40,086 *yuan*).[9]

Fou Ts'ong as a Jean-Christophe for China

Fou Ts'ong was born into a comfortable household in 1934, which included a servant and owned such machines as a radio and a phonograph, on which Fou Ts'ong's mother, Zhu Meifu, enjoyed listening to Western classical music.[10] Since the three-year-old Fou was fascinated by the music, his parents decided that his mother should teach him to play the piano.[11]

Fu Lei concluded that he had a special responsibility as he grew increasingly aware of his young son's musical gift. Just as Fu was bringing the fictional *Jean-Christophe* to China's readers, so must he nurture China's own Jean-Christophe to artistic maturity. At seven, Fou began piano lessons with an old family friend, the mathematician Lei Dan, who had studied for three years at the Shanghai Conservatory and was an old classmate of He Luting, the winner of Alexander Tcherepnin's composition contest. Fu Lei sold his wife's jewelry in order to purchase a suitable instrument for his musical son.

When Fou Ts'ong was eight, Fu Lei decided that no school could educate his son properly. He withdrew his son from school so that he might oversee his studies directly at home. This drastic step combined Confucian educational tradition and conscious emulation of James Mill's education of John Stuart Mill.[12] Like James Mill, Fu Lei prepared a rigorous course in his culture's classics. Fu Lei's pedagogical method was also that of Mill.

> My method of instruction was never to lecture, but rather to have the child first prepare, and then discuss the material himself; I would only make hints from the side about the parts he did not understand, in order that he might discover the correct answers himself. Nor did I correct his mistakes, but rather allowed him to discover questions, so that he might on his own accord become aware of contradictions. My goal was to cultivate the child's intellectual ability and basic logic.[13]

Fu Lei brought in tutors for mathematics, English, and of course, the piano.

Fu Lei held traditional Chinese musical culture in open contempt. Although Fou Ts'ong's mother enjoyed Chinese opera, Fu Lei would only occasionally indulge his wife by accompanying her. "These antiques are merely things for a musical museum or an opera museum; not only can they not be reformed, they ought not be reformed." Fu explained to his son that because music is "virginal" in China, it can develop freely, unlike painting, which has over a thousand years of tradition weighing down upon the spirits of young artists. Moreover, music has scientific methods, making it the art for modernizing China.[14] Just as the fictional Jean-Christophe had helped Europe develop a music to accompany its industrial progress, so was the real Fou Ts'ong to be nurtured to fulfill his destiny of bringing modern music to China.

At nine, Fou Ts'ong began studying with Mario Paci, the Italian conductor of the Shanghai Philharmonic, proudly described by Fu Lei as transmitter of Lizst's musical tradition, but who had so bitterly disappointed Xian Xinghai. When Paci died in 1947, Fou tried several teachers, but none was sufficiently prestigious; each was found wanting by Fu Lei, so the young pianist mostly studied on his own.[15] Fu Lei encouraged his son with inspirational talks about the childhood labors (and subsequent adult successes) of Beethoven, Mozart, and Chopin. The intellectual environment was certainly stimulating, and visits by Fu Lei's literary friends, and such painters as Liu Haisu and Lin Fengmian, provided sophisticated conversation for young Fou's eavesdropping.[16]

Fu Lei may seem the image of Confucian propriety to Chinese, but to a Western reader the regime he imposed on his son seems cruel. Fou Ts'ong was forced to practice seven or eight hours daily. When the sound of the piano stopped, Fu Lei would emerge from his study to find out why. Fu Lei also came out when he thought that his son's playing was not good enough: "Whenever he did not practice hard I locked up the piano, telling him he need not practice anymore. Each time he stood at the piano crying pitiably."[17] Such harshness was evident in other aspects of family life; Fou Ts'ong and his younger brother Fu Min both knew to remain silent when their father was at home, playing games only when he left.

Fu Lei's stern regime lasted for seven years. In 1948 the family moved from Shanghai to Kunming, in the southwestern province of Yunnan. Fou Ts'ong, then fifteen, rebelled, refusing to work on his academic studies, playing the piano "chaotically," and then swearing never to play the piano again.[18] Fou Ts'ong's punishment was to be sent back to school with the common herd. When the rest of the family returned to Shanghai in 1949, Four remained in Kunming, living with a family friend for a year of high school, and then entering university in 1950. For three years he did not study the piano, playing only occasionally to accompany choral groups. But the heavy hand of the father was felt in the son's alternative to music: he enrolled in Yunnan University's foreign languages department.

Even Fou's mother thought that Fu Lei was too strict with their children.[19] Fou Ts'ong's younger brother Fu Min was also interested in music, and was excited by the gift of a violin that had been left behind by a departed member of the Shanghai Jewish community. But later, in 1953, Fu Lei refused to allow him to take the entrance examination for the Shanghai Conservatory's middle school. Fu Lei reduced his younger son to tears, telling him that he was too old, that he did not have the talent to be a musician, and that Fu Lei was only willing to give up one son to music.

Fu Lei's arrogance is clearly expressed in a 1954 letter to Fou Ts'ong, then in Warsaw:

> Do not forget: your family environment from childhood until now is not only unique in China, but is exceedingly rare anywhere in the world. Who teaches a young arts student so much *morality* in addition to the arts? I have complete trust in you; the seeds that I have sown for so many years will one day flower in you—I am but a tool for morality and art, while your character is that of a brilliant artist![20]

In 1951 Fou Ts'ong returned to Shanghai, his family, and his music. In his father's account, Fou Ts'ong returned chastened: "Then (Fou Ts'ong was 17), I determined that Fou Ts'ong could specialize in music, because he could work hard."[21] He studied with Bronstein, a Russian on the Shanghai Conservatory faculty, but she emigrated to Canada the next year. From this time Fou Ts'ong had no teacher until August 1954, when he began studying in Poland to prepare for participation in the Chopin competition.

Bourgeois Intellectuals at the Beginning of Communist Rule

Life in the Fu household was Westernized, sophisticated, and intense. Fu Lei's cosmopolitanism was shown by his pipe, his phonograph, and his first editions of Balzac. Joseph Levenson once suggested that French literary interests defined a rarified extreme among the varieties of Chinese cosmopolitanism.

> And what was more cosmopolitan, anyway, then to be a French, not an English transltor? The relative eclipse of France in the twentieth century, except in culture, made French the language of the purest cultural sophisticate; English speakers were more likely, and more than likely, to be just gross, utilitarian lackeys, serving imperialist business and politics, not Shakespeare.[22]

However, Fu Lei also proudly displayed the Chinese intellectuals' set of the *Twenty-four Histories* of China's past dynasties.[23] Fu Lei, like many modern Chinese intellectuals, was middle-class in many ways easily understood by Westerners, but he also had a mandarin side concerned with moral responsibility, in his case focused above all on the cultivation of his son. It is important to bear in mind the multifaceted heritage of intellectuals in the People's Republic, with their shifting and often intangible mixture of capitalism, foreign culture, Confucian education, patriotism, and desire for social reform. Within most intellectuals these values and orientations coexisted uneasily and in varying proportions.

The political environment for music in the early 1950s promised great change and was fundamentally benign. Many of those intellectuals with the greatest wealth or closest ties to Chiang Kaishek fled to Hong Kong, Taiwan, or the United States. But the great majority remained on the Chinese mainland, while others returned to China from studies in the West, often somewhat anxious about the new government's bumptious origins but patriotic and hopeful about reforming Chinese society. They were encouraged by peace, the expansion of the education system, the end of inflation, and the creation of steady employment for musicians and other intellectuals. Edwarda Masi describes their special position:

> They constituted an emergent bourgeoisie in a country that had not known bourgeois development; they were the children of colonialism. They welcomed sympathetically the new government which was restoring national identity and dignity to China. At the same time, in seeking ways to legitimize their own role, they perceived a universal model in the history of Europe and were inclined to adopt European culture as their own—both its Western and Soviet versions.[24]

Many Communist Party leaders wanted to continue the populist cultural policies of Yan'an, but were not successful. The difficulties of adapting from music of rebellion to music of the establishment are well documented in set of forty-five reports on musical activities for 1950.[25] In Shanghai there was a series of meetings for conservatory faculty and symphony members on topics such as "Does music have a class nature?", "Is there any value in concerts for workers, peasants, and soldiers?", and "What is meant by scholasticism?" A study of participation in organized choirs in Shanghai showed that only thirty percent of the singers were workers, while the majority were middle-class office workers, students, and "others." Cultural officials were anxious about the ease with which many musicians cast aside Chinese national music in favor of the European classics. But the Shanghai Music Workers' Association had no income of its own to work on such projects because of a economic disruption, reinforced by Chiang Kaishek's bombings. Cultural officials in Hebei complained about the difficulty of producing high-quality political songs on a national scale, in contrast to the local propaganda work with which they were familiar. The victorious revolutionaries were pleased to have access to broadcasting and recording technology, but they were unfamiliar with the use of these tools, and had to depend upon urban middle-class specialists for aid.

Because of these problems, Western music remained the preserve of the urban, cosmopolitan elite after the victory of the Communist Party in 1949. Although Xian Xinghai had made herculean efforts to end the cultural isolation of the cosmopolitan intellectuals, the gap between their culture and the rest of China may have increased in the early years of Communist administration. As the revolution became institutionalized, it assumed an urban and increasingly bureaucratic quality that began to obscure the populist policies of Yan'an. Certainly in the arts, Yan'an populism gave way to renewed emphasis upon the cosmopolitan side of this great contradiction in modern Chinese culture. Many May Fourth figures became leaders of the new cultural organizations that were established after 1949.

On the eve of Communist victory, Mao gave a hint to the imminent rise in the status of Western culture when he employed piano playing as a metaphor for dealing with problems of Party administration. As Communist rule expanded throughout China, Party committees often had difficulty handling their mounting work load. Mao advised Party officials:

Learn to "play the piano." In playing the piano all ten fingers are in motion; it won't do to move some fingers only and not others. But if all ten fingers press down at once, there is no melody. To produce good music, the ten fingers should move rhythmically and in co-ordination. A Party committee should keep a firm grasp on its central task and at the same time, around the central task, it should unfold the work in other fields. . . . Some play the piano well and some badly, and there is a great difference in the melodies they produce. Members of Party committees must learn to "play the piano" well.[26]

For most musicians, the ambivalence seen in Xian Xinghai's career continued. Musicians were patriotic, eager to build a modern China, but also oriented toward foreign culture, so that integration with the culture of peasants and workers was a remote goal. As the Communists moved into the cities, the relevance of Yan'an populism declined, as if its great achievement had been tactical in winning a temporary alliance with the peasants of the interior.

Middle class dreams of a new China were accompanied by occasional political turmoil, but it seemed mostly to affect business or arts other than music. The Party did call for artists to reform their thinking to remove the influence of the exploiting classes, but music seemed to unimportant, compared to literature and film, for the Party's attention.[27] The motion picture industry, always a center of political controversy, conducted a campaign criticizing *The Story of Wu Xun* in 1951, while members of the politically central literary community were embroiled in a controversy over how to interpret the *Dream of the Red Chamber* and the writings of the critic Feng Xuefeng.[28]

Yet there were musical casualties as the Communists remade Chinese society. Psychiatrist Robert Lifton decribes the case of "Grace Wu," a music student he interviewed after her flight to Hong Kong in 1954. Wu, a Christian piano student, attended Beijing's Yanjing University, an American missionary institution. Her lack of enthusiasm toward the revolution comes through in her account of her unwilling accordion performance before a group of workers.

After the first piece they didn't know enough to applaud. On the second piece they applauded at a pause. I stopped and they stopped. I started and they began to applaud again. I got mad. I refused to play to the ignorant workers. The Communists tried to apologize, saying, "We had no idea they were so uneducated."[29]

Criticism of her capitalist family background and conflict over her American piano teacher contributed to profound psychological distress, manifest in diarrhea, fevers, and other physical ailments.

For most musicians, these tensions existed vaguely in the background but did not obviously impinge on their lives. For Fou and his family, modern music was Western music, art with a scientific foundation. China's growth as a modern nation was measurable by its attainment of international standards in music, and the new regime was enhancing the status of their music. Fu Lei's 1955 account of Fou Ts'ong's education refers in passing to some study of political theory from 1951 to 1952, but this is the only discernible trace of political life to be found in the years just after Liberation.[30] It may well be, however, that the subtle strains of life under a still uncertain new regime intensified Fu Lei's meanness toward his children.

The Chopin Prize

The revolution severed ties between China's musicians and the cultural centers of Western Europe. But the position of Western-style musicians was in fact strengthened as the People's Republic of China developed new bonds to eastern Europe. The Soviet Union, East Germany, Czechoslovakia, Poland, and Hungary were all major centers of European musical culture. These governments used music in cultural diplomacy to consolidate relations with their new Asian ally. Along with this diplomacy came a whole new musical support system, complete with teachers, competitions, and scholarships. Although China's musicians had to change many of their foreign connections after 1949, the Paris Conservatory and the Eastman School of Music held no musical advantages over the music schools of Leningrad and East Berlin. And the musical cultures of eastern and central Europe are perhaps even closer to the great Viennese classical tradition than those of Britain or the United States. Even before 1949, the Slavic school of musicianship was already well represented in China by emigrés who had fled Russia during the Russian Revolution.

After 1949, Soviet musical stars such as David Oistrakh and Sviatoslav Richter toured China, and a number of Soviet experts moved to China to teach in the conservatories. A Czech was the first conductor of Beijing's Central Philharmonic, staying for two years after its establishment in 1956.[31] Much eastern European music was performed in China in the 1950s, including the works of such modernists as Bartók, Kodály, Shostakovich, and Prokofiev.

Some Party leaders continued to suspect that Western classical music was unhealthy, but the new Soviet model helped overcome doubts that the socially prominent circle of Chinese Chopin aficionados posed a threat to the new regime. By 1954, the Chinese state sponsored a celebration of the 150th birthday of so relatively obscure a composer as Glinka, showing that cosmopolitanism was not dead but now leaned on a new set of foreign friends.[32] An indication of the extent to which Western music was viewed through Soviet eyes can be seen in the *People's Daily* article commemorating the two hundredth anniversary of Mozart's birth, which opens with a quotation from Rimsky-Korsakov's opera *Mozart and Salieri*. Mozart is praised as a musical nationalist for his pioneering use of German in opera. And Mozart's departure from Salzburg is presented as an act of rebellion against the control of music by a moribund feudal order.[33]

Fou Ts'ong's musical education was both erratic and eccentric. His road to Warsaw was smoothed by an outstanding musicianship which emerged despite his lack of systematic tutelage. Politics played an equally apparent role in this stage of Fou's career. His first stage appearance, in 1952, was a performance of Beethoven's "Emperor" Concerto with the Shanghai Philharmonic. The revolution meant that Chinese artists no longer suffered the slights endured by Xian Xinghai. The eighteen-year-old artist gained the attention of Beijing officials who were looking for young musicians to enter the piano competition of the 1953 "Fourth World Youth and Student Peace and Friendship Festival" in Romania. Fou went to Bucharest as one of a group of four hundred young Chinese, led by Youth League Secretary Hu Yaobang (later to be head of the Communist Party from 1981 to 1987). There he won third prize, an impressive accomplishment for a musician with so little experience. Fou, however, compared his bronze plaque unfavorably with the gold prize won by a Chinese flutist.[34]

Fou gave additional performances in East Germany and Poland. The Poles judged his playing to be so good that they invited him to participate, in 1955, in the fifth Chopin International Piano Competition in Warsaw, and also offered him a scholarship to study at the Warsaw Conservatory. The Chopin Competition is one of the most important events in the piano world. Held only once each five years, it offers young pianists an opportunity to attract attention to the benefit of their careers. Winners of the first prize in recent decades include Maurizio Pollini, Martha Argerich, and Krystian Zimmerman.

He Luting made a speech at a ceremony marking Fou's departure from Shanghai.[35] Fou went to Warsaw to begin his studies before the competition, preparing his program under the supervision of his Polish teacher, Drzewiecki.

In 1955 a jury of over forty experts listened to seventy-four pianists from twenty-four nations. In order to minimize national ties between judges and contestants, the musicians played behind screens in the first two of the three rounds of competition. The Chinese judge was an old family friend, Ma Sitson, president of the Central Conservatory. The competition was considerable; the first two prizes were won by the Polish Adam Haraciewicz and the Soviet Vladimir Ashkenazy, both of whom have enjoyed subsequent musical fame. Fou won the third prize in addition to a special award for his performance of Chopin's mazurkas.[36]

Fou Ts'ong immediately became a Chinese national hero. Third prize may not sound so impressive in itself, but Fou was the first Asian musician to be honored in an important international competition by Westerners for playing European music.[37] For all the controversies that have accompanied judgments at international music competitions, the Chinese government in the 1950s and the 1980s has placed great stock in them as opportunities for achieving recognition. Indeed, there are few other such arenas in which the accomplishments of China's young musicians can be presented to a skeptical Western musical establishment. Fou had demonstrated that Chinese musicians could play better than Westerners in their home continent of Europe. From this point, Fou Ts'ong's career was a matter of interest to the Party's chief leaders.[38]

The Chopin prize was a matter over which cosmopolitans and Marxists could easily agree, at least in 1955. For urban intellectuals, Fou Ts'ong's success was a badge of their own ability to participate in the world culture which they held so dear. For the leaders of the Communist Party, the Chopin Competition was a diplomatic encounter, in which Fou's performance demonstrated that China could achieve great things after expelling the imperialist powers. In the push for more musical success, some leaders became concerned that even in so remote an institution as the Lanzhou Northwest Teachers' Academy, where pianos were in short supply, many piano students cut political study classes in order to practice. Some skipped breakfast or ate it in the practice rooms, while others got up in the middle of the night to practice.[39] For cosmopolitans like Fou Lei, the answer was to buy more pianos and to appreciate the diligence of the music students rather than to wonder how they had travelled so far from the traditions of Yan'an.

Fou Ts'ong's triumph in the Chopin Competition was personal as well as national; it capped a new independence from his domineering father. Fou Ts'ong's journey to Warsaw in 1954 to prepare for the competition marked a new life away from Fu Lei as he remained in Poland to study at the Warsaw Conservatory after the competition. Fou Ts'ong's departure upset the always tense power relationship between father and son and Fu Lei was soon writing grotesque apologies.

> Last night in bed, I thought over your childhood. . . . From your childhood setbacks to your present successes, I know that I did not help you, but I made many serious mistakes as a papa. In my whole life I have never done anything shameful to friends or society, it is only to you and your mother that I have committed so many harmful acts.— These matters are often on my mind this year, only these past few days I cannot get them out of my head. It is pitiful to reach forty-five years of age, and only then genuinely become aware of the nature of fatherhood.[40]

Even this apology contains a self-pitying whine, putting Fu Lei back in the center where he had always insisted on placing himself. This theme continued over the next twelve years.

We only have the father's half of the correspondence, but can easily imagine that Fou Ts'ong was happy to be living apart from his family again. Fu Lei was full of advice, including normal parental requests for more letters, but also critical of his son's calligraphy and instructing him to provide sufficient identification on the European photos he sent home. He also ungraciously complained that an illustrated book sent as a gift was not worth the price Fou Ts'ong paid.[41]

More oppressive are Fu Lei's efforts to manage his son's musical career from Shanghai: Fou Ts'ong should stay in Poland rather than study in the Soviet Union; he should study more music theory. Fu Lei was unable to distance himself from Fou Ts'ong's musical career. Fu Lei maintained a private correspondence with his son's piano teacher in Warsaw, and wrote to Zhou Weizhi at the Chinese Ministry of

Culture, demanding that Fou *not* be allowed to take part in international competitions. When he discovered that young Fou had taken up his career plans independently with the Ministry of Culture, he reproached him with the charge that Schumann and Mozart had been better sons to their fathers.[42]

Mao and the Music Workers

The Party's policies toward music and other arts were inconsistent in the first years after 1949. China's new leaders had more urgent political priorities, and their own rough experiences in Yan'an were contradicted by the professionalism of the Soviet model. But between 1955 and 1958, China's musicians were brought into the political world in a dramatic series of three political movements.

Hu Feng

In 1955 the literary critic Hu Feng, a Communist, was labeled a counterrevolutionary amidst such fanfare that even the dreamiest musician must have taken notice.[43] The journal of the Musicians' Association warned that many had regarded music as immune to counterrevolution, but people like Hu Feng resisted changes in music education: they "opposed opening the schools' doors to workers, peasants, and soldiers; they spread among their students the reactionary theory of cosmopolitanism."[44]

Nineteen-fifty-five was a nervous year for many intellectuals. Fu Lei wrote some uncharacteristically political letters to his son in Poland, sending him copies of Mao's essays "On Practice" and "On Contradiction." In December, he sent a political letter so radically different in tone that he must have intended for it to be read by prying eyes, and perhaps also to alert Fou Ts'ong to changes in the political climate, as family friends came under fire during the Hu Feng Campaign.[45] Fou Ts'ong, who had undoubtedly grown in political sophistication when he was on the road in eastern Europe with Hu Yaobang in 1953, made a radio speech to China after the Chopin prize in which he said that his "success cannot be separated from the nurturing of the Communist Party."[46]

The campaign against Hu Feng encouraged dormant populists in the music world to criticize excesses of cosmopolitan taste, such as the popular waltzes of Johann Strauss. "Wine, Women, and Song" was held to express sentiments inappropriate to a socialist society; like capitalism's insidious jazz, Strauss's waltzes rendered their listeners passive, devoid of political will.[47] What were cosmopolitans to think? Few of them liked jazz, but Strauss was surely different, as his music was played for ladies and gentlemen, with violins instead of saxophones. Where were the boundaries of permissible music? Reassuringly printed facing the attack on Strauss in the journal *Renmin Yinyue* was an introduction to Beethoven's "Moonlight" Sonata by a Soviet authority.

Populists encouraged musicians to cleanse themselves by aiding in the great project to collectivize agriculture, which began in 1955. Musicians could help by going down to the countryside, singing folk songs, and organizing young peasants into music troupes and choirs.[48] As a reminder of the revolutionary tradition in music, Xian Xinghai's name was frequently involked as a model for the musical cosmopolitans.[49]

Some cosmopolitan musicians grumbled. Fu Lei's friend, Central Conservatory President Ma Sitson, was emboldened to write of Xian that at Yan'an, "some of his works were completed within a few hours. Strictly speaking, some of Xinghai's compositions are still lacking in art and insufficiently mature."[50] Ma felt he could speak so bluntly of the Party's musical hero because he had provided Xian with letters of introduction when he departed for France. Few of the cosmopolitans wanted to leave Shanghai and Beijing for the countryside. *People's Music* attempted to answer their complaints, denying that most peasants only knew two or three old songs and could not easily be taught new ones, or that it was only in wartime that the peasants could be roused through song.[51]

One Hundred Flowers

The nervousness induced by the Hu Feng campaign was calmed in the optimism of the Hundred Flowers movement of 1956 and the first half of 1957.[52] "Let a Hundred Flowers Blossom, Let a Hundred Schools of Thought Contend" was the slogan for a complex episode in the history of the Chinese intelligentsia. The Communist Party had successfully completed the socialist transformation of agriculture, industry, and commerce, and was feeling quite secure in its leadership of the People's Republic. It assumed that collectivization, by strictly limiting private property, would bring an end to class struggle. In the absence of landlords and capitalists to offer patronage, China's intellectuals would perforce become more closely tied to the workers and peasants.[53] Politically the critical powers of the intellectuals could be harnessed for the good of the nation. Mao's plan was to encourage them to speak up and suggest improvements. Not only would the Party be strengthened by such criticism, but the modern culture of the intellectuals could be more directly applied to the problem of industrializing China.

For the Fu family, the Hundred Flowers was presaged by a December 1955 visit by two important Party intellectuals: Wu Qiang, and novelist Zhou Erfu, secretary of the East Chinese United Front Department.[54] The callers offered the family better living quarters (which were declined as unnecessary), and solicitously asked Fu Lei's opinions on the questions of higher intellectuals, music, and painting.[55] The Party also began a major drive to recruit intellectuals, although Fu Lei was not asked to join.

The sanctity of the Western musical classics was affirmed on several occasions as the Party sought to cultivate the intellectuals' good will. Although no one defended Strauss waltzes, the bicentenary of Mozart's birth was celebrated in *People's Daily*. Fu Lei was probably not alone among the cosmopolitans in grumbling privately about the Marxist tone of the Mozart commemoration, but he was happy that the classics were given protection, and he wrote a series of radio programs on the life of Chopin.[56] The Shanghai Symphony, which had been rehearsing above a fish market since the 1930s, was at last given new quarters.[57]

In contrast to the intellectuals' cosmopolitan, Westernized tastes, many in the Party elite had old-fashioned Chinese aesthetic values.[58] Mao Zedong was typical. He had no discernible interest in European classical music; his own taste in art turned to literature, calligraphy, and Chinese opera. Yet he heard the sounds of piano music from his Zhongnanhai residence in the early 1950s; Mao's old friend and neighbor, Zhu Zhongli, the wife of Wang Jiaxiang (ambassador to the Soviet Union and head of the Party's International Liaison Department), bought a piano for her daughter.[59] The tastes of senior Party officials sometimes showed signs of becoming a bit bourgeois.

In the spirit of Hundred Flowers conciliation, Mao Zedong, Zhou Enlai, Zhu De, and Chen Yun attended ceremonies for National Music

Week in 1956.[60] Mao also spoke to the leaders of the Musicians' Association in August.[61] Mao addressed the "music workers" to clarify the continuing tension between artistic populism and cosmopolitanism. His characteristically rambling speech attempted to strike a balance. He attacked complete Westernization, but appreciated the benefits which scientific principles learned from foreign countries brought to Chinese culture. Mao distinguished art from a science such as medicine, which is universal.

> Western medicine is really effective in curing illness. There is no question of national form in operating on the stomach, removing the appendix or taking aspirin. Nor has the use of Chinese angelica and rhubarb anything to do with national form. But there is a question of form, of national form, in the arts. The arts are inseparable from the customs, feelings and even the language of the people, from the history of the nation. There is a large measure of national conservatism in the arts which can persist for even thousands of years. . . .
>
> Chinese beancurd, beansprouts, preserved eggs and Beijing duck are Chinese specialities and no other country can compare in their production; they can be spread internationally. Cuisine and clothing differ from country to country. What is worn in India is quite different from what is worn in China and is suited to the Indian environment. Chinese people eat with chopsticks while Western people use knives and forks. It wouldn't make sense to say that it is wiser and more scientific to use knives and forks and backward to use chopsticks.

In some respects Mao, the old populist, adopted the cosmopolitans' own analysis. Mao distinguished four class cultures in China: the modern culture of the bourgeois intellectuals, the archaic culture of the landlords, the technical skills of the workers, and the backward, illiterate culture of the peasants. "Although China's bourgeoisie and their intellectuals are few in number, they have modern culture and we still need to unite with them." Mao's populism was restrained in 1956. He rejected as absurd the idea that "old-style minstrels" could run specialized music schools, a task which must be left to the bourgeois musicians. Mao urged them to pay more attention to China, to apply their foreign learning to national needs, but he also reminded the musicians of the infusion of foreign music in the Sui and Tang Dynasties.

> The playing of foreign music hasn't meant the loss of our own music; our own music has continued to develop. If we can digest foreign music

and absorb its strong points, this will be beneficial to us. The indiscriminate rejection and the wholesale absorption of Western culture are both wrong.

Mao did not resolve the contradiction of cosmopolitans and populists. He gave more support to those seeking to fashion a new national music than to Chopin enthusiasts, but his words were encouraging even to the latter, especially as China's intellectuals entered the heady days of the Hundred Flowers.

Throughout 1956 Fu Lei was increasingly active in public as the leading representative of the formerly bourgeois intelligentsia. He had held a leading position in the Shanghai branch of the Chinese Writers' Association since 1951; in 1955 he became a member of the Shanghai Municipal Committee of the Chinese People's Political Conference, a "united front" body especially concerned with former capitalists, intellectuals, and Overseas Chinese. By 1957 Fu was made a secretary in the secretariat of the Shanghai Writers' Association.[62] In March of 1957, Fu Lei went to Beijing, honored as a nonparty representative to participate in the Communist Party's National Propaganda Conference.[63] Fu was picked as a spokesman because of *Jean-Christophe* and Balzac, and because of the fame of Fou Ts'ong, as well as to encourage less self-assured intellectuals to become activists as well.

Fu Lei's spirits remained high through most of the Hundred Flowers campaign. He sent Fou Ts'ong copies of speeches by Premier Zhou Enlai, Party Propaganda Chief Lu Dingyi, and others dealing with the question of intellectuals, with the highlights marked in red.[64] Fu enjoyed new political status, and a busy series of meetings on music, publishing, and cultural policy. Some of the policies under discussion included establishing special hospitals and food stores for intellectuals (so that they would not have to wait in line with others), and new homes for three thousand of the ten thousand higher intellectuals in Shanghai (so that they might have quiet studies in which to work). We do not know what Fu Lei said in his speeches, but he wrote to Fou Ts'ong that the state should pay more attention to music than to sports, that the general public needs to be educated about the nature of musical work so that it will understand the needs of artists. Fu Lei also wrote a report on arts publishing, insisting that it cannot be run on the same basis as ordinary enterprises.[65] Fu Lei's excitement was palpable: "We are truly entering the atomic age; the tempo is so fast that not everyone can keep up. There really are too many things to do, write, read, hear, and discuss."[66]

Fou Ts'ong could only try to grasp these events from Warsaw. As his father's letters careened from depression to exuberance, the political changes in China between 1954 and 1958 must have seemed both mysterious and frighteningly unstable. Fou must have been pleased to learn, however, that some talked of choosing him to represent China in the new International Tchaikovsky Competition which the Soviet Union planned to begin in 1958.[67]

As musicians responded to the Party's invitation for criticism, they raised a broad range of complaints. There was no proper concert hall in Shanghai, and there were too few concerts by Chinese artists, in contrast to visitors from eastern Europe.[68] Others complained of "sectarianism" which made it difficult for some composers to be published. He Luting protested that *People's Music* was not professional enough, and should be turned into a specialized musical journal. Singers told of the problems in staging *La Bohème,* when the Ministry of Culture ignorantly rejected the Experimental Opera Theater's request for more orchestral players by pointing to the fact that Chinese opera troupes only needed a few instrumentalists.[69]

Fu Lei as a Rightist Element

The Hundred Floweres movement ended abruptly. Many senior Party leaders, such as Peng Zhen and Liu Shaoqi, had reservations about the value of encouraging criticism of the Party. As the complaints escalated, Mao changed course. The Hundred Flowers were followed by the Anti-Rightist movement, a systematic effort to tame the now unruly intellectuals by identifying target individuals as "rightist elements," enemies of socialism against whom popular criticism could be directed. There were several degrees of being a "rightist element." Thousands of intellectuals lost their jobs, many to be exiled to distant provinces for twenty years. Many more received less harsh treatment, sometimes a cut in pay, often merely the public humiliation of being labeled. Some were labeled as rightists because of things they said during the Hundred Flowers, but others were selected merely on the basis of their associations or past history, such as the soprano Zhang Quan, who had returned from the Eastman School of Music to contribute to building a new China, only to be exiled to labor reform in Heilongjiang.[70]

Fu Lei did not lose his job, but he did lose his dignity when he became an object of criticism as the movement broadened beyond its initial targets.[71] Much of the attack on Fu centered around his arrogant attitude toward raising a prodigy. Two Shanghai newspapers printed an article entitled "Use Fu Cong's Upbringing to Refute Fu Lei's False Theory." Fu had failed to give sufficient credit to the Party for creating an environment for musical talent, and his home education scheme must have offended many populist minded Chinese, as did his self-satisfaction about his sophisticated friends.

While Fu Lei was being criticized in Shanghai, Fou Ts'ong first underwent criticism among the Chinese students in Warsaw, then was recalled from Poland to take part in rectification in Beijing.[72] After writing a self-criticism, Fou Ts'ong returned to Poland to continue his studies, as the censure of his father intensified. Fu Lei was the object of ten criticism meetings, and had to write three self-criticisms before one was accepted. By April 1958, as the movement was being concluded, Fu Lei was labeled a "rightist element." His wife reported that he lost seven pounds, his vision was affected, and his health so upset by his humiliation that a physician prescribed four months of rest. Depressed, he remained in bed refusing to see outsiders. He hinted ominously of suicide, deciding against it for the sake of his younger son, Fu Min, then twenty-one years old.

Despite Mao's reassuring speech to the music workers, China's cosmopolitans proved surprisingly vulnerable once simmering antipathies to them were tapped. The cosmopolitan intellectuals had to often displayed their arrogance, and they demanded special privileges which did little to endear them to other Chinese. Nor was China's long suffering at foreign hands easily forgotten; during a period of growing cultural nationalism a group trying to bridge diverse cultures risked being taken for agents of foreign interests. For some Chinese the confusion was innocent and ignorant. For others, it was willful and convenient. Many in China's political elite, resentful of the cosmopolitans' Western ways and unwilling to share power with them, found it useful to use intellectuals as scapegoats for all of China's problems. The novelist, Zhou Erfu, who had visited Fu Lei at the beginning of the Hundred Flowers to offer better housing and solicit his views, published a novel in 1958 attacking Shanghai's bourgeoisie, whose symbols were Western clothes, imported cigarettes, fox-trots, and of course, the piano.[73]

Fou Ts'ong's European Exile

Fou graduated from the Warsaw Conservatory in December 1958, as China became deeply involved in another political campaign: the Great Leap Forward. The Great Leap, which sought to substitute the physical energy of China's masses for scarce investment capital, was filled with populist rhetoric which promised little good for elite artists.[74] Fou was already distanced from his homeland by his father's rightist label and his own recall to China for self-criticism. He decided not to return to China, but to seek political asylum in London. Fou later said that he felt that he was "driven to climb Mount Liang" (forced into rebellion, like the warriors of the classical novel, *Shuihu Zhuan* [The Water Margin]), fearing that he and his father would be forced to criticize one another if he returned to China.[75] Fou was aided in his departure by a friend, Zamira Menuhin, the daughter of violinist Yehudi Menuhin, whom he married in 1960.[76]

At a press conference in January 1959, Fou spoke cautiously, protecting himself and his family members still in Shanghai, by asserting that "I have absolutely nothing to do with politics, I neither favor nor oppose the Communist Party. I really have no interest in politics. I came to the West in order to continue my musical study without impediment." He also said that he fled to protect his pianist's hands from mandatory physical labor, but did not mention his desire to protect his Chopin from Chinese populism.[77] He also complained about low wages earned by professional musicians in China. His wages were only 70 *renminbi* (equal to the wages of an ordinary factory worker), no matter how many concerts he played. Fou also expressed his disdain for He Luting's "The Cowherd's Flute," which he was happy not to have to play again.[78]

Soon after his arrival, Fou's London career was boosted in storybook fashion when the London Symphony Orchestra quickly needed to find a substitute soloist for the ailing American pianist Gary Graffman.[79] Marriage into the glamorous Menuhin family was also an asset for the otherwise little-known Chinese pianist trying to succeed in the West's musical world. Fou was soon touring the globe, performing in

South Africa in 1961 and in the United States and South America the following year.[80] Fou rejected three invitations to perform in Taiwan, a step which might well have harmed his family and friends in China.[81]

In Shanghai, an old friend was sent to break news of the defection to Fu Lei, who went into shocked seclusion, requiring months to recover through the consoling therapy of calligraphy.[82] It is difficult to disentangle the emotional and political damage of Fu Lei's rightist label status from that of his son's defection. Fu's new Balzac translation found no publisher in 1958. He had no salary, but was able to draw advances on royalties. One publisher suggested that he publish under a pseudonym (much like the U.S. movies made by the Hollywood Ten), a suggestion which he proudly refused to consider.[83]

Foreign Minister Chen Yi expressed concern about the Fu Lei family.[84] Chen Yi was the Red Army commander who had sent a piano to Yan'an during the war against Japan; among China's leaders he was perhaps the most sensitive to the uses of Western culture in diplomacy. Despite Fu Lei's rightist status, his son's career had been a matter of state since 1953, and Chen Yi was concerned that Fou Ts'ong not become a public opponent of the Chinese government, and that he not go to Taiwan. An uncle of Fu Lei who was a ranking Shanghai municipal official visited to encourage Fu Lei to resume correspondence with his son.[85] Nearly a year after Fou Ts'ong's flight to London, Fu Lei wrote an awkward letter declaring that "I am confident that the fatherland's gate will always be open to you."[86]

But because of the family's dual disgrace, Fu Min, the younger brother, was forced to withdraw from the Beijing Foreign Affairs Institute, ending his dream of a career as a diplomat. Although Fu Lei's rightist label was formally removed in September 1961, when Fu Min graduated the following year from the Foreign Languages Institute, he was assigned to be a high school teacher, crushing his hopes of becoming a translator of foreign literature.[87] Even then it was difficult to find a school willing to take him. He was finally hired by the well-known Beijing First Girl's Middle School, whose principal concealed his identity from other faculty and students.[88]

Fou Ts'ong maintained contact with his family, sometimes by telephone, but above all by letter. The tense relationship between the father and son continued at long distance, colored now by the burden of filial disloyalty. The letters are full of talk about music and culture. Fu Lei wanted to know if his son's Steinway was seven or nine feet long, discussed Sviatoslav Richter's lack of grace in playing Schubert, and offered his opinions about Artur Schnabel, Debussy, and Charlie Chaplin's memoirs.[89] He also provided much lofty talk of emotion and the responsibilities of ART, braced by uplifting quotations from Balzac. Fu Lei was a little envious of his Chinese Jean-Christophe Krafft, who found success in his art by transcending national pettiness. Fu Lei was predictably thrilled by his son's marriage to Menuhin's daughter. When their son was born, Fu Lei named his grandson Linsiao.

But this martinet father's hectoring streak persisted. He continued to correct Fou Ts'ong's calligraphy, and urged him to write rough drafts of his letters in order to improve his Chinese. He nagged about the proper settings on his son's camera, and about writing thank-you notes. He even meddled in decisions about housing in London, in an apparent bit of rivalry with Menuhin ("In this matter, you cannot take your father-in-law's opinion too seriously"). He even assigned poor Zamira the task of reading *Jean-Christophe*.[90] Nor did he spare Fu Min his haughty intrusions. When Fu Min translated a couple of chapters from a history of the English language, Fu Lei subjected his handiwork to a twenty-four page critique.[91] Fu Lei had a high regard for his achievements as a correspondent. He assigned each letter its own catalog number, and had his wife copy and save each one.

Fu Lei wrote to London expressing political optimism again in 1961 at Zhou Enlai's Guangzhou speech on literature and art, which opened up a new period of relative relaxation for artists.[92] The next year he raised the possibility of Fou Ts'ong's return, citing well-connected friends who insisted that the Party recognized Fou Ts'ong's "patriotic spirit," and hoped that he would return. They discussed a visit more concretely for 1966, when Fou Ts'ong had scheduled a series of performances in southeast Asia, but this depended upon the decision of central political leaders, who were of course then busying themselves with the Cultural Revolution.[93]

Fu Lei worked on more translations, including Rolland's *Life of Michelangelo,* some Maupassant short stories, and plays of Molière.[94] But as China turned leftward on the eve of the Cultural Revolution, the Shanghai literary critic Yao Wenyuan (later notorious as one of the Gang of Four) found *Jean-Christophe* a dangerous book.[95] One is surprised that it took this long, especially as Yao had been one of Fu's critics in 1957. According to Fu Min, his father said, "I was hurt by Yao Wenyuan during the Anti-Rightist movement, and now Yao is

This 1985 postage stamp shows a Beethoven-like Xian Xinghai, with a background of music from his *Yellow River Cantata*. It commemorates the eightieth anniversary of Xian's birth. This stamp was provided by Marc Blecher.

"Campus of Lu Xun Academy of Arts and Literature," by Lu Qun. *Jiefanqu Muke* [Woodcuts of the Liberated Area] (Beijing: Renmin Meishu Chubanshe, 1962). This former Catholic church was the headquarters of the Lu Xun Arts Academy in revolutionary Yan'an during the war against Japan. Here Xian Xinghai trained many of China's next generation of politically engaged musicians.

Communist film composer Nie Er accompanies actress Chen Yanyan in Shanghai, 1933. *China Pictorial* (June 1982).

China's celebrated novelist Ding Ling plays the *pipa* in a studio portrait with her mother. *China Pictorial* (October 1980).

"A Graduation Portrait," by Li Cunsong. This 1956 cartoon mocks the rage for Western music in China's conservatories and the concomitant rejection of Chinese music. The solitary *erhu* player on the right is outnumbered by his classmates who have studied Western instruments. *Manhua* 64 (March 1956).

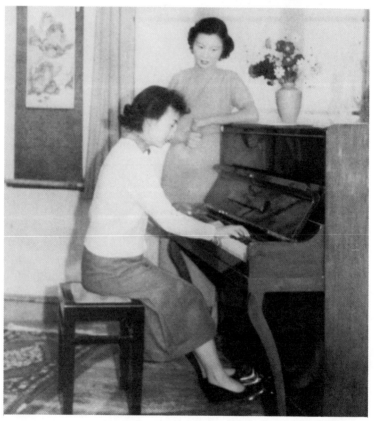

Above, left. Piano manufacturers: This 1958 woodblock by Wu Fan shows a young worker "Testing the Piano." In fact, the small homes of most middle-class Chinese cannot accommodate grand pianos. China did not manufacture them at that time, much less in the artist's home, inland Sichuan province, which still has no piano factory. *Renmin Ribao Heibai Banhua Xuan* [Selection of Black and White Woodblocks from *People's Daily*] (Beijing: Renmin Ribao Chubanshe, 1963).

Below, left. Piano consumers: A cultivated young middle-class woman plays a Chinese-built piano in this 1958 advertisement for "Xinghai" pianos. *China Pictorial* 101 (1958).

Piano prodigy Fou Ts'ong tries to win the approval of his stern Francophile father, the translator Fu Lei. *China Reconstructs* (April 1957).

Left. Fou Ts'ong at the 1955 Chopin Competition in Warsaw, where he was the first Chinese artist to be honored for performing European music in its homeland. *China Reconstructs* (April 1957).

Below. Although Red Guards initially attacked the piano as an instrument of imperialism, virtuoso Yin Chengzong helped save it from destruction. After Yin played for China's political elite in 1968, Chairman Mao Zedong showed his endorsement by standing to the right of the young pianist for a photo with other performers and Communist Party leaders Kang Sheng, Zhou Enlai, Lin Biao, and Jiang Qing. *China Pictorial* (September 1969).

Above, right. "The East Is Red," by Niu Wen. This 1959 woodblock shows the harmonium, a missionary legacy, reaching China's southern minority peoples. *Renmin Ribao Heibai Banhua Xuan* [Selection of Black and White Woodblocks from *People's Daily*] (Beijing: Renmin Ribao Chubanshe, 1963).

Below, right. Political campaigns of the 1960s and 1970s brought Western instruments and choral singing to China's countryside, in many cases for the first time. Here Composer Li Huanzhi leads peasant youth in song in 1964. *China Pictorial* (June 1964).

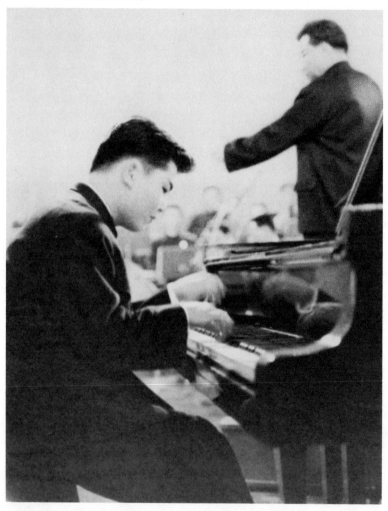

Yin Chengzong performing his *Yellow River Concerto* with Beijing's Central Philharmonic Orchestra. A film of this piece introduced piano music to hundreds of millions of peasants during the Cultural Revolution. *China Pictorial* (July/August 1971).

Pianist Liu Shikun looks pensive as a delegate to the 1979 National Artists Conference. Liu was spending less time playing the piano and more time managing the political faction of Marshal Ye Jianying, his aging father-in-law and China's head of state. Xieyingjia xiehui, ed., *Wentan Fanxing Pu* [A Guide to the Stars of the Arts World] (Beijing: Zhongguo Shehui Kexue Chubanshe, 1980).

Four young musicians of a People's Liberation Army ensemble are joined by their boss to play for the troops on China's southern coast. Marshal Ye Jianying, seated at the far left, plays the *erhu*. A military man with cultural pretensions, Ye also wrote poetry and was the father-in-law of piano virtuoso Liu Shikun. *China Pictorial* (October 1977).

The nightmare of China's cosmopolitans: a whole family of accordionists. Wang Piyun, center, is a member of a People's Liberation Song and Dance Ensemble. Her father was a pre-Liberation harmonica virtuoso who managed a German-owned Hohner Mouth Organ Factory. *China Pictorial* (December 1980).

Liu Shikun performs with the Central Philharmonic Orchestra in 1977. *China Pictorial* (February/March 1977).

"They laughed when I sat down at the piano": "The New Master of Piano Art," by Chen Qingxin and Xu Qinsong. This late Cultural Revolution fantasy shows a proud young member of a south China ethnic minority standing before her instrument and her delighted neighbors. *Meishu* 1 (1977).

"Village Song," by Zheng Weilu (Willow Aglialoro). This 1987 oil painting is based on a solitary saxophonist whom the painter heard practicing in a remote village. Anti-Western professors at the Xi'an Art Academy criticized both the painting's style and content, refusing to allow Zheng to graduate. Reproduced with the permission of the artist.

even redder; departing a little early would be better than falling into this guy's hands again.''[96]

Fu Lei and his wife, Zhu Meifu, ''departed a little early'' on September 2, 1966. Their joint suicide occurred at the fierce beginning of the Cultural Revolution, at the height of the Red Guard campaign to smash the ''Four Olds'' (old thoughts, culture, habits, and customs). A group of Red Guards from the Shanghai Conservatory had searched their house from August 29 until noon on September 2, taking as their slogan ''Down with the Old Rightist Element Fu Lei!'' They were searching for letters from Fou Ts'ong, whose defection they regarded as traitorous. In an old trunk, which the Fus were storing for others, Red Guards found an old mirror with a picture of Chiang Kaishek on its back; leafing through an old magazine, they found a picture of Song Qingling, Sun Yatsen's widow. On the morning of September 2, with over twenty big character posters denouncing the family pasted on the wall of their home, Fu Lei and Zhu Meifu, deprived of sleep, were forced to stand on a bench in their doorway wearing dunce caps and to endure the humiliation of public criticism. After the Red Guards had finally departed, Fu Lei told their servant that they wished to rest, then wrote ten suicide notes. Zhu Meifu took poison, then hanged herself. Fu Lei took poison, and was found the next morning sitting at his desk.[97]

The Fus's ashes were claimed from the Shanghai crematorium by a thirtyish woman claiming to be a stepdaughter. Legend has it that in fact she was a neighbor who had enjoyed listening to Fou Ts'ong practice the piano (although it had been twelve years since Fou had lived with his parents). The Fu family servant did not recognize her when she brought the ashes home, so her identity remains unknown.[98]

Fou Ts'ong was naturally shaken by this double suicide. ''Lamentable'' was his remark to a Japanese reporter who asked him later that month why he had left China at such a young age.[99] But in his continuing European exile, his concerns were much more those of other Western musicians, rather than the issues facing Chinese artists during the Cultural Revolution. Fou worked on such ordinary matters as building his career in a strange land, and avoiding exploitation by his manager.[100]

Fou's personal life was troubled. His marriage to Zamira Menuhin ended in divorce.[101] A second marriage in 1969 to the daughter of a Korean diplomat lasted only four months.[102] Fou made some unfortunate remarks in which he alleged that Jews dominated the London musical world, often making it difficult for an outsider to break through their cliquishnesss.[103] Such remarks did little to endear Fou to British musicians, and may have contributed to a decline in his concert opportunities.[104] The remarks probably reflected his own isolation as a Chinese musician in Europe without family support.

> I think my biggest problem is that I am fighting alone. I am certainly not a chauvinist. Art, literature, and music especially ought not be divided according to nationality. But my steady ideal is this: if a Chinese conductor could land a post with a major American orchestra, and if, in addition, a [Chinese] violinist could gain an international reputation and live in Europe, that would be good. We could [all] look after each other and cooperate together; for instance I could play piano concerti under the conductor, and perform chamber music with the violinist.[105]

In his exile Fou sought to ameliorate his isolation by frequent visits to Hong Kong. Security precautions were tight during Fou's first visit in 1965, but they relaxed as he returned frequently as a participant in the annual Arts Festival.[106] To show his gratitude, Fou donated a Steinway for Hong Kong's concert hall in 1972.[107]

In Hong Kong, Fou was treated as a celebrity. He was no longer Jean-Christophe, but "China's Chopin," a reference not only to his skill with mazurkas and polonaises, but also to how Chopin, too, left his native land to live in exile. The phrase also refers to Fou Ts'ong's reputation as a romantic. His intimate life, both real and imagined, has been chronicled in a way that is unusual for a Chinese personality. Romantic entanglements with Argentine pianist Martha Argerich (a 1965 Chopin prize winner), Korean violinist Kyung-hwa Chung, Hong Kong movie star Xiao Fangfang, and Hong Kong pianist Zhuo Yilong have been subjects of speculation. Hong Kong journalists sometimes suggest that residence abroad, far from the traditional propriety of Chinese families, encourages Fou's allegedly unrestrained romantic life.[108] Fou did marry Zhuo Yilong, a pianist of overseas Chinese merchant origin, who was born in Xiamen. She studied in Hong Kong as a youth, and later at the French National Conservatory and the Royal Conservatory of Music in London, where she now teaches.[109]

Fou's patriotism was questioned as well. The Polish Chopin, it was said, lived and died in France without taking French citizenship, but Fou Ts'ong bore a British passport; Fou was also criticized for his mockery of He Luting's "The Cowherd's Flute."[110] Fou defended his British citizenship (which he acquired in 1964), arguing that his work demanded that he have a passport for his work, although he would always be Chinese.[111] As for his criticism of He Luting, Fou in exile had kind words for the music of only one Chinese composer: Chou Wen-chung (Zhou Wenzhong), a student of Varèse and professor at Columbia University. Hong Kong reporters also accused Fou of having difficulties in remembering Chinese words, sometimes mixing English with Chinese (a common enough experience in Hong Kong's neocolonial culture, but no less galling for the pianist).[112]

Return to China

Fou Ts'ong returned to China in 1979 and was honored by the government as a professor at the Central Conservatory. This public rehabilitation of the former defector must be understood as part of a broader post–Cultural Revolution restoration of the bourgeois intelligentsia of which the Fu family is a prime representative.

Even before the Cultural Revolution, Fou Ts'ong considered performing again in China. By the time of Nixon's trip to China, Fou openly discussed with reporters his patient conviction that he would return in a few years.[113] The Chinese government approached Fou delicately about returning to China, with subtle negotiation on both sides. In November 1978, two years after the end of the Cultural Revolution, a delegation from the Chinese arts education delegation visited London. It leader was Wu Zuqiang, then vice-director of the Central Conservatory and a composer from a celebrated literary family. Wu was also a pianist, who had been a foreign student in the Soviet Union when Fou Ts'ong was in Warsaw. Wu and the delegation attended Fou's recital in Queen Elizabeth Hall. This was the first time any Chinese officials had heard Fou play for twenty years, and signaled the first step in his rehabilitation.[114]

Fou had to eat his 1959 sneering words concerning He Luting's little piano piece. He began telling interviewers that it was the only outstanding Chinese piano music: "There is only He Luting's 'Cowherd's Flute.' I have always liked this; because I especially like it, I decided to perform it."[115] Perhaps Fou's new attitude reflected compassion toward He Luting, who suffered greatly during the Cultural Revolution. Perhaps it revealed a desire to mollify He Luting, who had been restored to his powerful position as president of the Shanghai Conservatory. Whatever his motive, Fou signaled his contrition by including "The Cowherd's Flute" in the program for his Chinese listeners at Queen Elizabeth Hall in 1978.[116]

Fou then wrote to Deng Xiaoping, saying that he wanted to return to China in order to visit his younger brother.[117] Some Party leaders felt that Fou had betrayed his country, and resisted forgiving him. But this opposition ended when Deng Xiaoping and his supporters defeated the last important radical leaders in December 1978. Fou's invitation was approved in the same wave of reform that led to the posthumous rehabilitation of Liu Shaoqi. In order to prepare people for a change in policy toward Fou, there were hints in the press, such as a 1979 letter to the leftist Hong Kong magazine, *Dongxiang,* urging that Fou Ts'ong be permitted to return to China, as he had done nothing wrong and his conduct abroad had not hurt China.[118] Fou's return to China was linked to a public memorial service for his father and mother. Such services were common for prominent victims of the Cultural Revolution, and by the conventions of Chinese filial piety provided a logical occasion for Fou to return to Shanghai.

Fou Ts'ong and Chinese cultural officials reportedly agreed to the following conditions prior to his return. First, the news of Fou's return was to be included in reports of the memorial service. Second, Fou was to perform public concerts in Beijing and Shanghai, with open ticket sales (in fact, the concerts were restricted to invited audiences). Third, there was to be a television interview, though it did not receive the advance publicity which had been negotiated. Fou did not demand a salary, but his expenses were met, a car was made available, and two hundred *yuan* per month pocket money was offered for incidental expenses (an ordinary factory worker might earn half this amount in a month).[119]

Three hundred people attended the memorial service for Fu Lei and Zhu Meifu in April 1979, sponsored by Fu Lei's old organizations, the Shanghai Literature and Art Federation and the Shanghai Branch of the Chinese Writers Association. The Propaganda Department of Communist Party Central Committee, the Ministry of Culture, the Ministry of Education, the State Publishing Bureau, the Federation of Literary and Art Workers, and the Writers Association all sent floral wreaths.[120] After public acknowledgement of error in judging Fu Lei, his exonerated ashes were placed in the Shanghai Revolutionary Martyrs' Tomb.[121] Such ceremonies have many purposes: they provide an official apology to surviving family members, and signal to all that the disgrace of victim and relatives has ended. More broadly, rituals of public rehabilitation implicitly censure the officials who made the initial judgments and apprise others that they may now bring similar cases forward for review.[122]

Fou Ts'ong only stayed ten days in China, but this was the beginning of a more regular integration with Chinese society[123]; he returned to China annually between 1979 and 1986. In January 1980 Fou lectured at Beijing's Central Conservatory, where he also gave a popular series of four concerts, performing Debussy, Scarlatti, Schubert, and Beethoven—all composers who were not played during the ten years of the Cultural Revolution. The Polish ambassador attended, and the music was punctured by sounds of cassette recorders clicking in the audience. Fou also spent eight days at the Shanghai Conservatory, where he coached four pianists about to enter international competition.[124] He has since become an adjunct professor at the Central Conservatory while retaining his British citizenship.

Fou Ts'ong's rehabilitation was more a political than a musical event, accompanied at each step by well-managed propaganda. A flood of favorable interviews and profiles appeared in China and in the Hong Kong press (much of which makes its way back into China). For instance, the Communist *Wenhui Bao* of Hong Kong quoted Fou in 1980:

> I often feel remorse and pain about my leaving China. No matter how you put it, I am one of China's millions of intellectuals. In the Cultural Revolution they endured serious torment, but I avoided this disaster. This seems unfair.[125]

Fou claims that he keeps two books always at his bedside, *Jean-Christophe* (which he has read over five times), and *Dream of the Red Chamber*. Earlier in the rehabilitation process, he claimed a fondness for the poetry of Mao Zedong, a literary taste that seems to have been sated.[126] Most of the articles, in fact, say little about music, but much about the cultivated intellectuals represented by the Fu family.

After the double suicide the two brothers lost contact with each other. But in 1979, Fou Ts'ong helped his younger brother come to London. Fu Min had been labeled a "practicing counterrevolutionary" in 1968, largely because of his family background. Fu Min aided the cause of family rehabilitation in 1980 with a letter from London to the *People's Daily:* "Even though the West is ahead of us, in the end it is capitalist, and its future is hopeless." This may have been especially politic given his wife's desertion to marry an Englishman, casting new doubt on the family's commitment to China. After the rehabilitation, Fu Min's new respectability was marked by his election as representative to the People's Congress for his district in Beijing.[127]

The publication of Fu Lei's letters responded to a popular curiosity in China about the old bourgeois intellectuals and about the lurid tragedy of the Fu family. The collection of nearly two hundred letters by Fu Lei to his children became extremely popular, especially among young people. Nearly all the letters are to Fou Ts'ong, who brought back to China the letters he had saved in London. Fu Min destroyed all but two of his immediately after his parents' death, burning them in the stove of Ma Sitson, in order to avoid difficulty with Red Guards.[128] The first readers of the letters were Red Guards of the Shanghai Conservatory. After they seized the copies carefully made at Fu Lei's direction by Zhu Meifu, they later borrowed them from the files of their rebel organization to read under the guise of "investigation."[129] These copies were probably gathered later by China's public security officials, who still hold much material taken from private homes during the Cultural Revolution.

The Family Letters of Fu Lei are popular in China allegedly because Fu Lei is such a model of old-fashioned virtue. But one wonders if Fou Ts'ong published them to justify his defection, perhaps unconsciously letting all readers understand that he was fleeing not only China's politics but the obsessive love of a tyrannical father.

Fou Ts'ong remains a very political musician. After repairing his relations with the mainland, he began to perform in Taiwan. At first this seems to have occurred with the encouragement of mainland authorities as part of their long-term campaign to unite all Chinese. He even played the music of He Luting in his initial Taiwan performance in 1982.[130] But his subsequent performances may not have been so clearly sanctioned by Beijing. Fou played again in Taiwan in 1985, to great acclaim. After the purge of Hu Yaobang as head of the Chinese Communist Party at beginning of 1987, Fou refused to play in the People's Republic in an apparent act of protest. Hu, who was fired in the wake of widespread student demonstrations, had been Fou's earliest patron, in the eastern European tour of 1953.[131] The Guomindang immediately claimed Fou as its own, referring to him as a great pianist of the ''Republic of China.''[132]

Fou Ts'ong once again made peace with the Communist political authorities, performing in Shanghai in 1988.[133] But, like most Chinese musicians, his career as an artist continues to follow channels shaped by political reaction to his background of social privilege.

4

Science versus Revolution in the Modernization of Music

The great project of modernizing Chinese music has proceeded without pause throughout this century, but its progress has been filled with bitter controversy. Individual careers have been made, ruined, and then revived as both politicians and musicians have fallen out over modernity's true measure. Cosmopolitan lovers of Beethoven and populist composers of mass mobilizing songs have shared an antipathy to China's premodern music. But in the decade before the Cultural Revolution, populist and cosmopolitan currents increasingly diverged. As the high tide of Maoism swept across China, the European classics were silenced, yet the Westernization of music gained new momentum. The victorious populists, in fact, dealt even harsher blows to China's traditional music than had the cosmopolitans, as they updated instruments, harmonized melodies, and spread choral singing, adapting Europe's musical technique while rejecting its musical repertory. This chapter examines the politics of musical modernization up to the beginning of the Cultural Revolution.

China's Music Establishment

The leaders of musical institutions shared a mission to spread the Westernized music they learned in the decades before 1949. Despite their varied backgrounds and differing visions of China's future, they regarded China's traditional music as old-fashioned, or even as a reactionary impediment to national progress. Their patriotic task was to oversee the modernization of Chinese musical culture, ruthlessly if necessary. When Xian Xinghai faced this issue, he alternately developed two sides of his musical personality. Since 1949 these have become distinct political currents.

One group has channeled its cultural iconoclasm in support of the West's elite tradition of art music, arguing that China will be modern when it fully takes part in international musical culture, when its pianists are recognized around the world for playing Liszt and Beethoven, and when Chinese composers have themselves written great orchestral works. From this perspective, Europe's musical art must be emulated because it is scientific. Science is evident from the technology of the musical instruments, from the use of harmony, and from the association of this music with scientifically advanced societies. In contrast to this open respect for the European classics, another group of musicians has argued that music is modern when it is revolutionary. Faithful to Xian Xinghai's populist side, such musicians eschew Beethoven in favor of updating China's own instruments and singing style, and adding harmony as they use music to mobilize (and modernize) the workers and peasants of the People's Republic.

The tensions between these two groups have often been restrained partly because of their common commitment to reforming China's feudal musical tradition, but also because not all musicians can be simply and permanently categorized. For instance, the Korean-born musician Zheng Lucheng, who composed such songs as ''In Praise of Yan'an,'' ''Korean-Chinese Friendship,'' and ''Beautiful Qingdao,'' as well as settings of poems by Mao Zedong and Chen Yi, does not appear very cosmopolitan. Yet when Zheng returned from a visit to East Germany in 1951, he brought as gifts to his son editions of Beethoven sonatas and piano reductions of Beethoven's nine symphonies. This Yan'an songsmith also enjoyed Bach and Chopin, whose bust he kept atop his piano before the Cultural Revolution.[1] Yet differing approaches to modernizing music are sometimes more sharply defined, as a look at the presidents of three conservatories shows.

Beijing: Ma Sitson

At the cosmopolitan extreme was the president of Beijing's Central Conservatory, Ma Sitson.[2] Ma had been one of China's distinguished musicians before Liberation. Like Xian Xinghai, Ma was a Cantonese

violinist, who had studied at Lingnan and in Paris, where he helped
the older Xian find a violin teacher (the Paris Conservatory reports
finding no evidence that Ma had been a student, despite claims in
some Chinese sources).[3] But as the son of a Guomindang official,
Ma's background was privileged. And he was no revolutionary, serving the Guomindang instead of the Communist Party before 1949. During
the war, Chiang Kaishek's government invited him to set up the first
all-Chinese symphony orchestra in Chongqing, and later sent him on
a cultural mission to the Soviet Union.

At Liberation, Ma was in Hong Kong, but the Communists invited
him to return to head the conservatory (which they moved from the
Guomindang capital of Nanjing first to Tianjin, then to Beijing). This
was something of a united front gesture, intended to reassure other
non-Party intellectuals, such as Ma's old friend, Fu Lei. Ma held highly
visible honorific posts: vice-chairman of the All-China Federation of
Literature and Art, vice-chairman of the All-China Music Association,
and member of the committee to design China's new national flag.
These assured him high prestige, special treatment, and opportunities
to travel abroad. He was a leader of the Sino-Soviet Friendship Association, and a member of the jury that heard Fou Ts'ong in the 1955
Chopin compeition. Ma's international connections included his younger
brother, also a violinist, who had become a U.S. citizen. Mistrusted
by musicians from Yan'an, Ma responded by criticizing some of Xian
Xinghai's works as "still lacking in art and insufficiently mature,"
bold words against their patron saint.[4] After the antirightist campaign
of 1957, Ma became a figurehead at the Central Conservatory, but he
continued to draw his full president's salary, supplemented (until 1963)
by frequent concert perfromances. His compositions were frequently
performed, and his "Longing for Home" preceded each braodcast to
Taiwan.

Shenyang: Li Jiefu

Ma's populist antithesis was Li Jiefu, a Communist and president of
the Shenyang Conservatory, in Manchuria's Liaoning province.[5] Jie
Fu (like many Chinese artists, Li Jiefu used his given name for professional identification) was a vetern of Yan'an. A self-taught musican
who learned folk instruments in his youth, Jie Fu began composing
anti-Japanese songs in 1937 in Yan'an. As a member of an army pro-

paganda troupe during the war, he stayed close to his populist roots, returning to his native Manchuria and eventually becoming head of the Shenyang Conservatory, an institution never held in high regard by the more cosmopolitan musicians of Shanghai and Beijing.

Jie Fu and his longtime collaborator, An Po, described the northwest in an enthusiastic report on musical conditions after the Communitst victory. They said that modern instruments were easily obtainable (probably referring to pianos left behind by families of the defeated Japanese imperialists, no doubt including young Seiji Ozawa's first piano), and that "very many" music cadres had transferred from the old liberated areas because of early liberation of Manchuria. This mix made Shenyang the center of modernizing music in the Yan'an tradition. In addition, the Korean War put the northeast on the front line, with the campaign to "Resist America, Aid Korea" stimulating a demand for new anthems to stir resistance to a new foreign menace to China. Moreover, under Japanese occupation, many of the social positions that in Shanghai were filled by middle-class Chinese had been in foreign hands, leaving a shortage of middle-class people demanding Western art music. The mood in Manchuria was positive: "A great number of comrades who had no opportunity in the old liberated areas to study complex compositional techniques and forms have already written serviceable music with orchestra—cantatas, opera arias, and some orchestral pieces." For Jie Fu, modern music grew out of the marching songs of Xian Xinghai. A firm supporter of the Party's left, Jie Fu regarded peasants and workers as his audience, not the urban middle class. He wrote an opera, *Man of Steel* based on six months he spent at the Anshan Iron and Steel company in 1961, and he was well known for his satirical song "The American Moon" (which mocked bourgeois Chinese for believing it to be rounder and brighter than the moon shining over China).

Shanghai: He Luting

He Luting, president of the Shanghai Conservatory, occupied a position between Ma and Jie Fu.[6] Born in Hunan in 1903, He combined activism for revolutionary change, cultural iconoclasm, and enthusiasm for European classical music in much the same way as Xian Xinghai, with a similarly odd mix of Communism, movie music, and service in Yan'an. Had Xian lived, he might well have enjoyed a career similar to that of He Luting, whom he knew in the 1930s.

He Luting's revolutionary activism began in the Haifeng Soviet, a Communist-led peasant revolt in Guangdong in 1927. Like many radicals facing the Guomindang's counterrevolutionary terror, he then dropped out of political activity. He never studied abroad, but while enrolled at the Shanghai Conservatory in 1934 he won a first prize in Alexander Tcherepnin's piano composition contest for his "The Cowherd's Flute." Radicalized anew by the Japanese invasion, He joined the mass song movement, wrote music for patriotic movies (including some songs to words by Tian Han), and worked with the Communist New Forth Army in East China, where Chen Yi (later foreign minister) became his patron. He conducted Ma Sitson's orchestra in Chongqing, and later went to Yan'an. There, after Xian's departure, he joined the Communist Party and led the orchestra that had been established there by 1945. After Liberation he was made president of the Shanghai Conservatory, chairman of the East China Branch of the Musicians' Association, and vice-chairman of the National Musicians' Association. He Luting's fame rested on pre-Liberation songs, especially his popular "Song of the Guerrillas" of 1937. He wrote less music after 1949, although his "Night Party" (a musical description of the Chinese New Year celebration) is frequently performed. He Luting came under fire during the 1957 antirightist campaign, but he was spared the fate of Fu Lei by Chen Yi, soon to be China's foreign minister. Chen and He had ties going back to the New Fourth Army, which were renewed when Chen became mayor of Shanghai after Liberation.[7] In some ways He Luting combined the strengths of Jie Fu and Ma Sitson: Party membership and revolutionary credentials joined with an enthusiasm for Europe's high musical art that He's Shanghai constituency demanded. This combinatioin made him a central figure in China's musical politics.

The musical differences represented by Ma Sitson, Jie Fu, and He Luting had profound political implications, which sometimes festered before the Cultural Revolution, but which more often seemed insignificant when compared to their shared mission of modernizing musical culture. Many of their differences were concealed behind the cult of Nie Er and Xian Xinghai, who were men for all seasons in Chinese politics. The sharpest tension within Chinese musical culture had not been between the symphonies of the Paris Conservatory and the mass songs of the revolution, but between the apostles of *modern* music (of whatever form) and their true enemy, the parochial and feudal music of traditional Chinese culture.

The Administrative Autonomy of Music

The administrative organization of the music world separated Westernized music both from Chinese opera and from traditional ballad singing *(quyi)*. This meant separate professional associations, administrative hierarchies, meetings, and publications all joined by common links to the Communist Party Propaganda Department. The most important organization for Western-style musicians was the All-China Federation of Music Workers, which was established in 1953. In 1957 there were 590 members, 208 of whom were also in the Communist Party.[8] Sometimes this separation worked to the disadvantage of music, as when cultural officials favored Chinese opera, which apparently was true in Guangzhou. Western music might have developed more strongly in this old treaty port, but the Cantonese opera is extremely popular and dominates local arts.[9] But the musical establishment more often used this administrative autonomy to ignore resistance to their modernization program from the opera or ballad-singing constituencies, who had no formal voice in the music bureaucracy.

In addition, few senior leaders of the Communist Party cared much about European classical music, which also enhanced the administrative flexibility of the music establishment. Chen Yi and Kang Sheng have been the only notable enthusiasts, but their major political intervention was to support the publication of music for the aristocratic *qin* (zither) rather than to promote the European classics.[10] Western music has not claimed the political and aesthetic attention of the Party's leaders in the same way as literature and Chinese opera, topics which have divided the Central Committee on several occasions. In contrast to the low official emotional involvement with Western music, Peng Zhen battled with the Left concerning the reform of Beijing opera in the 1960s, Chen Yun traveled about Suzhou with tape recorders to capture the voices of old ballad singers, and Deng Xiaoping remarked to his physician: "If you don't see Sichuan opera, you don't understand civilization."[11]

Foreign music had only a utilitarian appeal to Party leaders. In the 1950s they strove to win international recognition in all fields, and to this extent accepted the music establishment's view that symphonic music was a valid criterion by which to judge modern culture, especially when it was reinforced by the Soviet example. After the collapse of Sino-Soviet relations, however, Zhou Enlai supported an ensemble specializing in performing third-world music, the Oriental Song and Dance Troupe. But again, although this was useful for China's diplomacy, Zhou took no personal interest in it.

The musical leadership operated with considerable exclusiveness, as we can see from criticisms that emerged during the Hundred Flowers movement. Angry musicians complained that the federation was controlled by composers and theorists who had little concern for the needs of ordinary musicians. The leaders made it difficult to get into the federation, and difficult for nonmembers to publish music.[12] A leader of a brass band complained of snobbery toward his ordinary but necessary music.[13] He Luting acknowledged that publication was a problem, but at the same time proposed reserving *People's Music,* the official journal of the federation, for professionals, leaving the amateurs to publish in the mass magazine *Song.*[14] The cosmopolitans of the music establishment weathered the Hundred Flowers criticisms of elitism; many of their critics were punished as rightist elements for their trouble. But eventually snobbery would be their undoing.

Music Leaps Forward

The Great Leap Forward was primarily an economic campaign, in which Mao and other Party leaders tackled China's poverty by substituting labor, which was abundant, for capital, which was scarce.[15] The Leap itself was a failure, resulting in three years of famine and economic depression, although it prefigured a more measured Maoist strategy for economic growth that brought steadier progress in the 1960s and 1970s. Beginning in 1958, the Leap was profoundly nationalist, as China began rejecting the Soviet approach to socialism. The preceding antirightist campaign silenced some of the most cosmopolitan musicians and frightened many more, preparing the way for the populist turn of the Great Leap Forward.

The Leap was concerned with producing large quantities, in the arts as well as in heavy industry. China's musical achievements were recounted in vulgar but effective terms in honor of the tenth anniversary of the new state. The number of advanced music schools had increased from four to eighteen. Fifteen new special elementary and secondary schools had been created for young musicians. The number of professional musical organizations increased from 3 to 148. In ten years China had published thirty musical periodicals, as well as over two thousand musical titles in sixty million volumes. Thirty-two million records were pressed, in thirty-five hundred titles. In addition, ninety-four Chinese had won international competitions, seventy musical groups toured abroad, and ninety-two foreign groups performed in China.[16]

The Party called upon musicians to build this record of achievement. Just as the Leap urged workers and peasants to increase their output of steel and grain, so too were artists caught up in an effort to increase production quotas sharply.[17] The Shanghai Musicians' Association set the pace in song writing to inspire the masses, with an initial goal of one thousand songs that was then raised to fifteen hundred. The next day, the Shanghai Writers' Association decided to contribute 150 texts each week to be set to music, only to have the number raised after discussion with the masses. The figure for the Shanghai Conservatory was originally set at six hundred, then increased to 1734. This sort of quota-busting continued until the whole city agreed to a music quota of 3873 new compositions for the year. Ding Shande, vice-president of the Shanghai Conservatory, announced his personal plan for two years at a Beijing forum: allowing for six days a week of administrative duties, he would compose one symphony, one opera or oratorio, one symphonic overture, ten instrumental pieces, twenty art songs, fifty songs for the masses, and thirty children's pieces. Similar silliness went on elsewhere; the Song and Dance Troupe of the Army's General Political Department increased initial quota of 500 pieces to 1545, and the Central Experimental Opera Theatre "realistically" planned 1379 works for the year.[18]

All this music was intended to inspire an audience of workers to greater production achievements. Choirs in Shanghai increased their own production (performance) quotas in order to contribute to economic growth.[19] Lest China's musicians miss the significance of these new activities, *People's Music* reminded its readers fondly of the Party's mass mobilizing arts troupes of the 1940s.[20] The difference was that, earlier, revolutionary musicians had strengthened China's political will in wartime, but in the Great Leap they were to arouse workers for overtime.

Some used populist music to accompany radical politics. Students from the Shanghai Conservatory wrote big character posters to criticize the bourgeois lifestyles of some of their fellow students, and to attack the conservatory's purchase of expensive imported equipment as a waste of state funds.[21] But despite the Leap's proletarianization of musical creation, and its invocation of the spirit of Yan'an, it was not nearly so hostile toward bourgeois culture as was the Cultural Revolution.

The diversity of cultural activities indicated that no one artistic faction dominated. "Culturally, the Leap in Shanghai was not antibourgeois. . . . In February 1959, the annual spring sales advertized 'Hawaiian electric guitars' and perfumed bedsheets."[22] Musical cosmopolitans used the Leap for their own purposes, going all out to mount the first all-Chinese performance of Beethoven's Ninth Symphony, which was presented as a patriotic achievement, as its performers no doubt felt it to be.[23] The Leap even had room for the small band of enthusiasts for the ancient *qin*. Beijing *qin* aficionados taught in a "spare time" school, and planned a new journal, *Qin Research,* which would, however, have politically restricted distribution.[24]

The Leap intensified the search for an authentically national music for China. "National music"[25] did not refer to the music of the minority nationalities, although that music was included within its embrace. It referred to music which was somehow distinctively Chinese, long a stated goal of music officials. But national character could mean anything from reviving the music of Confucian ritual to composing piano concertos on Chinese themes. The search for "national" Chinese music gained momentum as the Leap increasingly divided China from its Soviet ally.

A Great Leap formula for national music made it clear that this was no revival of traditional forms: "Chinese folk melodies + western professional technique = national musical culture."[26] The most successful composition using this approach was the violin concerto *Liang Shanbo and Zhu Yingtai,* composed jointly in 1959 by Chen Gang, a composition student at the Shanghai Conservatory, and He Zhanhao, a violinist who had played in the Zhejiang Provincial Yue Opera Company. Sometimes called the *Butterfly Lovers Concerto,* this work tells one of China's most popular love stories by adapting Shaoxing opera tunes into a flashy if sentimental display piece.[27] Audiences were enthusiastic about the concerto, but it was nonetheless disparaged from two sides: cosmopolitans sneered at its pentatonic melodies and its easy popularity, while populists were upset by its use of a romantic story that prettified the feudal order. The score was full of Italian markings, but *sostenuto, cadenza,* and *andante cantabile* merely irritated the populists while failing to mollify indignant cosmopolitans.

Some members of the Central Philharmonic resisted the policies of the Leap, claiming that their orchestra was international in nature; its main responsibility should be to perform foreign music instead of newly written Chinese pieces of low quality. Moreover, they should perform in concert halls, not factories and villages. They asked if Soviet orchestras were required to perform for peasants, and complained that sending players to popularize music in the countryside undermined the goals of raising the level of appreciation and attaining international standards. Some complained that the orchestra played better before the beginning of the Leap.[28] It should be remembered that the Central Philharmonic had only been established in 1956; many of its members feared that it lacked both a tradition of performance and bureaucratic clout needed to keep it from declining into an ensemble little resembling the orchestras of Vienna, Prague, or Leningrad. Perhaps it was in order to silence such grumblings that members of the Soviet Union's visiting National Symphony Orchestra were photographed in physical labor at Beijing's Ming Tombs Reservoir project.[29]

While everyone suffered economically with the collapse of the Great Leap Forward, cosmopolitan critics were heartened by the abandonment of its cultural policies. Mao withdrew from daily decision-making; Liu Shaoqi, Deng Xiaoping and other central leaders, although they had supported the Leap, attempted to undo some of its damage by experimenting with household farming and expanded peasant markets. Meetings of artists and cultural officials in Guangzhou and elsewhere resulted in a new, looser Party policy toward the arts. The "Ten Points on Literature and Art" was circulated in 1962 by the Ministry of Culture and the All-China Federation of Literary and Art Circles. It proposed less administrative interference with art, better working and living conditions for artists, and steps to "satisfy the people's righteous requirement for art appreciation."[30]

A Populist Victory

The cosmopolitan revival after the Great Leap Forward was brief, and within a few years musical populists were firmly in control. The Great

Leap Forward had altered the standoff between cosmopolitan and populist musicians in important ways. It strengthened institutions sympathetic to a more populist reading of culture. Local and provincial cultural bureaus, Li Jiefu's Shenyang Conservatory, and the vast musical apparatus of the General Political Department of the People's Liberation Army were all encouraged by the Leap's turn to mass mobilization. Cosmopolitans in the Musicians' Association and in the conservatories of Beijing and Shanghai had paid little attention to the mass song tradition in Shanxi's backward Xiyang County, for instance. Xiyang was not yet famous as the home of Dazhai, the agricultural model of the next two decades, but its cultural cadres were proud of their Yan'an-style music, and were pleased when their story was told to others during the Leap.[31]

The Europeanized musicians were more seriously weakened by changes in China's foreign policy. Unhappy at the Leap's repudiation of the Soviet model for industrialization, Khrushchev retaliated by withdrawing Soviet technical advisors from China in 1960. A thousand economic projects were halted when Soviet experts rolled up the blueprints and flew back home. Less notorious was the withdrawal of Soviet and eastern European musical experts from their assignments as visiting faculty and consultants throughout China's musical world. Such a sudden loss of expertise was damaging enough, but even worse was the loss of eastern Europe as a legitimate model for musical activity.

Mao Zedong was dissatisfied with the direction taken by Liu Shaoqi, Deng Xiaoping, and other leaders; he led a drive to return the Chinese Communist Party to its revolutionary roots. By 1962, Mao called upon Communists "never to forget class struggle," marking a turn to the left which culminated in the Cultural Revolution. Musicians and other intellectuals found the politics of the early 1960s very confusing, as the arts became first more relaxed, then radicalized, then both at once. Eventually the Maoists prevailed, and musical life had to adjust sharply, as artists tried to imagine what kind of music fit into a revived revolutionary spirit.[32] By 1964 the new slogan demanded that music "become revolutionary, national, and popular (*geminghua, minzuhua, qunzhonghua*)."[33] The slogan placed "national" between "revolutionary" and "popular" to indicate that it meant leftist, populist music honoring the traditions of Yan'an.

The Decline of European Classical Music

Populist musicians had been interested not in the art of Europe but only in its technique. Their growing political weight resulted in attacks first on specific composers for being unhealthy, then upon the entire repertory. As early as 1959 a *People's Music* article named some harmful twentieth century composers: Schoenberg ("reflects the emptiness and cruel heartlessness of capitalist society"), Stravinsky (reactionary in both content and musical form), and Hindemith (expresses capitalism's "declining character and coldness of interpersonal relations") were all found wanting, although some of the music of Debussy, Honegger, Scriabin, and Strauss might not be harmful.[34] In fact, Schoenberg, Stravinsky, and Hindemith have little following in China, so middle-class tastes were not seriously threatened by such discussion. But Debussy was popular, and a few years later he was the first European composer to merit his own political campaign. Yao Wenyuan, then still a literary critic in Shanghai, disliked Debussy's rarified sounds and led a campaign against musical impressionism's bourgeois features in 1963.[35] From this point, musicians began to worry about selecting politically safe music for their programs.

One musician sketched a pseudopopulist line of defense for his cosmopolitan colleagues. In the past, a minority of intellectuals had selfishly kept the pleasures of Beethoven to themselves. China's musicians had erred in placing European music at the heart of world music history, not recognizing contributions of other nations, and they had approached great composers without considering their social context and relations to the people. As a result music had become politically divorced from the people as well as artistically formalistic. Europe's progressive and healthy music should be performed openly, while incorrect and reactionary music could be set aside for reference use by professionals.[36] Despite the vigor of this argument, the appeal to the examples of Nie Er and Xian Xinghai, and a profusion of quotations from Marx and Lenin, it was too late to promise that cosmopolitan musicians would do better in the future. Other cosmopolitans were more blunt, complaining that the turn to the left would lower artistic standards and make music "bumpkinlike."[37] At the Shanghai Conservatory, President He Luting resisted the campaign against Debussy, called Yao Wenyuan a "hatchetman."[38]

China's split with the Soviet Union brought the European classical repertory to its lowest state. After Liberation, Soviet Communists had replaced Christian capitalists as the major support for Western music, but after 1960 Chinese cosmopolitans stood alone for the first time. They tried to make the most of China's foreign policy of solidarity with the Third World, performing music of the oppressed. But their hearts were not in it as they included among the Cuban and African songs a "Mexican Serenade," and "Old Man River" as a "jewel of world folk music." [39]

These musical controversies should be taken seriously. One can easily dismiss some, like the Debussy campaign, as silly and trivial. But the isolation of the cosmopolitan musical community from the great mass of the Chinese people was real, as was its foreign orientation in a period of Chinese national isolation. No one in the People's Republic seriously felt that unchecked performances of Beethoven symphonies might somehow restore China's bourgeoisie to power, but it was not so unreasonable to wonder if European classical music might distract the urban middle class from the problems of China's workers and peasants.

By 1964 even the home ground of the cosmopolitans was becoming radicalized. Five Beijing cosmopolitan professors attacked the blind worship of Western classics as bourgeois. They charged that one of their colleagues had berated a student for daring to inquire about Beethoven's deficiencies, and that faculty instructed their students to choose foreign composers as their models, rather than to write in a national style. Students from peasant backgrounds, they said, were intimidated into losing touch with the people. [40]

One troubled student from the Central Conservatory took his dilemmas directly to Mao Zedong, writing him about how he should deal with Western classical music, suggesting that China should stage a festival of Asian, African, and Latin American music. Chen Lian felt emboldened to write because his father had been at Yan'an, which is probably why Mao answered him in September 1964. Mao's response included a phrase that was to become an important slogan of the Cultural Revolution: "Make the past serve the present, make foreign things serve China." Mao also instructed that the conservatory should solve its problems by holding discussions among faculty and students. [41] This exchange was never published openly, although it circulated among musicians. At this same time Chen published an article attacking foreign romantic and religious songs, making it clear that Mao had intervened to support musical populism.[42] Mao's letter signaled the end of free performance of Western music. A brief but persuasive rectification occurred in the Musicians' Association, whose journal published no more rearguard defenses of European composers.[43]

The Renewal of Revolutionary Song

M⋅ sic's move to the left featured a predictable revival of the revolutionary mass song tradition of Xian Xinghai. It had never died, of course, but had shared prominence with other kinds of music in the 1950s. On the eve of the Cultural Revolution, mass song became the preeminent form of music in China, producing a great deal of group singing for a country that had not one professional choir before 1949.[44]

The most prominent composer of the early 1960s was Jie Fu, president of the Shenyang Conservatory. He applied the old art of mass revolutionary song to the new task by setting Mao Zedong's poems and other words to music, accompanied by native instruments. A three-day conference on his work was held in April 1964, making Jie Fu the 1960s model for music, just as Dazhai and Daqing were to inspire agriculture and industry.[45] As early as 1958, Jie Fu had experimented in teaching Western-style musicians to adapt their techniques to Chinese music.[46] Jie Fu's 1964 "We Are Marching on a Great Road" became a basic song for the army, where many of his other songs were popular: "People's Communes are Good," "Revolutionaries are Always Youthful," "This is the Letter Written by My Brother." The Western pedigree of this music is impeccable, as it mated the hymns of the YMCA to the marches of the Russian Red Army, but it is not music for urban intellectuals.[47] Reaching out to this audience, Jie Fu wrote "Child of Havana" to a Latin beat, in which a father tells his child how mother was killed by Yankee imperialism.

One of Mao's important political bases was the military, where Defense Minister Lin Biao had effectively introduced a radical political revival. Mao's campaign to recapture the spirit of revolution was first propagated in this army of peasant recruits, who early were taught to sing eleven revolutionary songs.[48] By 1964 all Chinese were urged to "Learn from the People's Liberation Army." For musicians this meant that the army's vast musical organization became a model for turning to nativist and populist forms.[49]

Maoists intended for the nation to learn military discipline and revolutionary politics as China sang the army's songs, but it also learned Western harmony, choral singing, and musical notation along the way. As old songs by Nie Er, Xian Xinghai, and others were revived, so new songs were written on such subjects as the model soldier, Lei Feng. The mass singing movement tried to win active involvement of ordinary people, rather than passive listening to professional singers, by promoting song contests among work units. Unions and propaganda department trained special singing instructors. Workplaces stopped limiting their choruses to the best singers, in order to involve more people. Singing squads led movie audiences in revolutionary songs before the shows began. And model choral units, such as Shanghai's Yangshupu Power Plant, pulled out all the stops, forming six choirs of four hundred personnel.[50]

Given the amount of politically inspired singing in China since the 1930s, it is striking that the Western art of choral singing had only imperfectly penetrated the nation's villages by 1965. Chan, Madsen, and Unger report that residents of Guangdong's Chen Village were required to sing revolutionary songs twice a day as part of a political campaign.

> Chen Villagers had never sung in unison before. Many were embarrassed to do so, especially the older men. Only the younger ones were ready to try out their voices. But the only songs they had ever known were from the popular Cantonese operas. They found the new tunes and words strange.[51]

Revolutionary songs also assumed instrumental form, with new prominence for the populist accordion. Imagine the feelings of conservatory piano faculty at the news of China's first all-accordion concert, in Beijing in 1963. Massed and solo accordionists, many of them spare-time aficionados, performed revolutionary songs as well as music from *The White-Haired Girl*. The accordion is portable and relatively inexpensive, well suited to spreading sturdy tunes throughout the nation. There were over ten million Chinese playing the accordion by 1963, although the musical establishment had previously paid little heed to the artistic interests of the urban petty bourgeoisie. The Tianjin Municipal Musical Instruments Factory had been turning out accordions for years, yet players of their instruments felt the sneers of cosmopolitan pianists.[52] Accordionists received official encouragement only in China's most populist periods. Thus the Great Leap Forward had brought articles on how to repair broken accordions.[53] In ordinary times, cosmopolitan musicians quietly preferred that these instruments remain broken.

Some senior Party leaders found that a few revolutionary songs went a long way. Hu Qiaomu felt that songs tied too closely to specific political campaigns were boring and ineffective.[54] But Liu Shaoqi praised the mass song movement on the utilitarian grounds that supported it in Yan'an: "The most economical thing is to sing revolutionary songs. It calls for no monetary expenditure and it elevates the spirits. It is most economical."[55]

Modernizing the Tools of Music

The eclipse of the European classics encouraged a broad renewal of interest in China's own music. The Musicians' Association sponsored a conference on the music of the *qin* in 1963, but this had too feudal a flavor to persist.[56] In a more populist vein, a new Academy of Chinese Music opened in Beijing in March 1964, where faculty and students would be free to work without the supervision of Beethoven-fanciers. Its head was Jie Fu's collaborator, An Po, transferred to Beijing from Liaoning, where the melodies of Yan'an still echoed most loudly.[57]

The "improvement" of China's traditional musical instruments has been on the agenda of musical cosmopolitans throughout this century. In the 1920s, Liu Tianhua (1895–1932) experimented with the *erhu*. A student of Western music theory and violin, he extended the possibilities of the instrument by applying violin technique.[58] By the mid 1930s, reformers altered instruments by increasing their volume, extending their range, tempering scales, etc. More frets were added to the *pipa*, and native instruments began to be combined into new orchestras patterned after European models of concert music. Western harmonies, compositional forms, and cadenzas also appeared.[59] The long history of Chinese music is filled, of course, with adaptations of instruments. But this twentieth-century movement is different because it claims science as its guide.

After Liberation, the reform of instruments accelerated as most musical leaders considered it an urgent need. Fifty different modernization projects were presented to a 1954 conference. Modifications were encouraged because of the supposedly "unscientific" principles used in making folk instruments. A little science can make a louder sound by substituting metal or nylon for the silk strings on the *erhu* or *pipa*.[60]

Cosmopolitans like He Luting treated this movement with condescension: although richly colored, China's traditional but unscientific folk instruments cannot produce precise pitches. He proposed that the Ministry of Light Industry help by systematically investigating how to produce reformed national instruments, which could then be modernized in the European manner. "At present each nation has its own national musical instruments, national orchestras, but all civilized nations have pianos, violins, and symphony orchestras."[61]

The pace of instrumental reform increased again after the Great Leap, when the Musicians' Association exhibited 140 modified musical instruments in Beijing.[62] Native instruments were played in orchestras, replicating the European bourgeoisie's search for greater volume of sound. Experimenters on both continents experimented with traditional instruments in order to coax from them greater volume and a more blended sound quality. Some of the technical developments were even identical, such as replacing hard sticks with soft ones for striking percussion instruments (gongs for China, kettledrums for Europe) in a way that blends more euphoniously with the rest of the orchestra.

The army cultivated ensembles of national music, more popular with its peasant recruits than in the conservatories. Most of the army's musical ensembles established units playing national instruments, although Western-style marching bands remained, as soldiers did not want to march to the sound of clappers and gongs.[63] The Jinan Military Region's Vanguard Song and Dance Troupe National Music Ensemble was the army's exemplar for advancing the cause of national music.[64] The Vanguard Ensemble traveled to Beijing for a series of forty concerts in 1964, demonstrating how its members had experimented with various frets, sizes of instruments, and construction materials to remake old instruments with richer, more flexible sounds. Such ensembles of national instruments were themselves a sign of modernity, as these sounds were not normally combined in this way. Many of the reformed instruments were also used to play bass and tenor parts new to Chinese instrumental music.

The "keyed wooden flute" (*guanzi*) of northern China provides an example of the problems inherent in adapting traditional instruments to the demands of modern music.

Chinese folk artists through the centuries evolved such a fine technique on this flute that they could even imitate falsetto singing and the natural human voice on it, but when used for stage accompaniments or in modern orchestras it is too loud and strident for gentle melodies and fails to harmonize with the other instruments. Moreover, the eight finger-holes produce a diatonic scale only, not the different keys and semitones required by modern instrumental music.

Zhang Jigui of the navy's political department art ensemble solved these problems by designing a bigger flute, with fourteen fingerholes and a harder mouthpiece. Similarly, the Vanguard Ensemble made an "enlarged set of gongs," adding semitones by increasing the number from nine to twenty-nine, making the tone mellower, and introducing a soft stick. The Kazakh *dumbra* was improved by making it in five sizes, with different pitches for harmony in ensembles. Steel strings replaced sheepgut strings on the highest-pitched *dumbra,* and all were given bigger sound holes for greater volume.[65]

Just as there was a modernizing prejudice against traditional instruments, so there was a similar effort to modernize singing technique. A longstanding debate between proponents of Chinese and Western vocal styles was relabeled by cosmopolitan musicians as a question of "scientific vocal technique in the 1950s."[66] Cosmopolitans favored the vocal styles and techniques of La Scala, regarding the lighter, more nasal native tradition of singing as unscientific, backward, and harmful to the vocal chords. Of course the highly cultivated voices of European opera are no more natural than those learned through years of training for Chinese opera: both are acquired techniques and tastes, having little to so with the sounds untrained people make when they sing. But the cosmopolitans argued for "science," even if it was not popular with Chinese audiences. "The high-pitched notes in the Sichuan songs in some passages are really too high. When you hear it you feel that the singer is making superhuman efforts and the sound is very much forced. The public may like it, but this is not scientific."[67]

In 1963 there was a new round in the conflict over singing style. But unlike the modernization of instruments, which united cosmopolitans and populists, the populists refused to condemn native singing styles, for obvious political reasons. Proponents of foreign vocal production were concentrated in the conservatories, while advocates of native singing style tended to work for local song and dance ensembles or the increasingly powerful People's Liberation Army. The nativists complained of intimidation by the Western-style singers, who told folk singers that they could attain a higher level of art by learning to sing like Europeans. The populists prevailed after Guo Lanying (an early star of *The White-Haired Girl*), gave a series of recitals in Beijing, followed by a conference on her very Chinese singing style, complete with discussion of her "scientific" vocal production.[68]

Musical modernization was combined with political radicalization on the eve of the Cultural Revolution. The dazzling performances of the army's Vanguard Song and Dance Ensemble inspired one microbiologist at the Academy of Sciences to repudiate the European classics which he once loved, but which caused him to waste much previous time. "If you listen to more Western bourgeois classical music, it slowly muddles your class viewpoint for understanding problems." As an example, the scientist referred to the ideology of "universal brotherhood" in the choral movement to Beethoven's Ninth Symphony. It holds forth an illusion of progress without conflict: "if the world can truly achieve affection among its peoples, then cannot conflict be rooted out and eternal peace be established throughout the world?"[69]

The role of the Chinese army in musical modernization had a parallel in nineteenth-century Europe. Berlioz, Rossini, Meyerbeer and other nineteenth-century European composers were enthusiasts of the inventions of Adolphe Sax (1814–1894), the Belgian-born instrument maker. Sax had as his great patron the French army, which was concerned with the condition of its bands. In addition to the saxophone family, Sax also developed groups of saxhorns (euphonium, flügelhorn, cornet) and saxotrombas (a short-lived instrument devised for cavalry bands), and experimented with bassoons, trombones, clarinets, and tympani. Sax used modern technology to attain mellifluously blended sounds, greater chromatic range, and increased volume to satisfy the growing middle-class audience.[70] Berlioz demanded that the Paris Conservatory help modernize French music (which he thought old-fashioned compared to German music) by introducing courses in the saxophone, ophicleide, bass tuba, and saxhorn.[71]

The notion of progress popular in Europe a century ago today underlies the continuing Chinese drive to modernize musical instruments, which is tinged with a fully romantic sense of struggle against difficult odds that will conclude in some sort of glorious music of the future, much as many Chinese believe that developments in European music culminated in Tchaikovsky. The question of preserving a sample of China's musical past simply does not arise, just as it did not in the mind of Berlioz in regard to French music. There are still many peasants in China living in material conditions little different from those that gave rise to the opera and the traditional musical instruments of the Qing dynasty. While this is true, neither cosmopolitans nor populists are likely to find musical nostalgia compatible with their quest for modernity. He Luting did not recognize himself when he quoted an anonymous critic of the music establishment: "The current leaders are all foreign musicians; they talk about national music, but in fact they eradicate national music under the pretence of enriching it." [72]

"The East Is Red": A Change of Anthems

The Cultural Revolution in music did not begin abruptly with some arbitrary political event, such as Beijing University's posters of May 1966. The explosion, when it came, reflected tensions that had long been building within musical circles. The musical fanfare which opened the Cultural Revolution, however, was certainly "The East Is Red," an old revolutionary song which became the movement's anthem. This stirring hymn was the title piece of a musical extravaganza for the fifteenth anniversary of the establishment of the People's Republic on October 1, 1964. *The East Is Red* told the history of China's revolution in song and dance, drawing upon mass song classics and vigorous dancing to spread Mao's message that the lessons of past struggle were relevant to China's continuing problems. [73] The song, written in 1942, was based on a northern Shaanxi folk song by a poor peasant named Li Youyuan (1903–1955). It was popular at Yan'an, but had been sung less frequently after Liberation, probably in deference to Party leaders who might object to its words:

> The East is red, the sun has risen. China has produced Mao Zedong!
> He works for the people's happiness, he is the people's savior.

The song's zealous words and stately melody were the perfect musical accompaniment to the new Mao cult. [74]

In fact, China was soon to need a new national anthem. Nie Er's sturdy "March of the Volunteers" had done good service since 1949, but the politics of the Cultural Revolution rendered it unsuitable. Its words had been written by Tian Han, the former patron of Nie and Xian Xinghai, who had become a leading cultural administrator in the People's Republic. When he was swept from power early in the movement, "The East is Red" became China's unofficial anthem. Meetings opened with solemn unison singing of this paean to Mao. The clock of Shanghai's former customs house was adjusted so that "The East Is Red" sang forth in place of the Westminster chimes left behind by the British. The Central People's Broadcasting Station began its day with "The East Is Red," played on a set of bells cast over two thousand years ago in the Warring States period. And when the Chinese sent their first satellite into space in 1970, it broadcast "The East Is Red," washing an entire planet in the purifying sounds of heightened revolutionary consciousness.[75]

Western-style music was not the chief battleground for China's artistic conflicts in the Cultural Revolution. Far more energy was probably being expended on the question of reform of Chinese opera, which pitted Jiang Qing (Mao's wife) and Ke Qinghshi, the mayor of Shanghai, against Peng Zhen, the mayor of Beijing, in a better contest over the direction that this popular art form should take.[76] Nonetheless, music was critical, not so much because of the numbers of people involved, but because of intimate involvement of the people with politically suspect foreign culture.

On the eve of the Cultural Revolution, Shanghai's musical climate could be seen in its annual May music festival. Two hundred pieces were performed in thirty-eight concerts, to an audience of over one hundred thousand. Unusually, seventy percent of the four thousand performers were workers, peasants, and soldiers. The militantly populist program featured various musical versions of Mao's poems, including both foreign-style choral settings and Suzhou ballads.[77]

Conservatory students were confused. In Beijing, over eighty percent of the Central Conservatory students participated in groups studying Mao's writings.[78] Much like students at other elite schools, radicalized piano students at the Central Conservatory became worried about such questions as "How can Western instruments serve the worker-peasant-soldier masses?" As they tried to reconcile their politics to their professional studies, they hauled a piano into the countryside, where they turned popular revolutionary songs into piano music and wrote new pieces reflecting village life.[79]

Most of China's musical institutions were eventually paralyzed by the conflict between those who joined the call to make cultural revolution and those who either resisted the call or became targets of the movement. The presidents of the Shanghai and Central Conservatories were attacked with special force. Their stories convey some of the bitterness, fear, and long-repressed hostility which the Cultural Revolution unleashed among musicians.

Shanghai: He Luting

He Luting was one of the earliest targets of the Cultural Revolution in Shanghai. By June 1966, Shanghai's newspapers criticized him by name, indicating a high-level decision to concentrate the movement against him.[80] In June, Maoists and conservative Party officials were still struggling for control of the Cultural Revolution. The latter tried to protect themselves against Maoist attack by sacrificing some of their more outspoken underlings. He received forewarning of the pending assault. A loyal conservatory graduate worked in the Shanghai Cultural Revolution Liaison Office, and He's daughter used her friendship with him to obtain copies of secret files assembled for her father's case. Despite this knowledge, he was unable to ward off the attack.[81]

It is unclear why Shanghai's political elite chose He Luting as a scapegoat to deflect criticism from themselves, although his past conflict with Yao Wenyuan over Debussy rendered him particularly vulnerable.[82] He Luting's elitist attitudes and his clear preference for European musical models made him vulnerable to attack in a period in which these values were under fire. The political isolation of the Westernized musical community made him an easy person to sacrifice.

He Luting may also have been selected as an early target because of his personal history. In 1940 He had argued that European music should be taught to the masses, who did not object to Western musical techniques and welcomed new musical experiences. In the rectification at Yan'an, He was attacked fiercely by Meng Bo, Mai Xin, and Lu Ji, all revolutionary mass song specialists and critics of excessive Europeanization. He is said to have departed early from the liberated area because of the criticism.[83] Chinese sources are hazy about just when He Luting was in Yan'an (offering dates between 1941 and 1943), which may reflect a desire to mask this past unpleasantness. If the story is true, it is very possible that his past enmities over Western music returned to burden him over two decades later. Acting on such long-held grudges was not rare in the Cultural Revolution.

Some of the charges against He Luting are either trivial or are ritualistic references to a history he shared with hundreds of Communists in the 1930s, such as accusations that he betrayed the Party after 1927, that he had worked with Tian Han, and that he studied with Huang Zi (a member of the Guomindang Propaganda Committee) at the Shanghai Conservatory. Other points of criticism are more substantial, and center around He Luting's advocacy of European classical music.

He told his students that Chinese music was backward because China has not passed through a stage of capitalist development. This resulted in a sense of melody inferior to Europe's. He tried to interest his students in absolute music, and invited them into his home to listen to his private recordings of European music.[84] In 1956 He had complained that Chinese instruments "have no fixed pitch and their pitch is narrow. We possess no bass instruments like the cello and the double-bass. In these respects we are behind the West. If we refuse to learn from it, we shall be the losers."[85]

He pushed international competitions, pitting one performer against another in individualistic struggle. Training students with such bourgeois motivations was compared to planting "time bombs" who would eventually ruin the music world with their selfish quest for fame.[86] He also criticized the policy of sending musicians to factories and villages for political work.[87]

He derided the revival of the mass song movement as the work of the "arabic number faction," referring to the simplified notation used to teach political songs. He dismissed these songs as "accompaniment for slogans in arabic numbers," claiming on another occasion that revolutionary music is "quickly written, quickly sung, quickly forgotten, quickly lost."[88]

He was haunted again by his 1934 composition for Tcherepnin, "The Cowherd's Flute," that had so annoyed Fou Ts'ong. Someone publicized the memories of an old peasant who really had tended water buffalo in the 1930s, making his childhood sound less idyllic than He's five minutes of musical chinoiserie. Worse, He had unfortunately boasted in a 1937 interview that Tcherepnin had played "The Cowherd's Flute" for Adolph Hitler.[89] Critics also faulted He for reviving some of the songs he had written for the movies in the 1930s, which allegedly had a bourgeois air about them.[90]

He also claimed "The East Is Red" as his own composition, including it in a 1957 edition of his songs. In fact, He Luting had made an arrangement of Li Youyuan's song in 1945, which "forced a dubious harmony upon it. He insisted on the so-called specialized techniques of music, using Western eighteenth and nineteenth century harmony, polyphony, and sloppy accompaniment to grind away the revolutionary spirit of the original tune."[91] Even if He Luting did not consciously steal credit for the Maoist anthem, his treatment of a peasant musician's work seems cavalier.

He Luting was fortunate that he was not charged with another plagiarism. One of his most popular compositions was the wartime "Song of the Guerrillas," which bears an uncomfortable resemblance to the eighteenth-century English tune "The British Grenadier." The song was well-known in East Asia early in this century from Japanese school songbooks.[92] Chinese artistic traditions are not so concerned with individual property rights as are our own, and have more relaxed conventions about borrowing and adapting the work of others. But it certainly would have been embarrassing during the Cultural Revolution for it to be shown that He had lifted his best-known tune from the British Imperial Army.[93]

At the end of the summer, He Luting's home was ransacked by Red Guards, who destroyed music by European masters as they sang music by his rival—Jie Fu's setting of Mao's words, "A Revolution Is Not a Dinner Party." He was forced to appear before several mass-criticism meetings, and to parade in a circuit around the conservatory wearing a signboard around his neck.[94] He Luting's supporters gathered materials and prepared petitions after December 1966 to reverse his verdict.[95] This apparently backfired, resulting in a televised mass-criticism meeting for He in April 1968. He used the occasion to make a public remonstrance for his mistreatment, which included a beating at the hands of ten Red Guards.[96]

Beijing: Ma Sitson

In Beijing, Ma Sitson was also an early victim of the Cultural Revolution, probably for similar reasons. The sixty-four-year-old president of the Central Conservatory was even more openly elitist (he refused, like Fu Lei, to allow his children to attend public schools) and isolated (his last concert had been in 1963, before the radical tide washed over the world of music). He also had never joined the Communist Party, marking him as a highly vulnerable bourgeois intellectual. The Left's charges against Ma are not available, but we do have his own account of his experience. At the outset of the Cultural Revolution, Ma and eighteen others from the Central Conservatory were held for fifty days of thought reform. Then they were returned to the Conservatory for a mass criticism session on August 9, where they were treated harshly, forced to wear duncecaps, and lashed by Red Guard belts. This was followed by 103 days in a "cowshed"—actually a small building formerly used to store pianos. In addition to political study, Ma was made to clean toilets, and each evening he had to sing:

> I am a cow-headed monster, I have sinned, I have sinned.
> I must submit to the people's dictatorship,
> Because I am an enemy of the people.
> I must be very frank,
> If I am not, smash me to bits.

The song "ended on the seventh note with a crescendo to make it sound ugly!" By September, interest in Ma had waned, and he was allowed to spend some, then later all evenings at home. But on his first return home, he found that his records and books had been destroyed or confiscated, and that out-of-town Red Guards were using his home for a barracks.[97]

Ma fled China in January 1967, first by disguising himself as a poor peasant, and then paying for an illegal boat trip into Hong Kong for Guangdong. He sold his story to *Life* magazine, and later testified against the perils of Red China to the U.S. House Internal Security Committee. The first installment of his two-part *Life* article was printed as a pamphlet by the Central Conservatory Red Guards, and was later widely reprinted throughout China, ostensibly for political study, but probably also for profitable sale on the streets to the curious, given the fame of its author.[98] This pamphlet did assure that Ma Sitson's name would be regarded as treasonous for some time to come, as did the fact that the Guomindang began to broadcast his song "Longing for Home" to the mainland, reversing the direction of the musical propaganda.

Shenyang: Li Jiefu

The most populist of the conservatory presidents began the Cultural Revolution by offering a new set of Mao-quotation songs. He also set to music Lin Biao's directive to the army: "Study Chairman Mao's writings, follow his teachings, act according to his intructions and be a good soldier of Chairman Mao."[99] Yet as the Red Guard movement grew and struck out at almost any figure in authority, Jie Fu also came under attack. But the new Cultural Revolution group in charge of the radical movement defended him as a good comrade with healthy tunes, and he was soon rummaging the works of Chairman Mao once more, in search of material for songs.[100] Jie Fu no doubt received some political protection from Minister of Defense Lin Biao; Huang Yongsheng, commander of the Guangzhou military region and a major supporter of Lin Biao, was the husband of Jie Fu's sister.[101] If for no other reason, Jie Fu should be remembered in music history for his most outrageous song title: "This Brand-New Art Form with Revolutionary Significance Is Helping to Spread the Thought of Mao Zedong and Deepening its Influence among the People."[102]

New Musical Leadership: Yu Huiyong

The Cultural Revolution brought down many of China's leaders, but it also provided upward mobility to new ones. When the rebel forces from the Shanghai Conservatory eventually selected a new leader (as a "responsible person" of the conservatory's Revolutionary Committee), they chose a thirty-five-year-old professor named Yu Huiyong. The Shanghai Conservatory was closed after 1967, but Yu went on to higher positions, rising to become China's minister of culture before the Cultural Revolution ended.[103]

Yu Huiyong followed a different road to the conservatory from that of He Luting.[104] He joined the revolution as a youth in Shandong, performing in a cultural work team on the eve of Liberation. He was sent to the Shanghai Conservatory when intellectuals were under pressure to admit more students of worker-peasant backgrounds to their institutions. Yu was older than most students; he was also already a Party member and had a better class origin than most students from intellectual families. But the latter had been practicing European instruments since they were children; Yu and other students transferred from cultural work teams tended to be shunted into the Department of National Music, on the theory that anyone could handle such low-grade material.[105]

After graduation, Yu was retained as a composition teacher in the Department of National Music. Other conservatory faculty presumed that he was there only because of his political credentials, and mocked him as the "melody composer" and for his poor understanding of the European arts of harmony and accompaniment. Yu was clearly a second-class member of the conservatory faculty, and must have accumulated much resentment toward the snobbery of He Luting. Yu's cosmopolitan critics presumed that his interest in native music reflected his lack of ability to learn "real" music. This may well represent a snooty cosmopolitan unwillingness to believe that anyone might prefer traditional Chinese music. The conservatories were the centers of modernizing zeal; faculty and students alike shared a deep prejudice against traditional instruments, some saying that "It is only blind 'sellers of songs' on the street who study the *erhu!*"[106] Yu responded by complaining in an article of the contempt with which his Eurocentric colleagues treated Chinese folk music, and of continuing prejudice against singers and performers from working backgrounds.[107]

Yu Huiyong's resentments made him enthusiastic about the movement to revolutionize Beijing opera, where his compositional skills were welcomed rather than mocked. He helped with the music for *Taking Tiger Mountain by Strategy,* and was the principal composer of the music for *On the Docks* in early 1965. *On the Docks* was a project of Shanghai's Beijing Opera Troupe; it was the first of the model operas to be set after liberation, and featured the struggle of militant stevedores (coolies before 1949) against counterrevolutionary sabotage. It was much loved by Jiang Qing, and it is on this project that Yu came to her attention.[108] Despite her zeal for reforming opera and music, Jiang had no formal training. Yu Huiyong became her most important adviser on musical topics, which led to ever-higher bureaucratic office.

At the outset of the Cultural Revolution, the Red Guards of the conservatory attacked Yu, both as a professor and as a specialist in the feudal arts of traditional music, just as they were taking part in the campaign against He Luting.[109] His association with Jiang Qing and other radicals protected him, however, and after the conservatory ceased functioning, Yu became head of the Shanghai Municipal Cultural Bureau (and secretary of its Party committee), then deputy director of the State Council Culture Group, a member of the Central Committee, and, in 1975, minister of culture. As Yu's influence expanded, he became the leader of China's new populist music establishment.

Yu Huiyong's example as a modernizing Chinese musician shows that it is inaccurate to dismiss the leftist music policies of the early 1960s simply as anti-Western. Yu's rise must be understood in terms of the class issues in Chinese culture. Cosmopolitan musicians, with their middle-class values, were culturally and socially isolated from China's workers and peasant majority. Their musical preferences led them to social snobbery as they tried to maintain their version of artistic standards that were not meaningful or acceptable to large numbers of Chinese. Cosmopolitans went along with Maoist programs, such as sending musicians to field and factory or admitting worker-peasant students, but they did so begrudgingly. They could never adjust to Maoist suspicions of expertise because their professional identities were given legitimacy primarily by their specialized musical knowledge and skills. When broader social and political tensions exploded in 1966 in the Cultural Revolution, it is not surprising that the musical cosmopolitans were picked as an easy target for the wrath of the Red Guards. Moreover, their victimization worked for several months to shield conservative Party leaders as Liu Shaoqi and Deng Xiaoping.

The turning point in the conflict between populism and elitism in Western musical circles was not the Cultural Revolution, but the years immediately preceding that movement. The Cultural Revolution was more dramatic and brought about important changes in personnel and institutions. But the leaders of cosmopolitan music owed their fall more to their elitism than to the drive to Westernize China's music that they shared with their adversaries, and which continued throughout the decade of the Cultural Revolution.

5

Court Pianist to the Cultural Revolution: Yin Chengzong

Westerners popularly believe that the Cultural Revolution eradicated their music in China, but this is not correct. The music of the Cultural Revolution followed the trend established by 1964, although with greater violence and chaos: European classics were banned, but cultural revolutionaries propagated a music that was in fact highly Western in its technique, harmonic structure, instrumentation, and emphasis on choral singing. Music was an important part for the new art which Cultural Revolution leaders proposed to replace the old. Yin Chengzong is a pianist whose career flourished during the Cultural Revolution. His career offers a glimpse into an emotionally charged world in which for a while the piano, as an emblem of the bourgeoisie, was in danger of obliteration. Partly through Yin's efforts, the piano was transformed from a target of revolution into a positive symbol of radical change in Chinese culture. As Yin responded to the challenge of the Cultural Revolution, he certainly introduced the piano to more people than any musician since Franz Lizst.

A Virtuoso for the Revolution

Gulangyu Island is the most charming part of the Fujian city of Xiamen. Before the revolution, when Xiamen was a treaty port, Gulangyu was where foreign merchants maintained their homes and foreign consuls their offices. The Chinese who lived there were intimately connected to foreign culture, especially music. Today the people of Xiamen still proudly identify Gulangyu as China's "musical island." Automobiles and trucks are banned from its streets, allowing visitors and residents alike pleasant walks, on which they may smell the island's flowers, gaze at its curious Sino-Western architecture, and hear the sounds of piano music floating on the air. Some of the island's five hundred pianos were left behind by foreigners, others were brought by Overseas Chinese returned to Fujian; still others have been purchased in the most recent wave of piano popularity in China.[1]

Gulangyu is proud of its many musicians, but the small island's most famous musical child is Yin Chengzong, who was born there in 1941.[2] Yin's father was a prosperous merchant, with overseas Chinese connections; he had lived in Singapore, returning to Xiamen to sell a variety of products ranging from soy sauce to photo supplies and stocks. Yin's father enjoyed the luxury of a concubine, who was Chengzong's mother. The family was feudal in its structure yet modern in its foreign outlook. Yin Chengzong's aunt married the first president of Xiamen University, a noted reformer of education. Yin's oldest half-brother studied architecture in the United States, returning to Gulangyu to design an American-style house for the Yin family; a half-sister was an Oberlin graduate who returned to China and made recordings of church music, a very bold venture for a Chinese woman of the time.

The first piano Yin knew was a player piano which was in the house when he was a young child; it was later removed, leaving no music for a few years. The Yin family was Christian; young Chengzong sang in churches, and took his first piano lessons at the age of seven from the wife of a Chinese Protestant preacher. The Yins eventually purchased a piano from Shanghai; Yin still had vivid memories of the night the instrument was delivered, when his older sister played the "Blue Danube Waltz" by candlelight because of a power failure. Within a few months, young Yin could play the Strauss waltz by ear. Within two years he was accompanying a children's choir on Xiamen radio and had performed a solo recital.

This was at the time of Liberation, which brought good things for Yin. The newly established Xiamen Musicians' Association recognized the talent of their local prodigy, and when he was twelve, arranged for him to study as a boarding student in the middle school attached to the Shanghai Conservatory. Like other advanced arts institutions, the Shanghai Conservatory drew many of its students from a special preparatory school, where the gifts of young musicians could be cultivated by China's best teachers as well as by foreign experts from the Soviet Union.

The end to China's civil war was less happy for Yin's home city. When the Guomindang armies retreated to Taiwan, they held on to Jinmen island (Quemoy), which is within shouting distance of Gulangyu. With U.S. support, the Guomindang built Jinmen into a massive underground fortress. This rearguard harassment of the new People's Republic put Xiamen on the front line of conflict with Chiang Kaishek and his U.S. backers. Yin's native city was transformed from a busy seaport, curious about foreign ways, into a military bastion, where the People's Liberation Army became the dominant cultural influence.

Yin's education in Shanghai was also caught up in world politics. His task was to become good enough to win international recognition for China. China's musical and political establishment placed great importance on winning foreign acceptance in culture as a way around China's diplomatic isolation. Cultural leaders correctly determined that a focus on the piano would bring success sooner than the lengthier process of cultivating orchestras and singers.

School life was punctuated by the successes of other Chinese pianists in foreign competitions. Fou Ts'ong's showing in the 1955 Chopin Competition was a model for all young Chinese musicians. Liu Shikun showed that this was not a fluke when he won second prize in the 1958 Tchaikovsky Competition in Moscow, after having won third prize in the 1956 Liszt Competition. In addition, Li Mingqiang won prizes in the Smetana and Enescu Competitions, and Gu Shengying won honors in Geneva and in the Sixth World Youth Federation Festival Piano Competition. China's press was full of pride at the prowess of its musicians in international competitions: "when our young pianists take part, they nearly always win a prize." These accomplishments were measured against the West's three hundred years of piano culture. The success of triumphing over European musicians was especially sweet, and China gave ample credit to Soviet advisors who helped train young Chinese artists.[3]

In Shanghai, Yin thought to meet Fu Lei, both as the father of his older keyboard colleague and as the translator of *Jean-Christophe*, which Yin admired as much as any intellectual Chinese adolescent. But the 1957 antirightist campaign broke out and the meeting never took place.

As a target of the campaign, Fu Lei was not receiving visitors, and even young Yin came under some mild criticism for his family's Christian religion.

Fou Ts'ong's 1959 defection threw the music world into turmoil. It was in that same year that Yin won his first international competition, taking the first prize in the Piano Competition of the Seventh World Youth Festival at Vienna, with a program of Liszt, Beethoven's "Appassionata" Sonata, and Mozart's Sonata K. 330. Upon his return to China, three recordings of his playing were issued in Beijing, and the eighteen-year-old Yin became something of a celebrity. China's embarrassment at losing Fou Ts'ong heightened its eagerness to celebrate the success of a new musical star.

Yin was only a second year student in the Shanghai Conservatory's Senior High School, where he was coached by two Soviet teachers, Tatulian and Krafchenko. With their help and the support of the Central Conservatory, he left China in 1960 to study in the Soviet Union, despite growing political tensions between the two nations. There were nine Chinese students at the Leningrad Conservatory with Yin, and several hundred Chinese studying elsewhere in the city. Bad feelings between China and the Soviet Union provoked frequent political debates between the Chinese students and the Soviet classmates.

Yin was a student at the Leningrad Conservatory in April 1962 when he repeated Liu Shikun's feat of winning second prize in the Tchaikovsky Competition. That year the first prize was shared by Vladimir Ashkenazy and John Ogdon; Yin shared second place with the American, Susan Starr, an unlikely political pairing that was largely ignored by the Chinese press. In the competition, Yin played Bach, Mozart, Scriabin, Rachmaninov, Chopin, Liszt, Tchaikovsky, and a Chinese piece, the suite from the ballet *The Mermaid,* by Wu Zuqiang and Du Mingxin.[4]

In his 1962 summer vacation, Yin enjoyed a triumphal return to China, with concerts in Beijing and Shanghai.[5] Yin rested in Gulangyu in preparation for another year at the Leningrad Conservatory. There his family purchased a piano for him, one left behind by a capitalist family that fled to Hong Kong in 1949. This instrument had been owned by Zhuo Yilong, the granddaughter of Yin's paternal aunt and later the wife of Fou Ts'ong—another reminder of how small and interconnected the European music community in China is.[6]

His triumph continued in the Soviet Union, where he gave fifty or sixty concerts after winning his prize, including performances with the Leningrad and Moscow Philharmonic Orchestras. Despite the political tensions between the two nations, Soviet audiences loved Yin, regarding him as nearly their own, for he had studied with Soviet teachers for six years in China and another three in Leningrad.

Yin was summoned back to China from Leningrad in June 1963. Two months earlier, Vladimir Ashkenazy had refused to return to Moscow from London, no doubt raising memories of Fou Ts'ong among Chinese cultural officials, although there is no reason to believe that Yin ever threatened to bolt for the West. Another factor in recalling Yin was the now open hostility between China and the Soviet Union, as Khrushchev mocked Chinese departures from the Soviet model for economic growth and Mao accused his recent Soviet allies of bullying China and promoting revisionism.

When Yin returned to China in the summer of 1963 he worked and studied at Beijing's Central Conservatory; two years later he was assigned to work in the Central Philharmonic Society. The Central Philharmonic is not only a symphony orchestra; it also includes a large chorus, solo singers and instrumentalists, several conductors, and its own staff of composers. The Central Philharmonic grew from two hundred members in 1957 to five hundred in 1986; its musicians perform in various combinations, giving some of its concerts a flavor of early–nineteenth-century European performances, where orchestral works might alternate with vocal or instrumental solo pieces.[7]

Yin arrived at a time of considerable confusion. Artists in the early 1960s had enjoyed rather good treatment. This was the time of the "three highs" policy, which promised artists high wages, high royalties, and high perquisites. Even when many rural Chinese were suffering malnutrition during the famine that followed the Great Leap Forward, professional musicians and other artists were given special meat rations in order to maintain their energies. Yet favoritism for artists was collapsing rapidly as China moved toward Cultural Revolution. The split with the Soviet Union led to a withdrawal of Soviet specialists in all fields. Soviet conductors and piano teachers returned home, and opportunities to listen to visiting Eastern European performers declined drastically. Without the eastern European weight, China's musical community was left to stand on its own at a time when the urban middle class was under increasing suspicion. National policies to recapture the embattled political consciousness and revolutionary energies of Yan'an further revealed the social isolation of the urban middle-class audience.

Yin immediately joined the ongoing controversy over European classical music. What was the place for a piano in a radicalized Chinese culture? Many held that the piano was the ultimate bourgeois instrument. China's newest star joined other European-style musicians in adapting revolutionary folk and mass songs to the piano. Yin was fond of Chinese opera, and the political problems facing the classical repertory encouraged him to try his hand at composing new pieces that would reflect Chinese culture.

Yin, although still a student, was increasingly celebrated; he was received by Mao Zedong at the 1964 Spring Festival. Yin toured China playing two very different recital programs. One consisted entirely of Chopin, in preparation for his possible participation in the 1964 Marguerite Long Piano Competition in Paris. This program was presented to such foreign audiences as businessmen attending the Guangzhou Trade Fair. The other program consisted of all Chinese music, including some of Yin's own compositions, a "*Yangge* Dance," and "Fishing People Sing of the Communist Party" (the folk tune on which the latter was based was entitled simply "Fishing Song," but the times demanded a title of reddish hue). This program was praised in the national press.[8] Yin did not go to Paris; instead, he went to live with peasants outside of Beijing, as part of a political movement. The Cultural Revolution was about to begin, and the moment was not auspicious for international piano contests. The Ministry of Culture cancelled Yin's trip, groundlessly fearing that he might defect.

Jiang Qing as a Patron of Symphonic Music

Yin's experiments in writing Chinese music for the piano coincided with the musical interests of the woman who would become his most important patron, Jiang Qing, Mao's wife. Jiang Qing's activities in the reform of Chinese opera are well known.[9] Less famous are her efforts in the realm of symphonic music, which she counted as a second "stronghold" that she helped capture "with all my heart and all my strength."[10]

Jiang Qing's enthusiasm for the arts has often been ridiculed since her fall from power in 1976, but it is clear that her interest was deep.[11]

As a young woman of fifteen, she encountered European music through piano lessons, like many Chinese in the 1920s, including the deposed emperor, Pu Yi. Her three months of piano study in 1929–1930 at the Shandong Experimental Arts Academy were not happy; her teacher "struck her wrists with sticks in order to regulate her style." As a result she never progressed beyond playing scales and simple exercises.[12]

Music continued to be important after Jiang Qing moved to Shanghai in search of a career in the movies. She supported herself in 1933 as a singing teacher at a YWCA night school for cigarette workers, introducing songs to her students by playing them on the *erhu*.[13] Xian Xinghai was still in Paris, but these lessons could well have included some of the revolutionary songs of Nie Er. She later knew Xian in Yan'an, where she studied at the Lu Xun Art Academy while he was composing his *Yellow River Cantata*.[14] She was probably hostess for the farewell dinner given by Mao when Xian departed for Moscow.

After Liberation Jiang Qing worked briefly in the Ministry of Culture's film bureau, but did not pursue an active political role in cultural policy until the Maoist revival in the 1960s. Up to that time, she restricted her artistic impulses to cultivating her hobby of photography. Leaders of the cultural establishment resented her reentry into politics, which they saw as unwarranted meddling in their affairs. Before the Cultural Revolution Zhou Yang sarcastically cried: "Let Jiang Qing be the Minister of Culture!"[15]

Zhou never took Jiang Qing seriously until it was too late. Other officials were more cooperative, including Minister of Defense Lin Biao. In February 1966 Lin arranged for Jiang Qing to preside over a Forum on Literature and Art for the Armed Forces. This Shanghai meeting, reminiscent of Mao's Yan'an Forum, provided Jiang Qing with a national platform for advocating her favored model works of art, which included several operas and the new *Shajiabang Symphony*. Mao revised her speech three times before Lin Biao distributed it.[16]

Jiang Qing agreed with Mao that dead "emperors, princes, generals, ministers, scholars and beauties" filled China's opera stages.[17] Similarly, foreign music prevailed in China's concert halls. Neither placed living Chinese workers and peasants at the center, and neither art grew from the new socialist economic base built since the revolution. Jiang Qing maintained that Soviet revisionism had grown because Stalin "uncritically took over what are known as the classics of Russia and Europe and the consequences were bad." [18]

Jiang Qing did not claim to know much about music. She even struggled to teach herself to read music again in the 1960s. [19] She had the Central Philharmonic send a piano to her home, but soon returned it in frustration when it became apparent that her piano lessons were too far in the past to be recalled. Jiang Qing claimed to be making investigations of music on Mao's behalf, which seems likely, as Mao had intervened in the Central Conservatory disputes in 1964, although he had never revealed any personal passion for music. Jiang Qing referred repeatedly to Mao's 1956 "Talk to Music Workers," claiming that Mao was considering revising and publishing it, but he never did. [20] Officials of the Ministry of Culture treated her with a combination of indulgence (arranging for visits with musicians) and suspicion (trying to bar her from meeting orchestra leaders and requesting reports on Jing's comments and activities). [21]

Jiang Qing's Program for Music Reform

Jiang Qing addressed musicians several times in the year after November 1964. This was at the height of the public discussion of how to make music national, and followed Yao Wenyuan's criticism of Debussy. Jiang's extensive but unorganized remarks reveal a coherent plan for joining European musical technique to Chinese culture. Ten major points emerge from her comments. [22]

1. China's musicians must find a course independent of both Western bourgeois standards and native feudalism: "The 'foreign tiger' and 'native tiger' are both ferocious, but we must not be bound by them." [23]
2. Western music is politically unhealthy. *Madama Butterfly* describes the shaming of Japanese women by American imperialism, and *La Traviata* dignifies prostitution. "Capitalism's music is headed for destruction, you do not want to go die along with the foreigners." [24]
3. However Chinese folk songs are not a satisfactory basis for creating a new musical culture. When the Ministry of Culture encourages folk songs, no one sings revolutionary songs any more.

Moreover, some of the folk songs are off-color. Chinese opera offers a more satisfactory basis for a new road in culture.[25]

4. International musical competitions are capitalist at the core, and tempt young artists with bourgeois prizes. Perhaps China should consider staging its own international festival of Asian, African, and Latin American music. Nevertheless, China does receive some benefit from musical competitions "from the standpoint of international relations."[26]

5. The question of singing technique is still unresolved. Western singing emphasizes sound, but "when people sing Western opera, it seems as if something is in their mouths, so that the words are all indistinct." Chinese singing emphasizes words; its combination with Western technique "can create the world's best singing method."[27]

6. The modernization of instruments must proceed, but with caution. Unreformed national ensembles cannot perform revolutionary music effectively, as the *erhu* cannot compare to the violin in richness. "I hear that the 'Vanguard Song and Dance Troupe' has reformed the *sheng* by making it from metal, enlarging its sound. Is it true that they have put metal strings on the *erhu*?" Because capitalist industry developed early, there has been time to develop a complete set of industrialized instruments in the West, while Chinese instruments are still handicraft products. At the same time, Jiang Qing was suspicious of reforming instruments to the point that they lose their special color; someone had made a *suona* (a double-reed instrument) of the bass range so absurdly long that it bumped the floor.[28]

7. The problem is not musical instruments, which are tools, but the music which is performed on them. Most "Chinese" instruments except the *qin* are of foreign origin. "National instruments still need many years of reform, why can the already developed Western instruments not be used? We should use foreign things to serve China." When a French-horn player arrived in the countryside from his conservatory, the peasants did not like his foreign music, but when he used his foreign instrument to play Chinese songs he became popular. Similarly, the piano has a powerful sound, but little repertory which the masses enjoy hearing. "[Liu Shikun] plays very well, but the workers do not understand when he plays Liszt."[29]

8. Music is bound up in a system of social snobbery. "We must smash foreign dogmatism. Symphonic music is in fact a formalistic thing; the various movements have no internal connections. Not only do Chinese listeners not understand it, but Caucasian working people do not understand it, and a great many bourgeoisie themselves also only pretend to understand in order to demonstrate how civilized they are." Musicians should take advantage of political movements to see China and learn more about their own country, reducing some of their social isolation.[30]

9. Western musical instruments should be protected. Jiang Qing criticized the rectification of musical ensembles of 1963, during which many Western instrumentalists were dismissed. She asked Lin Biao to protect them in the military, where the air force was most successful at retaining its wind and string orchestras. Each province should have its own orchestra. It is a pity to make musicians change occupations, as they have studied for many years to acquire their skills.[31]

10. Chinese opera needs European musical instruments. Chinese music is too simple and limited, and sometimes conveys the wrong flavor, as when the "Internationale" is played by native instruments in *The Red Lantern*.[32]

After Jiang Qing's fall from power in 1976, her enemies attacked her distaste for folk songs, which they represented as a dislike for the art of the masses. This is true, but her discomfort with rural folk culture is typical of the urban intelligentsia, and especially true of the symphonic musicians who celebrated her downfall.[33] Her program for music was rooted firmly in the tradition of cultural modernization patronized by China's middle class throughout this century.

The Shajiabang Symphony

Jiang Qing's most important institutional connection was with the Central Philharmonic, whose conductor, Li Delun, had been her friend in Shanghai in the 1930s. When she visited the orchestra on January 27, 1965, she encouraged its members to join her in making a symphony from the recently successful revolutionary opera *Spark Among the Reeds*. After listening to demonstrations of all of the orchestra's instruments to see if they were suitable for playing Beijing opera tunes, she invited the musicians to join her the next day at a performance of *Spark Among the Reeds,* which was later known as *Shajiabang.*[34]

The opera takes place in Shajiabang village, on the shore of Yangcheng Lake in Jiangsu Province. There, during the War of Resistance, eighteen wounded soldiers from the Communist New Fourth Army are recuperating. The local Communist underground conceals the warriors from the raids of Guomindang and Japanese forces, which are routed at the end of the opera. This work, created in 1958 as a Shanghai opera, was staged by Jiang Qing's allies as a Beijing opera for the 1964 National Opera Festival in the capital. There an enthusiastic Mao changed its name and urged "that the opera should end with the people's army fighting its way into the enemy's den." [35]

Jiang Qing was intensely involved in the creation of the *Shajiabang Symphony.* On September 25, 1965, she offered twenty-six suggestions, including opinions about the application of Beijing opera tunes and advice about which of the New Fourth Army's marches to use in the symphony's conclusion (she no doubt wanted to avoid using any music composed by Shanghai Conservatory President He Luting, who was attached to the New Fourth Army). The collective efforts of the Central Philharmonic produced a nine-movement work, scored for a large orchestra of piccolo, pairs of flutes, oboes, clarinets, bassoons, four horns, two trumpets, three trombones, tympani, tambourine, clappers, gongs of two sizes, cymbals, harp, *jinghu, erhu, pipa, suona,* and strings, plus a chorus and vocal soloists. Its movements take their names from action in the opera, such as the second movement, "Soldiers and People are as Fish to Water." [36]

But this "sparkling gem of art in the treasure-house of proletarian literature and art" [37] was not completed without resistance. Cultural officials mocked the symphony, claiming that it would take twenty years for peasants to understand symphonic music. They refused to assign composers to the project, denied rehearsal time, and told the singers that using Chinese singing style would ruin their voices. But the music was completed in time to be performed for National Day (October 1), 1965.[38] Maoist critics hailed a new dawn in symphonic music.

> For centuries the contents of the so-called "classics" of symphonic music were none other than the stories of gods, ghosts, landlords and aristocratic ladies set to music. They also upheld the sacredness of the individual and the primacy of love, and dwelt on dreams, death, the

graveyard and such like themes. Other works of a similar pattern seem to us to have been written by degenerates or madmen! In short, symphonic music was an art reflecting the decadent spiritual physiognomy of the bourgeoisie; an art upholding bourgeois rule and oppression; upholding private ownership and individualist concepts.[39]

In contrast, the new symphony was hailed as a celebration of people's war, that filled the concert hall with an unaccustomed "smell of gunpowder."[40] But of course some of the European bourgeoisie's most vulgar music offered the cheap thrill of counterfeit gunpowder, from Beethoven's *Welllington's Victory* to Tchaikovsky's *1812 Overture*.

Red Guards Assault the Piano

Yin did not join the Central Philharmonic until 1965, and did not take part in the *Shajiabang* project. As part of the Four Cleanups campaign of 1964–1965, Yin was one of thousands of young people sent to the countryside to learn correct politics from the poor and lower-middle peasants. After eight months he managed to have a piano brought to his village outside Beijing, which he used to play folk music and revolutionary songs, and to accompany choral singing. Yin kept in touch with musical developments in the city. Jiang Qing asked the *Shajiabang* opera company to go to Jiangsu's Yangcheng Lake in 1965 to live among (and better understand) the peasants who had inspired the opera. Early the next year, Yin asked permission also to go to Yangcheng Lake in order to adapt the new symphony for piano. But Li Ling, the Central Philharmonic's Party secretary, opposed Yin's turn from the classical repertory and denied the request. Yin remained in the countryside until the Cultural Revolution began in 1966. Lin Mohan of the Ministry of Culture advised him that he was "playing the piano too nervously and too intensely; you should prepare some more lyrical things." Yet the peasants enjoyed his music, and Yin later claimed that it was in the village that "I realized that the future of the piano depended on whether or not we could compose works which expressed our people's feelings and which they loved to hear."[41]

The Cultural Revolution's initial burst of political energy was a poorly focused outrage against all things that were ancient because they were feudal, all things that were Western because they were bourgeois, and all things that were Soviet because they were revisionist. The harshest and most chaotic period was the short-lived campaign against the "Four Olds" in August and September of 1966. Bands of newly organized Red Guards roamed the streets of China's cities in a crusade against old customs, old habits, old culture, and old ways of thinking. In practice these Four Olds were associated with educated elites, families such as Fu Lei's, whose homes were subject of raids by high school and university students looking for physical evidence of bourgeois ideology.

Many Red Guards believed that family origin was the ultimate test of one's revolutionary or counterrevolutionary credentials.[42] This view, in fact, protected many of Mao's enemies within the Party bureaucracy, whose origins were politically pure, and who were able to use the theory of family origin to deflect Mao's attacks toward those who had ties to the old middle class, who had relatives in Taiwan, or who had been labeled as rightists in 1957. Maoist leaders opposed this view, but were never fully able to persuade political activists to adopt Mao's more elusive standard of class as indicator of political behavior. Much of the destruction and violence of the early Cultural Revolution was actually by conservative Red Guard organizations which made scapegoats of the old elites to protect their own bureaucrat parents against Maoist attacks. After October 1966, when Red Guards turned increasingly against bureaucratic power-holders, the most openly "royalist" Red Guard groups were broken up, and there was less interest in the old bourgeoisie.[43] But until October, the campaign against the Four Olds was a reign of terror against the old bourgeoisie, and even after the main thrust of political activism shifted from this group, its members remained easy targets throughout the ten years of the Cultural Revolution.

Jiang Qing's strong views about the positive role that the piano might play in China were not widely known in 1966. Young Red Guards, urged to go out and make revolution, regarded the piano as a symbol of bourgeois affectation and loyalty to imperialism. Many urban middle-class families watched Red Guard mobs smash their pianos to pieces. Other families, eager to remove evidence of musical counterrevolution from their homes, sold their pianos to second-hand furniture stores for a fraction of their rapidly declining value.[44] Even at the Central Conservatory, Red Guards pulled pianos out into the school's corridors and sealed their keyboards shut; they also boarded up the conservatory's museum of the history of musical instruments.[45]

Red Guard raiding parties also enjoyed destroying recordings of European classical music. Beijing University official Tang Yijie had accumulated a collection of classical records sold in haste by Guomindang loyalists fleeing to Taiwan at Liberation, only to see them smashed by Red Guards in August 1966.[46] The Central Conservatory's collection of records and instruments was saved by faculty and students who divided them up for hiding.[47] One Guangdong music lover first buried his record collection. Later, when things had quieted down a bit, and he could no longer do without Mozart and Brahms, he unearthed some of his favorite recordings and listened to them with a rare pair of headphones. Even then, he stored the records atop kindling in his stove, so that he might claim that he was preparing to burn them, should Red Guard raiders reappear.[48]

Most Red Guards were as suspicious of pianists as they were of pianos. Yin Chengzong was severely criticized early in the Cultural Revolution, not only for his status as a virtuoso pianist but also for his Christian family background. Rebels from the Central Philharmonic even visited Gulangyu to gather materials on Yin, returning to Beijing with allegations that his father had collaborated with the Japanese during the war.[49] Red Guards also criticized Yin for pro-Soviet "revisionism," on the strength of a photograph of Nikita Khrushchev congratulating Yin for his success in the Tchaikovsky Competition. Indignant Red Guards threatened to beat Yin with their belts and lock up him in a "cowshed," a fate averted only by the intervention of friendlier members of the "revolutionary masses."[50]

Yin's problems were mild compared to those of some other pianists. Fan Jilin, China's most noted piano teacher and head of Shanghai Conservatory piano department, was beaten by her former students.[51] Shanghai pianist Li Mingqiang, fourth-prize winner in the 1960 Chopin Competition, was locked up early in the Cultural Revolution, and not allowed to perform publicly until after 1976.[52] Liu Shikun, China's other Tchaikovsky Competition prize winner, was sent to Beijing's Taicheng prison.

Perhaps the greatest loss to Chinese music, however, was Gu Shengying, Yin's friend and counterpart as piano soloist with the Shanghai Philharmonic.[53] Gu, another of the outstanding pianists of the People's Republic, chose suicide to escape from political harassment. Gu was born in Shanghai in 1937. Her mother was a university graduate in French literature, and her father was an interpreter. Shengying means "holy infant," which suggests that the family was Christian like Yin's. Growing up in a house filled with over twenty thousand books, Gu Shengying became well read in both foreign literature and the Chinese classics. Not surprisingly, Fu Lei was a family friend, and presented her with autographed copies of each of his books. Fu Lei encouraged her music, and in 1953, at the age of sixteen, Gu Shengying performed a Mozart concerto with the Shanghai Philharmonic. After study with a visiting Soviet teacher, Gu was sent to Moscow for advanced training. Gu joined Fou Ts'ong as an international prize-winner, taking first place in the 1957 Sixth World Youth and Student Festival, second prize in the 1958 Geneva Tenth International Music Competition, and a prize in the 1964 Queen Elisabeth International Piano Competition in Belgium.

In China, like the West, many more women play the piano than men, yet fewer women are encouraged to pursue professional careers. Gu became China's most prominent female pianist; her international success was rewarded by promotions in the Shanghai Philharmonic, and she became a member of Chinese Musicians' Association, deputy secretary of the Shanghai Philharmonic Youth League Committee, and a member of the Youth League Committee of the Shanghai Municipal Cultural Bureau. She responded to the leftward trend of Chinese politics in the 1960s by accompanying the orchestra to the countryside as accompanist and as a member of its chorus. Nor did she neglect to play Chinese piano music: she devoted an entire recital to music by Chinese composers in August 1963, including pieces with such titles as "Chairman Mao Comes to Our Village." [54]

But Gu's professional success and political activism were clouded. She had no boyfriends at an age when it is unusual for a Chinese woman to be single; she lived at home, giving her salary to her mother. Her father was in remote Qinghai, serving a twenty-year prison term imposed during the antirightist campaign of 1957, a movement which also ruined the careers of her teacher, Ma Gesun, and her friend, Fu Lei. Perhaps it was these connections that made her a target of the Cultural Revolution. Gu criticized statements by rebels in the Shanghai Philharmonic, but no one recalls exactly what she said. One of the orchestra's radicals accused Gu of being a "secret agent" for capitalist roaders. He struck Gu in the face at a meeting of the orchestra, and pulled her hair to force her to confess her guilt before a portrait of Mao Zedong. Perhaps Gu Shengying could see no end to political pressure. At home her mother was distraught, and her younger brother could not find work. Following the recent examples of Fu Lei and of Yang Jiaren, her old piano teacher, Gu Shengying filled her apartment with gas on January 3, 1967, killing herself, her mother, and her brother.

Yin Chengzong Resurrects the Piano

The darkest moment for the piano fell during the several months following the campaign against the Four Olds in the autumn of 1966. Yin then decided to fight back to restore his reputation, to protect both his instrument and his livelihood. He worked with other pianists, including Gu Shengying, who traveled to Beijing only two weeks before her suicide to discuss with Yin how they could make revolution in piano music.[55] With Gu dead, Liu Shikun under arrest, and Fou Ts'ong in exile, Yin was alone among China's piano virtuosos. In a dramatic gesture, he took the piano into the streets as a practical demonstration that it had a place in the Cultural Revolution.

Taking the Piano into the Streets

Red Guard demonstrations had become a serious strain on the citizens of Beijing. The capital had become a center for Red Guards from around the country, some coming on earnest political pilgrimages, others simply taking advantage of an unusual opportunity for "revolutionary tourism." Full of youthful high spirits, they disrupted traffic and often crossed from political ardor into hooliganism. In order to calm the city, Zhou Enlai and other central authorities attempted to restrict street propaganda by Red Guards from arts units, including the Central Philharmonic, instructing them not to waste state funds in their propaganda work, but to make revolution in a more economical manner. Most important, they were told to get off the streets and return to their units. Going down to villages and factories to transform their world views was important, but must be carried out "in an organized and planned way."[56] Yet other voices urged artists to get out of their studios and theaters and "make their way to factories, the countryside, and places where the sharpest struggle of the great proletarian cultural revolution is waged."[57] The Red Guards proved difficult to contain in the welcome spring weather of 1967. Conservatories and other musical institutions had ceased operation and their members were often at loose ends. Moreover, young musical rebels were under pressure to prove themselves revolutionary. Some composed songs with such improbable titles as "All Our Literature and Art Are in the First Place for the Workers, Peasants, and Soldiers," and "The Revolutionary Struggle on the Ideological and Artistic Fronts Must Be Subordinate to the Political Struggle."[58]

During this combination of spring fever and revolutionary ferment Yin began his campaign for the piano's political respectability. Yin and other members of the Central Philharmonic's Mao Zedong Thought Propaganda Team loaded a piano on the back of a truck and drove it to Tiananmen Square on May 12, 1967, for a rally celebrating the twenty-fifth anniversary of Mao's "Talks at the Yan'an Forum." Yin entertained Red Guard demonstrators by playing music from *The White-Haired Girl*, as well as such current revolutionary songs as "The Peasant Congress has Convened," and "Long Life to Chairman Mao!" The next day this curious traveling piano show returned, and Yin played music from *Shajiabang*. The Central Philharmonic's piano propaganda troupe later performed in Beijing's factories, nearby villages, and army bases, all to demonstrate that the piano could play a role outside the concert hall.[59]

Revolutionary Opera on the Keyboard

After the success of his Tiananmen demonstration, Yin continued experimenting with new music for the piano. He had only learned in April that Jiang Qing had recommended three years earlier that revolutionary opera be adapted for the piano, as her talks had been suppressed by the cultural establishment. He and other Central Philharmonic rebels were excited to discover such a high-level justification for their outdoor concert. If Yin was to continue as a performer, he needed a repertory to play which was politically acceptable in the China of the Cultural Revolution. In addition, "ultra-left" voices in the music world continued to belittle the piano and urge that it be smashed, giving him ample motive for creating new scores to replace the hopelessly bourgeois European classics.[60]

Yin won new fame and respectability by his piano version of arias from *The Red Lantern*, perhaps the most popular of the model operas. Its simply story describes a small town under Japanese occupation.

Railway worker Li Yuhe uses his lantern for sending secret messages to nearby guerrillas. After Li and his mother are tortured and killed, his teenage daughter Tiemei succeeds in transmitting the secret code to guerrillas. The Li's are in fact unrelated by blood, but have been united by class loyalty into a revolutionary family, full of noble purpose.

The new piece began to take shape in a performance on National Day (October 1), 1967, when Yin responded to audience demand for opera music. He sent a tape of this and his piano version of *Shajiabang* to Jiang Qing. By this time the Central Philharmonic had become a model artistic unit, as Jiang Qing relied on her old friend Li Delun to help her transform Chinese culture. As a sign of Jiang Qing's favor, the Central Philharmonic began to perform in the uniform of the People's Liberation Army, and the formerly long-haired musicians received military haircuts.[61] Jiang Qing liked the music, but in November wrote instructions for improvements. Yin began to work with the two principal singers from *The Red Lantern,* Qian Haoliang and Liu Changyu; the three of them sent Jiang Qing another tape in May 1968.[62]

Yin set eight arias from the opera, three of Li Yuhe, and five of Tiemei. Beijing opera vocal style and Chinese drums combined with a Lisztian virtuosity on the keyboard. Indeed, Liszt himself set a precedent for Yin's project in his piano paraphrases on such popular operas of his day as *Lucia di Lammermoor, Don Giovanni,* and *Rigoletto.*

The completed work's premier performance was at a concert in Beijing's Great Hall of the People on July 1, 1968, in celebration of the forty-seventh anniversary of the founding of the Communist Party. Sponsored by the Cultural Revolution Group, the concert also featured a performance of the *Shajiabang* Symphony. After the concert, Mao Zedong, Lin Biao, Zhou Enlai, Chen Boda, Kang Sheng and Jiang Qing posed for photos with the performers, including radiant Yin, who stood next to Mao. The happy pianist held a book of *Quotations from Chairman Mao Zedong* along with the rest of the crowd.[63]

This performance made Yin a national figure in music for Cultural Revolutionary China. The *People's Daily* of July 6 celebrated the concert with articles by Yu Huiyong, Li Jiefu, and Yin Chengzong. Yin acknowledged the dubious historical origins of his instrument: "The piano, this musical instrument extolled by the bourgeoisie as the 'king of music,' and the 'pearl atop the crown of musical art,' is the stubborn fortress of Western musical instruments." Even though the piano was used to spread bourgeois ideology and to corrupt young artists with the temptations of fame and foreign travel, Yin still asked, "but as the piano is built by the laboring people, why can it not serve the people, serve proletarian politics, serve socialism?"[64]

The new music was not very popular with the urban middle class, but it was not intended to be. Its purpose was to popularize pianos among groups formerly excluded from hearing modern European musical instruments. A model peasant from Hunan complained of the classical piano repertory: "stuff which made us feel sick when we heard it. Now we are taking a new liking to piano music as we listen to *The Red Lantern*. Our revolutionary determination keeps soaring and our enthusiasm for work mounting as we go on listening to it."[65]

The great publicity given to *The Red Lantern with Piano Accompaniment* was integrated into a broader effort to find limited uses for other forms of bourgeois art. Yin's piano music was paired with a famous new oil painting, *Chairman Mao Goes to Anyuan,* by Liu Junhua, a student at the Central Institute of Arts and Crafts."[66] Many Chinese radicals regarded both piano music and oil painting as terminally bourgeois. But by 1968 both oils and pianos were praised as useful techniques which could be adapted for Chinese subjects, largely because of their technical power. The Anyuan painting "retains the special features of Western oil painting in its richness of colour, in being true to life and skillful in characterization. It also assimilates the explicitness, the emphasis in the placing of the figure and the elaborate detailed touches of traditional Chinese paintings." Similarly, Yin's *The Red Lantern* "incorporates the basic features of the ringing, powerful melodies of the Peking opera with its clear-cut rhythm. It brings into play the peculiar qualities of the piano—its wide range, power, clarity and expressiveness."[67]

By 1968 China's leadership wanted to end popular fears that all foreign objects and ideas were condemned as bourgeois or revisionist. Yin's *The Red Lantern* was held up as a model which synthesized the best of Chinese and foreign artistic techniques. Chinese culture of that period offered other examples, such as medicine, which sought to combine Western technique with such native medical practices as herbal drugs and acupuncture.[68]

Yin's music spread across China on records made by the new Beijing Gramophone Records Plant. Workers of the former Beijing Playing-Card Factory had demanded to change products as the Cultural Revolution raised their consciousness.[69] Like the virtuoso Yin, these former makers of gambling devices needed a healthier product if they were to maintain their livelihoods during the Cultural Revolution. China's official press hailed Yin's music.

> This is a song of victory for the thought of Mao Zedong. The piano which had always been a tool serving the reactionary ruling classes found its way out of feudal courts and palaces and bourgeois mansions and halls and for the first time mounted the theatrical stage of the workers, peasants and soldiers. The success of the piano music *The Red Lantern* gives a new lease on life to this Western instrument which was isolated from the people for so long that it was practically on the brink of extinction, turning it into a weapon for the proletariat.[70]

Yin Writes a Piano Concerto

Alone among China's virtuoso pianists, Yin had not been overwhelmed by the currents of the Cultural Revolution, and had played a major role in limiting its virulent xenophobia. A 1969 postage stamp portrayed Yin playing his piano for proletarian revolution. He partook of the rarified atmosphere of the Cultural Revolution arts elite. Jiang Qing, who was fond of assigning new names, changed Yin's given name from Chengzong, which means "Support the Clan," to Chengzhong, which is a more revolutionary-sounding "Respect the Masses." Yin sometimes identified himself by his given name alone, along with other successful radical musicians, such as the singer (Qian) Haoliang and the composer (Li) Jiefu. For all the Cultural Revolution's repudiation of individualistic competition and striving for personal, rather than collective success, Yin was very much a celebrity.

Yin became the deputy leader of the Central Philharmonic and was a member of the 1975 National People's Congress. Despite his celebrity, Yin received no special favors in housing, unlike some Chinese artists. Rumors linked him romantically to Liu Changyu, the ingenue actress who sang Li Tiemei to Yin's accompaniment. Other more scurrilous suggestions hinted that he owned his position to an amorous bond with Jiang Qing, a calumny repeated about nearly every prominent male artist or athlete during the Cultural Revolution.[71] Such allegations pained Yin, but demonstrated that he had attained that level of celebrity which inspires such gossip. Even in revolutionary China, audiences imagined virtuoso pianists to be busily amorous, in the manner of Chopin or Liszt.

Yin's next big project was to compose a piano concerto. Jiang Qing had suggested even before the Cultural Revolution that Xian Xinghai's 1939 *Yellow River Cantata* could be turned into a piano concerto, avoiding the reliance upon folk songs that she found objectionable in Liu Shikun's *Youth Piano Concerto* of 1959.[72] Yin took this project as his own. Jiang Qing's patronage made it politically acceptable, while using the music of Xian Xinghai signaled to the Western music community that Xian was still held in high esteem (in the Chinese aesthetic tradition, Yin's borrowing themes from Xian was an act of homage, not plagiarism). If the piano was to be played, a Chinese concerto was necessary. The Cultural Revolution was not an easy time for a virtuoso; only by wrapping his technique in this sacred hymn of the revolution could Yin justify maintaining and developing his brilliant piano artistry.

In 1969, "under the personal guidance" of Jiang Qing, Yin and three other members of the Central Philharmonic formed a team to compose a *Yellow River Concerto*. They left Beijing and spent several weeks living in the loess caves of an old revolutionary base on the banks of the Yellow River. Following the modern Chinese tradition of artists going down to the countryside, they interviewed old peasants about the war against Japan, lent their muscle to help boatmen row and tow their vessels upstream, and listened to northern Shaanxi folk tunes played on a bamboo flute. And of course they studied the writings of Marx, Lenin, and Mao Zedong.[73]

The cultural revolutionaries honored Xian's memory when they reworked the *Yellow River Cantata* into a piano concerto, thereby putting Xian's music into a more cosmopolitan form than even he had imagined when he composed it in Yan'an by experimenting with the *erhu* and jars full of spoons. The concerto was full of pianistic bombast, resounding with the echoes of late-nineteenth-century romanticism. Its use of revolution to bridge East and West is clear in the coda, which blends "The East Is Red" and the "Internationale." The result was a new music, programmatic and politicized, to replace Europe's Chopin and Brahms.

The 1970 concerto was flashy, sentimental, and patriotic, but to many Western listeners it sounded gaudy. Harold Schonberg of the *New York Times* dismissed it as "movie music. It is a rehash of Rachmaninoff, Khachaturian, late romanticism, bastardized Chinese music and Warner Brothers climaxes." [74] But Yin did not write the *Yellow River Concerto* for Westerners; it was written for Chinese ears, where its notes reached two different audiences.

First, for piano-playing sophisticates, the *Yellow River Concerto* "gave piano students and performers at least one thing to play, and for a period of two or three years, all anyone could hear coming from every piano in China, was the *Yellow River Concerto*." [75] If the music did resemble Rachmaninoff and Khatchaturian, this only contributed to the popularity of Yin's music in China, where the Russian musical imprint had been powerful. Second, for peasants and workers, the *Yellow River Concerto* was an accessible introduction to European music, in a patriotic and politically unimpeachable form, supported by the full might of the Chinese state. Untold millions of peasants watched a film of Yin playing his concerto; most had never before heard or seen a piano. This was a music education project of historically unprecedented scope.

The concerto's Westernizing impact was reinforced by the parallel drive to introduce European instruments into Chinese opera orchestras. *Taking Tiger Mountain By Strategy,* for instance, had an orchestra of seven violins, two violas, cello, bass, oboe, clarinet, two trumpets, two horns, and Western timpani in addition to the traditional Chinese ensemble. [76] Jiang Qing, like other musical modernizers, regarded the sounds made by Chinese instruments as thin, in contrast to the richness of Western music. She considered only China's percussion instruments superior to Europe's. [77] In fact, the European instruments were often silent for long periods in the model operas, although they dominated the heroic sections. [78] The piano even made inroads into the traditional ballads of Suzhou; performers were required to replace their traditional accompaniment with an ensemble of piano, cello, and accordion, making it impossible for balladeers to continue their normal tours. [79]

A wood block entitled *The New Master of Piano Art* illustrates the ideal of the Cultural Revolution's music policy: a young peasant woman, by her dress clearly a member of a south China minority, stands proudly by a piano beneath the palm trees. Her fellow peasants smile warmly and applaud her, with traditional instruments at the side of picture ready to be joined in harmony with the modern, industrial, and now proletarian notes of the piano. [80]

Taken literally, the picture is absurd. Figuratively, however, it represents the radicals' efforts to demystify music. Maoists such as Minister of Culture Yu Huiyong praised amateur rather than professional musicians, and published books and articles to instruct the amateurs how to compose music.[81] Radical propaganda belittled the idea that music depended upon genius or special artistic inspiration. A typical account described a barber with only a grade school education who joined a spare-time song and dance ensemble in the People's Liberation Army. He panicked when he was assigned the task of writing a song. But his comrades helped by asking, "Were you just as helpless when you started to learn haircutting?"

> Although hair dressing and creative writing are two different things, both follow the same theory that from practice comes true knowledge and skills. Accordingly, he studied seriously and comprehended the aspects of the particular subject he had in mind. He also humbly sought advice from other comrades, made repeated revisions of his draft, and eventually succeeded in producing works acceptable to the masses.[82]

Many Chinese eventually tired of the *Yellow River Concerto*, but at the time it was a welcome departure from the ubiquitous model operas. The Central Philharmonic played about eight concerts each month, but with only one program: the *Yellow River Concerto*, the *Shajiabang Symphony*, and *The Red Lantern with Piano Accompaniment*.[83] That is a lot of *Yellow River*, even for its biggest fans. The music shortage was acute, as radical cultural officials were reluctant to approve new music (or any art) unless they were certain that it would pass the most stringent ideological test. Yin composed new piano music in 1972 in preparation for a forthcoming tour of Japan; he based his music on the ancient Chinese pieces *Meihua San Nong* [Three Variations on the Plum Blossom] and *Shimian Maifu* [Ambushed from All Sides], but neither was approved for performance by Yao Wenyuan.[84] Instead of new music, there was a revival of old songs by approved composers, especially Xian Xinghai.[85]

Yin deserves credit also for helping China avoid the harsh musical punishment of accordion music. The ultra-left in music had long sought to propagate the accordion as a modern, inexpensive, and portable instrument, but had continually suffered the snobbery of piano enthusiasts.[86] When Yin introduced the piano version of *The Red Lantern*, Shenyang's radical composer Jie Fu seized the occasion to ask: Now that the piano has been brought into the Chinese opera, why not the accordion, as well?[87] In its sometimes perverse way, the *Yellow River Concerto* helped protect the musical tastes of the urban intellectuals against a far worse fate, as accordion fever spread during the high tide of Maoism. Ye Wa, a Beijing student, took an accordion with her when she went to northern Shaanxi in 1970. The instrument was not new, but had been obtained by Ye Wa's artist sister in a trade for some paint. Peasants in this remote region were so unfamiliar with Western music that they approached her for permission to touch the strange instrument, which Ye and her friends used for entertainment, playing *The East Is Red,* Soviet marches, and Tchaikovsky's *Swan Lake.* When Ye obtained a factory job near Xian in 1972, her accordion was leaking air; patched with abundant strips of adhesive tape, the instrument served the factory propaganda team. Despite its battered condition, Ye could still sell it to a friend in 1978 for ten *yuan,* a quarter of her monthly wages.[88]

Jiang Qing's interest in music reminds us that musicians had been better off when no central leader cared about them, Jiang Qing was intelligent and lucid, but also shrill, vindictive, and personally petty. Her tastes were naive, embracing not only her revolutionary model operas but also *The Sound of Music.*[89] It is inaccurate to attribute the artistic limitations of the Cultural Revolution to her personal quirks, but her idiosyncracies did have a heavy impact. One European casualty of the Cultural Revolution in music was the tuba. Li De-lun told Toronto Symphony Conductor Andrew Davis in 1978 that Jiang Qing once expressed her dislike for trombones: " 'I don't like them,' she said. 'They are not to play anymore.' " Li thought quickly and convinced her that it had been the tuba, rather than the trombone, which had annoyed her. "He thought, rightly so, that it would be better to lose the tuba than the trombones. . . . And that is why he conducted with no tubas for at least 10 years. Madame Mao never noticed the difference."[90]

The renewed official approval of European instruments took an international dimension, for the People's Republic used musical diplomacy as it moved out of international isolation after 1971. Yin Chengzong, as China's premier pianist, enjoyed rare opportunities to travel abroad. China had last used his talents for diplomatic ends in the early 1960s. Between 1971 and 1975, Yin performed in Japan, North Korea, Albania, Yugoslavia, Romania, and Venezuela. The Lin Biao incident curtailed plans for him to play in Italy, France, and England.[91]

He also played with such outstanding visiting orchestras as the London Philharmonic, the Vienna Philharmonic (under Claudio Abbado), and the Philadelphia Orchestra (under Eugene Ormandy), each of which performed the obligatory *Yellow River Concerto* to honor their Chinese hosts. Philadelphia Orchestra members privately called it the "Yellow Fever Concerto," suggesting some limits to international understanding through music, as did the bizarre Chinese decision to have Yin play "Home on the Range."[92]

Music as a Refuge from the Cultural Revolution

While Maoist music was never distant from Maoist politics, it offered a kind of shelter of calm amidst ceaseless partisan conflict. For Chen Gang, composer of the *Liang Shanbo and Zhu Yingtai Violin Concerto,* music offered solace. "When I passed the difficult days of the Cultural Revolution, I very much loved to listen to Mahler's Fourth Symphony. The Symphony's slow movement was a kind of consolation; a great many human things are ultimately similar."[93] For others, such as Yin, the twists of the Cultural Revolution eventually permitted full-time music-making. Yin was a star in China's musical world, but when we look at more ordinary musicians, we see that the Cultural Revolution enabled thousands to use their musical talents to find better, more interesting employment than their less musical peers.

After 1970 the legitimacy of European instruments had been reaffirmed, even if the European classical repertory was still off limits. Musical proficiency offered an escape from grueling peasant labor for thousands of urban youth. Two policies converged to make this possible. First, urban youth were sent by the millions to live in the countryside. Just as Yin Chengzong had spent several months in 1964– 1965 living among the peasants, so were millions of youth recruited or assigned to go to the countryside, to steel themselves by learning hard labor and learning from the peasantry. Radicals endorsed this policy for its ideological value, and more conservative officials found it a useful mechanism for removing disruptive Red Guards from China's cities after 1967.[94]

Second, Maoist leaders placed a high value on political work in China's ideological superstructure. Mao maintained that a revolution in culture—including ideology, education, and the arts—was essential to prevent the erosion of China's earlier revolutions in politics and economics. This emphasis upon ideological reform took many forms. The memorization of Mao's writings is one of the most notorious. Another was the reorganization of China's artists into propagandists for Maoism. Such policies required musicians to help China sing and dance down the voluntarist road to revolution.

Thousands of young Chinese who had studied Western instruments used their bourgeois skills to join existing song-and-dance troupes, while the establishment of new ensembles created a heavy demand for capable singers and instrumentalists. One of the first indications of the new status of European instruments was the sudden demand for violins. From being accursed symbols of imperialism in 1966, the fiddle had become a ticket out of the rice paddies by 1972, when it became impossible to buy a violin on the open market.

Jiang Qing favored a model village outside of Tianjin, Xiaojinzhuang, where peasants specialized in music and poetry. Cultural activities raised the spirits of the peasants, which helped them increase production and resist the blandishments of revisionism. In fact, Jiang Qing arranged for People's Liberation Army soldiers to come to Xiaojinzhuang during the agricultural busy season to work in the place of preoccupied singing peasants.[95]

With this kind of encouragement, many local units established musical ensembles in the 1970s, and many young Chinese used every connection they had to become performers so that they would not have to work as peasants. One official of the Ministry of Light Industry made a public self-criticism that he had aided his elder son, who had learned to repair violins and pianos and to make cellos, obtain a position with an opera troupe in the People's Liberation Army. But many more pulled strings for their musical children and got away with it.[96]

Without minimizing the humiliation and physical torment suffered by many musicians, it is fair to point out that some escaped any attack, while others were assaulted for their political allegiances rather than for their artistic activities. Central Conservatory violin professor Zheng Xianghe was not attacked, even though he had been Ma Sitson's student before Liberation. Zheng apparently stayed clear of politics; moreover, he obtained a long-term hospital certificate from a physician and entered the hospital four times for bad health.[97] Composer Zheng Lucheng had a hard time, but because of his loyalty to purged Minister of Defense Peng Dehuai, not because of his artistic activities.[98] Li Delun, conductor of the Central Philharmonic, remained unscathed, and that orchestra's new young conductor, Chen Zuohuang, began learning his craft during the Cultural Revolution while leading a labor union song-and-dance ensemble.[99]

A Red Guard and His Violin

Xiao Tiqin is a violinist, born in Guangzhou shortly after Liberation.[100] His father was a church musician with connections to the music world. Xiao began violin lessons at eight. His story conveys something of the different flavor of music of the Cultural Revolution among musicians who were neither purged nor so celebrated as Yin Chengzong.

Xiao's boyhood teacher was a militant cosmopolitan named He Andong, who had denounced China's traditional music during the Hundred Flowers movement. His words earned him a rightist label, and he lost his post as chairman of the South China Region Music Institute. Unlike many rightists, He Andong did not remain silent. Told to sweep the streets to reform his thoughts, he appeared in an outlandish costume: combining pants in the style of the Tang dynasty with a Western jacket to demonstrate his opposition to the blending of Chinese and Western music, he carried a broken *erhu*. After a year of such passive resistance, he was told to stop sweeping.

He Andong had been wealthy before Liberation, and had a big house with a piano. Purged from his musical post, he worked making packaging until after the Cultural Revolution. He gave lessons to several private students, which extended beyond the boundary of approved music activities. Students came in groups of ten or so, some paying as much as fifteen *renminbi* per month, others paying nothing. He Andong would play a few bars of music on his piano, asking the student to repeat them on the violin. For texts, He used music of Ysaë, Paganini, Mozart, and Beethoven, all of which was coming under fire as the Cultural Revolution drew near. In his teaching he stressed the purity of the Western classics, which he contrasted to the limited expressiveness of China's own music.

These lessons, coupled with some useful connections, enabled Xiao to pass the examination to enter the Guangzhou Conservatory's middle school. But the Cultural Revolution began before he could graduate, changing his musical experiences drastically. Xiao became a Red Guard, playing a shrill folk flute called a *tizi* in a propaganda team. He forsook his violin because other radicals regarded it as a "black" instrument, while the *tizi* not only made a loud noise, but was considered "red."

Like many Guangzhou Red Guards, at the end of 1968 Xiao was sent to Hainan, a large, semitropical, frontier-like island which for centuries has been a place of political banishment. With his Red Guard companions, Xiao worked alongside peasants in unfamiliar and grueling agricultural labor, supposedly steeling his ideology in the process. After a year and a half, local leaders noted Xiao's musical background and arranged for him to play the violin in a propaganda team. Xiao's bourgeois talent and careful training of his reactionary teacher finally enabled him to escape manual labor, albeit in order to propagate revolution.

Xiao spent over four years traveling with the Hainan Autonomous Prefecture's Cultural Work Team. The hundred members included an orchestra of thirty and a "creation team" of eight, as well as singers, dancers, and technical personnel for electrical equipment. Most were children of intellectuals and capitalists; few were peasants. Some peasants had been recruited for training, but only one singer and one dancer had enough talent to stay with the company, whose musicians generally held peasants in contempt. Political pressure to recruit more peasants merely resulted in educated youth being passed off as peasants for the troupe.

Nor were there any ethnic minorities in the ensemble, despite the fact that it served a minority prefecture. Indeed, except when the troupe performed in county capitals, there were mostly Miao Chinese in the audiences instead of Han. In a strange political-musical charade, the one hundred former Red Guards from Guangzhou would dress up in Miao costumes and present Sinicized versions of Miao songs and dances to an audience whose ancestors had originally created them. The Miao appreciated the attention, which showed greater respect for their customs than most Han work teams paid them. But the music of the Miao was not only Sinified but Westernized, as these modernizing Chinese from Guangzhou added harmony and Western instrumentation. Hainan would have been a good spot for the woodcut, *New Master of Piano Art*. The only thing that kept Xiao's troupe from adding a keyboard to the minority music was the difficulty of transporting this great piece of middle-class furniture across Hainan's remote mountains.[101]

Xiao reported that the propaganda for the Miao was rudimentary. The Miao in one region had destroyed a newly installed electrical system, claiming that it contained devils. Xiao's ensemble performed there, singing about the advantages of electrification, at least a more straightforward task than using art to clarify the Maoist critique of revisionism for an audience of Han peasants.

Xiao was fascinated by the exotic Miao. Puritanical Han Chinese view the southern minorities as sensuous children of nature. Xiao's eyes widened as he reported that Miao men shared their wives with their guests, that Miao women stood up to urinate, and that Miao youth serenaded each other from opposite mountains each March, meeting later to make love in the valleys below.

Xiao's life was much softer than that experienced by most former Red Guards. His only agricultural labor was a bit of comradely help extended to peasants during the agricultural busy season. The musicians ate better food than was available to most Chinese, with extra meat to put strength into their performances. They also had the chance to travel. The ensemble not only served all of Hainan, but also gave performances in mainland Guangdong, and also made trips to Hunan and Guangxi (where they dressed like Miao, of course). Other educated youth sent down to Hainan were not allowed to visit the mainland for two years. It is easy to see why interest in learning to play Western instruments picked up so briskly later in the Cultural Revolution.

Xiao Tiqin quit the propaganda troupe in 1973 and returned illegally to Guangzhou. There he capitalized on the new interest in European music by giving private lessons on the violin. That year it was impossible to purchase a violin in Guangzhou. The piano, while restored to respectability, was less popular because of its greater expense and because the violin was of greater utility in gaining entry to propaganda troupes. But not all students had such specific motives. By this time mastery of European instruments also increased one's social standing.

Xiao taught two types of students: children of intellectuals, and children of high officials. Following the model of his own teacher, He Andong, Xiao taught students in groups. Each week he met two classes for two hours each, assuring him an income equal to an industrial worker's. His students gave him ration coupons. He found his students through introductions; one condition of instruction was a promise by the students that they would not disclose that they paid Xiao. Xiao included music from the model operas in his teaching materials to protect himself against possible criticism, although he encountered no problems. The public security bureau knew what he was doing, but did not bother him, apparently reasoning that he was causing no harm. Somewhat riskier were underground concerts, in which as many as one hundred people would meet secretly to listen to music performed in someone's home.[102] Three or four times per month Xiao would meet to listen or perform in this unusual concert setting. The audience consisted of educated youth and young teachers, but also included some officials and Party members, who would conceal their identities. A few people in Guangzhou were apprehended; some spent two or three months in jail, but most only had to endure a bit of inconvenience.

Xiao Tiqin, like many artists during the Cultural Revolution, cannot be classified easily. He admired He Luting as China's best composer, and was indignant at the *Liang Shanbo and Zhu Yingtai Violin Concerto*. While resentful of the Cultural Revolution's disruption of his life, he approved of Jiang Qing's mission to destroy old Chinese music completely and begin anew with a mix of Western and Chinese instruments. Similarly, he thought it was good for the Cultural Revolution to reverse the ordinary urban–rural relationship in the arts by sending talent to the countryside instead of draining it into the cities.

Xiao's experience was not unusual; after the initial attacks on Western music for its bourgeois associations, the Cultural Revolution created a demand for musical skills which enabled many to endure the movement with greater comfort than would otherwise have been possible. This is only one of many ironies of cultural politics in China, but it is one which affected common musicians as well as celebrated artists such as Yin Chengzong.

Purge and Rehabilitation

When Mao Zedong died on September 9, 1976, Yin's career collapsed. Jiang Qing and three other of Mao's closest followers were arrested. In a major redirection of China's cultural policy, those who had been victimized by the radicals returned to positions of influence, and artists who had flourished during the Cultural Revolution took their place in oblivion.

Yin Chengzong was banned from playing the piano, separated from his new bride, and placed under "isolated investigation." He was not formally imprisoned, unlike several members of Jiang Qing's entourage, such as Yu Huiyong. Yin cooperated with his interrogators, and after several months he was allowed visits from his wife, pianist Tao Zongshun. Yin was never publicly criticized by name, but he was not permitted to play the piano for the four years his case remained under investigation.[103] Some intellectuals privately criticized Yin as an political opportunist, while others faulted him for sincerity in his radical politics. Many simply resented his high status and opportunities to perform when many other professional artists were silenced. Those who shared Yin's views were in no position to defend him directly.

Yin's 1980 rehabilitation was preceded by rumors and press accounts designed to prepare public opinion for possible controversy. Several Hong Kong writers valiantly attempted to distance Yin from the Cultural Revolution. The most ludicrous effort argued that Yin's lack of enthusiasm for the Cultural Revolution could be seen in the film of the *Yellow River Concerto,* where Yin played with closed eyes, and by his not scoring a piano part when the finale quotes the part of the "East Is Red" that calls Mao the "people's savior." Yin's true political sentiments were alleged to be discerned in the score for the piano version of the *Red Lantern;* there the conflict between Left and Right is represented by the two hands of the pianist; in one climactic moment, Yin uses five fingers of his conservative hand, but only three of his radical digits.[104] Other reporters argued more simply that Yin had been very young when the Cultural Revolution began, and was easily deceived by Jiang Qing, or that Yin's service in fighting to protect the piano was his great and saving achievement.[105]

Restoring performance privileges to Yin provoked debate. Some members of the Central Philharmonic did not want to readmit Yin; their objections had the support of some in China's cultural establishment, and were overcome only after considerable discussion. As he resumed his career, Yin was an advisor to two of China's piano manufacturers, the Beijing Xinghai and Guangzhou Pearl River piano factories. Eventually Yin decided to try performing in the United States, where his massive talent would receive no interference from past political turbulence.

Yin's wife, Tao Zongshun, preceded him to the United States in 1980, when she became a student at the Manhattan School of Music. Yin's emigration was eased by his elder half-brother (now deceased) who lived in California. Eugene Ormandy introduced Yin to Harold Shaw, who became his first American manager and also helped bring him to America.

Yin is full of ambition to restore his career, but it takes time for a Chinese pianist to build a reputation in the United States. When Yin was at the height of his fame, China and the United States shared no cultural relations, so he never won an American audience. Most Americans also retain residual racism by which Asian performers are not easily imagined to be the best players of European music. Moreover, Yin's revolutionary pianism is a curious specialty to bring to the United States; most Americans simply do not know what to make of his unorthodox background.

But Yin has been playing frequently, impressing both audiences and music critics, and steadily recreating his career as a virtuoso. New York City is his base, where he lives with his wife and ten-year-old daughter, who also studies the piano—but her father says he will never compel her to become a professional musician.

Yin's technique may be at his peak. He continues to astound audiences with showpieces such as Liszt's *Fantasy on Don Giovanni,* yet his playing has also become more introspective as he learns new repertory more popular in the United States than China, such as Brahms' F-minor Sonata or Schumann's *Fantasiestücke.* Nowadays he plays in settings very different from those of his triumphs during the Cultural Revolution. San Francisco's "Today's Artists" series programs a private weekend of music each summer in the Oregon coast town of Yachats; a chartered plane flies wealthy California music patrons to Oregon, where they enjoy some of their favorite artists. Yin, who has played to great success in San Francisco, was one of the recent invited performers. His wealthy American patrons made social demands on their virtuoso, adding a new set of extramusical constrictions to those he learned while making worker-peasant-soldier music in China.

Yin's permanent residence in the United States has some of the flavor of an informal exile, but he has maintained his Chinese ties. His hometown of Xiamen has resumed its open stance to foreign ways, symbolized by the construction of a new pier on Gulangyu Island, built in the shape of a grand piano. The Yin family remains well placed in Xiamen, where his brother-in-law is now vice-mayor. Yin was invited to return to Gulangyu for a 1987 music festival to be sponsored by Xiamen's American Camel cigarette factory. He was unable to take part, although he was pleased to receive the invitation. In September 1987, Yin's photograph was displayed in the lobby of the Beijing Concert Hall, demonstrating clearly that his name is no longer clouded in China.

Yin is now cautious in his political views, suggesting that he has few political beliefs. When he does discuss his experiences during the Cultural Revolution, he explains that he was "driven to climb Liang Mountain," using the same phrase by which Fou Ts'ong described his defection: Liang Mountain was the stronghold of the heroic bandits of the classic Chinese novel, *Shuihu Zhuan* [Outlaws of the Marsh], who were compelled to their fates by the actions of their government.[106] Yet a Chinese virtuoso cannot escape the world of politics. Yin is still breaking through political barriers in his musical life. In 1986 he became the first pianist from the People's Republic of China to perform in South Korea, a nation with which Beijing is now cultivating better relations. His concert with the Seoul Philharmonic was telecast throughout Korea. Plans to perform a series of recitals in Taiwan in 1988 fell through at the last minute; if they are resumed later, they will mark the first musical contact between Taibei and Beijing. Yin also admits to a desire to perform again some day in the Soviet Union, where he still has friends and admirers. He could not return to Leningrad without political approval from both China and the Soviet Union, but such a journey would fit Yin's continuing activism in the mediation between China and the music of the West.

6

The Red Aristocrat: Liu Shikun

Two of the three great virtuoso pianists of the People's Republic of China won second prizes in the Tchaikovsky Competition. Liu Shikun's distinction was in 1958, the first year of the contest; Yin Chengzong's prize was four years later, in the second Tchaikovsky Competition. Although Yin and Liu have enjoyed good personal relations, Chinese politics has pulled them in opposite directions. While Yin enjoyed enormous success during the Cultural Revolution, Liu spent seven years of that decade in jail. And when Yin was purged in 1976, Liu resumed his career to enormous acclaim. Liu was married to the daughter of Ye Jianying, one of the Revolution's senior military commanders; the ups and downs of his career as a musician can only be understood as a part of the internal conflicts within China's new political elite.

A Marriage of Artistic and Political Elites

Liu was born in 1939, and received early pressure from his father, a music-loving capitalist from Tianjin. The elder Liu was a graduate of the Shanghai Conservatory, who sometimes beat his son in regard to his music. Not long after Liberation, Liu entered a special elementary school for musically talented children, attached to the newly established Central Conservatory. The Soviet experts who taught him arranged for a brief period of study in Moscow. The seventeen-year-old

161

Liu, in Budapest in 1956 before the anti-Soviet uprising, won third
prize in the International Liszt Competition, bringing home a ghoulish
token: a lock of Liszt's hair awarded by the Hungarian government.[1]
Liu was still in Europe during China's Hundred Flowers movement,
performing in Prague's famous Spring Music Festival in 1957. A few
months later he returned to China, where he caused a sensation when
he played Chopin and Liszt in a Beijing concert given by his high
school.[2] Liu's Soviet teachers urged him to enter the Tchaikovsky
Competition in 1958; Fou Ts'ong's hopes of competing had been ended
by his father's political disgrace, and Yin Chengzong was then only
fifteen. The American, Van Cliburn, and the Briton, John Ogden, shared
first prize. When the tall, gaunt young Chinese won second prize, his
homeland's community of Western-style musicians reacted with the
same enthusiasm that greeted Fou Ts'ong's Chopin Competition prize
in Warsaw three years earlier.

Liu returned to China to the mass mobilization of the Great Leap
Forward, which he joined enthusiastically. He went to work in the
countryside, but the Party paid special attention to the protection of
his hands, which had been a concern voiced by Fou Ts'ong upon his
defection.[3] During the Leap, the twenty-year-old Liu composed a *Youth
Piano Concerto*. This piece anticipated efforts by his seniors to combine Chinese and Western music. The concerto's melodies were based
upon northern Chinese folk tunes; an orchestra of Chinese instruments
accompanied Liu's piano.[4] Continuing to grapple with the poor fit between European music and Chinese culture, Liu joined with twenty or
so other Beijing pianists to find suitable Chinese music, figure out how
to assess nineteenth-century European composers, and raise the art of
accompanying in China.[5]

In 1962 Liu married Ye Xiangzhen, a student at Beijing's Central
Opera Academy, a daughter of Ye Jianying, one of China's senior
political and military leaders.[6] When China adapted the Soviet system
of military rank to its former guerrilla troops in 1955, Ye Jianying was
one of ten soldiers to receive the highest rank of marshal. His service
to the revolution was considerable. This son of a wealthy Hakka merchant from Guangdong had secretly joined the Communist Party while
at the Whampoa Military Academy. Later he participated in the ill-
fated Guangzhou Commune Uprising in 1927. After military training
in the Soviet Union and Germany, he sided with Mao in the political
debates along the Long March, and was chief-of-staff of the Eighth

Route Army during the war against Japan. After Liberation, he was the first Communist mayor of Beijing, and later served as mayor of Guangzhou and governor of his native province of Guangdong. Ye had worked closely with Mao, Zhou Enlai, and Lin Biao, three of the dominant political figures of the 1960s, so his political star was rising at the time of the marriage.[7]

Ye Jianying had many cultural pretensions of his own, and was more pleased than many generals might have been to have a celebrated musician as a son-in-law. When Ye was head of the Red Army School in the Jiangxi Soviet, he was a strong participant in the revolutionary drama movement, showing an early commitment to the use of art for raising political consciousness.[8] Ye was proud of his calligraphy; after Liberation he often presented inscriptions in his own hand to honor exemplary military units, factories, and farms. And he was a poet in his spare time. As his power grew, newspapers sometimes flattered him by printing such verses as his 1956 "Yumen 1" (Yumen is an oil field in Gansu Province):

> Factory buildings dot the Gobi Desert,
> Where very modern people wear very modern clothes.
> Already they have applied various isotopes to peaceful construction
> projects.[9]

Ye's poetry may not be very good, but he was an arts enthusiast. He was a patron of education in the Hakka capital of Meizhou, in Guangdong. Ye had traveled to Southeast Asia as a young man and later studied in Europe, giving him more cosmopolitan experience than most other senior leaders of the Communist Party. Liu was an attractive match for the daughter of this culture-craving marshal. Liu had joined the Communist Party in 1959, earning political acceptability, and his efforts to compose Chinese music for the piano showed a sensitivity to current nuances of Party arts policy.

The marriage of Liu to Ye Xiangzhen has a political significance beyond the personal bond between a pianist and a general's daughter. Relations between the old bourgeoisie and the emerging Communist Party elite were complex. The tensions between them are well known, and often erupted into acts of political suppression, in which bourgeois intellectuals such as Fu Lei were the inevitable losers. But there was another side of cooperation and kinship between the two groups. Liu Shaoqi's marriage to a daughter of the capitalist Wang family of Tianjin is one example; the marriage of Liu Shikun into Ye Jianying's family is another. In China's great cities bourgeois and bureaucratic families shared a similar style of life and sent their children to the same elite schools, bringing the two groups into constant interaction. Communist attitudes toward the urban middle class are inevitably intricate, because many revolutionary leaders have themselves come from urban middle-class or capitalist homes. In some periods, the Party has consciously cultivated the business class and its associated intelligentsia. Deng Xiaoping's reform program has occurred within such a period, but the origins of Communist cooperation with capitalists and intellectuals extend much earlier in the history of the People's Republic. Past collusion of the two elites is often forgotten, overwhelmed by the virulence of the Party's drive against capitalist remnants during the Cultural Revolution.

Despite his youth, Liu was already an internationally recognized pianist; he was a soloist for the Central Philharmonic and did not require the patronage of a powerful general to boost his career. Still, the marriage did not hurt his musical career, at least at first. In the fall of 1962 Liu performed in Hong Kong, with other outstanding Chinese musicians, including Gu Shengying. *People's Music* proudly quoted two English listeners who allegedly were overheard to say: "It certainly is not simple for these young Mainland musicians to play European music so successfully," and "Such culture! They've shot down the U-2 airplane!" [10]

Liu was not only good at impressing foreigners with Chinese mastery of European culture, he also responded actively to the rising Maoist demand for more national music. In 1963, in Beijing, Liu played the first piano recital in which all of the music was by Chinese composers. He included his own fantasy on a theme from *The White-Haired Girl,* his *Youth Concerto,* and music by He Luting and Ding Shande. [11] In recognition of his political activism, Liu was elected to the Third National People's Congress in 1964. This Communist virtuoso was also invited to perform to a select audience of top Party leaders in the auditorium at Zhongnanhai. [12]

At the same time, Ye Jianying's influence in political and cultural affairs was also growing. On the eve of the Cultural Revolution, when the novelist Mao Dun was replaced as minister of culture, Ye Jianying was deeply involved in selecting as his replacement a general named Xiao Wangdong, who brought many army associates with him to his new post. All of these appointments were approved by Ye, representing the Party's Military Affairs Commission.[13]

The First Imprisonment of Liu Shikun: Factional Politics

Pianist and Marshal as Cultural Revolution Targets

The Cultural Revolution did not go well for Liu Shikun. Like Yin Chengzong, Liu was criticized for his chosen profession. But while Yin was eventually able to overcome attacks upon his capitalist family, Liu was unable to escape being a pawn in radical enmity toward his powerful father-in-law.

In the summer and fall of 1966, Liu was under severe attack. He was declared a "second-rank ghost and monster" at one mass rally, and at another he had to wear a paper hat labeled "Counterrevolutionary Musician Liu Shikun." While the Central Conservatory's Red Guards kicked him and spat on him, Liu was made to kneel and confess to shaking hands with Khrushchev and surrendering to Soviet revisionism. Speakers accused him of seeking fame and capitalist comfort. While under "investigation" at the conservatory, Liu was made to clean floors and toilets with President Ma Sitson. Conservatory Red Guards taunted Liu with a nasty serenade:

> Liu Shikun you bastard,
> Now you can surrender.
> If you do not tell the truth,
> You may quickly die. . . .[14]

Liu was sometimes subjected to brutal treatment, but it is not true that Red Guards broke his arms or fingers in order to destroy his ability to play the piano, as was widely reported in the West.

Ye Jianying's politics intensified Liu's difficulties. Ye Jianying began the Cultural Revolution as a supporter of Mao, and was never toppled from his posts. However Ye spent much of the movement locked in fierce battle with his former friend, Lin Biao, leader of the dominant and most radical faction within the People's Liberation Army, and with civilian radicals, such as Jiang Qing. Ye participated in the "February Adverse Current" of 1967, when a group of senior officials attempted to slow the Cultural Revolution and protect their bureau-cratic subordinates.[15] Ye negotiated some limits to cultural revolution-ary activities in the army, but paid a heavy price. Radical activists suspected that he was planning armed intervention against them and raided his home, tearing up the floorboards in a fruitless search for hidden weapons and radio equipment. By April wall posters bore such messages as "Chop Off Ye Jianying's Tentacle Extending to the Field of Literature and Art!" His daughter's alma mater, the Central Opera Academy, set up a "Liaison Center to Drag Out Ye Jianying." Ye's five children, their relatives and servants eventually were arrested and detained for periods ranging from one to six years.[16]

Red Guards from the Central Conservatory directed the attack on Liu Shikun. Liu's capitalist family background seems to have been less important in these attacks than his family relationship with Ye, who was regarded by many radicals as a leading revisionist.

> Liu Shikun is a person who has intimate relations with the counter-revolutionary revisionist black line in literature and art. He has still not made any criticism of this black line in literature and art. Counter-revolutionary revisionist elements Zhou Yang, Xia Yan, and Zhao Feng made him a so-called red and expert model soldier. This kind of "model soldier" must be overthrown.

The Red Guards deprived Liu of his political rights and organized a small group to investigate his case.[17]

Early in the Cultural Revolution, children of prominent officials or-ganized their own exclusive Red Guards units. Ye Jianying's son, Ye Xuanning, was a member of the most notorious of these, the "United Action Committee."[18] Its members strutted about wearing insignia corresponding to the bureaucratic ranks of their parents. United Action members were among the most vicious persecutors of the former bour-geoisie, as they hoped to deflect the tide of the Cultural Revolution from their parents and their privileges.[19] The Central Conservatory initially had a similar "royalist" Red Guard group, which included the son of the famous scholar-official, Guo Moruo.[20] But United Ac-tion and other blatantly elitist Red Guard groups were disbanded as the Cultural Revolution increasingly changed its target from the old bourgeoisie to revisionist officials within the Party.

As various groups contended for leadership over cultural institu-tions, a radical named Qi Benyu established close ties with the Central

Conservatory and with Liu's inquisitors, the Mao Zedong Thought Combat Team Revolutionary Committee General Service Station.[21] Along with Yao Wenyuan and Zhang Chunqiao, Qi Benyu was a member of the new Central Cultural Revolution Literary and Art Small Group, with which Jiang Qing supplanted the paralyzed Ministry of Culture in May 1967. Jiang Qing was its head; a cellist of the Central Philharmonic, Lu Gongda, was the member responsible for music.[22]

Over a year after his inquisition had begun, in November 1967, representatives of the Central Conservatory were still discussing Liu's case with Jiang Qing and Chen Boda.[23] One story maintains that Liu and Ye Xiangzhen left Beijing for Guangzhou early in the Cultural Revolution, only to be accused by Jiang Qing of preparing to flee to Hong Kong. In this version, Ye was released, but Liu received a twelve-year sentence.[24] Liu was ultimately placed in Beijing's Taicheng prison (later home to Jiang Qing). The major purpose of his imprisonment seems to have been to use him as a hostage in order to put political pressure on Ye Jianying.[25] Liu's jailers tried to persuade him to write materials denouncing Ye, who remained free and active in China's political leadership.[26]

Artists supporting the Cultural Revolution were themselves internally divided. In 1968 Qi Benyu was overthrown as a member of a shadowy "May 16th Corps," alleged to be conspiring against Mao.[27] This conspiracy may not in fact have existed, but it was used to break the radical Left of the Cultural Revolution. The cellist Lu Gongda killed himself after being accused of being Qi's confederate. But this shakeup did not help Liu Shikun. Most of those branded as May 16th leaders were civilians; thus Lin Biao's influence was enhanced by their fall.

Lin Biao did not have serious musical interests. He maintained that "singing a good song is, in fact, also attending an important political class."[28] Lin's idea of a "good song" was a march, many of which were provided by his chief supporter in the music world, the old composer and head of the Shenyang Conservatory, Jie Fu. Jie Fu's music was heavily influenced by Soviet military tunes, and Chinese radios featured a steady diet of thumping marches until Lin Biao died in 1971, when his plane crashed in Outer Mongolia as he allegedly was fleeing a failed coup attempt.

Jie Fu had set Lin Biao's words to music, and was rumored to be the choice for minister of culture if Lin became chairman of the Com-

munist Party. According to one story, Jie Fu had even composed a
new national anthem for the plotters. Jie Fu was arrested after Lin's
death, and the gentler sounds of the Chinese flute, *erhu,* and other
native instruments began to be interspersed amidst more martial music.[29] In order to shore up political unity in the wake of a major split
within the Party, Mao backed a musical campaign to study two songs
from the revolution's past days of glory and struggle: the "Internationale" and an old Red Army song from the Jiangxi Soviet, "The Three
Main Rules of Discipline and the Eight Points of Attention."[30]

Rehabilitation

Ye Jianying replaced Lin Biao as defense minister (although this formal title was not restored until 1975). Lin's death also increased the
power of a group of Mao's civilian advisors: Jiang Qing, Zhang Chunqiao, Yao Wenyuan, and Wang Hongwen, later identified as the Gang
of Four. Their chief advisor on the arts was Yu Huiyong, formerly of
the Shanghai Conservatory. Ye Jianying's relations with this group
were bad, which no doubt explains why Liu Shikun's release from jail
was delayed for well over a year. In one petty feud in 1972, a group
of leftist artists visited a Shandong coast guard station for a period of
rest and writing. Ye Jianying ordered the writers expelled, arguing that
they had no authority to barge into a military installation. Zhang
Chunqiao was livid that his followers were treated like spies, and demanded self-criticism from the army. Arguments over this incident
persisted for two years.[31]

When Liu was finally released from Taicheng Prison in 1973, he
was housed in a well-appointed army guest house.[32] Top leaders of
the Party received him, including Mao and Jiang Qing, whom Liu
subsequently blamed for prolonging his detention. Liu claims that Mao
had inquired of him three times, but we do not know the content of
the Chairman's remarks.[33] It seems likely that no one had sufficient
incentive to push for his release until 1973, when Zhou Enlai intervened for reasons of foreign policy. China was beginning to end its
international isolation, and Zhou pressed for an active foreign policy
of cultural exchange to complement China's recent admission into the
United Nations and new relations with Japan and the capitalist West.
Zhou decided that China could then make use of two pianists.

Mao, impressed by Yin Chengzong's success with the *Yellow River*

Concerto, urged Liu to compose a "national piano concerto." A trop-
ical storm had recently struck Guangdong, devastating southern Hainan
Island. Liu took his inspiration from the struggle against this storm
and decided to adapt for the piano "Combatting the Typhoon," a 1964
composition for *zheng* by Wang Changyuan of Shanghai. Zhou Enlai
gave approval for Liu to go to Guangdong soon after the typhoon,
leaving travel arrangements in the hands of Ye Jianying. In Hainan,
Liu was inspired not by the destruction but by the energetic rebuilding
effort underway, which became the theme for his music.[34] But when
Liu completed the concerto in 1975, the Ministry of Culture decided
that it could not be performed in public unless it were rewritten as a
solo piano piece. Yu Huiyong reportedly harbored special hostility
toward Ye Jianying, which he vented on Liu.[35]

Liu's relations with Yin Chengzong were good, despite the possibilities for rivalry between two virtuosos with such different political
allegiances. When Liu returned to the Central Philharmonic after an
absence of seven years, Yin Chengzong, then at the peak of his career,
showed special concern for his well-being. Even China during the Cultural Revolution was big enough for two virtuoso pianists; Yin and
Liu collaborated in writing a 1974 article for *People's Daily* in which
they lent their voices to a national campaign against *Going Up to Peach
Peak Three Times,* a Shanxi opera which allegedly sought to defend
Liu Shaoqi.[36] In 1975 Liu joined Yin as a member of the Fourth National People's Congress, a public proclamation of his restored status.

Music and Cultural Revolution Foreign Policy

With the demise of Lin Biao, Zhou Enlai had a freer hand to reshape
China's foreign policy. China continued its 1960s emphasis on ties
with other developing nations, but also began to intensify its diplomatic and commercial relations with the capitalist world as it actively
sought counterweights to the Soviet Union. Cultural diplomacy was a
big part of the new foreign policy. After anticommunist Nixon visited
anticapitalist Mao, both sides invoked the sacred art of music to explain to their citizens why yesterday's enemies were not so evil: they
all spoke the international language of music. The orchestras of Philadelphia, Vienna, and London came to China and accompanied Yin
Chengzong in the *Yellow River Concerto* to prove that this was true.

Music without Titles

China's new diplomacy began to diverge from its domestic cultural politics, and to erode some of the tightest artistic restrictions. In 1973, the year of Liu Shikun's release, Chinese musicians could practice the works of European composers for the first time since the beginning of the Cultural Revolution, although, unlike visiting foreign musicians, they could not perform them in public. The London Philharmonic played Dvořák's Eighth Symphony, Brahms' Violin Concerto, and music by Haydn, Vaughn Williams, Elgar, and Beethoven; the Philadelphia Orchestra played Beethoven's Fifth Symphony, Brahms' First Symphony, and Dvořák's Ninth Symphony. These performances were the first of any European classical music in Beijing since 1968, when the Central Philharmonic Orchestra played "Vltava" from Smetana's *My Country* to show solidarity with the Czechs after the Soviet invasion.[37] The sounds of these long-forbidden pleasures made Chinese musicians eager for a break from their steady diet of home-grown revolutionary music.

Yu Huiyong of the State Council's "Culture Group" was the final arbiter of concert programs for Chinese performers. Yu was unhappy with the signs of a quiet return to the bourgeois music of Debussy and Beethoven. Foreign musicians, however, were under the authority of the Foreign Ministry, and Yu could not tell the Vienna Philharmonic what music to perform. More vulnerable, however, were a visiting violinist and pianist from Turkey, who played in China late in 1973. In the bureaucratic discussions over the approval of their proposed chamber music program, the radicals began to move against the reemergence of European "music without titles." This phrase referred to absolute music, or "instrumental music having no written title to indicate its content, such as 'Symphony No. 1,' 'Violin and Piano Concerto in G Major.' " Such "music came into being during a particular period of historical development, i.e., at the establishment of capitalist production relations," and "was held to be "inseparably associated with the historical development of the bourgeoisie."[38]

A report on the Turks' program circulated through the bureaucracy which identified the composers and explained the music, cautiously stating that "most of the musical works were composed under the influence of the bourgeois movement of enlightenment and that they

reflected the mental outlook of a newly emerging bourgeoisie in varying degrees.'' The report further noted that most of the works had no
profound social content, showing ''that most of the musical works to
be performed were relatively progressive, historically speaking, but
that they did not fully reflect the nature of society.'' Yao Wenyuan
added a comment to the report: the ''theoretical question of 'no social
content' and absolute music should be studied.''[39] The Turks played
their program in the end, probably unaware of the growing controversy of which they were a part. Had they known, they certainly would
have found it familiar: after a 1971 coup, the Turkish army banned
performances of Russian classics in order to protect the Turkish people
against Tchaikovsky-inspired subversion.[40]

China's radicals had seemed warmly welcoming to the Philadelphia
Orchestra in September 1973; Jiang Qing shook the hand of each player.
She requested of Eugene Ormandy that his musicians perform Beethoven's Sixth Symphony, the ''Pastorale.'' Beijing had no orchestral
parts, so a special plane was dispatched to fetch them from Shanghai.[41] In retrospect it seems that Jiang Qing wanted to compare Beethoven's programmatic symphony to his abstract ones.

Beethoven apparently flunked the program-music test, as the ensu-
ing campaign against the revival of European music eventually embraced both music without titles and program music as well. ''All
bourgeois music, programme and absolute, are weapons to shape opinion to serve the bourgeoisie for seizing and consolidating political
power.'' Untitled music is ''merely a means by which bourgeois composers conceal the class content of their works.'' But even when they
claim inspiration from such things as pines, fountains (the Philadelphia
Orchestra had performed Respighi), and moonlight, it masks ''the decadent, chaotic life and depraved sentiments of the bourgeoisie the
weird cacophony represents.''[42]

For half a year, European music was criticized as a germ that encouraged bourgeois sentiments.[43] Yu Huiyong, writing under the pseudonym of ''Chu Lan,'' found another opportunity to revenge himself
against the snobs of the conservatories.[44] Yu correctly argued that the
great tradition of European music from the late eighteenth and nineteenth centuries is associated with the emergence of the bourgeoisie.
Only slightly more controversial was Yu's view that musical titles alone
do not determine social content. ''Can the 'feelings' expressed in a

musical work have nothing to do with its composer's era, class and experiences of social life, political attitude, ideological tendency, world view, artistic stance, etc.?''[45]

Yu recalled the 1963 campaign against Debussy (instigated by Yao Wenyuan, and resisted by He Luting). Europe's classical music encompasses a theory of human nature which maintains that art can transcend class. To relax standards now would take China back to before the Cultural Revolution, when revisionists said: '' 'Let the people all enjoy' Western capitalist music's 'healthy and forthright compositions,' even to the point of nonsensically saying that classical music can 'inspire us today to struggle even more fiercely for peace, progress and for the glory of all humanity.' '' Yu held Beethoven to be a particularly menacing musical humanist.[46]

Westerners typically regard the campaign against untitled music as one of the zanier manifestations of the Cultural Revolution. Later, Yu Huiyong's critics said that he wanted to subvert cultural exchange and undermine Zhou Enlai.[47] There is some truth to this. Yu certainly was not to trying to stimulate cultural exchange with the West, although he favored and participated in musical exchanges with Third World nations.[48] The logic of the campaign does resemble the 1974 "Black Art Exhibition" which was more clearly directed against Zhou.[49] But the campaign against music without titles may not be so obscure as many others of the late Cultural Revolution. It purpose was, as Yu claimed, to keep up class consciousness in culture. World politics may have required concerts of European classics by foreign performers, but Yu wanted to remind China's urban middle class that these concerts did not signal the end of the Cultural Revolution's arts policies.

Moreover, the revival of European classical music was an implicit threat to Yu's program for model theatrical works. Yu and his coworkers had introduced European musical techniques in unprecedented ways, however much they rejected Western compositions. It was important to keep China's violinists busy playing works such as *The Red Detachment of Women,* rather than having them show their resistance by playing Mozart. The campaign was also motivated by a considerable amount of fear. Yu sincerely resented his former persecutors in the conservatory. He now persecuted them in turn, with a real appreciation of the power of elitist foreign culture to overwhelm his shallow-rooted efforts to fashion a new and revolutionary culture for China.

It is also important to recognize that Chinese instrumental music does in fact always bear titles, as it is much more closely bound to literary texts and conventions than European music. The cultural revolutionaries pushed Ying Chengzong and Liu Shikun to write the *Yellow River Concerto* and *Battling the Typhoon* precisely because such descriptive pieces found a response in Chinese audiences that European sonatas did not. Thus Yu Huiyong's personal pride in striking against European music was joined to national pride in China's own cultural traditions, and the stance which Yu adopted is more easily comprehended by Chinese than by Western readers. Calling attention to the lack of titles reminded the Chinese of the music's foreign nature.

The "Internationale"

The campaign was successful, and the purge of European classics so complete that when a German chamber ensemble performed in Guangzhou in 1975, the audience was given written instructions on when and how much to applaud.[50] Chinese virtuosos put away their Chopin études and Western music was once more driven back, with the curious exception of the "Internationale." This revolutionary hymn was written in 1888 by Pierre Degeyter, setting Eugene Pottier's poem from the Paris Commune of 1881. It has been an important song of the Chinese revolution ever since Qu Qiubai translated it into Chinese in 1923.[51] After the attack on European classical music, however, Chinese cultural officials treated it not just as a stirring revolutionary anthem, but as one of the highest points in the history of world culture. Yu Huiyong advised Chinese listeners to turn to the "Internationale" for good European music. Yu pointed out that it appeared in 1888, contemporary with Debussy. The "Internationale" "is the emblem of the rise of proletarian music," but Debussy, even with titles, "is the emblem of capitalist music already on the road to decline and decadence."[52] And Zhang Chunqiao claimed that "from the Internationale to the revolutionary theatrical works, the interval of more than a century was a blank."[53] The story of the composition of the "Internationale" was widely retold, and for a while, the pairing of Degayter and Pottier achieved a fame among China's hundreds of millions which will never be equalled by Mozart and Da Ponte, or Strauss and Hofmannsthal.[54]

The Conservatories Reopen

The very idea of a virtuoso was at odds with the ideals of the Cultural Revolution. The flashy pianism of Liu Shikun or Yin Chengzong, when labeled revolutionary, could dazzle audiences while it told a politically correct story. But the system which produced such performers was profoundly elitist, and was a target of the Cultural Revolution.

China's conservatories were reformed along the same lines as other institutions of higher learning. Instead of selecting pupils through a system of national entrance examinations and preparatory schools, students were to be drawn from the ranks of ordinary working people. The so-called "worker-peasant-soldier" students entered directly from the shop floor or the rice paddy, recommended by their fellow workers for their commitment to revolution. The intent of this policy was to open up opportunities for people who otherwise might never get to a university. In practice, many of the places marked for peasants went to urban youth who had spent a few years in the countryside. The new curriculum was highly politicized. Beijing's Central Conservatory was reopened as a part of a new "Central May 7th Arts University," following a trend to consolidate arts academies, opera schools, and conservatories into single units. The Shanghai Conservatory reopened with worker-peasant-soldier students in 1973.[55]

One can make a reasonable argument on egalitarian grounds for a rigorous affirmative action program, especially when such a small number of individuals receive higher education's benefits. But such programs in music need to begin at lower levels of instruction, and with a rich national program of music education. Policies to identify youthful musical talent, regardless of social background, would then increase the numbers of musicians from worker and peasant families. In the absence of a broadly based national system of music education, the radical reforms in the conservatories were not successful. By the time students are of university age, it is not too late to study music but it is too late to become a world-class virtuoso.

Many of the new students were held up to private scorn. The granddaughter of Chen Yonggui, leader of the Maoist model village of Dazahi, entered the new May 7 Arts University through the back door. When she could not pass the exam for the opera school, which was her first choice, she was put in the piano department, even though she could not read the five-line staff. After being caught stealing, she withdrew from the school. This story may not be accurate, but it is typical of the things said of the reforms by resentful urban middle-class music-lovers.[56] Whatever the truth of young Chen's case, the system was not designed to nurture virtuoso pianists.

The children of professional musicians had a much harder time entering the reopened conservatories, as they lacked either worker-peasant credentials or the political clout necessary to circumvent them. Many studied at home, often to better effect, as they studied the classics that had been purged from the conservatories. In addition, they had much more practice time, being free from the political meetings and physical labor of the schools. Musical units often competed hard to recruit such people, despite their lack of formal credentials.[57]

The Restoration of Cosmopolitan Musical Culture

Nineteen-seventy-six was an unusually tense year in Chinese politics. Zhou Enlai, who had skillfully mediated among the Party leadership's feuding factions, died in January. Ye Jianying feigned illness and withdrew from active leadership while Deng Xiaoping, who had been recalled to state service in 1973, was purged a second time after the April 5 demonstration in Tiananmen Square. Mao Zedong, enfeebled by Parkinson's disease, died on September 9. In October, Jiang Qing, Zhang Chunqiao, Yao Wenyuan, and Wang Hongwen were arrested in a sudden coup and denounced as a "Gang of Four." The triumvirate of conspirators responsible for this consisted of Ye Jianying, representing the People's Liberation Army, Prime Minister Hua Guofeng (who was also minister of public security), and Wang Dongxing, chief of army unit 8341, the praetorian guard which provided security for national leaders.[58] Hua was made chairman of the Communist Party, while Ye Jianying and Wang Dongxing rose to new heights of power.

Liu Shikun, happy to be rid of Jiang Qing, and full of praise for Hua Guofeng, began composing a new "choral suite" entitled *Unforgettable 1976*. Its four sections bore the following descriptive titles: (1) "The Chinese people mourn their great leader Chairman Mao and beloved Premier Chou Enlai"; (2) "Dark cloud over Peking"; (3) "Chairman Hua leads the Party and the country in smashing the Gang of Four"; and (4) "Chairman Mao's banner flies triumphantly across the land."[59]

The politics of the next five years steadily eroded the Left's power as officials purged during the Cultural Revolution returned to their posts, with Deng Xiaoping as their chief representative. Ye Jianying's political position was midway between Hua Guofeng, who sought to rule through a slightly moderated version of Mao's policies, and Deng Xiaoping, who wanted to renounce the Cultural Revolution completely.[60] A decisive Central Committee Meeting at the end of 1978 solidified Deng's victory, leading eventually to Hua Guofeng's forced resignation as head of the Party in 1981. In 1978 Ye gave up the Ministry of National Defense to become chairman of the Standing Committee of the National People's Congress, making him China's head of state until 1983.

Deng Xiaoping's political base was diverse but included considerable support from the urban middle class, anxious to end years of Maoist discrimination. Deng's program prominently restored to this class its honors and ended its most grievous abuses. In 1979 the rightist labels were removed from the heads of the hundreds of thousands of urban middle-class intellectuals who had been banished from their jobs in 1957. They received new jobs, and the minor political parties to which many had belonged were reactivated in a burst of united-front energy. Many received salaries lost during earlier political campaigns, fueling an unprecedented burst of consumption. Cities enjoyed a boom of new housing construction.

The urban middle class also resumed a separate cultural identity after ten years in which it had to make do with books, paintings, and music intended for an audience of workers and peasants. One of the reasons for the cultural restoration was simple entertainment, as the urban middle class had become bored silly with even the most polished art of the Cultural Revolution. But the restoration of this culture also symbolized the new rights and powers of the urban middle class. The process of cultural restoration was most apparent in literature, where it was quickly apparent that urban intellectuals were better at writing about their own experiences than trying to adopt the alien perspective of a peasant or worker.[61] Musicians were equally happy to perform once more the music of their own class, although they steadfastly denied that this was what they were doing.

In 1979, Ye Jianying spoke on the thirtieth anniversary of the People's Republic, when he proclaimed the Communist Party's renunciation of the Cultural Revolution. Ye described the Cultural Revolution as a calamity for which Mao must be blamed, thereby giving official endorsement to the theory of the two Maos: a good, inspiring, and revolutionary Mao who led China to socialism, and an impetuous, easily deceived Mao who presided over the Great Leap Forward and the Cultural Revolution.[62] The tension between these two images persists in the politics of the People's Republic.

Liu Shikun, as a child of the bourgeoisie and son-in-law of China's head of state, was well placed to play a prominent role in the restoration of a musical culture that had been shaped by the interaction of two elites. Both groups had suffered greatly during the Cultural Revolution; a generation after Liberation there was no danger of a capitalist return to power, and hostility between these two elites had diminished greatly.

The Repudiation of Music Policies of the Cultural Revolution

The initial changes merely abandoned the Gang of Four's institutions and artists for others that were not so very different. Jiang Qing's model village of Xiaojinzhuang, for instance, dropped from sight, replaced as a rural arts model by Shaanxi's Xiyang County, home of Dazhai and celebrated for its mass singing activities as early as the Great Leap Forward.[63] In a similar vein, Jiang Qing and her entourage were unconvincingly accused of crimes against the continuing leftist musical policies. They were said to dislike the "Internationale" and Xian Xinghai.[64]. Such accusations have a crazed desperation about them, as surviving leftists tried to distance themselves from Jiang Qing; this occurred while Hua Guofeng claimed that Jiang Qing and her supporters were agents of Chiang Kaishek. Foreign visitors heard officials earnestly blame all of China's musical deficiencies on the radicals, including China's lack of Western opera, even though this art had hardly flourished before the Cultural Revolution.[65]

More important, musical interests harmed by the Gang began to re-emerge. Enthusiasts for folk songs and national instruments, long ignored or repressed by the radicals of the Cultural Revolution, quickly re-established their unique link to the life of the masses.[66] The former system for music education was restored in 1978, discarding egalitarianism for a two-track system. The musically gifted could compete for entrance to the conservatories through examinations, although fewer resources were available for ordinary students. In the first year of the restored system, seventeen thousand students applied for one hundred places in the Central Conservatory.[67]

Several symbols heralded the newer order in music and politics. People stopped opening meetings by singing "The East Is Red." Nie Er's "March of the Volunteers" was restored as the national anthem, first substituting committee-written words for Tian Han's in 1978, and then returning to Tian's words in 1983.[68] Guangzhou Radio resumed its use of an extract from Beethoven's *Egmont Overture* to announce the weather forecast. The loudspeakers to which all of China was wired so that committee-determined music could be broadcast were disconnected, making it easier for the Chinese to avoid music if they chose.[69]

Although the direction of these changes is clear enough in retrospect, musicians were understandably confused by the rapid changes in policy. Arts officials were themselves divided about how far to go in restoring the order prior to the Cultural Revolution. Mao Zedong's 1956 "Talk to Music Workers," never openly published during his lifetime despite Jiang Qing's urgings, ironically was produced as a document for the reformers, a testimony to its essential ambiguity about the problems facing Western culture in China.[70] Less ambiguous was the campaign against the leftist slogan that "literature and art are a tool of class struggle."[71] Destroying the legitimacy of this viewpoint signaled all artists that their works would not be held to the rigidly political standards of the previous decade.

Personnel Changes

Jiang Qing's closest supporters were purged immediately after her arrest. Minister of Culture Yu Huiyong was arrested, and killed himself by drinking DDT; the Gang of Four was placed on public trial in 1980. Performers such as Yin Chengzong who had prospered during the Cultural Revolution were also purged. By this turn of political fortune, Liu Shikun became China's leading piano virtuoso, giving performances to crowds as large as eighty thousand. But not all leftist musicians were purged. Jin Yueqin, a nineteen-year-old worker at Shanghai's Number 6 Glass Factory, and composer of the popular "I Love Beijing's Tiananmen," was admitted to the Central Conservatory in 1978.[72] Conductor Li Delun proved himself to be a pre-eminent survivor in China's cultural politics. He suffered no penalties for heading the Central Philharmonic when it was one of Jiang Qing's model units, but he now conducts in tails instead of the uniform of the People's Liberation Army.

More notable were renewed careers by musicians who had been silenced during the Cultural Revolution, or who had been forced to play the music of song-and-dance troupes rather than the music of their choice and training. They were given new positions and honor, while the troupes quickly learned to sing and dance to the new tunes of post-Mao China.

Those who returned adopted as their symbol one who could not. Zhang Zhixin was a forty-five-year-old Party member and propaganda official in Liaoning who had been jailed for defending Liu Shaoqi. She was executed in 1975, her throat slit in order to prevent her from shouting slogans at the end, giving the tale of her martyrdom a gory fascination. Zhang was a violinist, as was her father, and composed several songs while in prison. Her family was from Tianjin, and Liu Shikun probably knew her, as her violinist sister was his coworker in the Central Philharmonic. Her death was the subject of a major campaign directed against Mao's nephew, Mao Yuanxin, the political boss of Liaoning who had signed her death warrant. In the propaganda that accompanied this campaign, Zhang was often portrayed with her violin, and her songs were reprinted and widely sung. Zhang's Maoist adversaries certainly understood the bond of music to politics proclaimed by her militant motto: "Use your violin as a gun."[73]

Gu Shengying, as a professional pianist rather than a propagandist, was probably closer to the hearts of most Chinese musicians. The Shanghai Philharmonic held a public ceremony rehabilitating her memory on January 4, 1979. Her aged father was allowed to return from Qinghai and was given housing in Shanghai, as well as recordings, press clippings, and photographs to replace those looted by Red Guards after his daughter's suicide.[74] But there was no way to replace the family he had lost.

The living rehabilitees included victims of the 1957 antirightist campaign as well as those who had been silenced during the Cultural Revolution, such as the president of the Shanghai Conservatory, He Luting.[75] But these groups were often at odds, as the latter had frequently participated in the attacks upon the former. Having them all work together in the same units again was as difficult in the music world as it was in other parts of Chinese society.[76] Other musicians were given greater political prominence. When the so-called "democratic" political parties that technically share power with the Communist Party were revived, several musicians joined with much fanfare, such as the violinist Sheng Zhongguo and the *pipa* virtuoso Liu Dehai, both of whom joined the Democratic League.[77]

The Rehabilitation of European Compositions

Liu Shikun gave an interview in July 1977 in which he uttered guarded words of praise for European composers: "We respect those who played a progressive role in their times and works from which we have something to learn artistically," he said, "but they are far removed from the life and struggle of the people in socialist China."[78] The pace of restoration proved to be so rapid that Liu's comments soon seemed too restrictive, and he and other musicians had to scurry to avoid being left behind.

The benchmark for the return of European music was Beethoven's symphonies. The fifth, of course, was the first to be performed, in March 1977. But the Central Philharmonic timidly announced its first performance by title only, without listing the composer.[79] Even after this breakthrough, radio officials had to seek the approval of cultural officials each time they broadcast a different Beethoven symphony, until all nine had been approved. Fortunately, the Chinese middle class has a greater passion for Beethoven than for Haydn.

China Rejoins the International Musical Community

Musical diplomacy resumed the course which had been interrupted by the campaign against music without titles.[80] Liu Shikun was involved in many of these new exchanges, either as a performer or as a representative of China's musicians. For instance, he met with a visiting Norwegian pianist, Kjell Baekkelund, in the spring of 1977.[81] The following year he toured the United States where he played *Battling the Typhoon* and a Liszt Hungarian Rhapsody with a traveling ensemble. The political nature of musical diplomacy was underscored after the establishment of diplomatic relations between China and the United States in 1979. In January, Deng Xiaoping, then visiting Washington, invited the Boston Symphony Orchestra to play in China. Although that orchestra's schedule is set three years in advance, the Bostonians were in China by March, with a $650,000 corporate subsidy. There the marshal's son-in-law performed Liszt's Piano Concerto No. 1 under the direction of the orchestra's conductor, Seiji Ozawa. Liu followed the orchestra back to the United States the next week for additional performances and a recording.[82]

Ozawa, who was born in Manchuria when it was under Japanese domination, is very popular in China as an Asian musician who has won success in the West. He has been supportive of efforts by Chinese musicians to improve their working conditions, as have many other foreign visitors. Yehudi Menuhin, who is the grandfather of Fou Ts'ong's child, has also visited China repeatedly, echoing the remarks of Ozawa and many of the Boston Symphony players about the poor quality of Chinese musical instruments.[83] Foreign visitors thus lent their support to Chinese musicians seeking better material support to enable China to be taken seriously in the international musical community. With the redirection of Chinese foreign policy, Isaac Stern and Yehudi Menuhin took the place occupied by Soviet and East European musical advisors in the 1950s.

At this time Fou Ts'ong returned to his homeland, as China sought also to utilize the talents of emigré Chinese to help bring its music up to international standards. Others such as the bass Si Yigui, a professor at Eastman Conservatory, and the composer Chou Wen-chung, resumed ties broken since the revolution. Chou's frequently performed music is influenced both by Chinese tradition and by his teachers, Varèse and Luening, suggesting ways for composers in the People's Republic to use the modernist musical vocabulary. Chou is a professor at Columbia University, where he established a Sino-American Arts Exchange Center.[84]

Even Ma Sitson, the Central Conservatory president who defected to the United States, was invited to return to China. When his brother, violinist Ma Sixiong, visited China in 1980, Ma declined an invitation to visit, but instead travelled again to Taiwan with much publicity and propaganda.[85] He died in Philadelphia in 1987 without having returned to his homeland. Many artists and intellectuals also chose to emigrate from China in the late 1970s, fearful that another era of radicalism might replace the looser rule of Deng Xiaoping.[86]

A Boom in Pianos

The minor resurgence of European instruments in the early 1970s paled in comparison to the piano boom of the following decade. The turn to the violin at the end of the Cultural Revolution reflected a utilitarian effort to escape agricultural labor. By the 1980s political and economic changes had reconstituted China's urban middle class, stimulating a more open and broadly based audience for European music. The older classical-music aficionados were joined by youth disposed to view Western culture as advanced, and a much larger group of people who found European music a badge of respectable social status much as Europeans themselves had in the early nineteenth century.

Deng Xiaoping rose to power by promising rehabilitation to disgraced officials. His reform policies have led to higher incomes for urban residents, especially by encouraging the re-emergence of a genuine urban petty bourgeoisie in the thousands of small enterprises that have blossomed in recent years. In addition, former capitalist families have been accorded new respect, partly in an effort to tap foreign investment, and partly in the hope that they may have skills to offer a more market-oriented economy. These groups have diverse origins and often conflicting interests, but they are bound together by their difference from the vast peasantry, by their shared commitment to an urban-based modernization of Chinese society, and by an emerging urban middle-class culture. The return of state officials to the road of embourgeoisement has been equally important. Mao interrupted this process fiercely, but in the 1980s Chinese officials increasingly put aside memories of revolutionary glory in favor of quiet, orderly lives resembling those of solid middle-class civil servants in other nations. Deng Xiaoping's favorite pastime is not music but bridge, which, like the piano, reveals a ready embrace for certain aspects of Western culture.

The spread of the piano throughout urban China represents a kind of embourgeoisement, a search for respectability, and celebration of family values that piano manufacturers in the West rode to fortune in the nineteenth century. Along with rising incomes, China's family planning policies have also encouraged the music boom. The single-child family is most common in cities, where the solitary children are likely to be indulged with piano lessons by doting parents and grandparents. Single children from urban middle-class families will be under special pressure to perform well in the examination system for higher education; many of their older relatives firmly believe that music lessons will promote intelligence in children. A recent description of a violin lesson for twenty-one students in Guangzhou revealed that most of the children were accompanied by their parents, who took notes and "often repeated the teacher's words in a low voice and gave their children extra instructions."[87] Such parental interest may have a darker side, which is rumored to have caused a notorious tragedy in Shanghai in 1987; pressed by his mother to excel in piano lessons, one child destroyed the family piano, then leapt to his death from his apartment window.

Instrument factories have been hard-pressed to keep up with demand. In 1986 customers had to wait between six months and two years for delivery of their new pianos. A new piano cost two thousand *renminbi* or more, well over a year's wages for an urban resident.[88] In addition to high prices, urban Chinese must sacrifice considerable space to own a piano in ordinarily crowded apartments; individuals only rarely own grand pianos. The shortage of instruments has encouraged the emergence of speculators in pianos, who purchase the instruments as investments rather than as machines for musical enjoyment.[89]

China's four piano factories in Guangzhou, Beijing, Shanghai, and Yingkou (in Liaoning) increased their production rapidly. They produced between thirteen and eighteen thousand per year between 1981 and 1983, but eighty percent of these were for export. In Ningpo, an old center of Chinese capitalism, a fifth factory was created from a former plant for sewing machine cabinets.[90] The Guangzhou Piano Factory, China's largest, employs nearly a thousand workers; it had only twenty when it was formed in 1956. Most of its Pearl River pianos sell for around twenty-five hundred *renminbi;* there is also an inexpensive model with only seventy-two keys. But piano inflation is so great that in 1988 one Pearl River piano sold for over five thousand *renminbi* in Fuzhou.[91]

The older instruments themselves embody the history of European music in China. Ms. Peng, a teacher of English in Zhengzhou, told me the saga of her piano,[92] which was made in England by a long-defunct manufacturer. How it made its way to China is unclear. Early in this century, Ms. Peng's grandfather, a Guangzhou capitalist, wanted his daughter to be cultivated in modern Western ways, and purchased the piano for her childhood music lessons. The instrument was still in the family when the young Ms. Peng moved north in the 1930s to marry a Beijing intellectual, whereupon the instrument accompanied her as part of her trousseau. After Liberation, the piano was confiscated as capitalist property, but Ms. Peng repurchased it from the state.

She then took it with her, at considerable inconvenience, first to Kaifeng and then to Zhengzhou, where there were few piano teachers for her own daughter, the third generation of young women to play on this imperialist instrument. Early in the Cultural Revolution, someone offered Ms. Peng a token price of one *yuan* to haul away the instrument, but Ms. Peng declined, choosing instead to hide it. The family moved the piano from the parlor into a smaller room, which they papered over until the Cultural Revolution ended. Now the same instrument is used for the piano lessons of the great-grandchild of its original owner.

Fan Qihua, a Shanghai language teacher, had a sadder story. Her German-made piano had also been long in the family. It was part of her dowry and she later gave it to her own daughter. But the piano was one of eight hundred seized from bourgeois households by Red Guards during the campaign against the Four Olds. Fan emigrated to the United States after the Cultural Revolution; nearly twenty years after her instrument was confiscated, she received word that it had been found in a Ningbo "cultural institution," and was returned to her relatives.[93]

The new status of European music has encouraged an unprecedented pride and activism by the music community. For instance, the first self-employed person accepted into the Communist Party in Shanghai was Luo Xinghai, a piano repairman of thirty years. Luo had turned down an offer to work in Hong Kong, and often repairs instruments for schools at no charge in addition to organizing other self-employed people to serve the elderly.[94]

Music and the Four Modernizations

But musicians did not find everything to their liking in the newly reconstituted middle-class culture. The lighter touch of cultural administrators was pleasant, but the decline of Maoist theories stressing the importance of revolution in the superstructure meant that music sank to a lower level of significance to the state. The great slogan of the post-Mao years, the "Four Modernizations," encouraged very practical interpretations. Without its political functions, music was of little practical use to many people.

In Chinese schools the new push for modernization meant that music teachers, like art teachers, were often drafted to teach mathematics and science. School administrators with limited budgets often chose science over the arts. An art teacher in Ye Jianying's home city of Meizhou reported that the Four Modernizations policy devastated music and painting instruction in his middle school. School administrators decided to end the second year of art and music in favor of additional science courses. The music teacher was ordered to stop giving exams so that students could have more time to study mathematics and science, since the arts were not covered on the newly revived university entrance examination.[95] Music teachers complained bitterly when they were reassigned to teach mathematics; eventually the Education Ministry took steps to protect classes in the arts.[96]

Even when a school had special music teachers, they often were poorly trained. Beijing has over four thousand primary schools, but only a few more than thirty of the music teachers have even attended middle-school music education classes. In 930 middle schools, only a few more than 20 of the music teachers have attended a university.[97]

Students also were drawn to scientific courses instead of the arts because the sciences might help them in modern careers. When senior high school students in Guangxi were asked to list their favorite subjects in 1983, thirty-three percent named mathematics, sixteen percent physics, and only two percent music, which ranked even below politics. A survey ﾃf students in elite Beijing University found that only ten percent couﾗ read the five-line staff, and only a quarter could read numbered musical notation.[98]

These problems made many musicians anxious about the future of music in China. A group of prominent musicians (including He Luting and Zhao Feng) prepared "A Proposal for Strengthening School Music Instruction," in which they complained that national leaders did not sufficiently stress music, schools did not emphasize music classes, equipment was inadequate and working conditions poor, qualifying standards for music teachers were too low, and the ideology of music education was backward. They also stressed the need for a reform of teaching methods. Without changes in music education, the classics would never be popularized, and training would be restricted to a few outstanding specialists.[99]

Music educators were outraged when three fingers were severed from the hand of Zhou Guangren, a professor of piano at the Central Conservatory and China's first pianist to win an international prize. She was moving a piano when its leg collapsed, mauling her hand as thoroughly as any industrial accident. Many asked why the fifty-four-year-old vice-chairman of the department had to serve as a piano-mover, and why the conservatory had to use an instrument in such bad condition.[100]

Financial stability for musical institutions has been another problem under the Deng Xiaoping reforms.[101] Arts ensembles have been urged to become financially self-sufficient, a demand that may be easier for a factory than for an orchestra. The Central Philharmonic has had to record film soundtracks for income, at the expense of rehearsal time for the music it wants to play. The Shanghai Symphony must divide into "light music groups" which provide background music in hotels and restaurants. Other music groups must use fewer members in order to balance their books, a practice which hits chorus members especially hard. Individual musicians also supplement their low incomes by moonlighting as teachers and pop performers, but this often exhausts them and they still cannot easily find the money for such necessary expenses as the replacement of old instruments.[102]

The Second Imprisonment of Liu Shikun: Spiritual Pollution

Liu's piano-playing flourished along with his father-in-law's power. But divorce and Ye's death stripped Liu of political protection. Liu was charged with a variety of misdeeds, many associated with his ties to the outside world, and was jailed once more.

Ye Jianying's position as an ally of both Hua Guofeng and Deng Xiaoping, plus his status as one of the most senior of China's surviving revolutionaries, assured him continued honor in his post as head of state. At the peak of his power, Ye received considerable fawning attention, such as the 1979 performance in Hong Kong by soprano Guo Shujen of a setting of Ye's poetry.[103] Liu Shikun continued to receive even more attention as a performer. A December 1979 solo recital in Hong Kong showed him in top form. Liu's commanding stage presence suited a rather brooding, hyperromantic style of playing. For this recital he played Bach, Mozart, Beethoven, Schubert, Matsuma, Liszt, and his own electrifying virtuoso piece, "Prelude and Dance."[104]

Liu's musical success was all the more impressive for being achieved with little practice time. Liu Shikun had become an informal political secretary for his increasingly feeble father-in-law. Ye, born in 1897, was only able to read token passages when delivering his public speeches, and even then he required a brace of nurses to hold his body upright. He was unable to manage his affairs without aid, yet his political position assured a steady stream of political demands. Liu Shikun spent much of his time receiving petitioners seeking favors of Ye Jianying. The pianist had become the manager of his senile father-in-law's political faction, making two or three weekly visits to present Ye with the requests he had screened. By 1981 Liu gave up performing altogether, and worked in the Ministry of Culture as deputy director for the Arts Bureau under the cartoonist Hua Junwu, with special responsibilities for music, dance, and fine arts. Yin Chengzong had aided Liu in 1973, and Liu repaid the favor by helping Yin return to the Central Philharmonic.[105] Liu's transformation from pianist to political adviser is reminiscent of Farinelli, the celebrated castrato who influenced the policies of Philip V and Ferdinand VI of Spain.[106]

Liu Shikun had so wedded his career to Ye Jianying that he could not survive the dissolution of his marriage in the early 1980s. Relations between Liu and Ye Xiangzhen had apparently been strained for some time. Ye Xiangzhen had become a movie director, relying on Ye's protection to make her 1981 film *Wilderness,* which was notable for pushing the limits of acceptable romantic dialogue.[107] Ye Xiangzhen was unhappy with Liu's extramarital affairs; in the scandal that accompanied their divorce, Liu was accused of a variety of bureaucratic, financial, and sexual misdeeds. Liu was said to have usurped Marshal Ye's authority, for instance, by showing restricted movies to local police in exchange for aid for his friends who were falsely described as "Ye's relatives." Liu was accused of smuggling old paintings out of China and smuggling consumer goods (such as refrigerators, cameras, tape recorders, and televisions) into China from Hong Kong. He was accused of establishing close ties with foreign businessmen on his trips abroad and sometimes using these connections for immoral purposes. One U.S. businessman is supposed to have agreed to return Liu's favors by sponsoring several students to the United States, an opportunity which Liu used for sending several of his lovers abroad. Liu allegedly used a five-room military guest house and a car belonging to the People's Liberation Army for his complicated affairs with several women, and used his influence in the Ministry of Culture to get jobs in the movie industry for one girlfriend. Liu's purported gifts of money to one lover were discovered after she made a messy effort to poison herself. Liu was then forced to make a (false) self-criticism over this affair in his work unit, the Central Philharmonic.[108]

It is impossible to assess these charges. Liu Shikun remains under a cloud, and those who know him are not eager to remind anyone of their relations with him. But like other aspects of Liu's career, these accusations must be viewed in a political context.

By the early 1980s, Deng Xiaoping's regarded Ye Jianying as an impediment to a more rapid overhaul of economy and society. Ye was old, and represented old-line Maoist thinking in the army, but he refused to surrender his political positions to younger, more reform-minded officials. The political resurrection of Deng Xiaoping had become possible only with the arrest of the Gang of Four, yet the three men who planned that action were more loyal to Maoist traditions than to Deng and his supporters. Wang Dongxing had been forced from power in 1978; Hua Guofeng in 1981. Only Ye remained.

Ye's family is widely believed to have abused its political position in corrupt ways. Ye had many well-furnished homes all over China. Some of his children were repeatedly accused of corruption, including such acts as smuggling gold and taking bribes while importing German electrical equipment. Other family members were raised to important political positions on the basis of their father's power. Ye Xuanping, for instance, was made mayor of Guangzhou, and his wife, Wu Xiaolang, became deputy mayor of Shenzhen. Ye Xuanning was placed in charge of Overseas Chinese affairs for Taiwan, Hong Kong, and Macao.[109]

The disarray in Liu's personal life provided an excellent opportunity for Ye Jianying's enemies to expose the life of privilege and influence-peddling that apparently characterized this grand family of the red aristocracy. It is common for China's leaders to use their positions to aid their children in ethically dubious ways. Of Deng Xiaoping's children, for instance, one son studies in a U.S. university, another heads China's national organization for the disabled, and a daughter earns thousands of dollars by selling her paintings to Hong Kong collectors perhaps more interested in political connections than watercolors. Such abuses of power become pigtails which one's enemies can pull. Liu Shikun became a pawn in a drive to dislodge Ye from his position of power, a repeat of his role in the Cultural Revolution. Indeed, Ye resigned as head of state in 1983, although he retained his membership on the six-man standing committee of the Political Bureau of the Communist Party.

A second set of issues made Liu more vulnerable. The opening of China's economy and culture to Western and Japanese influence has been controversial. Not all of China's leaders have wanted to proceed as rapidly as has Deng Xiaoping's reform faction. Some fear that unchecked foreign contracts will corrupt China. Artists who enjoy the privilege of foreign travel have often been accused of succumbing to temptation. In one 1981 case, an opera company from Chaozhou was caught engaged in massive smuggling when it returned from Hong Kong: its members hid watches in costumes and instrument cases, and concealed pornographic books and magazines in its music.[110]

In 1983 efforts to limit harmful influence from abroad congealed in a campaign to combat "spiritual pollution." This confused and inconclusive campaign led to criticisms of dancing, Hong Kong popular music, and Western style of dress. Liu was conveniently placed to serve as a negative example for the campaign.[111] The smuggling charges against Liu reminded all Chinese artists to be careful about what they carried to and from China.

The sexual charges against Liu had a similar impact. Some Chinese think that musicians are especially prone to sexual misconduct. Fou Ts'ong and Yin Chengzong have also endured envious and no doubt fanciful gossip about their amorous lives. Shortly after the Central Conservatory was revived in 1978, two students were expelled for a romantic affair, leading the head of the Party propaganda department to wonder why artists were so susceptible to the "evil wind" of reckless acts between men and women.[112] Chinese views of sex are puritanical by contemporary Western standards.[113] Whatever the truth of Liu's womanizing, he once again did not meet the standard set by the campaign against spiritual pollution. This, combined with the politically motivated embarrassment of the Ye family, was his undoing.

Liu was not arrested. Ye Jianying remained fond of Liu, despite the divorce, and protected the pianist. Even if their relations had soured, Ye would have expended much of his influence to avoid the shame of seeing his former son-in-law in prison. Liu gave up his political position and returned to music, his prestige badly battered. He appeared in March 1984 as one of fifteen international prize-winners to perform at a special concert in Beijing; although Liu was clearly the most eminent of these musicians, his Moscow prize was not mentioned by the press, a clear sign of his lowered status.[114] Soon after this concert, Liu began to devote most of his attention to business ventures instead of music.

Ye Jianying was finally forced to retire in 1985, but not before striking a final deal by which his son-in-law would be promoted from mayor of Guangzhou to governor of Guangdong province (both former posts of the father-in-law). His daughter, Ye Xiangzhen, went into business in Hong Kong. Ye apparently was too senile to be aware of the arrest of Liu Shikun on April 29, 1986.

Liu had been under investigation by the Beijing Municipal Public Security Bureau and the State Security Ministry, which had sent a female undercover agent to befriend Liu in order to gather evidence against him. His alleged crimes were drug smuggling and gold speculation. In February 1986 Liu received a telegram from Hong Kong, reporting that his mother had been hospitalized in a traffic accident, and urging him to come immediately. Public Security officials denied him permission to leave China, incorrectly suspecting that Liu planned to flee. After his divorce from Ye Xiangzhen, Liu married a singer of Japanese Overseas Chinese origin from the Central Philharmonic, fueling the suspicions of the police that he might bolt for Japan. At this point Liu began destroying evidence against him, flushing papers down the toilet and making late-night trips to dump garbage. No formal charges were filed out of respect for the ninety-year-old marshal. Ye Jianying's death on October 22, 1986 lead to renewed speculation that sentencing would soon take place.[115] In the summer of 1987 there was a rumor that Liu had been sentenced to seventeen years in prison, but in fact he was released, perhaps for lack of evidence.[116] An acquaintance of Liu in the United States reports that he now sits silently at home, depressed and uninterested in music. Liu is not yet fifty years old, but it seems unlikely that he will soon play the piano for the public again.

7

The Power of Music, the Music of Power

The great classics of European concert music are among the most powerful artifacts of our civilization in their capacity to move people to joy, tears, exhilaration, and a score of lesser, if steadier pleasures. Beyond its European homeland, this music's considerable aesthetic attractions are reinforced by the West's political and economic domination of the world during the past century. To ignore this connection or treat it merely as a curious coincidence is naive, and makes it impossible to understand the complex interrelationship between the sphere of musical pleasure and the political reality in which this pleasure lives and dies. Observed in its native habitat, this music at times does appear to soar serenely above the petty conflicts of a squalid world. But China's stormy reception of European classical music makes it difficult to treat art solely as a spiritual concern.

A Coda for the Pianists

The entanglement of music and politics has not been kind to China's three great virtuoso pianists. Their social origins are similar and they belong to a small, densely interconnected social and musical circle. What to do with the piano and other badges of elitist modernism during populist periods is a theoretical question if you are a member of the Central Committee, but not if you are a concert pianist. One of the distinctive features of the piano is that although it was an instrument invented to extend the expressive possibilities of human musicians, it has come to dominate its players. Ever since Robert Schumann crippled his hand with a device intended to strengthen his reach, virtuoso pianists have become extensions of their instrument; they must devote years to acquiring and maintaining physical technique, and their personal lives are shaped by the harsh demands of concert tours. As their skills cannot simply be put aside until the winds of populism subside, pianists face difficult political and aesthetic choices.

Each of the three pianists had a different bond to the political system. Fou Ts'ong remained intimately tied to the old bourgeois intelligentsia, Yin Chengzong rose with the rebels of the Cultural Revolution, and Liu Shikun joined the red aristocracy of high-level Communist bureaucrats. Not one of these career courses has permitted what Western music-lovers might recognize as a normal life as a pianist. Each artist suffered imprisonment or exile, and each has endured bitter public excoriation for his political ties. Indeed, since 1958 there has never been a time when one (and usually two) of these pianists has not been under a cloud. The harassment of musicians has come from all points in the Chinese political spectrum. Fou fled a China in which Mao Zedong was chairman of the Communist Party and Deng Xiaoping its secretary-general, Yin was banned from the concert stage by Hua Guofeng and gently allowed to emigrate under Deng Xiaoping, while Liu has been jailed by both Left and Right. Maoists have not been unique as persecutors of China's artists.

Musicians in the West also have their careers interrupted for a variety of reasons. Merely consider the non-Chinese top prize-winners in the 1958 and 1962 Tchaikovsky Competition. Van Cliburn, his talent apparently diminished, has not played a regular public concert since 1978, except for private performances for such friends as Ferdinand and Imelda Marcos; recently he played at the White House for Reagan and Gorbachev. Vladimir Ashkenazy has had a fine career, but his personal life was disrupted by his quiet defection to the West. John Ogdon went mad, suffering from visions of glowing crosses in San Antonio, paranoid fantasies about the implantation of electrodes into his body, and conspiracies by Adolf Hitler. After four suicide attempts he tried a musical return, much like a Chinese rehabilitation. Susan Starr dropped from sight; when last heard from she claimed that sexism harmed her career, not an implausible hypothesis when one contrasts the gender ratio of piano students to that of successful concert artists.[1]

The Chinese piano virtuosos are still young, both by international norms for pianists and by Chinese standards for artists and public figures of any sort. Fou Ts'ong, born in 1934, is the oldest, while Yin Chengzong is almost a full decade younger. Many twists no doubt remain to their careers. Fou Ts'ong has recently recorded several Mozart concertos with the Polish Chamber Orchestra for RCA, revealing a crisp and clean approach very much in accord with current European fashion for Mozart interpretation. Yin Chengzong has also recently recorded a collection of Chopin and Chinese music for Philips, which may well help him receive the recognition his formidable musicianship and prodigious technique deserves in the West. Only Liu Shikun seems lost to the world of music, at least for the time being. Chinese musical conditions have changed radically, suggesting that younger musicians may have an easier time than these three somewhat scarred pioneers. At least in the 1980s, China is working at healing past political wounds in the music world. Both Ma Sitson and (Li) Jie Fu were treated with dignity and respect in the press, presumably to please their cosmopolitan and populist followers.[2] The cult of Xian Xinghai still has many worshippers, but now nonrevolutionary musical pioneers share his honors.

The great classics of European music flowered along with the rise of the bourgeoisie to a position of political dominance, first with Europe and then around the globe. Along with empire came imperial musical culture, but at its furthest reaches there was barely any social foundation to sustain this music. In China, revolution jolted the ambitious but vulnerable urban middle class, including the three pianists considered here as its musical representatives. Virtuoso performers must always have a high tolerance for risk, but this is usually a bravery against the embarrassment of missed notes and messy trills. Each of these Chinese virtuosos has shown a kind of political courage beyond the normal calling of a professional musician.

Orpheus in the Under(developed) World

Among the popular pieties of Western culture is the notion that music constitutes an "international language." Great music is alleged to

transcend mean national boundaries, linking refined human spirits one
to another directly, without the meddlesome mediation of politics.
Movies and television documentaries have shown such performers as
Isaac Stern, Yehudi Menuhin, and the Boston Symphony in China,
appealing to our common humanity through the music of the masters.[3]

Our mass media's image of cultural exchange focus on the happiness that *our* music brings to China. Concealed beneath the happy
views of instruction in bowing and discussions of tempos is a proselytizing condescension resembling that of an English professor who,
with no thought that he might find pleasure in reading *Dream of the
Red Chamber,* expressed sorrow that the Chinese do not know Shake-
speare, much as nineteenth-century missionaries were once overcome
by China's unfamiliarity with Jesus. A similar condescension reso-
nates through this account from a *Christian Science Monitor* reporter
listening to the Mendelssohn Violin Concerto at the Shanghai Conservatory in 1980.

> A young man, eyes closed and brows lifted, moved his bow with the
> kind of fervour that makes nothing less than extraordinary sound. His
> teacher accompanied him on an old Moutri piano that was somewhat
> out of tune; somehow, it didn't matter. They were playing with feel-
> ing—with more passion than I'd seen in China up to that point. . . .
> Posters of Mao and Chairman Hua peered down over the young musi-
> cian's shoulders. I closed my eyes to listen. Here it is, I thought. In the
> past 10 years the heart of the Chinese people has been kept alive after
> all. . . . I was moved—so much that a tear escaped down my cheek. I
> brushed it furtively away.[4]

The world culture system is a system of power, in which China is
still weak enough that we accept its art only on our own terms. We
welcome landscape paintings and translated poetry which we then put
to our own purposes, such as opportunities for speculative investment
and the creation of comforting myths about Asian spirituality and com-
munion with nature. But we have found no use for China's rich indigenous musical culture, which remains opaque to Western audiences.
If Western governments were to promote the *pipa* and Beijing opera
in competition with some of the glories of our own musical civilization, we might understand more easily how bitter political controversies over music have arisen in modern China.

The international-language image is much loved by diplomats and
cliché-ridden politicians, who use it as courteous filler for ceremonial

occasions and as a convenient distraction from unpleasant political realities.[5] Even the mayor of Eugene, Oregon managed to purr that "the universal language of the arts has brought us together," when Soviet pianist Lazar Berman made a sudden appearance there in the spring of 1987. "Few in Lazar Berman's audience understood his words, but his language was unmistakably universal," exclaimed the newspaper of the University of Oregon.[6] Everyone was too polite to explain that Eugene's good fortune rested on the U.S. State Department's discovery that it was one of the few spots where Berman could perform without drawing demonstrators from the Jewish Defense League. In 1987, Vladimir Feltsman, a dissident Soviet pianist, was welcomed to the United States with fulsome praise for music's transcendence of politics; the boosts to his new career in the United States indicate quite the opposite.[7] But at the same time, the United States continued to deny a visa to Dang Thai Son, the Vietnamese virtuoso who won the 1980 Chopin Competition. Dang merely wants to perform in the United States, for which he has taken the trouble to learn the music of Charles Ives.[8]

The figure of Orpheus offers an alternative metaphor to remind us of our music's power to inspire and control. Orpheus, son of Apollo and Calliope, sang and played with such excruciating sweetness that he tamed the Furies of Hades in order to bring his beloved Eurydice back to life. A more openly sinister version of the Orpheus myth is the Pied Piper of Hamelin, who lured a whole city's children into captivity with his enchanting music. A suitably manic Orpheus for our times is the hero of Werner Herzog's movie, *Fitzcarraldo*. Fitzcarraldo wants to exploit the rubber of the Amazon jungle, but must overcome the fierce Jivaro headhunters. He charms the savage Indians into timidity by playing recordings of Enrico Caruso on his gramophone, so overwhelming them that they agree to pull his steamship over a mountain. Orpheus is committed to civilizing and dominating through the power of his art, even as he exploits those whom he seduces.

The irresistibly compelling music of Orpheus is conveyed to the Third World through our instruments, symphonies, and songbooks. Their power is so great that they entice first the elites and then whole populations into emulating our civilization. The mythical Orpheus eventually perishes when he seduces and then rejects a group of Thracian maidens, who angrily tear him limb from limb, throwing both his lyre and his head into a river. One is tempted for a moment to see Jiang Qing as a wrathful Thracian maiden, attacking the West's Orpheus through the Cultural Revolution. But we have seen that the Cultural Revolution, beneath its virulent opposition to individual works of European art, in fact pushed Western music's roots ever deeper into Chinese society. If even Chinese Communism makes room for piano recitals, can anyone escape seduction?

The Orpheus myth was once the West's standard cliché in the discussion of music and its power. Why did it fall into disuse, supplanted by the weaker metaphor of music as an international language? Before the rise of bourgeois music, Europe's composers and their aristocratic patrons were quite aware of music's awesome power. The elite music of court and church was a precious luxury, bearing a kind of majesty that even the most beautiful music has lost as it has become readily accessible to nonelite audiences. When Louis XVI ascended to the French throne in May 1774, Gluck was quick to send the new monarch a letter, seeking the continued patronage of the French royal house.

> When, following the example of the Greeks, Augustus, the Medicis and Louis XIV encouraged and supported the arts, they had a more important aim in view than that of providing further amusement and pleasure; they regarded that portion of human knowledge as one of the most precious links in the political chain; they knew that only the arts are capable of making men gentle without corrupting them and of rendering them prone to submission without debasing them.[9]

Gluck's language was flowery, but his appeal to the Orpheus-like power of music was sincere.[10] But the sense of music as a political rite diminished as the bourgeoisie became music's chief patron. Indeed, Berlioz, Gluck's greatest champion in the nineteenth century, had such a different consciousness that he mocked Confucian efforts to use music to spread morality. If only his guitar were like that of the Chinese sage, joked Berlioz, "think of the benefits I might have brought, the heresies I might have rooted out, the truths instilled, the noble religion founded, and the happiness we might all be enjoying now."[11]

By the late nineteenth century, the emotional link between music and the state had been attenuated. Late romantic music has the power to affect its listener's emotions intensely, but its message is more frequently personal rather than an overt comment on state affairs. Apart from Brahms' ineffectual *Triumphlied* in celebration of the Franco-

Prussian War, his music and his politics are separate. One would never know listening to a Brahms sonata that its composer belonged to a nutty club whose members vowed to pull Bismark's carriage into Berlin in place of their esteemed chancellor's horses.[12]

The Orpheus myth declined because it was less useful in a world where music was increasingly personal. Professional musicians were forging new self-identities as autonomous artists, and consciously rejected an ideology of state patronage. They retained the right to champion political causes, but these would be of their own choosing. Moreover, the musicians of high romanticism preferred to serve the *people,* not the state.[13]

With the spread of Western empire, the international-language metaphor proved comforting to both conquerors and subjects alike. The West's musicians, if they thought much about empire, preferred to imagine their art opening new opportunities for shared pleasure and enlightenment, rather than imagining its other use as a secondary aspect of an increasingly global web of social control. Musical cosmopolitans in China have a different motive for insisting on the international status of Europe's music: to identify it as Western is to acknowledge their own isolation and vulnerability, and reopen old accusations that lovers of Liszt are agents of imperialism. When China's Central Philharmonic toured the United States in 1987, conductor Chen Zuohuang illustrated this point by explaining his view of symphonic music to the *New York Times.* "I don't like to say it is purely a Western form of art. It is a universal form of language. Gradually it has become a universal language and has become a cultural treasure for the whole world."[14]

Of course this Western music is a cultural treasure, enjoyable outside its continent of origin. Yet it is also an ideology, a beguiling form of false consciousness. According to Theodore Adorno, "[i]f music really is an ideology, not a phenomenon of truth—in other words, if the form in which it is experienced by a population befuddles their perception of social reality—one question that will necessarily arise concerns the relation of music to the social classes."[15] Elsewhere, Adorno argues that a society's structure is visible from its uses of music, that "no matter where music is heard today, it sketches in the clearest possible lines the contradictions and flaws which cut through the present-day society."[16]

Another image beyond Orpheus is needed to describe the West's stance toward the music of the Third World. No Asian Orpheus has yet emerged to dominate us, because outside the myth Orpheus can only work his magic when his lyre is buttressed by trade, tanks, and television satellites. Perhaps the crude vitality of a strip mine better captures our objectification of Third World music, which becomes raw material for our cultural plunder, to be reshaped, processed, packaged, and used in an alien context. Copper, bananas, and sounds all receive the same treatment. We take a little Ravi Shankar from India, some African rhythms, or Balinese gamelan music to insert for a time into our own aesthetic, then discard them when the commercial value of their novelty is gone. Their shelf life is only slightly longer than a bag of potato chips.[17] In a world of musical equality, Westerners would learn to play Third World instruments properly, and understand the social meanings of the music. To be sure, we train ethnomusicologists to specialize in such arcana, much as we train other experts to know about diseases of the foot or to teach political science.

A Cycle of Nationalism and Internationalism

Imperialism and revolution have added a new twist to a traditional suspicion that foreign culture corrodes China's national essence: Chinese practitioners of foreign culture can be branded as "bourgeois" when their art is under fire. In intensely nativist periods, one demonstrates virtue by disliking Western music. Yet the Communist Party's commitment to use culture for its own political purposes enables Western-style violinists, pianists, and wind players to maintain their skills until Brahms is once more in style. Once this cycle is complete, cultural nationalism is expressed by vigorous efforts for Chinese to win prizes in international music competitons. China thus turns both hatred for Western music and proficiency in performing it to its nationalist needs as these gradually change.

The Continuing Westernization of Chinese Music

Despite the radical disjunctions for individual artists, the drive to spread European music has been a continuous feature of this century. Whether under populist or elitist form, more people are exposed to pianos, harmony, polyphony, and electronic *shengs*. The wave of modernization has far to go before it is spent; there is ample reason to suspect that it may again assume populist forms in which Chopin gives way to concertos for the *pipa*. But it is important to distinguish between superficially anti-Western episodes of cultural populism—such as the Cultural Revolution—and a longer process that changes China's music in ways that everyone still agrees to be modern.

However little respect the cultural revolutionaries had for the treasures of the European repertory, the movement spread Western harmony, instruments, and choral singing. Radicals claimed that formerly the piano was used

> largely to adorn the mansions and salons of the rich. Now the revolution in piano music by the proletariat, exemplified by the piano music *The Red Lantern* with Peking opera singing and the piano concerto *The Yellow River*, has liberated the instrument created by the labouring people and returned it to them, to serve the needs of the people.[18]

Rhetoric aside, this is not a bad description of the long-term diffusion of European music in China; state intervention has pushed populist pianos at the proletariat, in contrast to the market-driven spread of this music in its homeland a century earlier. The piano failed to take hold as an instrument of revolution, remaining bulky and bourgeois no matter how often it was set in a truck for Red Guard demonstrations or represented beneath palm trees. Yet in its peculiar way, the Cultural Revolution prepared the way for the cultural restoration which followed. Once the piano had been saved, could Chopin be far behind?

If the cosmopolitans prevail in their battle against traditional music, they owe much to the Cultural Revolution's destruction of folk arts, which the radicals also saw as rump manifestations of feudal culture.[19] Although foreign experts later could come to China to help restore previous standards in symphonic music and oil painting, there were no such experts to help restore such traditional folk arts as ballad singing and story telling.[20]

A musical pluralism prevails in China now, with performances of many musical types and regional genres. Through television, much of this music reaches larger audiences than ever before. State patronage has been extended to protect many dying forms. Chen Yun used his growing political power after the Cultural Revolution to promote his favored Suzhou ballads.[21] Archaeologists have recovered ancient instruments, and "feudal" sounds are being reconstructed as they never could have been during the Cultural Revolution. The army's Vanguard Song and Dance Ensemble, leader of the movement to modernize traditional instruments before the Cultural Revolution, is once more experimenting prominently with new and arresting combinations of sounds.[22]

Yet solo instrumental music, ballads, and even Chinese opera have all become cultural enclaves for middle-aged citizens. Some native forms are being propped up by their use for the tourist industry, but this is unlikely to be a force for maintaining purity of artistic traditions.[23] Minister of Culture Wang Meng worries about building a new audience for opera, which some argue should be videotaped for preservation before it dies out.[24] Although Jiang Qing's model operas are not often performed, the "Budding Hundred Flowers" opera troupe of Zhejiang has combined violin, bass, and electric organ with traditional Chinese instruments in order to win over new audiences for the old *yue* opera.[25] The disarray of musical tradition is obvious in other respects as well, as with the addition of instruments such as the cello and accordion to ensembles billed as performing "traditional" music.

Cultural Protectionism

The false and sentimental notion that music is an international language is the cultural counterpart of the doctrine of free trade; both theories appear most reasonable from the standpoint of nations strong enough to sell either their culture or their commodities in foreign markets. As economic protectionists find supporters among those damaged by foreign competition, so cultural nationalists can appeal for patriotic support against imported art.

Westerners often trivialize questions of cultural nationalism. We have a place for exotic native dances, which add color to tourists' slides and videotapes, but serious resistance to Western artistic domination is treated as nasty and uncivilized. Excesses of cultural nationalism seem illegitimate because they question the purportedly universal nature of Western culture within the historical context of imperialism.

The political importance of culture has increased in the late twentieth century. Xenophobia did not seriously threaten the old-fashioned empires of previous century. When it got out of hand, force could be applied, as in the Boxer uprising or the anti-imperialist boycotts of the 1920s. But today, sales of consumer goods are more important to the profits of multinational corporations, which depend upon the diffusion of "global" culture to stimulate global demand. Old-fashioned political and economic domination has been replaced by subtler patterns of neocolonialism in which openness to Western culture appears to have commercial significance. The growing business of selling information across national boundaries—news, satellite television broadcasts, motion pictures—is especially threatened by cultural nationalism.

The contradiction between the cultural nationalism demanded by China's revolution and the cosmopolitan tastes of China's urban elite has reproduced a dialectic found in other nations. Musical counter-movements to European art music have grown in other spots along the periphery of world capitalism. The musical history of Argentina has been punctuated by tension between its participation in such glories of European music as the operas staged at the *Teatro Colon*, and reactions against musical cosmopolitans, who have repeatedly been criticized for subjugating their nation to foreign interests.[26] The "patriarch of Argentine national music," Alberto Williams, returned from his European studies determined to develop Argentine culture by identifying with *criollo* heritage. He composed works with names such as "El rancho abandonado" and "Aires de la Pampa."

> I wanted to drench myself with the music of my land, in order not to be a foreigner in my own country. I wanted to write Argentine music. Not mere transcriptions, but art music with feeling, color, and native essence. And for that reason I went to the ranches of the province of Buenos Aires, to learn the songs and dances of the *gauchos*.[27]

Later, the regime of Juan Peron purged cultural cosmopolitans such as Borges and urged middle-class families to instruct their children in the *gaucho*'s guitar rather than the piano of Europe.

A better-known example is found in nineteenth-century Russia. Mili Balakirev, railway official and leader of the nationalist "Mighty Five" composers, opposed the Westernized conservatory style of Anton Rubinstein and Tchaikovsky. Balakirev and his nationalistic followers did not reject all that the music of Germany and France had to offer, "but he judged the sonata-form tradition to be an excrescence upon it, a damnable temptation to insincere note-spinning." Taking folk song and dance as his inspiration, Balakirev thought that "the very concept of a sonata-development involved the distortion and decomposition of themes for the sake of pattern-making."[28]

A classic problem in China's relations with the West has been how to import Western technical knowledge without eroding Chinese values in the process. The nationalistic approach of the Cultural Revolution was to detach European instruments and their techniques from the repertory which had given these instruments their shape. This approach was perhaps effective in the short run, but it simply led to a greater leap into foreign culture when political tides turned again to a more open posture toward the West.

The Plucky Chinese as International Underdogs

Asia's role in the production of European music is now quite substantial. The equipment used—whether pianos or compact disk players—is likely to come from Asia. Japanese, Korean, and Chinese musicians are also more frequently enjoying careers that are genuinely international. China's struggle for international recognition of musical successes must work against a subtle but pervasive racism. This sometimes take simple forms, such as the inability to distinguish Asian musicians, who are alleged to look alike and have names that are difficult for Westerners to remember. Some stereo enthusiasts—those who spend tens of thousands of dollars in search of the perfect tweeter—believe that Japanese-made equipment "can't reproduce American music accurately because Japanese audio engineers design with Japanese music in mind." [29] Even among other Asians there is often a feeling that Europeans can best play the great nineteenth-century classics. According to a Japanese banker living in Jakarta,

> An Indonesian complained to me that when the NHK Philharmonic came to Indonesia and played Beethoven—yes, it did give the impression that standards are high in Japan. But he told me that when Indonesians want to hear Beethoven, they will invite an orchestra from the Netherlands. "If the NHK Philharmonic visits, naturally it would play Japanese, Korean, or Chinese music, we think," he said, "but you Japanese are white at heart." [30]

Americans were once in China's position, at the periphery of European civilization and recipients of its musical condescension. Tocqueville, Stendahl, and others commented with horrified fascination on our lack of music. When the first American piano prodigy went to Paris for instruction in 1842, the thirteen-year-old Louis Moreau

Gottschalk was denied entry into the conservatory with a contemptuous snort toward his nation—"nothing but a land of steam engines." Many Europeans found it difficult to accept the success of American-built pianos at the 1867 Paris Exposition.[31] More recently, Van Cliburn's first prize in the 1958 Tchaikovsky Competition enabled American musicians to be taken seriously by European audiences and impresarios, and also by themselves, with the effect of a musical sputnik in reverse.[32]

Many musicians disparage the international competition circuit, where the goal often seems to be to play more notes faster than anyone else. Jorge Bolet, head of the piano department at the Curtis Institute, describes competition pianists with disdain: "They never miss a note, never take a chance, and never have ideas of their own. Go to one of the big international competitions—everybody plays alike."[33] Yet this often shallow system remains important to China. Competitions, for all their shortcomings, remain the only way that a non-Western musician can gain respect, by beating Westerners at their own musical games. Even Bolet, who was born in Cuba, might find this to be true today. China's cosmopolitans have persuaded the politicians that music's great value for China is not spiritual but practical: China's world standing will rise as young musicians enter and win international music competitions.

Chinese have been especially embarrassed by their backwardness in musical technique and technology. Many Chinese were distressed in the 1950s that visiting Soviet orchestras performed Chinese music better than the Central or Shanghai Philharmonics, and a generation later they are unhappy that the technically best recordings of Chinese symphonic music are made in Japan.[34] That industrializing China cannot quickly match the technical standards of the Soviet Union or Japan should not be a surprise. Musical standards in Europe at the turn of the nineteenth century were poor, for many of the same reasons that they are problematic in China today.[35] Chinese pride has been boosted by the fact that the Central Philharmonic's cycle of Beethoven symphonies have been recorded by a *French* company, Editions Printemps Musical.[36] The Central Philharmonic's successful 1987 tour of the United States also enhanced musical self-esteem, as Americans began to realize that this Chinese orchestra could offer performances of Western classics that were not merely competent, but, at their best, exciting and intriguing.[37]

Two Museums of Music

In the West the great tradition of European classical music seems to have run its course. There are many exciting performers of music written one or ten generations ago, but there is little audience for new compositions. Concert halls resemble museums, in which pieces by dead composers are brought out for exhibition. It is a joke that contemporary pieces must be placed second on the program by any soloist or ensemble: when new music opens a concert, many in the audience will come in late, but if it is the final selection, they will depart early. Even our composers are beginning to give up: minimalist John Adams, composer of the opera *Nixon in China,* confesses that

> All of my music has this feeling of *deja vu.* The issue of vanguardism, the whole avant-garde, has burned itself out. As we approach the end of the century, there is an exhaustion of this intense need to run to the barricades, to forge ahead to the future.[38]

Concert life on capitalism's periphery has different problems. China's musical cosmopolitans are still full of confidence in the progress of their art, which they regard as a force against feudalism. But there is considerable skepticism about modernism in European music, leaving the music of high romanticism in a supreme position. The warhorses of European musical culture are preferred for the same reasons that they are favored in provincial cities in North America: they are famous, therefore they must be good. This audience bias has makes it difficult for Chinese composers to establish a following, especially when they must deal with politically charged issues such as instrumentation or the use of a pentatonic scale.

It is as if there are two museums of music, each changing its exhibitions but moving in different directions.[39] The West's perception of its own great tradition is under constant renovation, as new music is raised to "classic" status, as once-popular composers are played less frequently, or as forgotten works and styles of interpretation are rediscovered. China's protracted isolation and the different social meaning that these classics assume in Asia mean that the gap between the two museums is increasing. Recent Western fascination with antique instruments and eighteenth-century performance practices, or with the recovery of bel canto singing technique, are countered by Chinese restorations of the music culture of the 1940s and 1950s. Without cultural isolation, Liu Shikun's hyperromantic piano style might have been ground away by the weight of recordings, visiting performers, and modern texts. China's musical museum is showing new interest in Schoenberg; is China about to begin a serialist period, a generation after its heyday in West?[40]

China has yet to approach the postmodern musical consciousness now popular in the West, where much energy is expended in stripping away the reforms of the nineteenth century to discover how the music of Mozart or Bach may once have sounded. A Chinese violin teacher, true to Max Weber's thesis that the middle class in an industrializing society "modernizes" its music, lectured a student during a visit to East Germany.

> I feel German students not only persist in using but study in depth the bowing and fingering used in the days of Bach, Beethoven and Mozart. I agree with you and admire this, but I hope my students will be able to adjust their bowing to meet the needs of modern audiences and the requirements of the acoustics in grand music halls. I hope they will not unconditionally use the original style of bowing.

The Chinese violinist reported somewhat sadly: "The student nodded when I said this but I did not know whether he accepted my suggestion or not."[41]

In China, a robust and forward-looking movement to improve traditional musical instruments continues to endanger the nation's rich musical tradition; European musicologists shocked a delegation of Chinese musicians in 1979 by attacking them for presenting as "traditional" music that had in fact been highly Westernized.[42] Politics explains the weakness of the curatorial spirit among China's musicians. Europe's *ancien régime* is sufficiently distant that no one is made nervous by reconstructing its music, while China's revolution is still too close or too incomplete to allow much slackening of the drive toward musical modernization. Whatever musical modernization may mean, it rejects the culture of the past.

A Resurgent Urban Middle Class

The music we superficially share, when it travels to China, is no longer ours. Because it is embedded within a system of power, our music must assume different functions in China, where it has now created its own history of sentiments, loyalties, and resentments. Some Westerners have hoped what some Chinese politicians have feared: that lovers of Mozart would form a fifth column which could intensify the West's influence within the heart of the People's Republic. But this misses the truth that music's meaning exists only within the culture where it is performed and heard. Tens of thousands of Japanese sing Beethoven's setting from the Ninth Symphony of Schiller's *Ode to Joy* in enormous festivals each New Year.[43] But this continued annual exercise will not make them any less Japanese, just as the 1970s Western enthusiasm for the music of Ravi Shankar did not somehow make us more Indian.[44]

Although urban intellectuals were cowed by the Cultural Revolution, Deng Xiaoping's reform program has restored their honor and their political self-confidence. An ironic measure of their power is that their separate social identity is publicly denied as post-Maoist theorists insist that they have become a part of the working class, although this honorific formulation is not apt to persuade many factory workers. Other components of the reconstituted urban middle class include the entrepreneurial households of the Deng reforms, a remnant of the old bourgeoisie, and the stolid civil servants of the post-Mao bureaucracy.

The postrevolutionary high point of the urban intelligentsia was the autumn of 1986, before Hu Yaobang was forced to resign as general secretary of the Communist Party in January 1987, following a month of student demonstrations. Fang Lizhi, an astrophysicist and vice-president of the Chinese University of Science and Technology, was a spokesman for intellectuals until he was dismissed from his post (and from the Party) after the demonstrations. Fang argued that Marx's theory of class was only applicable to the nineteenth century, and that in the modern era, intellectuals "who own and create information and knowledge, are the most dynamic component of the productive forces, this is what determines their social status." With this, Fang said what many intellectuals have long thought, that they are the leading class in China, and that they have special responsibilities to lead the benighted masses. When asked what characteristics the advanced class should have, Fang responded that

> Generally speaking, people, who have internalized the elements of civilization and possess knowledge, have hearts which are relatively noble,

their mode of thought is invariably scientific and they therefore have a high sense of social responsibility or even self-sacrifice. They also have grievances and may be discontent. Their point of departure is not their personal interest, but social progress.[45]

Around the same time appeared a plea for legislation to protect the position of intellectuals, arguing that they are the most dynamic, least conservative, and most courageous part of the working class, in an era when the number of manual laborers is declining.

Intellectuals have inherited the cultural legacy of mankind, and keep on searching for new ideas for scientific and cultural development. They have volunteered to quietly dedicate their lives to China's moderniza- tion. Undoubtedly, intellectuals are the most revolutionary component, the backbone and mainstay of China's working class.[46]

The new urban middle class uses mastery of European music (part of the "cultural legacy of mankind") in a quest for respectability that looks downright bourgeois. Three examples illustrate the continuing importance of European music to these intellectuals.

Li Zhengtian, a painter on the faculty of the Guangzhou Fine Arts Academy, became famous as one of the three authors of the "Li Yizhe" political manifesto of 1974.[47] Released from jail, Li abandoned polit- ical activism at the behest of his new wife, the daughter of an officer in the People's Liberation Army. The officer's wedding gift was a piano, much welcomed by Li, whose own passion for music was in- stilled by piano lessons from his mother, herself a labor activist and member of the Communist Party. Above this piano hangs Li's own abstract painting in homage to the music of Chopin.[48]

Wang Meng, a writer who was purged as a rightist in 1957 but who has now become China's minister of culture, describes in one of his stories an intellectual blessed with new housing and consumer goods, including a Japanese Sharp stereo, on which he listens to the "theme song of the Oscar-winning *Love Story*, . . . the low notes of the cello warm and solemn." The intellectual, Song, urges Beethoven's Ninth Symphony on his son, who would rather listen to "black spirituals." Once his wife "put on some music, Schubert's *Trout*. In a fit of alien- ation from its beauty, Song thought of fish sizzling in the pan."[49]

The novelist Zhang Xiangliang describes in *Mimosa* the release from a Qinghai prison camp of a rightist from a capitalist family. His stand- ing as a "bourgeois intellectual" is indicated by a stream of references to foreign literature (Goethe, Byron, Anderson, Pushkin, Whitman, and Marx), but also to Western music, which keeps resounding in his mind: he hears Verdi's Requiem, Brahms' Lullaby, and even Louis Armstrong. At the novel's climax, as the hero hovers between suicide and reaching for *Capital,* he finds musical solace in terms that might bring a blush to Romain Rolland.

> The thick mist lifted, a ray of sunshine filtered through the treetops like a flashing golden sword. The soft notes of a piano could be heard. Fate knocking at the gate! It sounded uneasy yet strangely resolute. Presently a French horn trumpeted a charge. Powerful, stirring music engulfed me like the waves of a sunlit sea. It seemed to be expressing Beethoven's determination to grapple with fate and not let it subdue him.[50]

And one can of course look at the concert-going behavior of urban Chinese to make the same point. In June and July 1986, Luciano Pavarotti filled the ten thousand seats of the Great Hall of the People eight times, including an initial concert followed by seven performances of *La Bohème* with the Opera Theatre of Genoa. Pavarotti is the most popular foreign singer in China ever, and was received by Party chief Hu Yaobang.[51]

The cosmopolitans at last have a proper concert hall in Beijing, the first constructed since Liberation.[52] The hall occupies choice real estate in the block across from Zhongnanhai. Composer and Central Committee member Wu Zuqiang is rumored to be responsible for the success of this project. As music-lovers climb the stairway to the lobby of the Beijing Concert Hall, they pass oil portraits of Xian Xinghai and Nie Er. The first faces honored are thus Chinese, but in the lobby at the top are arrayed paintings of Beethoven, Mozart, Haydn, Bach, Tchaikovsky, Brahms, and Debussy. The sense of being in a shrine is braced by the news that Chuck Berry's "Roll Over Beethoven" has been banned in China, cut from a radio show of American popular music because of disrespect for the composer.[53] Yet, as Chinese cosmopolitans arrived for concerts in September 1987, before they entered the new hall they could hear a reminder of musical populism wafting on the late summer air, as the Beijing clock chimes played "The East Is Red."[54]

The cosmopolitans, from their position of restored influence, are reevaluating earlier populist drives to transform China's music. *The Yellow Earth* is a film which describes a soldier sent to a village around

Yan'an to gather folk songs. The movie shows the harshness of peasant life, including its suspicion toward outsiders, superstition, ignorance, and fatalism, and is a far cry from Maoist celebrations of the revolutionary spirit of northern Shaanxi peasantry.[55]

In a similar vein, Wang Meng wrote a story about an old Eighth Route Army cultural instructor.

> In 1949, singing revolutionary songs they had liberated China. . . .
> And each time their armed forces entered a city, they danced the folk
> dances of Yan'an and beat waist-drums. Dancing with red silk they had
> liberated the whole mainland. They thought they were ushering in a
> golden age of justice, morality and prosperity.

The sadness of the old revolutionary is heightened by his dismay at the popularity of Hong Kong popular music: "After thirty years of education, of singing 'Socialism Is Good' and other revolutionary songs, the whole country was being swept away by 'the loneliness of love'!"[56]

The Cultural Gap

Just as Beethoven and Wagner have symbolic meaning in the West even for those who do not know their music, so in China does Western music spread from the cosmopolitans in ever-weakening concentric circles, as other groups discover that status may be won through foreign music. Today these circles extend far indeed; the current Chinese press makes much of peasants buying pianos and forming their own brass bands.

The 1986 movie, *The Fascinating Village Band,* based on an incident in Liaoning's Jinxian county, tells the story of farmers who have earned enough money to have some disposable income for music. But their efforts to start a band encounter obstacles from city snobs and fellow villagers who think that peasants have no business playing Western music. In the end, it is a triumph of tubas and saxophones, of modern-thinking peasants wearing Western suits and neckties. The village in Jinxian is remembered by the film's director as extremely poor a decade ago, when even more prosperous farmers could only play *suona* or other traditional Chinese instruments, and did not have the necessary cultural background to desire Western instruments.[57] Several senior Party leaders attended the movie's premiere, indicating their support for this example of wholesome socialist culture, which they pressed hard to receive the 1986 "Golden Rooster" (China's Oscar) as the best film of the year.[58] Other articles continued the theme, attributing a shortage of pianos and other Western instruments to peasant musical shopping sprees, as modern Western instruments displace the *erhu* and dulcimer under the economic reforms.[59]

It is indeed unprecedented for peasants to show so much active interest in European music, but these stories are limited to the most prosperous areas. The reality of cultural life for most peasants is much starker. Three hundred of China's two thousand counties had no libraries in 1985. Forty percent had no regular television service. Only seventeen percent of the villages received the provincial daily newspaper on its day of publication. "Cultural and information facilities in rural areas have gone unimproved during the implementation of the present reforms."[60]

The cultural gap between urban cosmopolitans and China's peasant majority remains enormous. What has changed is the political symbolism centered around this gap. Peasants appear to honor the urban middle class when they form brass bands, much as the children of city people were once made to honor the peasantry with their labor as they were sent down to the villages during the Cultural Revolution. Western high culture has been reinstated as a emblem of modernity, much as earlier cosmopolitans regarded it as a revolutionary alternative to China's feudal high culture.

China's cultural gap is also a class gap, which poses limits to the expansion of European music. Concerts and even recordings remain concentrated in a few major cities, echoing the situation regarding access to Western painting, dance, or literature. In 1978, when a long-awaited series of thirty-five classics from Chinese and world literature was published, one quarter of the books were allocated for the capital.[61] But even within the cities, and with rising incomes, there is often too little leisure time to permit artistic pastimes. Urban workers have one free day per week, which is so filled with chores that "commonly there is only half a day left for walking in parks, going to movies, window shopping, or simply socializing with friends."[62] And of course the cost of instruments remains high; a piano requires over a year's wages by an urban worker, equivalent to conditions in Europe in the middle of the nineteenth century.

In Europe, one of the successes of the first Viennese school was its ability to appeal to several levels of musical taste at once, as its composers included in their symphonies and concertos an alternation of simple dance rhythms, songful melodies, and sonata technique that permitted counterpoint and other sophisticated devices.[63] One wonders if this can be repeated in China, where this music, by reason of its foreign origin, seems homogeneous and distant from China's own musical tradition. Rather than providing a musical source of social unity, the urban middle class seems to condescend to others who like this music, but puffs up its own self-pride when they find it difficult.

It is important to recognize that while art is still more readily available for citizens with higher incomes than for the poor, one of the great accomplishments of the Communist government lies in raising cultural standards throughout the population. China's lack of a truly wealthy class makes it difficult to imagine some of the more outrageously luxurious manifestations of European music, such as the aluminum grand piano of the dirigible *Hindenburg*, especially designed for entertainment of airship passengers.[64] Despite the grumblings of foreign visitors and Chinese professionals about the poor quality of Chinese-made musical instruments, the government seems determined to keep costs low, in order to enable ordinary people to afford music. Yet middle-class Chinese are eager to jettison public discussion of the class aspect of culture, however important class distinctions may be to the sociology of music in contemporary China.[65]

Cosmopolitans and Moral Music

Many Westerners assume that when China's artists and intellectuals enjoy our art, they must also share the political values which this art represents in the West. Such scholars presume that there is a restive bloc of Chinese liberals who are eager to reform China's culture under the slogan of "art for art's sake." While musicians and other artists have certainly stood against specific policies of the Chinese government (for example, through participation in the public repudiation of the Cultural Revolution), the great majority remain deeply politicized and profoundly oriented toward state service in their values and behavior. One must distinguish between artists criticizing the state from a position of moral autonomy (the tradition of Qu Yuan), and a purported necessary linkage between art and political liberalism.

The imprint of Confucian theories that music influences morality is still strongly felt.[66] It was obvious enough in Maoist uses of music, but even the restored cosmopolitans are a long way from art for art's sake. New books on music appreciation reveal a very traditional Chinese insistence that good music creates good morals. Symphonies are said to be better than popular music, warranting state support because symphonies will make their listeners into better people. The new music appreciation recommends sticking to the West's great tradition of program music, which is easier to evaluate in moral terms. This attitude resembles that of the cultural revolutionaries, who denounced abstract sonatas and symphonies as bourgeois.[67] The ever-shifting dialectic between populists and cosmopolitans entered a new stage in the 1980s, when both groups were alarmed by the spread of "vulgar" popular music from Hong Kong and Taiwan. The populists regard these trivial songs of love as debased, while the cosmopolitans agree that inelegant popular songs are inferior to the ennobling music of nineteenth-century European symphonies.

The linkage of music and statecraft not only harmonizes with traditional Chinese notions of art as a source of power, but it also reflects the need of Third World nations to strengthen their own state power in order to deal effectively with imperialism. Europe's industrialization strengthened the bourgeoisie, which was often trying to escape state intervention. The Chinese state has been involved in industrialization from the outset, partly because of the weakness of China's own bourgeoisie, but also because of the greater pressures of international competition from strong, aggressive nations in Japan and the West. The consequences of this historical difference are constantly with us, but are often ignored as we continue to search for the missing Chinese liberals. Recall the words of the Cultural Revolution's musical martyr, Zhang Zhixin: "Use your violin as a gun!" This is no liberal; could Leonard Bernstein understand what she was talking about?

The West's own tradition of moral music is now so attenuated that we find it most prominently on the right, with fundamentalist preachers who play rock records backwards, hoping to discover words in praise of Satan, or with Allan Bloom, who maintains that "Rock music provides premature ecstasy."[68]

China's cosmopolitans wield the cudgel of music against two adversaries in two different ways: harshly, flailing violently against the remnants of feudal culture, and more gently, tapping politely at foreigners who have not yet recognized China's talents. Li Delun of the Central Philharmonic is one Chinese musician who prospered before, during, and after the Cultural Revolution. He now believes that "people need this product of the West to liberate their cultural thinking from 2,000 years of feudalism. Li has taken spreading classical music in China as his mission."[69] Beethoven's music, says Li, is of great use in opposing feudal thought, struggling for human rights, and liberating the individual.[70]

Joseph Levenson wrote his study of cosmopolitanism in Chinese culture during the high tide of Maoism, causing him to give his study the flavor of a funeral oration for a dead cause. The cosmopolitans are now back from the grave; their turbulent past gives every reason to anticipate that they will endure further shocks; Chinese culture simply has too much weight to be overturned. Their vigorous determination, however, gives some hope that something new and interesting will emerge from confidently juxtaposing European and Chinese musics.

One of China's great dynasties was the Tang, between 618 and 907, a period in which China was deeply influenced by extensive contact with foreign cultures. Li Delun might not appreciate quoting a poem from that feudal dynasty which prefigures our century's conflicts and their likely outcome.

> Made of silk strings and the wood of *wutong,*
> The *qin* pours forth the sound of antiquity.
> Bland and insipid? The sound of antiquity
> Appeals not to the modern ear.
> Its jade studs lack not lustre though long disused,
> On its red strings dust and dirt have gathered.
> For a long time it has been abandoned
> But its clear sound lingers in the air.
> For you I wouldn't refuse to play, 'tis true,
> But who else amongst us would care to listen!
> What have made it so, degraded it so?
> The barbaric oboe and reed flute from the West.[71]

Notes

Abbreviations

AFP   = *Agence France Presse*
FBIS   = *Foreign Broadcast Information Service*
JPRS   = *Joint Publications Research Service*
NCNA   = *New China News Agency*
SCMP   = *Survey of China Mainland Press*
SPRCP = *Survey of People's Republic of China Press*

1 Cosmopolitan Culture at Capitalism's Periphery

1. Beyond a distinctive set of instruments, Western music is characterized by functional harmony, performance by groups of musicians, planning (rehearsal), the concept of radical innovation, the use of notation as a control devide, an emphasis on virtuosity, and the emergence of music as an independent cultural domain (not bound to religion and other forms of ceremony). Bruno Nettl, *The Western Impact on World Music: Change, Adaptation, and Survival* (New York: Schirmer Books, 1985), 5.

2. Frank Harrison, ed., *Time, Place and Music: An Anthology of Ethnomusicological Observation c. 1550 to c. 1800* (Amsterdam: Frits Knuf, 1973), 168.

3. A picture of these Chinese musicians and their Portuguese bandmaster is in Jonathan Spence, *To Change China: Western Advisers in China 1620–1960* (Boston: Little, Brown, 1969), 123.

4. In the 1860s, German military advisors hired to help reform the army introduced drilling to song. Isabel K. F. Wong, "*Geming Gequ:* Songs for the Education of the Masses," in Bonnie S. McDougall, ed., *Popular Chinese Literature and Performing Arts in the People's Republic of China 1949–1979* (Berkeley: University of California Press, 1984), 114–15.

215

5. Jonathan D. Spence, *The Memory Palace of Matteo Ricci* (New York: Viking Penguin, 1984), 194–95, 197–200. Europeans recognized the curiosity of the mechanics of the keyboard instruments: Elizabeth I of England sent an organ and its maker to the Sultan of Turkey in 1598. See Rana Kabbani, *Europe's Myths of Orient* (Bloomington: Indiana University Press, 1986), 17–18.

6. Jean Baptiste Du Halde, *A Description of the Empire of China and Chinese-Tartary, together with the Kingdoms of Korea, and Tibet: from the French of P. J. B. Du Halde, Jesuit* trans. R. Brookes, 2 vols., London, 1738, 1741. Extract in Frank Harrison, ed., *Time, Place and Music,* 163.

7. Hong studied in Guangzhou with a Missouri Baptist, I. J. Roberts. See Wong, *"Geming Gequ:* Songs for the Education of the Masses," 113–14.

8. On the expatriate community, see Albert Feuerwerker, "The Foreign Presence in China," in John K. Fairbank, ed., *The Cambridge History of China,* vol. 12, part I (Cambridge: Cambridge University Press, 1983), 128–207. See also V. G. Kiernan, *The Lords of Humankind: European Attitudes to the Outside World in the Imperial Age* (London: Weidenfeld & Nicolson, 1969), 146–72.

9. "107-Year-Old Philharmonic Society," *Beijing Review* 29 (22 September 1986): 30.

10. W. Somerset Maugham, *On A Chinese Screen* (New York: George H. Doran Company, 1922), 14–16.

11. Alexander Tcherepnin, "Music in Modern China," *The Musical Quarterly* 21, (October 1935): 395.

12. Ma Ke, *Xian Xinghai Zhuan* [Biography of Xian Xinghai] (Beijing: Renmin Wenxue Chubanshe, 1980), 118.

13. Mao Yu-run, professor of composition, Shanghai Conservatory of Music, interview with author, Eugene, Ore., 27 October 1987.

14. S. Frederick Starr, *Red and Hot: the Fate of Jazz in the Soviet Union 1917–1980* (New York: Oxford University Press, 1983), 226–27.

15. Tcherepnin (as he spelled it after moving to the United States in 1949), was born in Russia in 1899, the son of a composer. Since his death in 1977 he is remembered as a skilled but minor neoclassical composer. A recent Schwann catalog shows recordings of ten of his compositions. See Zhang Jiren, "Qie'erpin yu Zhongguo di yinyue" [Tcherepnin and Chinese Music], *Ming Bao Yuekan* [Bright News Monthly] 165 (September 1979): 17–23; Tcherepnine, "Music in Modern China," 391–400; "Western Composer Nourished by Chinese Music," *Beijing Review* 28 (4 March 1985): 35.

16. Guo Zhiqu, *Zhongguo xiandai minzu yuepai di xianquje Jiang Wenye* [Jiang Wenye, Pioneer of the School of Chinese Contemporary National Music], (Taiwan), 22.

17. Qian Renkang, "Brief Introduction to The Composer," *Selection of*

Vocal Music of He Luting, Baili Record Company Cassette NB-3, 1979; Zhang, "Tcherepnin and Chinese Music," 19–23; Tchenepnine, "Music in Modern China," 399.

18. Zhang, "Qie'erpin yu Zhogguo di yinyue," 18–19.

19. Ibid., 19.

20. Artur Rubinstein, *My Many Years* (New York: Alfred A. Knopf, 1980), pp. 372–94.

21. Tcherepnine, "Music in Modern China," 394, 396; A. C. Scott, *Literature and the Arts in Twentieth Century China* (Garden City, N.Y.: Anchor Books, 1963), 131.

22. David Kanzler, *Japanese, Nazis & Jews: The Jewish Refugee Community of Shanghai, 1938–1945* (New York: Yeshiva University Press, 1976), 363–88. See also Renata Berg-Pan, "Shanghai Chronicle: Nazi Refugees in China," in Jarrell C. Jackman and Carla M. Borden, eds., *The Muses Flee Hitler: Cultural Transfer and Adaptation 1930–1945* (Washington: Smithsonian Institution Press, 1983), 283–89.

23. I am unaware of any Chinese going to Europe to learn its music before the early twentieth century, and do not know what to make of the indignant report of Franz Schubert's friend, Moritz Schwind, who wrote of the first performance of Schubert's A Minor Quartet, Op. 29, in 1824: "A Chinese sitting next to me thought it affected and devoid of style. I should just like to see Schubert affected! A single hearing, what can that mean to the likes of us let alone to such a gobbler-up of notes?" Quoted in George R. Marek, *Schubert* (New York: Viking, 1985), 153–54.

24. Mayching Margaret Kao, "China's Response to the West in Art: 1898–1937" (Ph.D. diss., Stanford University, 1972), 71–72.

25. William P. Malm, "The Modern Music of Meiji Japan," in Donald H. Shively, ed., *Tradition and Modernization in Japanese Culture* (Princeton: Princeton University Press, 1971), 260.

26. Arthur Loesser, *Men, Women and Pianos: A Social History* (New York: Simon and Schuster, 1954), 597.

27. Zhongguo Yishu Yanjiuyuan Yinyue Yanjiusuo, ed., *Nie Er* (Beijing: Renmin Yinyue Chubanshe, 1982), 45.

28. Shi Junliang, "Zhonggu yinyue sanshi nian (xia)" [Thirty Years of Chinese Music (Part II)] *Guanchajia* [Observer] 22 (August 1979): 54.

29. Guo Zhiqu, "Zhongguo xiandai minzu yuepai di xianquje Jiang Wenye" [Jiang Wenye Pioneer of the School of Chinese Contemporary National Music], (Taiwan), n.d., 17–27. The tone of this article is bizarre, as the author presents Jiang as a composer who supported Chinese nationalism, despite his enthusiastic participation in Japan's imperial culture. Under the name Bunya Koh, Jiang's *Five Sketches,* op. 4, *Three Dances,* op. 7, and *Bagatelles,* op. 8, were published in the "Collection Alexandre Tcherepnine" (Tokyo: 1936).

30. It is startling that Jiang was not punished for collaboration. Instead, after editing a hymnal for the Catholic church, he was appointed professor of composition at the new Central Conservatory after 1949. Less surprisingly, he was declared a rightist in 1957, to be rehabilitated only in 1976.

31. Max Weber, *The Rational and Social Foundations of Music* (Carbondale: Southern Illinois University Press, 1958).

32. Edwin M. Good, *Giraffes, Black Dragons, and Other Pianos: A Technological History from Cristofori to the Modern Concert Grand* (Stanford: Stanford University Press, 1982), 27–35. The piano strikes the strings with a hammer, unlike the harpsichord, which plucks its strings with a quill or plectrum.

33. Loesser, *Men, Women and Pianos*, 39–41.

34. Weber, *The Rational and Social Foundations of Music*, 122–123, 124.

35. On the transition from court to bourgeois patronage, see Henry Raynor, *A Social History of Music from the Middle Ages to Beethoven* (New York: Schocken Books, 1972), 290–355.

36. Jacques Attali, *Noise, The Political Economy of Music* (Minneapolis: University of Minnesota Press, 1985), 47.

37. Arnold Hauser, *The Social History of Art*, vol. 3 (New York: Vintage Books, 1962), 81.

38. William Weber, *Music and the Middle Class: The Social Structure of Concert Life in London, Paris and Vienna* (London: Croom Helm, 1975), 6.

39. Cyril Ehrlich, *The Piano: A History* (London: Dent, 1976), 16.

40. Hauser, *The Social History of Art*, vol. 3, 81–82.

41. Marek, *Schubert*, 77–78, 91–95, 182.

42. Loesser, *Men, Women and Pianos*, 164.

43. Hauser, *The Social History of Art*, vol. 3, 80–82.

44. Good, *Giraffes*, 142.

45. Anita T. Sullivan, *The Seventh Dragon: The Riddle of Equal Temperament* (Lake Oswego, Ore.: Metamorphous Press, 1985); Joseph Needham, *Science and Civilization in China*, vol. 4: Physics and Physical Technology, part I: Physics (Cambridge: Cambridge University Press, 1962), 214.

46. David Murray, "The Romantic Piano: Chopin to Ravel," in Dominic Gill, ed., *The Book of the Piano* (Ithaca: Cornell University Press, 1981), 84.

47. David Cairns, ed., *The Memoirs of Hector Berlioz* (New York: W.W. Norton, 1975), 283.

48. See Robert Donington, *The Interpretation of Early Music* (London: Faber & Faber, 1963).

49. Angus Heriot, *The Castrati in Opera* (London: Secker & Warburg, 1956).

50. Loesser, *Men, Women and Pianos*, 120.

51. Ibid., 131.

52. See Eva Rieger, " 'Dolce semplice'? On the Changing Role of Women in Music," in Gisela Ecker, ed., *Feminist Aesthetics* (London: The Women's Press, 1985), 135–49.

53. Stendahl, *Life of Rossini* (London: Calder & Boyars, 1970), 344–45.

54. Loesser, *Men, Women, and Pianos*, 386, 429.

55. Weber, *Music and the Middle Class*, 17, 46, 53.

56. Cyril Ehrlich, *The Music Profession in Britain since the Eighteenth Century: A Social History* (Oxford: Oxford University Press, 1985), 50–75.

57. William Weber, *Music and the Middle Class*, 93.

58. Ehrlich, *The Music Profession in Britain since the Eighteenth Century*, 67.

59. William Weber, *Music and the Middle Class*, 101–8.

60. Walter Wiora, "Of Art Music and Cultural Classes," in Edmond Strainchamps and Maria Rika Manites, eds., *Music and Civilization: Essays in Honor of Paul Henry Lang* (New York: W.W. Norton, 1984), 472–77.

61. Excellent reviews of China's musical traditions may be found in Liang Mingyue, *Music of the Billion: An Introduction to Chinese Musical Culture* (New York: Heinrichshofen Edition, 1985), and in the articles on Chinese music by Shigeo Kishibe, Liang Mingyue, Tsuen-Yuen Lui, Colin P. Mackerras, Rulan Chao Pian, A. C. Scott, Kate Stevens, and Bell Yung in Stanley Sadie, ed., *The New Grove Dictionary of Music and Musicians*, vol. 4 (London: Macmillan, 1980), 245–83.

62. Liang, *Music of the Billion*, 23–24.

63. R. H. van Gulik, *The Lore of the Chinese Lute: An Essay in the Ideology of the Ch'in* (Tokyo: Charles E. Tuttle, 1969), 1–2.

64. Ibid., 132.

65. Wen-Chung Chou, "A Visit to Modern China," *The World of Music*, 20 (1978): 42.

66. See Colin P. Mackerras, *The Rise of the Peking Opera, 1770–1870: Social Aspects of the Theatre in Manchu China* (London: Oxford University Press, 1972); and Colin P. Mackerras, *The Chinese Theatre in Modern Times* (London: Thames & Hudson, 1975).

67. Han Kuo-huang, "Titles and Program Notes in Chinese Musical Repertoires," *The World of Music* 37 (1985): 74–75.

68. van Gulik, *The Lore of the Chinese Lute*, 95.

69. Han Kuo-huang, "Titles and Program Notes in Chinese Musical Repertoires," 70–72.

70. Bell Yung, "*Da Pu:* The Recreative Process for the Music of the Seven-String Zither," in Anne Dhu Shapiro, ed., *Music and Context: Essays for John M. Ward,* (Cambridge, Mass.: Harvard University Department of Music, 1985), 370–84; Liang, *Music of the Billion*, 185–96.

71. Liang, *Music of the Billion*, 13, 21, 174–76.

72. Ibid., 27–28.

73. Alan R. Thrasher, "The Role of Music in Chinese Culture," *The World of Music*, 37 (1985): 3.

74. Thrasher, "The Role of Music in Chinese Culture," 3–17.

75. van Gulik, *The Lore of the Chinese Lute*, 44, 61–62. Van Gulik unhelpfully translates *qin* as "lute," arguing that the latter instrument had a similar connotation in European culture.

76. Yung, *"Da Pu,"* 370–71.

77. The legendary *qin* player Yu Boya (of 8th–5th century B.C.) befriended Ziqi, "the only person who could understand his music. When the latter died, Bo ya smashed his zither, and never touched the strings again, because no one else in the world could understand his playing." Yung, *"Da Pu,"* 381.

78. Kenneth J. DeWoskin, *A Song for One or Two: Music and the Concept of Art in Early China* (Ann Arbor: University of Michigan Center for Chinese Studies, 1982), 161.

79. *The New Grove Dictionary of Music and Musicians*, s.v. "China: I. General," Liang, *Music of the Billion*, 63, 82–84.

80. Liang, *Music of the Billion*, 31.

81. "China: I. General," 247; Bliss Wiant, *The Music of China* (Hong Kong: Chung Chi College, 1965), 38–39.

82. Tran Van Khe, "Chinese Music and Musical Traditions of Eastern Asia," *The World of Music* 37 (1985): 85.

83. van Gulik, *The Lore of the Chinese Lute*, 27.

84. DeWoskin, *A Song for One or Two*, 93, quoting the Han "Book of Music." DeWoskin (116) also retells

> the story of Duke Ling of Wei and his visit to Duke Ping of Qin. The two dukes forced their music masters to play *qin* tunes that were composed under the influence of morally reproachable lords or that were spiritually too potent for the unperfected virtues of the dukes themselves. As the performance went on, dark cranes appeared, an early warning of the cosmic disorder brought on by the playing. But the dukes persisted. There followed a torrent of rain and then a three-year drought that scorched the earth of Qin.

85. Helmut Wilhelm, "The Bureau of Music of Western Han," in G. L. Ulmen, ed., *Society and History: Essays in Honor of Karl August Wittfogel* (The Hague: Mouton, 1978), 123–35; Liang, *Music of the Billion*, 78–79.

86. Human ears may detect well over thirteen hundred pitch distinctions. Musical tonality is neither natural nor logical, but social, "a decision made against the chaos of pitch." Richard Norton, *Tonality in Western Culture: A Critical and Historical Perspective* (University Park: Pennsylvania State Uni-

versity Press, 1984), 58. Norton describes the role of the piano as an instrument for arbitrarily but effectively setting common tonality:

> The world of pitch is virtually infinite and—with the exception of the octave—irrational. Let us consider it. When we run our fingers over the keys of a finely tuned piano we bring into play one of the most finite systems of pitch data every [*sic*] created. Here are eighty-eight tones, each equidistant from its neighbor on either side, with the entire series precisely tuned to an international standard of frequency measure that is currently more accepted and widespread than the metric system.

87. Kenneth J. DeWoskin, "Philosophers on Music in Early China," *The World of Music* 37 (1985): 40.

88. DeWoskin, *A Song for One or Two*, 46–83.

89. Ibid., 81.

90. See Ibid., 82–83; Needham, *Science and Civilization in China*, vol. 4, 186–92.

91. *The New Grove Dictionary of Music and Musicians*, s.v. "China: IV. Theory," 261.

92. Richard E. Strassberg, *The World of K'ung Shang-jen: A Man of Letters in Early Ch'ing China* (New York: Columbia University Press, 1983), 190–91.

93. Nettl, *The Western Impact on World Music*, 78.

94. " 'Si Zhu'—Music to Live Forever," *Beijing Review* 30 (15 June 1987): 31–33; Thrasher, "The Role of Music in Chinese Culture," 11–17.

95. See Marie-Claire Bergere, "The Chinese Bourgeoise, 1911–37," in John K. Fairbank, ed., *The Cambridge History of China*, vol. 12, part I (Cambridge: Cambridge University Press, 1983), 722–825. A useful review of the academic literature on capitalism in modern Chinese history is William T. Rowe, "Approaches to Modern Chinese Social History," in Oliver Zunz, ed., *Reliving the Past: The Worlds of Social History* (Chapel Hill: University of North Carolina Press, 1985), esp. 270–83.

96. Y. C. Wang, *Chinese Intellectuals and the West 1872–1949* (Chapel Hill: University of North Carolina Press, 1966), vii.

97. Bonnie S. McDougall, "Writers and Performers, Their Works and Their Audiences in the First Three Decades" in McDougall, 273–74.

98. Vera Dunham, *In Stalin's Time: Middleclass Values in Soviet Fiction* (Cambridge: Cambridge University Press, 1976), 16. Dunham is of course discussing the Soviet Union after World War II, but in terms highly suggestive of China after the Cultural Revolution.

99. Weber, *Music and the Middle Class*, 7, 9, 120–25; Donald M. Lowe, *History of Bourgeois Perception* (Chicago: University of Chicago Press, 1982), 24.

100. Loesser, *Men, Women and Pianos,* 430.

101. David Plante, "Profiles (Sir Stephen Runciman)," *The New Yorker,* 3 November 1986, 72. Runciman, the great historian of Byzantium, was recruited to "go thump in the bass."

102. Marie-Claire Bergere, " 'The Other China': Shanghai from 1919 to 1949," in Christopher Howe, ed., *Shanghai: Revolution and Development in an Asian Metropolis* (Cambridge: Cambridge University Press, 1981), 1–34.

103. Ibid., 33.

104. Ibid., pp. 3, 12–13.

105. See Lin Yu-sheng, *The Crisis of Chinese Consciousness: Radical Antitraditionalism in the May Fourth Era* (Madison: University of Wisconsin Press, 1979). But many May Fourth intellectuals also found inspiration in radical strands of Neo-Confucianism rather than European culture. See Theodore Huters, "Blossoms in the Snow: Lu Xun and the Dilemma of Modern Chinese Literature," *Modern China* 10 (January 1984): 49–77.

106. Bonnie S. McDougall, "The Impact of Western Literary Trends," in Merle Goldman, ed., *Modern Chinese Literature in the May Fourth Era* (Cambridge, Mass.: Harvard University Press, 1977), 45.

107. Joseph R. Levenson, *Revolution and Cosmpolitanism: The Western Stage and the Chinese Stages* (Berkeley: University of California Press, 1971). See also the stimulating Levensonian analysis of George F. Fencl, Jr., "Confucian Music and Its Modern Fate: Communist Provincials and Chinese Cosmopolitanism," (Honors thesis, Harvard College, 1984).

108. *The New Grove Dictionary of Music and Musicians,* s.v. "China: I. General."

109. Nettl, *The Western Impact on World Music,* 3.

110. It is certainly true that Western composers have often worked in several nations, such as Handel in England, Boccherini in Spain, Martinů in France, and Bartók in the United States. But these national differences within a shared Western civilization are in no way comparable to the cultural gap between Europe and China.

111. Barbara L. Tischler, *An American Music: The Search for an American Musical Identity* (New York: Oxford University Press, 1986), 68–91. John H. Mueller and Kate Hevner, *Trends in Musical Taste* (Bloomington: Indiana University Humanities Series no. 8, 1942), 63–70, document the marked drop in German music and rise of French pieces in repertories of major U.S. symphony orchestras during World War I.

112. An excellent discussion of political abuses of music is Arnold Perris, *Music as Propaganda: Art to Persuade, Art to Control* (Westport, Ct.: Greenwood Press, 1985).

113. See Theodor W. Adorno, *Introduction to the Sociology of Music* (New

York: Seabury Press, 1976), and *Philosophy of Modern Music* (New York: Seabury Press, 1973).

114. Pierre Bourdieu, *Distinction: A Social Critique of the Judgment of Taste* (Cambridge, Mass.: Harvard University Press, 1984), 7, 11.

115. New York: W.W. Norton (1972), ix.

116. Needham, *Science and Civilization in China,* vol. 4, 214–28.

117. *The New Grove Dictionary of Music and Musicians,* s.v. "Accordion."

118. Although nineteenth-century Britain did. Customs regulations in 1853 referred to imported accordions "commonly called Chinese." Erhlich, *The Music Profession in Britain since the Eighteenth Century,* 101.

119. Hugh Honour, *Chinoiserie: The Vision of Cathay* (New York: E.P. Dutton, 1962), 225.

120. Harrison, *Time, Place and Music,* 189.

121. Arthur Livingston, ed., *Memoirs of Lorenzo da Ponte* (Philadelphia: J.B. Lippincott, 1929), 440–41.

122. The sixteen-year-old Franz Schubert, feeling boisterous, signed a 1813 wind octet as "composed by Franz Schubert, Chapel Master to the Imp. Chinese Court Chapppelll at Nanking, the world-famous resident of His Chinese Majesty." Marek, *Schubert,* 37.

123. Good, *Giraffes,* 110–12.

124. William Ashbrook, *Donizetti* (London: Cassell, 1965), 4, 252, 508; Alan Walker, *Franz Liszt: The Virtuoso Years 1811–1847* (New York: Alfred A. Knopf, 1983), 440–41.

125. Kabbani, *Europe's Myths of Orient,* 138. See the classic work on this subject, Edward W. Said, *Orientalism* (New York: Pantheon, 1978).

126. Judith Oringer, *Passion for the Piano* (Los Angeles: Jeremy P. Tarcher, 1983), 63.

127. "Chopsticks" spread so rapidly that in 1880, Rimsky-Korsakov, Borodin, Cui, Laidov, Liszt, and Scherbachev published a set of variations on its idiotic theme for four-hands piano in St. Petersburg. V. V. Yasttrebtsev, *Reminiscences of Rimsky-Korsakov* (New York: Columbia University Press, 1985), 545.

128. F. W. Gaisberg, *The Music Goes Round* (New York: Macmillan, 1942), 63.

129. Schoenberg insisted on *sprechstimme,* in the style of *Pierrot Lunaire,* but Thalberg wanted something more like *Tranfigured Night.* See Otto Friedrich, *City of Nets: A Portrait of Hollywood in the 1940's* (New York: Harper & Row, 1986), 31–34.

130. Billy Rose and Con Conrad, "Since Ma is Playing Mah Jong" (New York: M. Witmark & Sons, 1924).

131. A. C. Scott, *Mei Lan-fang: The Life and Times of a Peking Actor* (Hong Kong: Hong Kong University Press, 1959), 107.

132. Ehrlich, *The Piano*, 10, 35.

133. Good, *Giraffes*, 102.

134. Loesser, *Men, Women and Pianos*, 593–96; Andrew Clements, "Eccentric Pianos," Gill, *The Book of the Piano*, 249–51.

135. Good, *Giraffes*, 181–82.

136. William Brooks, "The American Piano," in Gill, *The Book of the Piano*, 174.

137. Ibid., 182. Unwanted pianos were again destroyed, for entertainment, in various American "happenings" of the 1960s.

138. Ehrlich, *The Piano*, 133–37. See also Jeanne Allen, "The Industrialization of Culture: The Case of the Player Piano," in Vincent Mosco and Janet Wasko, eds., *The Critical Communications Review*, vol. III: Popular Culture and Media Events (Norwood, N.J.: Ablex Publishing, 1985), 93–109.

139. *The New Grove Dictionary of Musical Instruments*, s.v. "Pianoforte."

140. Ehrlich, *The Piano*, 136–37.

141. F. W. Gaisberg, *The Music Goes Round*, 62–64. See also Pekka Gronow, "The Record Industry Comes to the Orient," *Ethnomusicology*, 25 (May 1981): 251–84.

142. Good, *Giraffes*, 241; Ehrlich, *The Piano*, 67, 197.

143. Ehrlich, *The Piano*, 197, 217, 220.

144. Oringer, *Passion for the Piano*, 81.

145. Electronic keyboard sales in the United States rose from 400,000 in 1983 to over one and a half million in 1985. Piano sales fell by 46,000 in same period. Dave Marsh and Rock & Roll Confidential, "Sampling sounds: Getting the most in the new machine," *In These Times*, 22–28 October 1986, 14.

146. Steven Flax, "Baldwin-United Back from the Dead," *Fortune*, 16 September 1985, 46–53.

147. Judith Oringer, "Imports Dominate Piano Market," *Los Angeles Times*, 3 September 1985.

148. Ehrlich, *The Piano*, 195, 199.

149. "Toward Top Quality," *Korea Trade and Business* 6 (February 1988): 4–6.

150. Li Quanmin, "Wo guo zizhi gangqinxian chenggong" [Our Nation's Success in Making Piano Wire], *Renmin Yinyue* (January 1960): 13.

2 The Ambiguous Legacy of Composer Xian Xinghai

1. My account of Xian's life is based on several sources, including a volume of Xian's own letters and other writings entitled *Wo Xuexi Yinyue de Jingguo* [My Course of Musical Study] (Beijing: Renmin Yinyue Chubanshe, 1980). Other sources include several works by Ma Ke, a fellow composer who wrote much of the music for the opera, *The White-Haired Girl:* Ma Ke, *Xian Xinghai Zhuan* [Life of Xian Xinghai] (Beijing: Renmin Wenxue Chubanshe, 1980); Ma Ke, ed., *Xian Xinghai Huazhuan* [Illustrated Biography of Xian Xinghai] (Beijing: Music Publishing Company, 1960); and Ma Ke, "Hsien Hsing-hai the Composer," *Chinese Literature* 12 (1965): 110–16. A more recent biography (Ma's was written in the 1950s) is Qin Qiming, *Xian Xinghai* (Wuhan: Changjiang Wenyi Chubanshe, 1980). Reminiscences by Guo Moruo and others are collected in *Huanghe Dahechang* [The Yellow River Cantata] (Beijing: Renmin Yinyue Chubanshe, 1978). Chen Yaxuan compiled a useful chronology *(nianpu)* in his 1956 book *Yinyuejia Xian Xinghai* [Musician Xian Xinghai] (reprint. ed., Hong Kong: Eryashe, 1978).

2. All Chinese sources agree that Xian was born in 1905. Yet photographs of both Xian's French identification papers and Soviet tombstone give 1909 as his date of birth. See Ma, *Xian Xinghai Huazhuan,* 17, 61. Xian reported to the Paris Conservatory that he had been born in 1911. Personal communication, Conservatoire Nationale Supérieur de Musique, 2 February 1988.

3. Hiroki Kani, *A General Survey of the Boat People in Hong Kong* (Hong Kong: Chinese University of Hong Kong, 1967), 3.

4. In fact, Xian first attended a free school run by the Lingnan Young Men's Christian Association. He entered Lingnan's secondary school in 1920, graduating in 1924, after which he entered the university. Ma, *Xian Xinghai Zhuan,* 14, 25.

5. This former preacher, identified only as "Professor B," was a pianist and a Hegelian, and holder of a German doctorate. He is mentioned in only one source, for apparent political reasons. Ma, *Xian Xinghai Zhuan,* 21–37.

6. Ma, *Xian Xinghai Huazhuan,* 5. The bass drum in the photo is labeled "Commercial Press Orchestra," suggesting either a borrowed drum or a confusion about ensembles. The brass band is described by Qin, *Xian Xinghai,* 15–16.

7. Qin, *Xian Xinghai,* 14.

8. See "Ming Huajia Situ Qiao Shishi" [Famous Painter Situ Qiao Dies], *Meishu* (March 1958); 46; Shen Congwen, "The Painter Situ Qiao as I Knew Him," *China Reconstructs* 29 (September 1980): 44–45.

9. An excellent introduction to Xiao, Zhao, and other early music reformers is Godwin Yuen, "Stylistic Development in Chinese Revolutionary Song (1919–1948)" (Ph.D. diss., Griffith University, Australia, 1989), ch. 5.

10. Qin, *Xian Xinghai*, 19–25; Xian Yuqing, "Xian Xinghai Zhongxueshi Ersan Shi" [Two or Three Things about Xian Xinghai's Middle School Years], in *Xian Xinghai Ziliao ji* [Compendium of Materials on Xian Xinghai], (n.p., n.d.), 29a; Sun Youlan, "Xian Xinghai zai 'Lingnan Daxue' ji qita" [Xian Xinghai at "Lingnan University" and Other Matters], *Renmin Yinyue* [People's Music] (January 1963), 17–20.

11. A. C. Scott, *Literature and the Arts in Twentieth Century China* (Garden City, N.Y.: Anchor Books, 1963), 130–31.

12. On Tian, see the articles in *Xin Wenxue Shiliao* [New Literary Materials] 4 (1983): 79–91: Chen Mingyuan, "Zong Beihua tan Tian Han" [Zong Baihua Discusses Tian Han]; Zhao Mingbi, "Tian Han tongzhi zai zuoyi wenhua yundong shiqi de ersan shi" [Two or Three Things about Comrade Tian Han in the Period of the Left-Wing Culture Movement]; and Hua Chenzhi, "Tian Han tongzhi yu 'Kangzhan Ribao' " [Comrade Tian Han and "Resistance War Daily"].

13. The Southern Society was closed by the Guomindang in 1930 for its left-wing activities. See *Cihai* [The Sea of Words], 1981, p. 314, and Ma, *Xian Xinghai Huazhuan*, 9; Ma, *Xian Xinghai Zhuan*, 52–54; Qin, 26–27.

14. Maurice Meisner, "Iconoclasm and Cultural Revolution in China and Russia," in Abbot Gleason, Peter Kenez, and Richard Stites, eds., *Bolshevik Culture* (Bloomington: Indiana University Press, 1985), 279–93; Levenson, *Revolution and Cosmopolitanism: The Western State and the Chinese Stages* (Berkeley: University of California Press, 1971). See also George F. Fencl, Jr., "Confucian Music and Its Modern Fate: Communist Provincials and Chinese Cosmopolitanism," (Honors thesis, Harvard College, 1984). On the intellectuals of the May Fourth Movement, see Chow Tse-tsung, *The May Fourth Movement: Intellectual Revolution in Modern China* (Cambridge: Harvard University Press, 1960); and Vera Schwarcz, *The Chinese Enlightenment: Intellectuals and the Legacy of the May Fourth Movement of 1919* (Berkeley: University of California Press, 1986).

15. Ma, *Xian Xinghai Zhuan*, 46.

16. "Pupian de yinyue" [Popularized Music], in Xian, *Wo Xuexi Yinyue de Jingguo*, 92–93.

17. Zhou Fanfu, "Wanjiu Zhongguo yinyue jiaoyu de zhongyao jianyishu [An Important Proposal to Save China's Music Education], *Jing Bao* [The Mirror] 102 (January 1986): 84.

18. Qin, *Xian Xinghai*, 27–30.

19. Wu Zhiqing, *Yinyuejia Xiaozhuan* [Brief Biographies of Great Musicians] (Singapore: Xingguang Yueqi Gongsi, 1975), 126. After Ma Sitson defected to the United States during the Cultural Revolution, mainland sources excised him from Xian's life.

20. Sterling Seagrave, *The Soong Dynasty* (New York: Harper & Row,

1985), 254. This extremely popular ballet had two hundred performances within its first two years, according to Boris Schwarz, *Music and Musical Life in Soviet Russia* (New York: Norton, 1972), 74. But it has always been resented by Chinese, including Mao Zedong, who refused to attend a performance when he visited Moscow in 1950. See Wu Xiuquan, "Sino-Soviet Relations in the Early 1950s," *Beijing Review* 26 (21 November 1983): 20.

21. Although Dukas was celebrated at the time, his reputation has since faded considerably. He is best remembered today as the composer of a minor warhorse of the symphonic literature, *The Sorcerer's Apprentice*, popularized by Walt Disney in the movie *Fantasia*, as the music to which the hapless Mickey Mouse struggles to bail water.

22. Xian's student compositions included a violin sonata, a piano suite, a sarabande for string quartet, and songs. See Xian, *Wo Xuexi Yinyue de Jingguo*, 20–22.

23. He lived with a fellow Cantonese student, Zheng Zhisheng. With three others, they formed a "French Returned Students Musical Association." Wang Zhenya, "Zheng Zhisheng Xiansheng shengping shiji linzhao" [The Rarity of Mister Zheng Zhisheng's Life Story], *Renmin Yinyue* 200 (November 1981): 31.

24. Xian, *Wo Xuexi Yinyue de Jingguo*, 7.

25. Ibid., 7, 20–21.

26. Qin, *Xian Xinghai*, 40–41. Xian's widow claimed in 1975 that he had been in contact with Communist Party comrades in Paris. See Qian Yunling, "Yi Xinghai" [Remembering Xinghai], in *Huanghe Dahechang* [The Yellow River Cantata] (Beijing: Renmin Yinyue Chubanshe, 1978), 80. Xian claimed in his 1939 application for Party membership that his thinking was changed by contact with Chinese workers in France, causing him to "resolutely sympathize with the Communist Party." See Xian, *Wo Xuexi Yinyue de Jingguo*, 83. There certainly was a tradition of radicalism among Chinese workers in France. Xian followed the participants of the highly politicized worker-student movement of the 1920s; its members included Deng Xiaoping, who first became a leader of the Chinese communist movement in France between 1920 and 1926. See Nora Wang, "Deng Xiaoping: The Years in France," *The China Quarterly* 92 (December 1982): 698–705.

27. Xian, *Wo Xuexi Yinyue de Jingguo*, 5–6.

28. According to a personal communication from the Conservatoire Nationale Supérieur de Musique (2 February 1988):

> His passage at the Paris Conservatoire was most unsatisfactory—in fact, virtually negligible. He was at the school barely 6 months, subsequently disappearing without giving the school any notification. . . . He entered on Jan 22, 1935, as composition student in class of Paul Dukas and was present at the June (1935) year-end exam; no result obtained. He then requested & was granted a leave of

absence from studies for 35–36 academic year. Having thereupon not resumed contact with the Conservatoire, he was expelled from the school in Oct. (letter of expulsion dated Oct. 12 36). All in all, a considerable waste of Conservatoire time & effort & apparently minimal appreciation on his part.

29. Qin, *Xian Xinghai*, 27, 64, 70–73; Ma, *Xian Xinghai Zhuan*, 118–121; Xian, *Wo Xuexi Yinyue de Jingguo*, 41–42.

30. Xian, *Wo Xuexi Yinyue de Jingguo*, 10. Xian even turned to a gypsy ensemble from Shanghai's night life in search of performers for his music. Qin, *Xian Xinghai*, 69. The orchestra did not completely reject Chinese music, however; in 1930 it had performed an overture by Huang Zi, professor at the Shanghai Conservatory and graduate of Oberlin and Yale. Xu Shizhen, *Huang Zi Zuopin shi Yanjiu* [Research on the Compositions of Huan Zi] (Taibei: Youshi Shudian, 1972), 1–3.

31. Zhang Jiren, "Qie'erpin yu Zhongguo de yinyue" [Tcherepnin and Chinese Music], *Ming Bao Yuekan* 165 (September 1979): 20; Qin, *Xian Xinghai*, 70–73; Xian, *Wo Xuexi Yinyue de Jingguo*, 24.

32. Qin, *Xian Xinghai*, 69.

33. Zhongguo Yishu Yanjiuyuan Yinyue Yanjiusuo, ed., *Nie Er* (Beijing: Renmin Yinyue Chubanshe, 1982); and Shi Junliang, *Nie Er Zhuanlue*, [Brief Biography of Nie Er] (Hong Kong: Shanghai Shugu, 1982).

34. Qin, *Xian Xinghai*, 80; Xian, *Wo Xuexi Yinyue de Jingguo*, 22.

35. This description is based on Isabel K. F. Wong, "*Geming Gequ:* Songs for the Education of the Masses," in Bonnie S. McDougall, ed., *Popular Chinese Literature and Performing Arts in the People's Republic of China 1949–1979* (Berkeley: University of California Press, 1984), 112–43. See also Godwin Yuen, *Stylistic Development in Chinese Revolutionary Song* (1919–1948).

36. Qin, *Xian Xinghai*, 39.

37. Liang Maochun, *Zhang Hanhui Zhuan* [Life of Zhang Hanhui] (Xi'an: Shaanxi Renmin Chubanshe, 1985), 113–59.

38. Xian, *Wo Xuexi Yinyue de Jingguo*, 9.

39. Zhongguo, 32–33.

40. Ma, *Xian Xinghai Huazhuan,* 20.

41. Ibid., 20; Qin, *Xian Xinghai*, 80–81.

42. Xian donated some of his new salary to needy musical friends. Xian, *Wo Xuexi Yinyue de Jingguo*, 10.

43. For an introduction to the politics of the Shanghai cinema in the 1930s, see Jay Leyda, *Dianying: An Account of Films and the Film Audience in China* (Cambridge, Mass.: M.I.T. Press, 1972), especially ch. 3. Leyda quotes a French journalist on the foreign control of Westernized film culture in Shanghai in 1934:

The company head is named Marcus Avadjian. He was born in Mosul and travels with an American passport. His assistant is Greek, but holds Portuguese citizenship. Their distributor is a deserter from the Russian navy. The board of directors of a rival firm is presided over by a Turk of Spanish nationality. Other members of this board: an Englishman expelled from England, a Filipino, a Russian, and an Armenian. (360)

44. Xian, *Wo Xuexi Yinyue de Jingguo,* 10.

45. Like Xian's music, spoken drama was a Western import to China. Chinese drama was traditionally operatic. Spoken drama thus had a very "modern" air to it in the 1930s.

46. Xian, *Wo Xuexi Yinyue de Jingguo,* 11.

47. Qin, *Xian Xinghai,* 130.

48. Qian, "Yi Xinghai," 72.

49. Ibid., 74; Li Ling, *Yinyue Mantan* [Informal Talks on Music] (Beijing: Renmin Yinyue Chubanshe, 1983), 56.

50. Qian, "Yi Xinghai," 73–74; Xian, *Wo Xuexi Yinyue de Jingguo,* 12.

51. Qian, "Yi Xinghai," 73.

52. W. H. Auden and Christopher Isherwood, *Journey to a War* (New York: Random House, 1939), 88.

53. The "tonic sol-fa notation" works by relative pitch, indicated by number: 1 is *do,* 2 is *re,* 3 is *mi,* etc. When a key is indicated, it becomes 1: thus in the key of G, 1 is G, 2 is A, and so on. Dots above and below numbers indicate higher or lower octaves, and the length of a note is shown by the kind of line printed beneath it. See the description in David Holm, "Introduction to Ma Ke's 'Man and Wife Learn to Read'," in John Berninghausen and Ted Huters, eds., *Revolutionary Literature in China: An Anthology* (New York: M.E. Sharpe, 1976), 79–80. Shen Xiao, in *Geyong Shouce* [Song Handbook] (Shanghai: Wenhua Chubanshe, 1953), 2, claims that the *jianpu* system was imported from Japan, but this sounds like an avoidance of the missionary role.

54. Li, *Yinyue Mantan,* 55.

55. Xian, *Wo Xuexi Yinyue de Jingguo,* 11–12.

56. Ibid., 13–14.

57. Qian, "Yi Xinghai," 75.

58. See Ellen R. Judd, "Revolutionary Drama and Song in the Jiangxi Soviet," *Modern China* 9 (January 1983): 127–60; Paul G. Pickowicz, *Marxist Literary Thought in China: The Influence of Ch'u Ch'iu-pai* (Berkeley: University of California Press, 1981).

59. Judd, "Revolutionay Drama and Song in the Jiangxi Soviet," 143.

60. Lu Ji, "Jiefangqu de yinyue" [Music in the Liberated Areas], in Zhonghua Quanguo Wenxue Yishu Gongzuozhe Daibiao Dahui Xuanchuanchu, ed., *Zhonghua Quanguo Wenxue Yishu Gongzuozhe Daibiao Dahui Jinian Wenji* [Collection of Documents Commemorating the National Congress of Chinese Literary and Art Workers] (Beijing: Xinhua Shudian, 1950), 206.

61. Judd, "Revolutionary Drama and Song in the Jiangxi Soviet," 153. See Pickowicz, *Marxist Literary Thought in China*, 192–209.

62. Zheng Lucheng, "Gechang Geming" [Singing Revolution], in Ding Xuesong, *Zuoqujia Zheng Lucheng* [Composer Zheng Lucheng] (Shenyang: Liaoning Renmin Chubanshe, 1983), 289. In contrast, Edgar Snow met a "very serious-minded" electrical engineer in the Communist base area who felt "These people spend entirely too much time *singing!* This is no time to be singing." *Red Star over China* (New York: Grove Press, 1961), 276.

63. Ellen R. Judd, "Prelude to the 'Yan'an Talks': Problems in Transforming a Literary Intelligentsia," *Modern China* 11 (July 1985): 394.

64. Ma, *Xian Xinghau Huazhuan*, 37.

65. Ma, "Hsien Hsing-hai the Composer," 113.

66. Qin, *Xian Xinghai*, 141.

67. Xian, *Wo Xuexi Yinyue de Jingguo*, 19.

68. Xian's friend, Li Ling, says that Xian "spoke extremely poorly." Li Ling, *Yinyue Mantan*, 59.

69. Qian, "Yi Xinghai," 76.

70. Xian, *Wo Xuexi Yinyue de Jingguo*, 30.

71. Ibid., 30–36.

72. Guan Hetong, "Shenqie ganren de gemin xinsheng" [Heartfelt and Moving Revolutionary Aspirations], *Guangming Ribao* [Enlightened Daily] (11 August 1977).

73. See Mark Selden, *The Yenan Way in Revolutionary China* (Cambridge, Mass.: Harvard University Press, 1971).

74. Li Huanzhi, "Yi 'Huanghe' " [Remembering "Yellow River"], in *Huanghe Dahechang*, 85; Qin, *Xian Xinghai*, 141.

75. Yuen, *Stylistic Development in Chinese Revolutionary Song (1919–1948)*, 299.

76. Xian, *Wo Xuexi Yinyue de Jingguo*, 15–16.

77. Wong, *"Geming Gequ,"* 125.

78. Qin, *Xian Xinghai*, 141–42; Guang Weiran, "Xian Xinghai tongzhi huiyilu" [Recollections of Comrade Xian Xinghai], in *Huanghe Dahechang*, 67–70.

79. Qian, "Yi Xinghai," 79–80.

80. Guang Weiran, "Xian Xinghai tongzhi huiyi lu" [Recollections of Comrade Xian Xinghai], in *Huanghe Dahechang*, 67–70; Qin, *Xian Xinghai*, 144.

81. Xian, *Wo Xuexi Yinyue de Jingguo*, p. 16.

82. Xian, *Wo Xuexi Yinyue de Jingguo*, p. 85.

83. Qian, "Yi Xinghai," pp. 76–77.

84. Qian Yunling, "Yi Xinghai," p. 82; Ma, ed., *Xian Xinghai Huazhuan*, p. 43.

85. Guang, "Xian Xinghai tongzhi huiyi lu," 65.

86. Qian, "Yi Xinghai," 78; Xian Xinghai, "Wei shenma yanjiu minge" [Why Study Folksong?], in *Wo Xuexi Yinyue de Jingguo*, 107–12. Bartók and other modernists, of course, had been gathering folksongs in Europe earlier than this.

87. Xian, *Wo Xuexi Yinyue de Jingguo*, 15–16, 110, 117; Qin, *Xian Xinghai*, 145.

88. See Judd, "Prelude to the 'Yan'an Talks,' " 377–408.

89. Quoted in Pickowicz, *Marxist Literary Thought in China*, 99.

90. David Holm, "The Literary Rectification in Yan'an," in Wolfgang Kubin and Rudolf G. Wagner, eds., *Essays in Modern Chinese Literature and Literary Criticism* (Bochum: Brockmeyer, 1982), 272–308.

91. Bonnie S. McDougall, *Mao Zedong's "Talks at the Yan'an Conference on Literature and Art": A Translation of the 1943 Text with Commentary* (Ann Arbor: University of Michigan Center for Chinese Studies, 1980).

92. Judd, "Prelude to the 'Yan'an Talks'," 377.

93. McDougall, *Mao Zedong's "Talks"*, 75.

94. Excellent analyses of the *yangge* movement are offered by David Holm, "Folk Art as Propaganda: The *Yangge* Movement in Yan'an," in Bonnie S. McDougall, ed., *Popular Chinese Literature and Performing Arts in the People's Republic of China 1949–1979* (Berkeley: University of California Press, 1984), 3–35; and Ellen R. Judd, "Cultural Redefinition in Yan'an China," *Ethnos* 51 (1986): 29–51.

95. Holm, "Folk Art As Propaganda," 23.

96. Ibid., 30.

97. Judd, "Cultural Redefinition in Yan'an China," 35.

98. Shen Cheng-zhou, "China's New Musical Play," *Chinoperl Papers* 11 (1982): 90.

99. *The White-Haired Girl* is a *geju* (song-play), in contrast to *huaju* (spoken-word drama, another twentieth-century importation from the West), or *xiqu*, the traditional Chinese opera, which in its various local forms, sets new texts to a set of traditional tunes that are repeated from opera to opera—in contrast to Western opera, in which musical novelty is more important than variation in text.

100. Ma Ke and Qu Wei, " 'Baimaonu' yinyue de chuangzao jingyan" [The Experience of Composing the Music for "The White-Haired Girl"], in Yan'an Lu Xun Wenyi Xueyuan, *Baimaonu* [The White-Haired Girl] (Beijing: Renmin Wenxue Chubanshe, 1962), 229–35.

101. Qin, *Xian Xinghai*, 144.

102. Ma, *Xian Xinghai Huazhuan*, 50. There are rumors in China that Xian failed the entrance examination for Moscow's Tchaikovsky Conservatory.

103. Xian, *Wo Xuexi Yinyue de Jingguo*, 41–50.

104. Ibid., 37.

105. Ibid., 43.

106. Qin, *Xian Xinghai*, 118.

107. Guo Moruo, Preface to *Huanghe Dahechang*, 2.

108. Qin, *Xian Xinghai*, 146.

109. Ma, *Xian Xinghai Huazhuan*, 51–61; Qin, *Xian Xinghai*, 146.

110. Ma, *Xian Xinghai Huazhuan*, 51–61; Qin, *Xian Xinghai*, 147; Chen, *Yinyuejia Xian Xinghai*, 33; Xian, *Wo Xuexi Yinyue de Jingguo*, 70–75.

111. Xian, *Wo Xuexi Yinyue de Jingguo*, 67–68, 82.

112. Guo incorrectly reported that Xian had cancer, however: Li, *Yinyue Mantan*, p. 58. I do not know why Guo could obtain Guomindang permission to return to China and Xian could not.

113. Ma, *Xian Xinghai Huazhuan,* 51–61; "Xian Xinghai guhui huidao zuguo" [Xian Xinghai's Ashes Return to His Native Land], *Renmin Yinyue* 216 (March 1983): 6.

114. Qian, "Yi Xinghai," 82; Qin, *Xian Xinghai*, 149.

115. Guo Moruo, Preface to *Huanghe Dahechang*. The movie is described in Leyda, *Dianying*, 166–68; it is also reviewed by Theodore Herman, "Portrait of a Nation on the Way," *The China Weekly Review*, 22 March 1947, 98–99.

116. Nie Er was the subject of a 1959 movie, starring Zhao Dan, the Charleton Heston of the Chinese Left. In the movie, Nie's story is more colorful than his life was in fact, according to Leyda, Dianying, 260–61.

117. Zhongguo Yishu Yanjiuyuan Yinyue Yanjiusuo, *Nie Er*, 76.

118. Ma, *Xian Xinghai Huazhuan*, 64.

119. *Yinyue Xinshang Schouce* [Handbook of Music Appreciation] (Shanghai: Shanghai Wenyi Chubanshe, 1981), 517–34.

120. Meng Po and Qiao Shutian, *Mai Xin Zhuan* [Life of Mai Xin] (Shanghai: Shanghai Wenyi Chubanshe, 1982).

121. See Merle Goldman, "The Political Uses of Lu Xun," *The China Quarterly* 91 (September 1982): 446–61.

122. Ma, "Hsien Hsing-hai the Composer," 116.

123. Qian, "Yi Xinghai." 71–83, especially 76.

124. "As the symphony was composed during the war years, it was not a perfect piece." This enigmatic remark does not adequately explain why Xian's symphony lay unplayed. Could it be so markedly worse than some pieces that were performed? Yu Hedeng, "Commemorating Top Two Composers," *Beijing Review* 29 (3 March 1986): 30. Xian's second symphony was performed by a student orchestra at the Central Conservatory in 1960, but has been little heard since. A. C. Scott, *Literature and the Arts in Twentieth Century China*, 136.

125. "Yinyuejia Zuotan 'ming i fang' [Musicians' Forum on "Contending" and "Blooming"], *Renmin Yinyue* (May 1957): 5.

126. The 1962 book was *Xian Xinghai Zhuanji* [Special Collection on Xian Xinghai], edited in two volumes by Huang Xiangpeng and Qi Yuyi of the Central Conservatory's Chinese Music Research Institute. See the editorial preface to Xian, *Wo Xuexi Yinyue de Jingguo*. The new edition of Xian's works is published by the Guangdong Publishing House for Higher Education. See Beijing *Xinhua* (English), 24 November 1986. On Xian's recordings, see *Zhongguo Baike Nianjian* [China Encyclopedia] (Beijing & Shanghai: Zhongguo Dabaike Quanshu Chubanshe, 1982), 558.

127. There is now a Xian Xinghai–Nie Er Musicians' Association, led by cultural populists, in opposition to the cosmopolitan-dominated Chinese Musicians' Association. Mao Yu-run, professor of composition, Shanghai Conservatory of Music, interview with author, Eugene, Ore., 27 October 1987.

128. Roxane Witke, *Comrade Chiang Ch'ing* (Boston: Little, Brown, 1977), 387.

3   The Defector: Fou Ts'ong

1. Fou Ts'ong uses a French romanization of his name, presumably following his Francophile father. It is Fu Cong in standard *pinyin* romanization.

2. Ye Yonglie, "Jiashu de wanjin" [Family Letters Worth Ten Thousand Pieces of Gold], *Baogao Wenxue Xuankan* [Selections from Reportage Literature] 2 (1984): 5.

3. Fu's father owned a very large estate of four hundred *mu* (over sixty acres). Yu Yi, "Fang Fu Cong" [Interview with Fou Ts'ong], *Xingdao Ribao* [Star Island News], 15 April 1973, in *Fu Cong Ziliao Ji,* [Collection of Materials on Fu Ts'ong] (n.p., n.d., in Library of Congress), 28.

4. Qiao Pei, *Zhongguo Xiandai Yinyuejia* [China's Contemporary Musicians] (Taibei: Tiantong Chubanshe, 1976), 134–36.

5. Fu translated *Jean-Christophe* in the 1930s. He spent two years revising this translation in the early 1950s. Ye Yonglie, "Fu Lei zhi si" [The Death of Fu Lei], *Baogao Wenxue* 2 (1986), in *Zhengming* 103 (May 1986): 36–39. The publication of *Fu Lei's Collected Translations* by Anhui People's Publishing House was announced in "Publishing News," *Chinese Literature* (Autumn 1986): 225. Fu Lei translated thirty-three works of foreign literature, including fifteen novels of Balzac. Fu Min, "Wo de fuqin—Fu Lei" [My Father—Fu Lei], *Dongxifang* 11 (November 1979): 72.

6. For details of Rolland's life, see William T. Starr, "Romain Rolland," in Jean-Albert Bede and William B. Edgerton, eds., *Columbia Dictionary of*

Modern European Literature (New York: Columbia University Press, 1980), 676–77; and *Dictionnaire des Litteratures Française,* (Paris: Bordas, 1984), S.V. "Romain Rolland," 1958–68.

7. Romaine Rolland, *Jean-Christophe* (New York: Henry Holt, 1913) runs to 1577 pages. Random House once published *Jean-Christophe* as one of its Modern Library "Giants," which suggests how popular Rolland's novel once was in the United States.

8. Rolland, *Jean-Chrisophe,* book 3, 349.

9. See "Kan, zui ede xiuzhengzhuyi gaochou zhidu!" [Look how criminal was the revisionist remuneration system!], *Wenge Fenglei* [Cultural Revolution Storm] (9 June 1969).

10. This account of Fou Ts'ong's youth is based upon the following sources: *Fu Lei Jiashu* [Family Letters of Fu Lei] (Hong Kong: Sanlien Shudian, 1984), 4; Fu Lei, "Fu Cong de chengzhang" [Fou Ts'ong's Upbringing], *Xin Guancha* [New Observer] 8 (1957), in *Fu Cong Ziliao Ji,* 31–32; Ye, "Jiashu de wanjin," 4–17; Ye Yonglie, " 'Taiyang dixia zui guanghui de shiye' " [The Most Glorious Occupation under the Sun], *Beijing Wenxue* [Beijing Literature] 6 (June 1985): 2–13.

11. Dong Fang, "Fu Lei fufu" [Mr. and Mrs. Fu Lei], *Mingbao Zhoukan* [Mingbao Weekly], 3 March 1974, in *Fu Cong Ziliao Ji,* 4.

12. See Chapter 1, "Childhood and Early Education," in *Autobiography of John Stuart Mill* (New York: New American Library, 1964), 25–47.

13. Fu Lei, "Fu Cong de chengzhang" [Fou Ts'ong's Upbringing], 31. Compare this to Mill's *Autobiography,* 38, 43.

14. *Fu Lei Jiashu,* 27, 35.

15. One of these teachers was the wife of Si Yigui (Sze Yi-kuei), the noted bass (and later professor of voice at the Eastman School of Music). Chen Fang, "Gangqin yiwai de Fu Cong" [Fou Ts'ong Beyond the Piano], *Xingdao Ribao,* 10 March 1974, in *Fu Cong Ziliao Ji,* 20.

16. Ye, "Jiashu de wanjin," 6; Jin Dongfang, "Ting Fu Cong yanzou, he Fu Cong xianliao" [Listening to Fou Ts'ong Perform, Chatting with Fou Ts'ong], *Mingbao Yuekan* 133 (1 January 1977): 15.

17. Fu Lei, "Fu Cong de chengzhang" 31–32.

18. Ibid., 13.

19. Dong Fang, "Fu Lei fufu," 4.

20. *Fu Lei Jiashu,* 21–22.

21. Fu Lei, "Fu Cong de chengzhang," 32.

22. Joseph R. Levenson, *Revolution and Cosmopolitanism: The Western Stage and the Chinese Stages* (Berkeley: University of California Press, 1971), 35.

23. Ye, "Taiyang dixia zui guanghui de zhiye'," 2–3; Jin, "Ting Fu Cong yanzou, he Fu Cong xianliao," 15.

24. Edoarda Masi, *China Winter: Workers, Mandarins, and the Purge of the Gang of Four* (New York: E.P. Dutton, 1982), 14.

25. Zhonghua Quanguo Yinyue Gongzuozhe Xiehui, ed., *Yijiuwulingnian de Yinyue Yundong* [The Music Campaign of 1950] Beijing: Zhongguo Tushu Faxing Gongsi, 1950), especially 27, 71, 76, 156–157.

26. Mao Zedong, "Methods of Work of Party Committees," *Selected Works of Mao Tsetung*, vol. 4 (Peking: Foreign Languages Press, 1967), 379.

27. For an example of early demands for reform, see Hu Ch'iao-mu, "Why Must Literary and Arts Workers Carry Out Ideological Reform?" NCNA Peking, December 5, 1951, in *Current Background* 156 (5 February 1952): 19–24.

28. See Merle Goldman, *Literary Dissent in Communist China* (Cambridge, Mass.: Harvard University Press, 1967), ch. 6.

29. Robert Jay Lifton, *Thought Reform and the Psychology of Totalism: A Study of "Brainwashing" in China* (New York: W.W. Norton, 1961), 347.

30. Fu Lei, "Fu Cong de chengzhang," 32.

31. A. C. Scott, *Literature and the Arts in Twentieth Century China* (Garden City, N.Y.: Anchor Books, 1963), 143.

32. Bonnie S. McDougall, *Mao Zedong's "Talks at the Yan'an Conference on Literature and Art": A Translation of the 1943 Text with Commentary* (Ann Arbor: University of Michigan Center for Chinese Studies, 1980), 19–20, discusses a mellower stance toward foreign cultural models in the revisions of Mao's speech after liberation.

33. Zhang Hongying, "Commemorating the Great Austrian Musician Mozart," *Renmin Ribao* [People's Daily] (27 January 1956).

34. Ye, "Jiashu de wanjin," 9; Qiu Zhen, "Cong Fou Ts'ong huojiang tanqi" [Speaking of Fou Ts'ong Winning The Prize], *Renmin Yinyue* 26 (April 1955): 29.

35. Ye, "Jiashu de wanjin," 9.

36. Qui Zhen, "Cong Fou Ts'ong huojiang tanqi," plus following news note. See also Ma Sicong, "Guanyu Fou Ts'ong dejiang" [About Fou Ts'ong Winning The Prize], *Renmin Yinyue* 27 (May 1955): 19.

37. The first pianist from the People's Republic of China to win honors in international competition was Zhou Guangren (now a professor of piano at Beijing's Central Conservatory of Music), at the Third World Youth Festival in Berlin in 1951, and later at the first Schumann International Piano Competition in 1956. See "Winning Musicians Show Their Talents", *Beijing Review* 27 (30 April 1984): 34.

38. Zhou Yang, for one, was involved deciding how long Fou Ts'ong should study in Warsaw. *Fu Lei Jiashu*, p. 113.

39. "Expose Bourgeois Thought within the Realm of Music," *Renmin Yinyue* 29 (July 1955): 8.

40. *Fu Lei Jiashu,* 142–43.

41. Ibid., 20, 107.

42. Ibid., 44, 46, 53, 55, 67, 114, 117.

43. The Hu Feng campaign is discussed in Goldman, *Literary Dissent in Communist China,* ch. 7.

44. "Suqing yinyuejie de yichie yinzang di fangeming fenzi!" [Eliminate All of the Music World's Hidden Counter-revolutionary Elements!], *Renmin Yinyue* 33 (October 1955): 1.

45. *Fu Lei Jiashu,* 68, 77–78, 91.

46. Ye, "Jiashu de wanjin," 9.

47. Wei Fang, "Ping 'Yuehan Shiqusi ji chi yuanwuqi" [A Criticism of "Johann Strauss and His Waltzes"], *Renmin Yinyue* 28–29 (November–December 1955): 70.

48. Zheng Lucheng, "Yinyue zuozhe xingdongqilai, huanjie nongyehua de gaochao" [Music Workers Mobilize, Welcome the High Tide of Agricultural Collectivization], *Renmin Yinyue* 28–29 (November–December 1955): 3.

49. See various articles in *Renmin Yinyue* in 1955 (the tenth anniversary of Xian's death).

50. Ma Sicong, "Jinian Nie Er, Xinghai" [Commemorating Nie Er and Xinghai], *Renmin Yinyue* (October 1955): 7.

51. Mou Sheng, "Tan yinyue xiaxiang wenti' [About the Question of Sending Music Down to the Villages], *Renmin Yinyue* 28–29 (November–December 1955), 6–7.

52. For background on this campaign and its aftermath, see Roderick MacFarquhar, *The Origins of the Cultural Revolution,* vol. 1: Contradictions among the People 1956–1957 (New York: Columbia University Press, 1974). Examples of the writing generated by the Hundred Flowers may be found in Hualing Nieh, ed., *Literature of the Hundred Flowers,* 2 vols. (New York: Columbia University Press, 1981).

53. Richard Curt Kraus, *Class Conflict in Chinese Socialism* (New York: Columbia University Press, 1981), 43–51.

54. Luo Bing, "Zhonggong gaoceng de taose xinwen" [Sex News from the Chinese Communists' Upper Ranks], *Zhengming* 101 (March 1986): 10.

55. *Fu Lei Jiashu,* 79.

56. Ibid., 80, 104.

57. Mao Yu-run, Professor of Composition, Shanghai Conservatory of Music, interview with author, Eugene, Ore., 27 October 1987.

58. Bonnie S. McDougall, "Writers and Performers, Their Works, and Their Audiences in the First Three Decades," in Bonnie S. McDougall, ed., *Popular Chinese Literature and Performing Arts in the People's Republic of China 1949–1979* (Berkeley: University of California Press, 1984), 282.

59. Zhang Wei, "A Start in Writing at the Age of 63," *Beijing Review* 31 (14–20 March 1988): 25–27.

60. "Women jiandaole Mao Zhuxi" [We Saw Chairman Mao], *Renmin Yinyue* (September 1956): 6–7.

61. Mao Zedong, "A Talk to Music Workers," *Beijing Review* 22 (14 September 1979): 9–15. The speech was not published until 1979.

62. Ye, "Fu Lei zhi si," 37. Ye, " 'Taiyang dixia zui guanghui de zhiye'," 4.

63. *Fu Lei Jiashu,* 110–15.

64. Ibid., 85, 101.

65. Ibid., 85, 104, 116. Fu published an article criticizing the Communists for excluding non-Party intellectuals from cultural leadership. See Fu Lei, "Dajia qide qiang dajia chai" [We all Built The Wall, Let Us All Tear it Down], Shanghai *Wenhui Bao,* 8 May 1957.

66. Ibid., 93, 101–2.

67. Ibid. 117.

68. Ding Shande, "Rang yinyue yishu wei zuguo de shehuizhuyi jianshe zuochu gengda di gongxian" [Let the Art of Music Make Even Greater Contributions for the Socialist Construction of our Homeland], *Renmin Yinyue* (February 1956): 1–3.

69. "Yanzoujia, gechangjia, zhihuijia gei yinxie ti yijian" [Players, Singers, and Conductors Give Opinions to Music Workers' Federation], *Renmin Yinyue* (June 1957): 5.

70. Ying Fen, "Ye tan Zhonguo yinyue sanshinian" [Some More Discussion of Thirty Years of Chinese Music], *Guanchajia* 22 (August 1979): 60–65.

71. This account of the impact of the Anti-Rightist movement on the Fu family is based on Dong, "Fu Lei fufu," 4; *Fu Lei Jiashu,* 117–119; Ye, "Jiashu de wanjin," 11; Ye, " 'Taiyang dixia zui guanghui de zhiye,' " 6.

72. Ye, "Fu Lei zhi si," 37.

73. Zhou Erfu, *Morning in Shanghai* (Beijing: Foreign Languages Press, 1962), 3–4:

> Mei Zuoxian took the lid off a tin of State Express cigarettes on the little round table and after taking one he fished out a silver-coloured cigarette case from the pocket of his European-style suit and calmly filled it from the tin. Then he picked up the silver-coloured Ronson lighter that was on the table, lit his cigarette and sat there smoking, looking contentedly across at the grand piano in the corner of the room.

74. See MacFarquhar, *The Origins of the Cultural Revolution,* vol. 2: *The Great Leap Forward 1958–1960* (New York: Columbia University Press, 1983).

75. Ye, "Fu Lei zhi si," 37. See also Lek Horton, "Taking Chopin to China," *Index on Censorship* 9 (February 1980): 47–48.

76. Yu, "Fang Fu Cong," 28.

77. Bi Jizhou, "Ji Zhongguo gangqinjia Fu Cong" [An Interview with Chinese Pianist Fou Ts'ong], *Jing Bao* 4 (10 April 1979): 62–64; Yu, "Fang Fu Cong," 28.

78. Yi Sheng, "Taochu gongdang guichang de Zhongguo gangqinjia Fu Cong" [Pianist Fou Ts'ong, who Escaped the Clutches of the Communists], 16 June 1959, in *Fu Cong Ziliao Ji*, 39; Bi, "Ji Zhongguo gangqinjia Fu Cong," 62–64.

79. Yi, "Taochu gongdang guichang de Zhongguo gangqinjia Fu Cong," 39.

80. *Fu Lei Jiashu*, 161, 224, 245.

81. Ye, "Jiashu de wanjin," 12.

82. Ibid., 11–12.

83. Ye, "Fu Lei zhi si," 37–38.

84. Ye Yonglie, "Ninnin qingshen" [Your Deep Feelings, Sir], *Baogao Wenxue Xuankan* 26.

85. Ye, "Jiashu de wanjin," 12.

86. *Fu Lei Jiashu*, 119.

87. Ye, "Jiashu de wanjin," 13.

88. The principal was Wang Qiqing, wife of the politician Wang Zhen. Ye, " 'Taiyang dixia zui guanghui de zhiye'," 4–5.

89. *Fu Lei Jiashu*, 124, 210.

90. Ibid., 139–40, 144, 262, 267, 272.

91. Ye, " Taiyang dixia zui guanghui de zhiye'," 5.

92. *Fu Lei Jiashu*, 206.

93. Ibid., 238, 269.

94. Fu, "Wo de fugin—Fu Lei," 72.

95. Lars Ragvald, *Yao Wenyuan as a Literary Critic and Theorist* (Stockholm: University of Stockholm, 1978), 107, in Marian Galik, "Foreign Literature in the People's Republic of China between 1970–1979," *Asian and African Studies 19* (Bratislava: Veda, 1983), 63.

96. Fu, "Wo de fuqin—Fu Lei," 72.

97. Ye, "Fu Lei zhi si," 36–39; Ye, " 'Taiyang dixia zui guanghui de zhiye'," 5–7; Ye, "Jiashu de wanjin," 13–14.

98. Ye, "Jiashu de wanjin," 14.

99. "Fu Cong yu Zhongguo" [Fou Ts'ong and China], *Xingdao Ribao*, 30 November 1970, in *Fu Cong Ziliao Ji*, 12.

100. Ye, "Jiashu de wanjin," 12.

101. His father-in-law still had kind words for both Fou Ts'ong after the

divorce, and Fu Lei's letters. See Yehudi Menuhin, *Unfinished Journey* (New York: Alfred A. Knopf, 1977), 202–3.

102. Chen Fang, "Gangqin yiwai de Fu Cong" [Fou Ts'ong Beyond the Piano], *Xingdao Ribao*, 10 March 1974, in *Fu Cong Ziliao Ji*, 20. Bi Jizhou, in "Ji Zhongguo gangqinjia Fu Cong," places Fou's second divorce in 1974.

103. Yu Mu, "Xiyang, Chuiliao, Xiaobang" [Sunset, Weeping Willows, Chopin], *Wenlin* [Literary Grove] 1 (1 December 1972): 6–7.

104. Bi, "Ji Zhongguo gangqinjia Fu Cong.", p. 64.

105. Yu, "Xiyang, Chuiliao, Xiaobang," 9.

106. Ai Yue, "Wo suo renshi de Fu Cong" [The Fou Ts'ong I Know], *Xingdao Ribao*, (4 July 1976), in *Fu Cong Ziliao Ji*, 16.

107. Bi Jizhou, "Shijie yitan de mingxing" [Stars of the Arts World], *Xingdao Wanbao* 26 February 1973, in *Fu Cong Ziliao Ji*, 7.

108. "Fu Cong de meimeng" [Fou Ts'ong's Dream], *Xingdao Ribao*, 17 January 1972, in *Fu Cong Ziliao Ji*, 7; Sha Lun, "Fu Cong de shenghuo yu xingge [Fou Ts'ong's Life and Personality], *Shibao*, 15 November 1975, in *Fu Cong Ziliao Ji*, 2–3.

109. Ye, "Jiashu de wanjin," 17; Chen Fang, "Gangqin yiwai de Fu Cong," 20.

110. Zhou Fanfu, "Fu Cong chonglin de ganxiang" [Reflections on the Eve of Fou Ts'ong's Visit], *Xingdao wanbao*, 3 September 1975, in *Fu Cong Ziliao Ji*, 3.

111. Tominaga Sohiko, "Fu Cong de fengcai" [Fou Ts'ong's Elegant Bearing], in *Fu Cong Ziliao Ji*, 23; Ye, "Fu Lei zhi si," 37.

112. Sha Lun, "Fu Cong de shenghuo yu xingge," 2.

113. "Fu Cong de meimeng," p. 7.

114. Ye, "Jiashu de wanjin," 15.

115. Jin, "Ting Fu Cong yanzou, he Fu Cong xianliao," 15.

116. Bi Jizhou, "Ji Zhongguo gangqinjia Fu Cong," 63. Fu made his peace with He Luting in person as well. See the picture in *Renmin Yinyue* 216 (March 1982): 31.

117. Ye, "Jiashu de wanjin," 15.

118. *Dongxiang* 6 (March 1979): 31.

119. You Sheng, "Jiekai gangqin dashi Fu Cong huijinghu zhi mi" [Solving the Mystery of Master Pianist Fou Ts'ong's Return to Beijing and Shanghai], *Jing Bao* 6 (10 June 1980): 30–31.

120. Ye, " 'Taiyang dixia zui guanghui de zhiye'," 11.

121. Ye, "Fu Lei zhi si," 39.

122. I thank Joe Esherick for making this point.

123. Ye, "Jiashu de wanjin," 15.

124. You, "Jiekai gangqin dashi Fu Cong huijinghu zhi mi, 31–33.

125. "Fu Cong tan zai fang Zhongguo ganshou" [Fou Ts'ong Discusses His Feelings about Returning to China], Hong Kong *Wenhui Bao* (4 August 1980).

126. Ye, "Jiashu de wanjin," 17; Bi Jizhou, "Ji Zhongguo gangqinjia Fu Cong," 64.

127. Ye, " 'Taiyang dixia zui guanghui de zhiye'," 2–13.

128. Ibid., 6; Fu Min, "Wo de fugin—Fu Lei," 72.

129. Ye, "Jiashu de wanjin," 13.

130. Ibid., 16.

131. Hu had been a supporter of Fou's rehabilitation. He issued a 1982 directive: "You ought to welcome this emigrant, who departed under special circumstances, 'to rejoin his unit'." Ye, "Fu Lei zhi si," 39.

132. "New York 'Rave' Notices for Chinese Pianist," *ChinaUpdate* (April 1987): 4.

133. An initial step was Fou's interview explaining his position in the Hong Kong leftist monthly, *Jing Bao*. See Mo Liya, "Langji tianya qinsheng fu yuguo" [Wandering to the ends of the earth, singing of the nation's sorrows with the sound of the *qin*] 119 (June 1987): 54–57. See also Dai Gang, "Shanghai: Season of Music and Dance," *Beijing Review* 31 (27 June–3 July 1988): 42.

4   Science versus Revolution in the Modernization of Music

1. Ding Xuesong, *Zuoqujia Zheng Lucheng* [Composer Zheng Lucheng] (Shenyang: Liaoning Renmin Chubanshe, 1983), 224–25, 263–65.

2. Bi Jizhou, "Wenge beiju de kunan yinfu Ma Sicong" [Ma Sitson, a Bitter Note in the Cultural Revolution Tragedy], *Jing Bao* 36 (July 1980): 67–69; Qiao Pei, *Zhongguo Xiandai Yinyuejia* [China's Contemporary Musicians] (Taibei: Tiantong Chubanshe, 1976), 47–50; Wu Zhiqing, *Yinyuejia Xiaozhuan* [Brief Biographies of Musicians] (Singapore: Xingguang Yueqi Gongsi, 1975), 126–29; Ma Sitson (Ma Szu-tsung) "Testimony," Hearings before the Committee on Internal Security, House of Representatives, Ninety-second Congress, First Session, 25 March 1971, 71–88; Ma Sitson, "We Are Slaves Who Have Been Betrayed," *Life,* 14 July 1967, 64–73.

3. Personal communications to author from the Conservatoire Nationale Supérieur de Musique, 25 January 1988, and G. Ermisse of the French National Archives, Ministry of Culture and Communication, 20 April 1988.

4. Ma Sicong, "Jinian Nie Er, Xinghai" [Commemorating Nie Er and Xinghai], *Renmin Yinyue* (October 1955): 7.

5. See An Po and Li Jiefu, "Yao changde geng dongqing, geng pubian, geng chijiu!" [Sing Even more Movingly, More Popularly, More Lastingly!],

in Zhonghua Quanguo Yinyue Gongzuozhe Xiehui, ed., *Yijiuwulingnian de Yinyue Yundong* [The Music Campaign of 1950] (Beijing: Zhongguo Tushu Faxing Gongsi, 1950), 43–56; Chen Ko, "The Story of a Revolutionary Composer," *China Reconstructs* 13 (November 1964): 34–37; An Po, "Cong 'tongsu yinyuehui' xiangdao muqian yinyue gongzuo yingzhuyi de wenti" [Considering Some Noteworthy Problems in Music at Present from A "Popular Music Concert"], *Renmin Yinyue* (March 1958): 12.

6. See *He Luting Pipan Wenti Huibian* [Collection on the Question of Criticizing He Luting] (Hong Kong: Ynagkai Shubao Gongyingshe, n.d.); *He Luting Ziliao Ji* [Collection of Materials on He Luting] (n.p., n.d., in Library of Congress); Liang Maochun, "Lun He Luting zuopin de xuanlu" [On the Melodies in the Works of He Luting], *Yinyue Yishu* [Musical Art] 3 (1984): 43–50; Notes to *He Luting Shengyue Zuopin Xuan* [Selections of Vocal Music Composed by He Luting] (Nanguo Cassette no. NB-3, 1979).

7. Mao Yu-run, professor of composition, Shanghai Conservatory of Music, interview with author, Eugene, Ore., 27 October 1987.

8. Wang Yuanfang, "Two Examples of Liu Xuean's Groundless Allegations," *Renmin Yinyue* (August 1957): 7.

9. Li Yinghang, head of the Guangzhou branch of Music Workers' Federation and Secretary of its Party Group, complained during the Hundred Flowers movement that the Guangzhou Cultural Bureau slighted music other than opera. See "The Anti-Party Conspiracy of Rightist Element Li Yinghang and Others Brought to Light," *Renmin Yinyue* (August 1957): 9; Yang Jingcheng, "Lift the Mask from Li Yinghang," *Renmin Yinyue* (September 1957): 15–16.

10. The two men jointly gave their backing to a book of *qin* music published in 1963, at a time when fedual remnants were viewed suspiciously. Kang wrote the characters for the cover, Chen inscribed the opening of the book. See *Qinqu Jichen,* vol. 1, part 1 (Beijing: Zhonghua Shudian, 1963).

11. See "Ch'en Yun is the Black Chief Commander of the Demons and Monsters of Literary and Art Circles," Peking *Ts'ai-mao Hong-ch'i* [Finance and Trade Red Banner], 15 February 1967, in *SCMP—Supplement* 175 (12 April 1967): 27–29; *How Vicious They Are! A Collection of Reactionary Utterances by Liu Shao-ch'i and Teng Hsiao-p'ing* (Beijing: Liaison Post for Criticizing Liu, Tend and T'ao, "Red Flag Commune" of Peking Railways Institute, Red Guard Congress, April 1967), in *SCMP—Supplement* 208 (26 October 1967): 26.

12. "Yanzoujia, gechangjia, zhihuijia gei yinxie ti yijian" [Players, Singers, Conductors Give Opinions to Music Workers' Federation], *Renmin Yinyue* (June 1957): 4; "Shuochule xinfuhua" [Words Spoken from the Heart], *Renmin Yinyue* (June 1957): 2–3.

13. Oyuang Feng, "Tongguanyue jeiduohua you shei guanhuai?" [Who Will Cultivate This Flower of Brass Bands?], *Renmin Yinyue* (May 1957): 6.

14. "Yinyuejia zuotan 'ming' 'fang' " [Musicians' Forum of "Blooming" and "Contending"], *Renmin Yinyue* (May 1957): 2–5.

15. For political background on this movement see Roderick MacFarquhar, *The Origins of the Cultural Revolution*, vol. 2: *The Great Leap Forward 1958–1960*. (New York: Columbia University Press, 1983).

16. "Shinianlai woguo yinyue shiye de fazhan" [The Development of Our Nation's Music over the Past Decade], *Renmin Yinyue* (October–November 1959): pp. 32–35.

17. See S. H. Chen, "Multiplicity in Uniformity: Poetry and the Great Leap Forward," in Roderick MacFarquhar, ed., *China Under Mao: Politics Takes Command* (Cambridge, Mass.: M.I.T. Press, 1966), pp. 392–406.

18. "Keep Apace of The Stride of Six Hundred Million People," *Renmin Yinyue* (March 1958): 3–5.

19. "Shanghai Song Movement in Full Swing," *Renmin Yinyue* (March 1958): 5–6.

20. Gao Kuzhou, "Inherit the Glorious Tradition of the Cultural Troupe," *Renmin Yinyue* (April 1958): 33–34.

21. Shao Tong, "Hengsao langfei, menggong baoshou" [Sweep Away Waste, Fiercely Attack Conservatism], *Renmin Yinyue* (March 1958): 6–7.

22. Lynn T. White III, "Bourgeois Radicalism in The 'New Class' of Shanghai, 1949–1969," in James L. Watson, ed., *Class and Social Stratification in Post-Revolution China* (Cambridge: Cambridge University Press, 1984), 159.

23. Prior efforts used mostly foreign musicians or were incomplete. See Li Ling, "Shidai de shengyin" [Sound of the Age], *Renmin Yinyue* (July 1959): 4–5.

24. "Dang de haozhao huacheng juda liliang" [The Party's Call Creates a Great Force], *Renmin Yinyue* (September 1959), 1.

25. *Minzu yinyue*. In Taiwan, *guoyue* is used to mean "national music."

26. Zhao Feng, "Develop an Education Criticism Movement of A Mass Character, Establish A Proletarian Music Education Curriculum," *Renmin Yinyue* (November 1958): 9.

27. He Zhangao and Chen Gang, " 'LiangZhu' de dansheng" [the Birth of "Liang-Zhu"], Shanghai *Wenhui Bao* (3 August 1959); Zhou Qian, "Tan Chen Gang de 'LiangZhu' xiao tichin xiezouqu" [About Chen Gang's "Liang-Zhu" Violin Concerto], *Guanchajia* [The Observer] 26 (December 1979): 72–75.

28. "What Is the Road That Our National Symphonic Music Should Develop?" *Renmin Yinyue* (June 1958): 28–29. Stern responses appeared in the next issue of *People's Music:* Lu Minde, "Symphonic Music Must Serve Pol-

itics," *Renmin Yinyue* (July 1958): 24–26, and letters from indignant readers, 26–27.

29. Ma Sicong, "Chinese Audiences Warmly Welcome the Soviet National Symphony Orchestra," *Renmin Yinyue* (June 1958): 32–33.

30. "Ten Points on Literature and Art" [Opinions on Current Literary and Art Work (Revised Draft)], *Issues & Studies* 8 (July–August 1972): 75–83, 98–104.

31. "Shanxi, Leaping along on Wings of Song," *Renmin Yinyue* (April 1958): 9–12.

32. On the relaxed policies of 1960 to 1962 and the Maoist backlash in culture, see Byung-joon Ahn, *Chinese Politics and the Cultural Revolution: Dynamics of Policy Processes* (Seattle: University of Washington Press, 1976), 161–81.

33. Zhao Feng, "Shilun yinyue geminghua he minzuhua, qunzhonghua de guanxi" [Some Ideas on the Relationship among Making Music Revolutionary, National, and Popular], *Guangming Ribao* (11 March 1964); Wang Yunjie, "Tan jiaoxiangyue de geminghua, minzuhua, qunzhonghua" [About Making Symphonic Music Revolutionary, National, and Popular], *Guangming Ribao* (29 March 1964).

34. Wang Yuhe, "Xiandai zichanjieji fandong yinyue liupian jianjie" [A Brief Introduction to Contemporary Bourgeois Reactionary Musical Schools], *Renmin Yinyue* (February 1959): 37–38.

35. Several articles summarized in "Guanyu Debiaoxi de taolun [xu]" [The Discussion of Debussy (continued)], *Renmin Yinyue* (December 1963): 37. See also *China News Analysis* 523 (3 July 1964): 5–7.

36. Chen Ying, "Bixu jiaqiang de zhandou—guanyu duidai Ouzhou gudian yinyue de yixie wenti" [We Must Battle Even More Fiercely—Some Problems Concerning the Treatment of European Classical Music], *Renmin Yinyue* (October 1963): 2–5.

37. Li Xingwen, " 'Tuchan gongsi' bian" [A Debate about the "Peasant Products Company"], *Renmin Yinyue* (December 1963): 23.

38. *He Luting Pipan Huibian,* 7, 39, 57.

39. Jiang Ying, "Zhongyang Yuetuan de Ya, Fei, Lading Meizhou yinyuehui" [The Central Philharmonic's Asian, African, Latin American Concert], *Renmin Yinyue* (March 1963): 21. Jerome Kern, of course, composed "Old Man River" for his *Showboat.*

40. "Zouchu jiaoxue bixu anzhao dang de wenyi fangxiang chedi gaige" [Education in Music Composition Must Be Thoroughly Reformed According to the Party's Direction for Literature and Art], *Guangming Ribao* (7 September 1964).

41. "Chronology of Events in the Struggle Between the Two Lines on the Cultural Front Since the Founding of the People's Republic of China Seven-

teen Years Ago," *Wen-hua Ke-ming T'ung-hsun* [Cultural Revolution Bulletin] 11, May 1967, in *Current Background* 842 (8 December 1967): 15; *Jiang Qing Tongzhi Lun Wenyi* [Comrade Jiang Qing Discusses Literature and Art] (May 1968), 72.

42. Han Chao and Ch'en Liang *[sic]*, "What are the Ill Effects of the Song Book '200 Famous Foreign Songs'," *Chung-kuo Ch'ing-nien Bao* [China Youth News] (5 September 1964), in *JPRS* 26,658 (1 October 1964): 7–8.

43. Chien Hsin, "Chao Feng's Ugly Face of Opposition to the Thought of Mao Tse-tung," *Kuang-ming Jih-pao* (22 January 1967), in *SCMP* 3872 (1 February 1967): 20.

44. Shi Junliang, "Zhongguo yinyue sanshi nian (shang)" [Thirty Years of Music in China (I)], *Guanchajia* 21 (July 1979): 68.

45. Lu Ji, "Zai doujengzhong chansheng de gequ—wei Jie Fu tongzhi gequji chuban erzuo" [Songs Born in the Midst of Struggle—Written for the Publication of Comrade Jiefu's Song Collection], *Renmin Yinyue* (December 1963): 2–6; "Liaoningsheng wenxue yishujie wei 'Jiefu gequ xuan' chuban juxing yinyyuehui, zuotanhui" [The Literary and Artistic World of Liaoning Province Stages Concert and Forum for the Publication of "Jiefu Song Collection"], *Renmin Yinyue* 133 (May 1964): 17–18; Liao Tushu, "Tan Jiefu Tongzhi wei Mao Zhuxi shici puqu de zuopin" [About Comrade Jiefu's Compositions Setting the Poems of Chairman Mao], *Renmin Yinyue* (October–November 1964): 32–33.

46. An, "Cong 'tongsu yinyuehui'," 12–13; See also An Po and Jie Fu, "Shinian gengyun, baihua qikai" [Ten Years of Cultivation, A Hundred Flowers In Bloom"], *Renmin Yinyue* (October–November 1959): 31–35.

47. Chen, "The Story of a Revolutionary Composer," 34–37.

48. "Jiefangjun quanguanbing zhixing Lin Biao Yuanshuai zhishi, xianqi dachang geming gequ de xin gaochao" [Officers and Soldiers of the People's Liberation Army Implement Marshal Lin Biao's Instruction, Set Off a New High Tide of Singing Revolutionary Songs], *Renmin Yinyue* (January 1961): 12–13.

49. Zhao Feng, "Huanhu Jiefangjun wenyi huiyen de chenggong" [Celebrate the Success of the Liberation Army's Arts Performance], *Guangming Ribao* (11 May 1964). Several prominent military musicians were featured in a symposium on the radicalizaiton of music reported in "Ruhe zhengque lijie yinyue geminghua, minzuhua, qunzhonghua jiqi huxiang guanxi" [How to Correctly Understand the Mutual Relations among Making Music Revolutionary, National, and for the Masses], *Guangming Ribao* (19 May 1964).

50. "Jing Hu geming gequ yue chang yue xiangliang" [Beijing and Shanghai Revolutionary Songs Are Ever More Resonant], Beijing *Dagong Bao* (9 February 1964); Guo Shuzhen, "Zouchu yinyueting, wei nongmin gechang" [Go Forth from the Concert Hall, Sing for the Peasantry], *Guangming Ribao*

(11 March 1964). See also the reports in "The Socialist Singing Movement," *Union Research Service* 33 (24 December 1963); and "Mass singing Activities in Shanghai," *Union Research Service* 42 (21 January 1966).

51. Anita Chan, Richard Madsen, and Jonathan Unger, *Chen Village: The Recent History of a Peasant Community in Mao's China* (Berkeley: University of California Press, 1984): 77.

52. Mao Di, "Ting shoufengqin yinyuehui suixiang" [Thoughts after Hearing the Accordion Concert], *Renmin Yinyue* (October 1963): 30.

53. Wang Yiting, "Fengqin de huangying bujunle dzenma ban?" [What to Do If An Accordion Reed Will Not Work], *Renmin Yinyue* (April 1958): 37–38.

54. Revolutionary Rebel Detachment of the Union of Chinese Writers, "Liu Shao-chi's Black Hand in the Realm of Literature and Art—The assorted crimes of Hu Ch'iao-mu," Beijing *Wen-hsueh Chan-pao* [Literary Combat Journal] 4, 14 April 1967, in *SCMP* 3942 (19 May 1967): p. 14.

55. "Liu Shao-ch'i's Counter-Revolutionary Revisionist Utterances on Culture and Art," in Peking *Hung-se Hsuan-ch'uan-ping* [Red Propaganda Soldier] 4, 10 May 1967, in *SCMP—Supplement* 259 (29 September 1967): 38.

56. "Zhongguo yinxie zhaokai qinqu dapu zuotanhui" [Musicians' Association Convenes Forum on Qin Music], *Renmin Yinyue* 129 (January 1964): 40.

57. An had been head of the Liaoning Provincial Cultural Department, chairman of the Provincial Musicians' Association, president of the Northeast People's Arts Academy, and associate of Li Jiefu. Ma Ke, "Huainian An Po, xuexi An Po" [Mourn An Po, Study An Po], *Renmin Yinyue* 144 (August 1965); 21–22; "Zhongguo Yinyue Xuean juxing jianyuan dianli" [Groundbreaking Ceremony for the Academy of Chinese Music], *Guangming Ribao* 22 September 1964).

58. *The New Grove Dictionary of Music and Musicians*, s.v. "China: V. Instruments," 270.

59. Alan R. Thrasher, "The Sociology of Chinese Music: An Introduction," *Asian Music* 12 (1981): 42–43.

60. "Zhongguo yinyuejiaxiehui dengdanwei zuotan yueqi gailian" [The Chinese Musician's Association and Other Units Hold Forum on the Reform of Musical Instruments], *Guangming Ribao* (17 November 1954); "Beijing zhuxing yueqi gailang zuotanhui" [Beijing Convenes A Forum on Improving Musical Instruments], *Renmin Yinyue* 6 (December 1954): 63; Zhang Jinde, "Yige xinxing minzu yuedui de chengzhang" [The Maturing of a New Style Nationalities Musical Ensemble], *Renmin Yinyue* 28 (June 1955): 22–24.

61. He Luting, "Minzu yinyue wenti" [The Question of National Music], *Renmin Ribao* (11 September 1956): 17–22.

62. *The New Grove Dictionary of Music and Musicians,* s.v. "China: VI. Since 1949," 280.

63. Li Wei, "Qianjinzhong de budui yinyue gongzuo" [Military Music Work in the Midst of Its Advance], *Guangming Ribao* (29 March 1964).

64. Liu Fengjin, "Yizhi minzu yuedui zai minzuhua fangmian zouguo de daolu" [The Road of Traveled by a National Music Ensemble in Nationalization], *Guangming Ribao* (18 March 1964); "Cong yinyuehui kan Qianwei Gewutuan minzu yueqi gaige" [See the Vanguard Song and Dance Troupe's Reform of National Musical Instruments in Concert], *Renmin Yinyue* (August 1962): 32; "Folk Music Concerts," *Chinese Literature* 2, (1964): 123–24.

65. These and other examples are discussed in Mao Chi-tseng, "Reform of Traditional Musical Instruments," *Chinese Literature* 8 (1965): 110–16. Similar reforms of musical instruments have taken place in Taiwan, where silk *zheng* strings have given way to metal. See the illustrations of instrumental innovations illustrated on page 10 of Liang Tsai-ping, ed., *Chinese Music* (Taibei: Chinese Classical Musical Association, 1964), especially the "quadran pipe fiddle," which looks like the joining of four drums to a cello.

66. Shi Ying, " 'Baihua qifang' zatan" [Mixed Comments on "Let A Hundred Flowers Blossom"] *Renmin Yinyue* (December 1956): 21.

67. Quoted from *China News Analysis* (21 July 1961), 4, in Kuo-huang Han and Lindy Li Mark, "Evolution and Revolution in Chinese Music," in Elizabeth May, ed., *Musics of Many Cultures* (Berkeley: University of California Press, 1980), 22.

68. "Xitan Guo Lanying duchang yinyuehui" [Happy Discussion of Guo Lanying's Solo Song Recital], *Renmin Yinyue* (December 1963): 16–22. See also Li Huanzhi, "Tantan minzu yanchang yishu de fazhan he tigao" [Chat about the Development and Elevation of National Singing Art], *Renmin Yinyue* (June 1963): 5–8.

69. Ma Tingheng, "Xiyang zichanjieji yinyue dui wo de duhai" [I was Poisoned by the Bourgeois Music of the West], *Guangming Ribao* (4 March 1965).

70. *The New Grove Dictionary of Music and Musicians,* s.v. "Sax," 530–31.

71. David Cairns, ed., *The Memoirs of Hector Berlioz* (New York: W.W. Norton, 1975), 318–319, 402–3.

72. He, "Minzu yinyue wenti."

73. See *Dongfang Hong Gequji* ["The East Is Red" Song Collection], (Hong Kong: Sanlien Shudian, 1965).

74. See Cai Cai, "Shengge 'Dongfang Hong' de bimo guansi" [A War of Words over the Hymn, "The East Is Red"], *Dongxiang* [The Trend] 28 (January 1981): 29; Wei Hsia-an, "The Most Powerful Song," *Chinese Literature*

1 (1970): 108–13; Zhongguo Minjian Wenyi Yanjiuhui, ed., *"Zhongguo Chuliaoge Mao Zedong"* ["China Produced a Mao Zedong"] (Beijing: Renmin Wenyi Chubanshe, 1951), 2; Jiang Qihua and Xiao Xinghua, "Renmin geshou Li Youyuan he 'Dongfang Hong' de yansheng" [The People's Songsmith Li Youyuan and the Birth of "The East Is Red"], *Renmin Yinyue* 1 (1978): 34–35.

75. *The New Grove Dictionary of Music and Musicians*, s.v. "Chimes"; Yue Sheng, "Bian Zhong" [*Bian* Bells], Beijing *Dagong Bao* (12 March 1964).

76. See Byung-joon Ahn, "The Politics of Peking Opera, 1962–1965," *Asian Survey* 12 (December 1972): 1066–81.

77. Tsung Chi, "The Seventh 'Shanghai Spring' Music Festival," *Chinese Literature* 8 (1966): 164–76.

78. "Duanzhengle wenyi fangxiang, zengqiangle gongnong ganqing" [A Corrected Direction in Literature and Art, A Strengthened Feeling for Workers and Peasants], *Guangming Ribao* (29 March 1964).

79. "Zhongyang Yinyueyuan shisheng jingchang wei gongnong yanzou" [Central Conservatory Faculty and Students Regularly Perform for Workers and Peasants], *Guangming Ribao* (31 May 1964).

80. Twenty-nine articles attacking him in the June 1966 issue of Shanghai *Wenhui Bao* have been reprinted in Hong Kong, giving ample documentation to the campaign against him. See *He Luting Pipan Huibian*.

81. See Lynn T. White III, *Policies of Chaos: Labels, Bosses, and Campaigns as Causes of China's Cultural Revolution* (Princeton: Princeton University Press, forthcoming).

82. This is the reason given in Xiao Shen, "Cong 'gua yige waiguo siren' dao da yixie Zhongguo huoren" [From "Grab a Dead Foreigner" to Hit Some Living Chinese], *Renmin Yinyue* (March 1979): 14–16.

83. See *He Luting Ziliao Ji*, 5; Liang, "Lun He Luting zuopin de xuanlu," 44.

84. *He Luting Pipan Huibian*, 22, 42, 48.

85. Quoted in Han and Mark, "Evolution and Revolution in Chinese Music," 22.

86. *He Luting Pipan Huibian*, 9, 22.

87. Ibid., 34, 43.

88. Ibid., 6, 28.

89. Ibid., 12, 86–87.

90. Jiang Baixun, "Zhonggong Shanghai Wenlian de fandang fenzi" [Anti-Party Elements of the Shanghai Federation of Literary and Art Workers], *Jinri Dalu* [The Mainland Today], (1 December 1966), in *He Luting Ziliao Ji*, 5.

91. *He Luting Pipan Huibian*, 16–17.

92. Even during the 1930s, some criticized the "Song of the Guerrillas" for being Western, not national. See Li Ling, *Yinyue Zatan* [Talks on Music], vol. 3 (Beijing: Beijing Chubanshe, 1980), 216.

93. This would not have been the first revolutionary expropriation of "The British Grenadier," which was reset with revolutionary words as "The New Massachusetts Liberty Song" in 1770. See Kenneth Silverman, *A Cultural History of the American Revolution* (New York: Thomas Y. Crowell, 1976), 145–46. The original words are: "Some talk of Alexander, and some of Hercules, / Of Hector and Lysander, and such great names as these; / But of all the world's brave heroes there's none that can compare, / With a tow, row, row, row, row, row, to the British Grenadiers." He Luting's words are: "We are crack shots, each bullet wipes out an enemy; / We are a flying army, fearing neither high mountains or deep rivers," etc.

94. "Kelien 'Jialing Jiangshang' de He Luting" [Pitiable He Luting "On the Banks of the Jialing River"], *Wanren Zazhi* [Everybody's Magazine] (12 September 1968), in *He Luting Ziliao Ji*, 2.

95. "Wei He Luting fanan jituan, huodong didian pianji Shanghai Zhuzhou Wuhan Nanjing Shaoyang" [Group for Reversing the Verdict on He Luting Active in Shanghai, Zhuzhou, Wuhan, Nanjing, and Shaoyang], *Xingdao Ribao*, 18 July 1968, in *He Luting Ziliao Ji*, 1.

96. According to one account, He was also given poisoned tea, but survived because of his strength. Li Yanwu, "Jiang Zhang Yao Wang de shiji" [How Jiang, Zhang, Yao, and Wang Gained Power], *Zhengming* 38 (December 1980): 14; *He Luting Ziliao Ji*, 3. Red Guards from the conservatory's middle school severely beat Jiang Ruishi, their principal (and He's wife). She was protected by one of her students, the stepson of actor Zhao Dan (star of the movie *Nie Er*). See Zhang Xinxin and Sang Ye, "Chinese Profiles," *Chinese Literature* (Spring 1986): 27.

97. Ma, "Testimony," 71–88; Ma Sitson, "Terror at The Hands of The Red Guard," *Life*, 2 June 1967, 22–29, 63–66; and Ma, "We Are Slaves Who Have Been Betrayed," 64–73.

98. Lu Ren, "Xiezhu 'pantao' de youdiyuan" [The Postal Worker Who Aided the "Deserter"], *Zhengming* 91 (May 1985): 76–77. The first part of the *Life* story was reprinted in the Soviet magazine, *Literature*, on July 19, 1967. From this source it was translated into Chinese. Under the title "Why I Escaped from China," Ma's account was published as a pamphlet in Guangzhou, and in the Beijing Red Guard magazine, *Shuangchen-yue* 1 (10 January 1968), in *Survey of China Mainland Magazines* 616 (25 March 1968): 10–15. The Red Guard version is quite accurate, omitting only a few of the abuses reported by Ma, and (understandably) his account of how he fled to Hong Kong. These omissions may well be in the Soviet version.

99. "Quotations from Chairman Mao Tse-tung' Put to Music at Shenyang

Musical Festival,'' NCNA-English Shenyang, 1 November 1966, in *SCMP* 3815 (4 November 1966): 27.

100. "Qi Benyu Tongzhi tan Li Jiefu de wenti" [Comrade Qi Benyu Discusses the Problem of Li Jiefu], Beijing *Zhandou Bao* [Fighting News] (23 February 1967).

101. Mao Yu-run, professor of composition, Shanghai Conservatory of Music interview with author, Eugene, Ore., 27 October 1987.

102. "Quotations from Chairman Mao Set to Music and Widely Sung," *Chinese Literature* 4 (1967): 138–39.

103. This discussion draws on my "Arts Policies of the Cultural Revolution: The Rise and Fall of Culture Minister Yu Huiyong," a paper for the Harvard University Conference on New Perspectives on the Cultural Revolution, May 1987.

104. Jin Dongfang, "Guanyu Yu Huiyong" [About Yu Huiyong], *Mingbao Yuekan* 131 (November 1976): 24–25.

105. The problem was not limited to Shanghai. A Guangzhou music professor also asserted that "The transferred children of workers and peasants cannot learn Western musical intruments, but they may study national music." "Lu Zhongren choushi" [The Stinking History of Lu Zhongren], Guangzhou *Dongfeng Wenyi* [East Wind Literature and Art] (31 January 1968). Lu also wanted to have a sixty percent quota on students from such backgrounds, who could, after graduation be sent to work in lower-level positions.

106. "Expose Bourgeois Thought within the Realm of Music," *Renmin Yinyue* 29 (July 1955): 8.

107. Yu Huiyong, "Peng Boshan—Sworn Enemy of Folk Music," *Renmin Yinyue* 30 (August 1955): 4.

108. "Expose and Criticize the Counterrevolutionary Crimes of Yu Huiyung, Sworn Follower of the Gang of Four," Beijing Domestic Service in Mandarin, 9 December 1977, in *FBIS* (14 December 1977): E14–18.

109. Even though Yu was on the sidelines, others from his department were active in the campaign against he Luting.

5 Court Pianist to the Cultural Revolution: Yin Chengzong

1. I visited Gulangyu in February 1986. See also Zhang Zeyu, "Xiamen—A Garden by the Sea," *Beijing Review* 29 (19 May 1986): 24; and Hong Lanxing, "Gulangyu: An Island of Pianos," *Beijing Review* 30 (6 July 1987): 32–33.

2. Biographical information on Yin Chengzong may be found in Huang Dalu, "Gangqinjia Ying Chengzong de youmeng" [The Nightmare of Pianist Yin Chengzong], Hong Kong *Guanchajia* [Observer] 41 (20 April 1981): 27–

29; Harold C. Schonberg, "A Chinese Pianist Resumes An Interrupted Career," *New York Times,* 25 Septebmer 1983; Wang Jinming, "Yin Chengzong de licheng" [The Career of Yin Chengzong], *Mingbao yuekan* 167 (November 1979): 28–34; Yan Qimei, "Yin Chengzong: you shi yige Li Lianying" [Yin Chengzong: Once Again a Li Lianying], Hong Kong *Dangdai* [The Present Age] 7 (15 March 1981): 43–46; Zhu Qingxin, "Luhuo huishen dao shaowen" [From Deep in the Stove's Ashes to the Warmth of Dawn], *Jing Bao* [The Mirror] (January 1983): 58–61. Yin has also written a brief autobiographical statement, available from his agent, Harold Shaw. I have supplemented these written materiials with interviews with Yin in New York City on May 13, 1987; Newport, Ore. on July 11, 1987; and Eugene, Ore. on Feburary 25–28, 1988.

3. Hong Shi, "Cong Li Mingqiang, Gu Shengying dejiang tanqi" [Speaking of Li Mingqiang and Gu Shengying Winning Prizes], *Renmin Yinyue,* (October 1958): 30. See also Zhong Dao, "Cong huode liangge yinyue yidengjiang tanqi" [Speaking of Winning Two First Prizes in Music], *Wenhui Bao* (18, September 1959).

4. Zhao Binguo, "Zai Qiekefusiki bisaihuishang de Yin Chengzong" [Yin Chengzong at the Tchaikovsky Competition Concert], *Renmin Yinyue* (July 1962): 23–24.

5. One grumpy European commented unfavorably upon Yin's romantic style, but perhaps captured his independent spirit.

> The Chaikovksy laureate showed his piano equipment this afternoon. A taste for the worst side of Liszt could be blamed on his Leningrad teacher, I suppose. A talent for extreme contrasts (thunder and whipped cream), the skill of a machine and the mannerisms of a ham, or an abbé. Are there courses in stage comportment in conservatories? Yin Chengzong looks like someone who listens to no one any longer—soon no one will try saying anything to him.

Jay Leyda, *Dianying: An Account of Films and the Film Audience in China* (Cambridge, Mass.: M.I.T. Press, 1972), 309.

6. Yin Chengzong, interview with author, Newport, Ore., 11 July 1987.

7. Alan L. Kagan, "Music and the Hundred Flowers Movement," *The Musical Quarterly* (October 1963): 427; "Thirty Years of Development," *Beijing Review* 29 (25 August 1986): 24.

8. Yi Ding, "Yin Chengzong de Zhongguo gangqin zuopin duzuohui" [Yin Chengzong's Solo Recital of Chinese Piano Works], *Renmin Yinyue* 136–37 (August–September 1965): 73–74.

9. See Byung-joon Ahn, "The Politics of Peking Opera, 1962–1965," *Asian Survey* 12 (December 1972): 1066–81; D. W. Fokkema, "Maoist Ideology and Its Exemplification in the New Peking Opera," *Current Scene* 10 (August 1972): 13–20; *Jiang Qing Tongzhi Lun Wenyi* [Comrade Jiang Qing on Lit-

erature and Art] (May 1968); *Jiang Qing Tongzhi Jianghua Xuanbian* [Selection of Speeches by Comrade Jiang Qing] (1 February 1968); Colin Mackerras, "Chinese Opera after the Cultural Revolution (1970–72)", *The China Quarterly* 55 (July–September 1973): 478–510; Colin Mackerras, *The Chinese Theatre in Modern Times* (London: Thames and Hudson, 1975), 196–211; Hua-yuan Li Mowry, *Yang-pan Hsi: New Theatre in China* (Berkeley: Center for Chinese Studies, 1973); Lois Wheeler Snow, *China on Stage* (New York: Vintage, 1972); and Constantine Tung, "The Hidden Enemy as Villain in Communist Chinese Drama," *Educational Theatre Journal* 25 (October 1973): 335–43.

10. "Jiang Qing Tongzhi zai Beijing Wenyi zuotanhuishang de jianghua" [Comrade Jiang Qing's Speech at the Beijing Forum on Literature and Art], 9 & 12 November 1967, in *Jiang Qing Tongzhi Lun Wenyi* [Comrade Jiang Qing Discusses Literature and Art] (May 1968): 176; Jiang Qing, "Wei renmin li xingong" [Do New Services for the People], 12 April 1967, in *Jiang Qing Tongzhi Jianghua Xuanbian* [Selected Speeches of Comrade Jiang Qing] (Guangzhou: Renmin Chubanshe, 1968), 41.

11. For example, Zhao Feng of the Central Conservatory: "She claimed she had deliberated on every note and every headgear for the ballet but she knows nothing about musical notes. In fact she does not even know how to read the musical score." "She is not a standard-bearer of revolutionary literature and art but a shameless pickpocket." Zhao Feng, "Musical Authority Calls Chiang Ching 'Plagiarizer'," Hong Kong *AFP*, 19 January 1977, in *FBIS*, 21 January 1977, E5–E6.

12. Ross Terrill, *The White-Boned Demon: A Biography of Madame Mao Zedong* (New York: William Morrow, 1984), 32; Roxane Witke, *Comrade Chiang Ch'ing* (Boston: Little, Brown, 1977), pp. 388–89.

13. Terrill, *The White-Boned Demon*, 53–54.

14. Witke, *Comrade Chiang Ch'ing*, 390.

15. *A Collection of Chou Yang's Counter-Revolutionary Revisionist Speeches* (Beijing: Liaoyuan Combat Regiment of Central Academy of Fine Arts, et al., n.d.), in *Selections from China Mainland Magazines* (24 March 1969): 15.

16. *Summary of the Forum on the Work in Literature and Art in the Armed forces with Which Comrade Lin Piao Entrusted Comrade Chiang Ch'ing* (Peking: Foreign Languages Press, 1968). A slightly different (earlier) version is in *SCMP* 3956 (9 June 1967): 1–15.

17. Chiang Ching, *On the Revolution of Peking Opera* (Peking: Foreign Languages Press, 1968), 2.

18. *Summary of the Forum on the Work in Literature and Art in the Armed forces with Which Comrade Lin Piao Entrusted Comrade Chiang Ching*, 14.

19. "This is something I really don't understand, but I'm studying it now." T'an Yuan-shou, "Comrade Chiang Qing Leads Us to Struggle," Beijing *Hsin*

Pei-ta [New Beijing University], 30 May 1967, in *SCMP—Supplement* 190 (7 July 1967): 18; Witke, *Comrade Chiang Ch'ing*, 388–89.

20. *Jiang Qing Tongzhi Lun Wenyi*, 66, 70. Jiang read this speech aloud at her 1966 PLA Forum, despite its relatively relaxed stance on European music.

21. *Jiang Qing Tongzhi Lun Wenyi*, 67–68.

22. I have drawn these remarks from "Jiang Qing Tongzhi dui yinyue gongzuo de yici jianghua [A Speech of Comrade Jiang Qing on Music Work], 18 November 1964; "Jiang Qing Tongzhi guanyu yinyue gongzuo de zhongyao zhishi [Comrade Jiang Qing's Important Instructions on Music Work], 14 January 1965; "Jiang Qing Tongzhi dui jiaoxiangyue *Shajiabang* de zhishi" [Comrade Jiang Qing's Instructions Concerning the Symphonic Music *Shajiabang*], in *Jiang Qing Tongzhi Lun Wenyi*, 63–66, 67–72, 73–81.

23. *Jiang Qing Tongzhi Lun Wenyi*, 63.

24. Ibid., 63–64.

25. Ibid., 63, 73.

26. Ibid., 64, 72.

27. Ibid., 63, 71.

28. Ibid., 69, 64, 65.

29. Ibid., 64, 69, 70. Because Liu Shikun was in political disgrace when this text was published, it refers only to "X X X," although the context makes Liu's identity clear.

30. Ibid., 65, 71–72.

31. Ibid., 69.

32. Ibid., 74.

33. Fu Hsin, "Behind Chiang Ch'ing's Utmost Dislike of Folk Songs," *Guangming Ribao*, 20 November 1976, in *SCMP* 6258 (13 January 1977): 195–96; See also Criticism Group of the Ministry of Culture, "Defend the Policy of 'Letting a Hundred Flowers Blossom and a Hundred Schools of Thought Contend'," *Guangming Ribao*, 22 April 1977, in *SPRCP*, 6334 (6 May 1977): 226.

34. Ch'en Ju-t'ang, "The Revolutionary Symphony 'Sha Chia Pang' Has Fought Its Way Out of the Old Camp," *Hung-ch'i* 8 (23 May 1967), in *Survey of China Mainland Magazines* 579 (12 June 1967): 17–19; Criticism Group of the Ministry of Culture, "Restore the Truth of History—Exposing Chiang Ch'ing's Crimes in Plundering the Fruits of Model Revolutionary Theatrical Works'," *Renmin Ribao*, 13 February 1977), in *FBIS*, 15 February 1977, K4; "Jiang Qing Tongzhi dui jiaoxiangyue *Shajiabang* de zhishi" [Comrade Jiang Qing's Instructions Concerning the Symphonic Music *Shajiabang*], in *Jiang Qing Tongzhi Lun Wenyi*, 73–81.

35. "Shachiapang" Revolutionary Fighting Regiment of the no. 1 Peking Opera Company of Peking, "Mao Tse-tung's Thought Illuminates the Road of Revolution of Peking Opera," in Chiang Ching, 44–55. See also Bell Yung,

"Model Opera as Model: From *Shajiabang* to *Sagabong*," in Bonnie S. McDougall, *Popular Chinese Literature and Performing Arts in the People's Republic of China 1949–1979* (Berkeley: University of California Press, 1984), 149; "A Great Standard-Bearer, a Dauntless Warrior: A Chronicle of Comrade Chiang Ch'ing's Activities in the Field of Literature and Art," *Issues and Studies* (October 1975): 92–93. The text of *Shajiabang* is in Snow, *China on Stage*, 126–90.

36. Kao Chang-yin, "A Brilliant Example of Making Foreign Things Serve China," *Chinese Literature* 11 (1968): 96–103. See the score published as *Shajiabang* (Beijing: Renmin Yinyue Chubanshe, 1976).

37. Kao, "A Brilliant Example of Making Foreign Things Serve China," 103.

38. Ch'en, "The Revolutionary Symphony 'Sha Chia Pang' Has Fought Its Way Out of the Old Camp."

39. Hsiao Min, "Pioneer of Symphonic Music of the Proletariat—In Praise of the Symphony 'Shachiapang'," *Chinese Literature* 5–6 (1967): 160.

40. The Fight Regiment for Mao Tse-tung's Thought and the "Red Rock" Corps of the Central Conservatory of Music, "A New Lease of Life for Symphonic Music," Beijing *Jen-min Jih-pao*, 3 June 1967, in *Current Background* 831 (24 July 1967): 43–47.

41. Yin Chengzong, "Yi Jiang Qing tongzhi wei guanghui bangyang, zuo yongyuan zhongyu Mao Zhuxi de geming wenyi zhanshi" [With Jiang Qing as a Glorious Example, Become a Revolutionary Literary and Art Worker Eternally Loyal to Chairman Mao], *Renmin Ribao* [People's Daily], 6 July 1968; Wang Jinming, "Yin Chengzong de licheng;" Yan Qimei, "Yin Chengzong: you shi yige Li Lianying," 43–46; "Shachiapang" Revolutionary fighting Regiment of the no. 1 Peking Opera Company of Peking, "Mao Tse-tung's Thought Illuminates the Road of Revolution of Peking Opera," Yin Cheng-chung, "How the Piano Concerto 'Yellow River' Was Composed," *Chinese Literature* 11 (1974): 97–102.

42. Richard Curt Kraus, *Class Conflict in Chinese Socialism* (New York: Columbia University Press, 1981), 115–41.

43. Hong Yong Lee, *The Politics of the Chinese Cultural Revolution* (Berkeley: University of California Press, 1979), 86–87.

44. Early in the Cultural Revolution, used pianos sold for as little as 100 or 200 *renminbi*, in contrast to 1981 prices of 1500 or 1600 *renminbi*. Ying Fen, "Ye tan Zhongguo yinyue shanshi nian" [Some More Discussion of Thirty Years of Chinese Music], *Guanchajia* 22 (August 1979): 63; Huang Dalu, "Gangqinjia Ying Chengzong de youmeng," 29.

45. Liang Heng and Judith Shapiro, *Son of the Revolution*, (New York: Vintage Books, 1984), 115–16.

46. Yue Daiyun and Carolyn Wakeman, *To the Storm: The Odyssey of a*

Revolutionary Chinese Woman (Berkeley: University of California Press, 1985), 85, 168.

47. Bai Yunfei, "Xiao tichin jiaoyujia Zheng Xianghe" [Master Violin Teacher Zheng Xianghe], *Guanchajia* [The Observer] 17 (March 1979): 69.

48. Anonymous interview with author, Hong Kong (October 1979).

49. Huang, "Gangqinjia Yin Chengzong de youmeng," 28.

50. Yin Chengzong, interview with author, Eugene, Ore., 25–28 February 1988.

51. Fan died of disease in 1968. Bai Yunfei, "Pianist Gu Guoquan Talks about Music," *Guanchajia* 16 (February 1979): 75–76.

52. "Guoji Xiaobang gangqin bisai jieshu, woguo Gangqinjia Li Mingqiang huo disiming [International Chopin Piano Competition Concludes, Our Nation's Pianist Li Mingqiang Takes Fourth Prize], *Renmin Yinyue* (March 1960): 38–39.

53. Liu Manqin, "Zhuming nugangqinjia Gu Shengying zhi si [The Death of the Famous Female Pianist Gu Shengying], *Zhengming* 23 (September 1979): 14–19.

54. "Gu Shengying, Bo Yibin juxing Zhongguo zuopin yinyuehui" [Gu Shengying, Bo Yibin Perform Concerts of Chinese Music], *Renmin Yinyue* (August–September 1963): 63.

55. Ying Chengzong, telephone interview with author, 2 March 1988.

56. "Zhou Zongli jiejian sige wenyi danwei geming zaofanpai daibiao shi de tanhua zhaiyao" [Summary of the Conversation when Premier Zhou Received Representatives from the Revolutionary Rebel Groups of Four Literary and Art Units]; "Regulations of the Central Committee of the Chinese Communist Party Concerning the Great Proletarian Cultural Revolution of Literary and Art Units," 17 February 1967, in Beijing *Wanshan Hongbian Red Mountain Everywhere*, 1 (April 1967): 2.

57. "More on Letting the Literary and Art Circles Quickly 'Fight' Their Way Out," Shaghai *Wen-hui Pao*, 5 February 1967 in *SCMP—Supplement* 170 (23 March, 1967):

58. Words and music are in *Chinese Literature*, 8 (1967), 201–202.

59. "Wenyi jianxun" [Short Dispatches on Literature and Art)], Beijing *Wenyi Hongoi* [Literature and Art Red Flag] (30 May 1967); Yin, "Yi Jiang Qing tongzhi wei guanghui bangyang, zuo yongyuan zhongyu Mao Zhuxi de geming wenyi zhanshi," Yin, "How the Piano Concerto 'Yellow River' Was Composed."

60. Yin, "Yi Jiang Qing tongzhi wei guanghui bangyang, zuo yongyuan zhongyu Mao Zhuxi de geming wenyi zhanshi."

61. Yan, "Yin Chengzong: you shi yige Li Lianying," 43.

62. Yin, "Yi Jiang Qing tongzhi wei guanghui bangyang, zuo yongyuan zhongyu Mao Zhuxi di geming wenyi zhanshi."

63. "Chairman Mao and Vice-Chairman Lin Biao Attend Musical Perfor-mance," *Chinese Literature* 9 (1968), 3–6. Yin and his fellow performers were honored by Chen Boda, Kang Sheng, Jiang Qing, Zhang Chunqiao, and Yao Wenyuan at a reception to reassure them on the eve of the concert. "Birth of Piano Music 'The Red Lantern' with Peking Opera Singing," *Chinese Lit-erature* 9 (1968): 7.

64. Yin, "Yi Jiang Qing tongzhi wei guanghui bangyang, zuo yongyuan zhongyu Mao Zhuxi de geming wenyi zhanshi."

65. "Birth of Two Gems of Art," *Chinese Literature* 10 (1968): 97.

66. See Liu Junhua, "Singing the Praises of Our Great Leader is Our Greatest Happiness," *Chinese Literature* 9 (1968): 32–40.

67. Ting Hseuh-lei, "Greet the New Era of Proletarian Revolutionary Lit-erature and Art," *Chinese Literature* 11 (1968): 89.

68. Ren Wenxin, "Biao shehuizhuyi zhi xin, li wuchanjiehi zhi yi" [Show Something New for Socialism, Innovate for the Proletariat], *Renmin Ribao,* 30 July, 1968.

69. "Gramophone Records of Piano Music 'The Red Lantern' with Peking Opera Singing," *Chinese Literature* 12 (1968): 119.

70. Jen Wen-hsing, "Blaze New Trails, Socialist and Proletarian—Something New and Something Distinctive," *Chinese Literature* 10 (1968): 4–5.

71. Terrill, *The White-Boned Demon,* 317.

72. *Jiang Qing Tongzhi Lun Wenyi,* 64.

73. Yin, "How the Piano Concerto 'Yellow River' Was Composed"; Yin Chengzong, autobiographical statement, 1987.

74. *New York Times,* 14 October 1973, quoted in Witke, *Comrade Chiang Ch'ing,* 459.

75. Yin Chengzong, autobiographical statement, 1987. From abroad, Fou Ts'ong praised the revival of the piano, even if he did regard Yin's composi-tions as musically backward. "Xianreng tuichu hongdengji dalu gechu lu-owule" [Mainland Music Becomes Backward by Still Promoting *The Red Lantern,*], *Xingdao Ribao,* 9 February, 1974, in *Fu Cong Ziliao Ji* (n.p., n.d.), 5.

76. Witke, *Comrade Chiang Ch'ing,* 417.

77. "Tong Zhongguo Jingjuyuan, Beijing Jingju Yituan bufen yanyuan de jianghua" [Talk with Some Performers of the Chinese Beijing Opera Acad-emy and the First Beijing Opera Troupe of Beijing], 1 May 1967, in *Jiang Qing Tongzhi Lun Wenyi,* 170.

78. Amateur performances often had no European instruments at all. *The New Grove Dictionary of Music and Musicians,* s.v. "China: Ill. Musical drama and narratives."

79. David Bonavia, *Verdict in Peking: The Trial of the Gang of Four* (Lon-

don: Burnett Books, 1984), 135. Jiang Qing was not unhappy if this curtailed a "feudal" form of music.

80. The woodblock is by Chen Qingxin and Xu Qinsong in *Meishu* [Art] 1 (1977): 27.

81. Bi Shuqin, *Tan Gremin Gequ Chuangzuo* [On Composing Revolutionary Songs] (Shanghai: Renmin Chubanshe), 1976).

82. Sparetime Singing and Performing Group, 2nd Company of a certain PLA Peking Unit, "Strip the 'Theory of Inspiration' of of *[sic]* Its Mysterious Cloak," *Chieh-fang-chun Wen-i* (Liberation Army Literature and Art 5 (1973), in *Survey of China Mainland Magazines—Supplement* 50 (28 December 1973): 10.

83. Yin Chengzong, personal communication to author, 10 May, 1988; see also Tim Brook, "The Revival of China's Musical Culture," *The China Quarterly* 77 (March 1979): 114.

84. Wang, "Yin Chengzong de licheng," 32; Yin Chengzong, personal communication to author, May 10, 1988. Jiang Qing was apparently interested in "Three Variations on the Plum Blossom," which she was later accused of using to make counterrevolution. See Wu Zhao, " 'Maihua sannong' yu Jiang Qing de yexin" ["Three Variations on the Plum Blossom" and Jiang Qing's Ambition], *Renmin Yinyue* 6 (1977): 10, 18–19.

85. "Concert Commemorating Nieh Erh and Hsien Hsing-hai, Two People's Musicians," *Peking Review* 18 (31 October 1975): 6.

86. Mao Di, "Ting shoufengqin yinyuehui suixiang" [Thoughts after Hearing the Accordion Concert], *Renmin Yinyue* (October 1963): 30.

87. Li Jiefu, "Zan gangqin panchang 'hongdengji' " [Praise "The Red Lantern" with Piano Accompaniment], *Renmin Ribao* (6 July 1968).

88. Ye Wa, interview with author, Eugene, Ore., 26 May 1988.

89. Witke, *Comrade Chiang Ch'ing,* 117.

90. James Barron, "Andrew Davis, the Model of a Jet-Age Conductor," *New York Times,* 16 April 1978. A somewhat different version of this story inspired American composer Brian Holmes' satirical piece for brass ensemble, "Tales of the Cultural Revolution."

91. Wang, "Yin Chengzong de licheng," 28–34; Yin Chengzong, personal communication to author, 10 May 1988.

92. Witke, *Comrade Chiang Ch'ing,* 457–59.

93. Bi Jizhou, "Chen Gang tan yinyue chuangzuo" [Chen Gang Discusses Musical Composition] *Jing Bao* 1 (10 January 1982): 68.

94. See Thomas P. Bernstein, *Up to the Mountains and Down to the Villages: The Transfer of Youth from Urban to Rural China* (New Haven: Yale University Press, 1977); Anita Chan, Richard Madsen, and Jonathan Unger, *Chen Village* (Berkeley: University of California Press, 1984).

95. "Poems from Hsiaochinchuang," *Chinese Literature* 9 (1976): 115–

21. "Chiang Ching and Hsiaochinchuang: Thoroughly Settle Accounts With the Renegade Chiang Ching's Counter-revolutionary Crimes in Hsiaochinchuang," Beijing NCNA Domestic Service, 11 January 1978, in *FBIS*, 17 January 1978, E1–E7.

96. Beijing NCNA Domestic Service, 18 February 1978, in *FBIS*, 21 February 1978, E20–E23.

97. Bai, "Xiao tichin jiaoyujia Zheng Xianghe," 68–69.

98. Ding Xuesong, *Zuoqujia Zheng Lucheng* [Composer Zheng Lucheng] (Shenyang: Liaoning Renmin Chubanshe, 1983), 3–51.

99. "China's First Ph.D. Conductor," *Beijing Review* (25 August 1986): 24.

100. I interviewed Xiao (which is not his real name) in Hong Kong, on November 12 and 13, 1979.

101. Mackerras reports persistent but less extreme Westernizing influences in the national music ensembles of the Mongols and the Uighurs. Colin Mackerras, "Traditional Mongolian Performing Arts in Inner Mongolia," *The Australian Journal of Chinese Affairs* 10 (July 1983); 31; and Colin Mackerras, "Uygur Performing Arts in Contemporary China," *The China Quarterly* 101 (March 1985): 58–77.

102. A young pianist recounted very similar experiences when she supported herself by giving private lessons in Guangzhou after 1971, including the private recitals. Interview with author, Hong Kong, 22 October 1979.

103. Yan, "Yin Chengzong: you shi yige Li Lianying," 43–46.

104. Wang, "Yin Chengzong de licheng," 32–33. Yin's inclusion of a reference to music of the Tang dynasty in *The Red Lantern* was similarly alleged to show that he wanted people to look to the past instead of the future.

105. Huang, "Gangqinjia Ying Chengzong de youmeng," 27–29; Zhu, "Luhuo huishen dao shaowen," 58–61.

106. When Yin visited me in 1988, he reacted with horror to a big newspaper picture of Jimmy Swaggart, the defrocked Christian demagogue, who reminded Yin too painfully of figures from China's Cultural Revolution. Yin read a draft of this chapter, and was unhappy to find so much discussion of politics.

6   The Red Aristocrat: Liu Shikun

1. Chen Rongqiao, "Wo he Liu Shikun chongfeng taiping shanxia" [Liu Shikun and I Meet Again beneath the Pacific Mountains] *Guanchajia* 11 (September 1978): 76–77; Yin Chengzong, interview with author, Eugene, Ore., 25–28 February 1988.

2. The Central Conservatory had moved from Tianjin to Beijing. For a

description of the conservatory and its high school, see Felix Greene, *Awakened China* (Garden City, N.Y.: Doubleday, 1961), 231–33.

3. Liu Shikun, "Wode chanzhang" [My Upbringing], *Renmin Yinyue* (October–November 1959): 47; Lao Zhicheng, "New Musical Talent is Maturing," *Renmin Yinyue* (August 1957): 39.

4. Liu's fellow composer was Huang Liangfei. Han Zi, "Xin Zhongguo jiaoxiangyue yishu de fazhan" [The Development of Symphonic Musical Art in New China], *Renmin Yinyue* (October–November 1959): 19.

5. "Zhongguo yinxie zai Jing huiyuan chengli gangqin xiaozu" [Beijing Members of the Musicians Association Establish Piano Group], *Renmin Yinyue* (April 1960): 37.

6. Ai Zhiyou, "Liu Shikun chule shenma shi?" [What Has Liu Shikun Done?] *Zhengming* 61 (November 1982): 18

7. See Wolfgang Bartke and Peter Schier, *China's New Party Leadership* (New York: M.E. Sharpe, 1985), 231–32; Zhou Tan, "Ye Jianying yu wenge de weimiao guanzi" [Ye Jianying's Subtle Relationship to the Cultural Revolution], *Jing Bao* 29 (December 1979): 32–34.

8. Ellen R. Judd, "Revolutionary Drama and Song in the Jiangxi Soviet," *Modern China* 9 (January 1983): 140.

9. Peking NCNA Domestic Service in Chinese, 1 August 1978, in *FBIS*, 2 August 1978, E4–E5.

10. Zhao Feng, "Women de fengge—'wenzhi binbin' " [Our Style—Gentle], *Renmin Yinyue* (February 1963): 14.

11. Zhao Feng, "Ting Liu Shikun Zhongguo zuopin yanzouhuihou de ganxiang" [Feelings after Hearing a Concert of Liu Shikun's Chinese Compositions], *Renmin Yinyue* (June 1963); 17–18; Hong Shigui, "Liu Shikun Zhongguo gangqin zuopin duzouhui tinghou" [After Hearing Liu Shikun's Recital of Chinese Piano Compositions], *Renmin Yinyue* (June 1963): 19–20; "Recital by a Young Pianist," *Chinese Literature* 9 (1963): 118.

12. Shi Wei, "Cong yanbo Beituofen 'diwu jiaoxiangyue' tan Zhonggong duidai xiyang gudian yinyue de taidu" [From the Broadcast of Beethoven's Fifth Symphony Talk about the Chinese Communists' Attitude toward Western Classical Music], *Guangjiaojing* 55 (April 1977): 10.

13. "Yeh Chien-ying's Criminal Activities in the World of Literature and Art," Beijing *Hung-teng Pao* [Red Lantern News] 3, 20 May 1967, in *JPRS* 41,884 (18 July 1967): 53–56.

14. Liang Heng and Judith Shapiro, *Son of the Revolution* (New York: Vintage Books, 1984), 116–21; Ma Sitson, "Terror at the Hands of the Red Guard," *Life*, 2 June 1967, 22–29, 63–66.

15. These leaders included Li Xiannian, Tan Zhenlin, Xu Xiangqian, and Li Fuchun.

16. Xi Chen, "A Great Struggle to Defend Party Principles—Revealing the

True Nature of a Major Political Incident, the 'February Countercurrent,' Concocted by Lin Biao and the 'Gang of Four', Tenmin Ribao, 26 February 1979 in *FBIS*, 28 February 1979, E7–E20.

17. Zhongyang Yinyue Xueyuan Mao Zedong Sixiang Zhandoutuan Geming Weiyuanhui Zongqinwuzhan, "Guanyu Liu Shikun wenti de shengming" [Proclamation on the Question of Liu Shikun] *Geming Fenglei* [Revolutionary Storm] (15 April 1967).

18. Luo Bing, "Deng Xiaoping zhihui de san da zhanyi" [The Three Great Campaigns under Deng Xiaoping's Command], *Zhengming* 74 (December 1973): 12–13.

19. Richard Curt Kraus, *Class Conflict in Chinese Socialism*, (New York: Columbia University Press, 1981) 120–31; David and Nancy Milton, *The Wind Will Not Subside: Years in Revolutionary China—1964–1969* (New York: Pantheon, 1976), 159–62.

20. Liang and Shapiro, *Son of the Revolution*, 117.

21. *Geming Fenglei* [Revolutionary Storm] (15 April 1967); see also the description of conservatory student and radical activist Peng Ming in Liang and Shapiro, *Son of the Revolution*, 234.

22. "Zhongyang wenge wenyizu zhengshi chengli" [Central Cultural Revolutionary Literature and Art Group Established], Beijing *Jianggangshan* 2 (19 June 1967)

23. "Chen Boda, Jiang Qing deng shouzhang jiejian sige yangbanxi danwei de zuotan jiyao" [Summary of the Conversation of Chen Boda, Jiang Qing, and Other Leaders In Receiving Four Model Opera Units], 9 November 1967, in *Jiang Qing Tongzhi Lun Wenyi* [Comrade Jiang Qing Discusses Literature and Art,] May 1968, 173.

24. Yan Qimei, "Yin Chengzong: you shi yige Li Lianying" [Yin Chengzong: Once Again a Li Lianying], *Dangdai*, [The Present Age] 7 (15 March 1981): 46.

25. Such is the speculation of Han Suyin, *Phoenix Harvest* (London: Triad Grifton Books, 1982), 69, 268.

26. Liu Shikun, "Nuli chuangzuo minzu de gangqin de zuopin" [Make Great Efforts to Create National Piano Compositions], *Renmin Yinyue* 1 (1977): 10.

27. On the May 16 Corps, see Maurice Meisner, *Mao's China: A History of the People's Republic* (New York: Free Press, 1977), 330–34, and Anne F. Thurston, *Enemies of the People* (New York: Alfred A. Knopf, 1987), 142–44.

28. Political Department of the Red Capital Machinery Plant Revolutionary Committee, "The Internationale Inspires Us in Fighting," Jiangxi Radio, 14 September, 1971, in *Union Research Service* 65 (12 November 1971); 183.

29. *China News Analysis* 1062 (3 December 1976): 6. Jie Fu reportedly

died from excitement after the arrest of the Gang of Four, as he was thinking of rehabilitation.

30. Three Main Rules: correct political direction, simple and arduous work-style, flexible strategy and tactics; Eight Points for Attention: speak politely, pay fairly for all purchases, return everything borrowed, pay for any damage, do not hit or swear at people, do not damage crops, take no liberties with women, do not ill-treat prisoners.

31. Hsieh Chen, "A Major Conspiracy to Oppose the Party and Usurp Army Leadership—Exposing the Truth of the So-Called 'Shantung Issue' Concocted by the 'Gang of Four'," *Renmin Ribao,* 12 March 1977, in *FBIS,* 24 March 1977, E12–E16.

32. Ai, "Liu Shikun chule shenma shi?", 18

33. Liu, "Nuli chuangzuo minzu de gangqin de zuopin," 10–12.

34. Lo Chiang, "New Piano Music," Chinese Literature 6 (1975): 110–13; Peking NCNA in English, 4 January 1977, in *FBIS,* 6 January 1977, E15; "Interview with Pianist Liu Shih-kun," Peking, NCNA in English, 7 July 1977, in *SPRCP* 6383 (19 July 1977): 61–63.

35. Peking NCNA in English, 4 January 1977, in *FBIS*, 6 January 1977, E15; "Interview with Pianist Liu Shih-kun," 61–63; Wenhuabu Pipanzu [Ministry of Culture Criticism Group], "Jie 'Sirenbang' sidang Yu Huiyong de laodi" [Expose the Unsavory Past of Yu Huiyong, Sworn Follower of the "Gang of Four"], *Renmin Ribao* (5 November 1977).

36. Yan, "Yin Chengzong: you shi yi ge Li Lianying," 46.

37. Leonard Marcus, "China Chronicles," *High Fidelity* 29 (August 1979): 69.

38. Ko Nan, "Historical Truth and Realistic Struggle—Is Untitled Music Something of No Class Character?" *Kwangming Daily,* 24 January 1974, in *FBIS,* 1 February 1974, B14.

39. Hu Pai-ping and Yu Chiung, "A Political Scheme Cannot be Covered Up with Unpleasant Noise—Commenting on the Gang of Four's So-Called Criticism of Absolute Music," Peking Domestic Service, 6 November 1977, in *FBIS,* 10 November 1977, E9–E10.

40. I thank Arif Dirlik for this information.

41. Roxane Witke, *Comrade Chiang Ch'ing* (Boston: Little, Brown, 1977), 457–58; Joseph Lelyveld, "China Denounces Respighi's Music," *New York Times,* 15 February 1974.

42. Chu Lan, "Grasp the Essence, Deepen the Criticism" reprinted as "Criticize the Revisionist Viewpoint in Music," *Peking Review* 17 (1 March 1974): 18–19.

43. Two collections of articles from this campaign are *Lun Yinyue de Jiejixing,* [On the Class Nature of Music] (Beijing: Renmin Yinyue Chubanshe, 1975); and *Pipan Guanyu Wubiaoti Yinyue de Xiuzhengzhuyi Guandian* [Crit-

icize the Revisionist Viewpoint of Music without Titles] (Guangzhou: Renmin Chubanshe, 1974).

44. I have discussed these issues in "The Rise and Fall of Culture Minister Yu Huiyong" (paper for the Conference on New Perspectives on the Cultural Revolution, Harvard University, 1987).

45. Chu Lan, "Yingdang zhongshi jeichang taolun" [We Should Pay Attention to this Discussion], in *Lun Yinyue de Jieiixing* [On the Class Character of Music] (Beijing: Renmin Chubanshe, 1975), 1–7.

46. Chu, "Shenru pipan zichanjieji de renxinglun," 12–23.

47. Hu and Yu, "A Political Scheme Cannot be Covered Up with Unpleasant Noise."

48. Yu Huiyong led a revolutionary opera troupe to Algeria in 1974. See Hou Dezhang, "Jiang Qing yangbantuan chuguo xianchou ji" [A Record of Jiang Qing's Model Opera Troupe Showing Its Incompetence Abroad], *Zhengming* 54 (April 1982): 68–71, and 55 (May 1982): 67–71.

49. Radicals seized paintings originally commissioned for new tourist hotels under Zhou Enlai's patronage; there was a notorious display of these negative examples of "reactionary" art. See Ellen Johnston Laing, *The Winking Owl: Art in the People's Republic of China* (Berkeley: University of California Press, forthcoming), ch. 8.

50. Anonymous, interview with author, Hong Kong, 13 November 1979.

51. Isabel K. F. Wong, "*Geming Gequ:* Songs for the Education of the Masses," in Bonnie S. McDougall, ed., *Popular Chinese Literature and Performing Arts in the People's Republic of China 1949–1979* (Berkeley: University of California Press, 1984), 119.

52. Chu, "Shenru pipan zichanjieji de renxinglun."

53. Han Mu, "A Farce on the Stage and Behind the Scenes," *Guangming Ribao,* 18 December, 1975, in *SPRCP* 6251 (4 January 1977): 62.

54. For example, see Ma Qilai, "*Guojige*" *Zuoje Baodiai he Digaite* [The Creators of the "Internationale," Pottier and Degeyter] (Beijing: Commercial Press, 1971); Liang Mao, "*Guojige*" *he Bali Gongshe Geming Yinyue* [The "Internationale" and the Revolutionary Music of the Paris Commune] (Beijing: Renmin Yinyue chubanshe, 1978); Hua Wen, "Salute to the Literature of the Paris Commune," *Chinese Literature* 6 (1971): 15–20. The composer Saint-Saëns came in for special criticism for his opposition to the Paris Commune. See Shi Wei, "Cong yanbo Beituofen 'diwu jiaoxiangyue' tan Zhonggong duidai xiyang gudian yinyue de taidu," 12.

55. Zhang Yaowen, "Yi zhandou renwu zuzhi yinyue jiaoyu" [Organize Music Education as a Mission of Struggle], *Renmin Yinyue,* 3 (1976): 25–29.

56. Ying Fen, "Ye tan Zhongguo yinyue sanshi nian" [Some More Discussion of Thirty Years of Chinese Music], *Guanchajia* 22 (August 1979), 64.

57. Ibid., 64.

58. Zhou, "Ye Jianying yu wenge de weimiao guanxi," 32–34.

59. "Interview with Pianist Liu Shih-kun," pp. 61–63; Liu, "Nuli chuangzuo minzu de gangqin de zuopin," 10–12.

60. Zhou, "Ye Jianying yu wenge de weimiao guanxi," 32–34.

61. Perry Link, "Intellectuals and Cultural Policy After Mao," in A. Doak Barnett and Ralph N. Clough, eds., *Modernizing China: Post-Mao Reform and Development* (Boulder, Colo: Westview Press, 1986), 81–102.

62. Ye Jianying, *Speech at the Meeting in Celebration of the 30th Anniversary of the Founding of the People's Republic of China* (Beijing: Foreign Languages Press, 1979).

63. See Kong Qing, "Xiyang ge ruhai" [The Songs of Xiyang are like the Sea], *Renmin Yinyue* 2 (1978): 29–30.

64. Peking NCNA in English, 30 March 1977, in *FBIS*, 30 March 1977, E4; Zhongyang Wuqi Yishu Daxue Yinyuexueyuan Chuangzuo Yanjiushi, "Fangeming wenhua weijiao de pochan" [The Bankruptcy of Counter-Revolutionary Cultural Encirclement], *Renmin Yinyue* 2 (1977): 6–8.

65. Marcus, "China Chronicles," 74.

66. Zhongguo Gewutuan Dapipanzu, "Jiang Qing pohuai minzu gewu zuize nantao" [Jiang Qing Cannot Escape Responsibility for Smashing National Song and Dance], *Renmin Yinyue* 1 (1977): 18–19; Wang Hanwu, "Guchui minzu xuwuzhuyi shi weile touxiang fubi" [Advocating National Nihilism is For the Sake of Capitulation and Restoration], *Renmin Yinyue* 12 (1977): 20.

67. Bi Jizhou, "Zhao Feng fang Gang tan dalu de yinyue jiaoyu" [Zhao Feng Visits Hong Kong and Discusses Mainland Music Education] *Jing Bao* 11 (November 1984): 78–79.

68. Sun Jen, "Ever More Resonantly Sing 'The March of the Volunteers'," *Renmin Yinyue* 214 (January 1983); 4–5.

69. See Huan Daoyi, "Gaoyinlaba naode women buneng xuexi he xiuxi" [Loudspeakers Keep Us from Studying and Sleeping], *Renmin Ribao* (3 September 1977); Yu Yizhen, "Cong yize xiaoxi xiang dao gaoyinlaba" A News Item Calls Loudspeakers to Mind], *Nanfang Ribao* [Southern Daily] (11 April 1979).

70. *Beijing Review* 22 (14 September 1979): 9–14.

71. For example, see Zhang Juhua, "Jianzhi wuchan jieji de dang de wenxue yuanze" [Support the Literary Principles of the Party of the Proletariat], *Shanghai Wenxue* [Shanghai: Literature] (July 1979): 74–78.

72. *FBIS*, 1 November 1978, E30.

73. Ouyang Mei, "Zhongguo dangdai de 'shengnu zhende' " [Contemporary China's "Saint Joan"], *Zhengming* 21 (July 1979); 26–28; "Why Was an Outstanding Woman Communist Killed?" *Beijing Review* 22, (27 July 1979): 19–21; Zhang Zhixin, "Shei de Zui" [Whose Crime?] *Gequ* (July 1979): 2;

Zhang Zhiqin, " 'Yao ba qin dang qiang shi' " ["Use Your Violin as a Gun"], *Renmin Yinyue* 173 (August 1979): 3–4. See the discussion of the campaign for Zhang's memory in Colin Mackerras, *The Performing Arts in Contemporary China* (London: Routledge & Kegan Paul, 1981), 173–74.

74. Liu Manqin, "Zhuming nugangqinjia Gu Shengying zhi si" [The Death of the Famous Female Pianist Gu Shengying], *Zhengming* 23 (September 1979): 14–19.

75. On He Luting's rehabilitation, see Xiao Ding and Xu Yin, "Yinggutou yinyuejia He Luting" [Hard-boned Musician He Luting], *Jiefang Ribao* [Liberation Daily], 13 January 1979; reprinted in *Renmin Yinyue* 167 (February 1979): 10–13.

76. One publicized case involved Li Chunyi, a music historian at Beijing's Music Research Institute. Li's probationary Party membership was revoked in the 1957 campaign. Yang Guang, then the office manager for the institute, was purged during the Cultural Revolution, as was Li, of course. When both men were rehabilitated in the later 1970s, Yang resumed his harassment of Li, allegedly still interfering with Li's Party membership and his plans for foreign travel. Ying Fen, "Yinyueshijia Li Chunyi shou yazhi" [The Suppression of Music Historian Li Chunyi], *Guanchajia* 38 (20 December 1980): 14–15.

77. "Democratic Parties Enrol New Members," *Beijing Review* 24 (25 May 1981): 6; "Non-Communist Parties Getting Bigger," *Beijing Review* 29 (1 December 1986), 5–6.

78. "Interview with Pianist Liu Shih-kun," pp. 61–62; Liu, "Nuli chuangzuo minzu de gangqin de zuopin," 10–12.

79. Contrasting accounts by foreigners then resident in Beijing are in Edoarda Masi, *China Winter: Workers, Mandarins, and the Purge of the Gang of Four* (New York: E.P. Dutton, 1982), 302–3; and Erwin Wickert, *The Middle Kingdom: Inside China Today* (London: Harvill Press, 1983), 126–28.

80. See the excellent account of the Toronto Symphony's 1978 visit to China in Tim Brook, "The Revival of China's Musical Culture," *The China Quarterly* 77 (March 1979): 113–21.

81. Peking NCNA in English 26 May 1977, in *FBIS*, 26 May, 1977, A9.

82. Beijing NCNA in English, 28 June 1978, in *FBIS*, 29 June, 1978, A1–A2; Beijing *Xinhua* in English, 19 March 1979, in *FBIS*, 20 March, 1979, B1–B2; "The Boston Goes to China," CBS Documentary, 27 April 1979.

83. Henry Scott-Stokes, "Ozawa Impressed With Upbeat China," *New York Times*, 20 June 1978.

84. For a profile of the center, see Ling Yuan, " 'Come On Over, the Climate Fine'," *Beijing Review* 31, (7–13 March 1988): 35–37.

85. Bi Jizhou, "Luoyi beishang de haiwai huayi yinyuejia" [A Continuous Stream Northward of Overseas Musicians of Chinese Origin], *Jing Bao* 50 (September 1981): 65, 67–69.

86. Bai Yunfei, "Xiaotiqin jiaoyujia Zheng Xianghe" [Master Violin Teacher Zheng Xianghe], *Guanchajia* [The Observer] 17 (March 1979): 68–69.

87. "Music Craze in Guangzhou," *Beijing Review* 30 (7–13 December 1987): 45–46.

88. Electronic organs are popular, costing a few hundred *renminbi*, and violins can be bought for between forty and seventy *renminbi*.

89. Americans also speculate in pianos, counting on their rising value as commodities. See Nancy I. Ross, "Imports Invade U.S. Piano Market," *Los Angeles Times*, 6 March 1987.

90. "Jianxian duanni de Zhejiang Gangqinchang" [The Gradually Learning Zhejiang Piano Factory], *Shijie Jingii Daoboa*, [World Economic Report] (24 March 1986); "Winning Musicians Show Their Talents," *Beijing Review* 27 (30 April 1984): 34.

91. Officials at Guangzhou Piano Factory, interviews with author, Guangzhou, 13 February 1986; Yin Chengzong, interview with author, Eugene, Ore. 25–28 February 1988.

92. Her name is not Peng, and she is from a different city. Interview with author, Eugene, Ore., 16 April 1987.

93. Beijing *Xinhua* in English, 9 April 1986.

94. "Self-Employed Man Joins the Party," *Beijing Review* (5 November 1984): 30.

95. Guangdong art teacher, interview with author, Hong Kong, 30 October 1979.

96. "Zhongxiaoxue ying jiaqiang yinyue meishu jiaoyu" [Middle and Elementary Schools Must Strengthen Education in Music and Fine Arts], *Guangming Ribao* (29 May 1979).

97. Zhou Fanfu, "Wanjiu Zhongguo yinyue jiaoyu de zhongyao jianyishu" [An Important Proposal to Save China's Music Education], *Jing Bao* [The Mirror] (January 1986): 85.

98. "Students Lack Artistic Training," *Beijing Review* 28 (26 August 1985): 32.

99. Zhou, "Wanjiu Zhongguo yinyue jiaoyu de zhongyao jianyishu," 84–85. American music educators have very similar concerns. Classical music fans make up only between three and six percent of the U.S. population, and little growth is likely without more music in schools. But there is anxiety over competition for resources with technical subjects. Paul R. Lehman, associate dean of the University of Michigan School of Music, hoped "that the new obsession with excellence and the interest in standards and quality will spread beyond English, mathematics and science to include music programs. But I am concerned that the renewed emphasis on academics will leave even less room in the schedule for music." Gene I. Maeroff, "Classical Music Not Their Thing," *New York Times*, 12 April 1984.

100. Bi Jizhou, "Zhuming gangqinjia Zhou Guangren duanzhi yiwai de qianyin hougou" [The Background and Consequences of the Accidental Severing of the Fingers of Famous Pianist Zhou Guangren], *Jing Bao* 32 (September 1982): 59–60.

101. See John Fitzgerald, "A New Cultural Revolution: The Commercialization of Culture in China," *The Australian Journal of Chinese Affairs* 11 (January 1984): 105–20.

102. Bi Jizhou, " 'Xiang qian kan' gei dalu yinyuejie dailai weiji" [The Crisis Brought to the Music World by "Looking toward Money"], *Guanchajia* 38 (20 December 1980): 46, 69; John F. Burns, "Chinese Conductor Revisits Home," *New York Times,* 4 September 1985.

103. Shu Zhaoqin, "Dui Zhongguo yishutuan de qiwang" [Hopes for the Chinese Arts Troupe], *Jing Bao* 7 (July 1979): 17.

104. I attended this recital.

105. Yan, "Yin Chengzong: you shi yige Li Lianying," 43–46.

106. Angus Heriot, *The Castrati in Opera* (London: Secker & Warburg, 1956), 95–110.

107. Link, "Intellectuals and Cultural Policy After Mao," 90.

108. Chin Min, " 'Ezhu yingxu chan wan gan' " ["Wicked Conduct Can Destroy Legions"], *Jing Bao* 2 (10 February 1983): 16–19; Ai, "Liu Shikun chule shenma shi?", 18.

109. Luo Bing, "Deng Xiaoping zhihui de san da zhanyi" [The Three Great Campaigns under Deng Xiaoping's Command], *Zhengming* 74 (December 1983): 12–13; Luo Bing, "Ye Jianying ciguan de beijing" [The Background of Ye Jianying's Resignation], *Zhengming* 65 (March 1983): 7–9; Luo Bing, "Da huanban yu taizidang" [The Big Personnel Shuffle and the Party of Crown Princes], *Zhengming* 94 (August 1985): 8; Chang Chuan, "Ye Jianying yu Liu Shikun daidu'an" [Ye Jianying and the Liu Shikun Drug-Smuggling Case], *Zhengming* 109 (November 1986): 11.

110. Huang Gongzhi, "Chaojutuan zousi'an de yubo" [The Implication of the Chaozhou Opera Company Smuggling Case], *Zhengming* 41 (March 1981): 17.

111. For background on this movement, see Thomas B. Gold, " 'Just in Time!' China Battles Spiritual Pollution on the Eve of 1984," *Asian Survey* 24 (September 1984): 947–75; Colin Mackerras, " 'Party Consolidation' and the Attack on 'Spiritual Pollution'," *The Australian Journal of Chinese Affairs* (January 1984): 175–86.

112. "Chang P'ing-hua's Speech to Cadres on the Cultural Front," *Issues & Studies* 14 (December 1978): 116–17. "They should have been better behaved. Although there is no regulation that school students cannot fall in love, is it worthwhile cultivating colleges [*sic*] students who decide to marry in a few months after they have been enrolled into a college, or those who are

swollen with pregnancy before marriage?'' ''Let me make it clear today that whoever acts recklessly in the relations between men and women and make them the talk of the town will be punished. We must put a stop to this evil wind.'' Zhang asked why artists are so susceptible to affairs. Perhaps, he decided, they yield to impulse too easily, or have more opportunities. They should avoid imitating Lin Liguo or Wang Hongwen.

113. See Beverly Hooper, *Youth in China* (Ringwood, Victoria: Penguin Books Australia, 1985).

114. ''Winning Musicians Show Their Talents,'' *Beijing Review* (30 April 1984): 34.

115. Luo Bing, ''Liangge jingren de da anjian'' [Two Startling Cases], *Zhengming* 105 (July 1986): 6–7; Luo Bing, ''Deng Xiaoping huishang piping Chen Yun'' [Deng Xiaoping Criticizes Chen Yun at a Meeting], *Zhengming* 108 (October 1986): 11; Chang, ''Ye Jianying yu Liu Shikun daidu'an,'' 11–12; Eric Pace, ''Marshal Ye Jianying Dies at 90; Had Been China's Head of State,'' *New York Times,* 23 October 1986.

116. Shi Shan, ''Liu Shikun yi huo shifang'' [Liu Shikun Freed], *Dongxiang* 40 (July 1987): 11.

7   The Power of Music, the Music of Power

1. Donal Henahan, ''What Makes a Gifted Artist Drop Out in Mid-Career?'' *New York Times* 17 August 1986; Brenda Lucas Ogdon and Michael Kerr, *Virtuoso: The Story of John Ogdon* (London: Hamish Hamilton, 1981).

2. For instance, see ''Violin Competition Features Chinese Works,'' *Beijing Review* 30 (1 June 1987): 32; ''Thirty Years of Development,'' *Beijing Review* 29 34 (25 August 1986): 24; Liang Maochun, ''Lun He Luting zuopin de xuanlu'' [On the Melodies in the Works of He Luting], *Yinyue Yishu* (Musical Art) (1984): 43.

3. See the excellent discussion in Merrilyn Fitzpatrick, ''China Images Abroad: The Representation of China in Western Documentary Films,'' *The Australian Journal of Chinese Affairs* 9 (January 1983): 87–98.

4. Bunny McBride, ''Releasing China's Musical Soul,'' *South China Morning Post,* 6 January 1980.

5. *Within* the West, the international language metaphor makes more sense. Boccherini, Mozart, Haydn, Cimarosa, Handel, Stravinsky, Bartók, Martinů, Hindemith, Britten, Schoenberg have worked in various Western nations, and their music is clearly intelligible throughout our culture. This is quite different from the cultural relations between the West and Asia or Africa.

6. Steve Lundgren and Lisa Kosse, ''Famed Soviet Pianist 'Speaks' Universal Language of Peace,'' *Oregon Daily Emerald,* 13 February 1987.

7. According to Mark Swed, "Emigré Pianist: Is on the Run—and Enjoying it," *Los Angeles Times,* 22 April 1988:

> As Feltsman stepped off the plane Aug. 18, he walked right into the American dream. The ubiquitous flash bulbs and bright television lights from the world's media were waiting for him. (It hardly hurt that Feltsman and his attractive wife are particularly photogenic.)
>
> Also waiting for him was the teaching post in New Paltz, with a comfortable salary of $80,000. Columbia Artists, the kingmaker among music managements, signed him. So did CBS Records, which had already released a tape of Chopin preludes that had to be smuggled out of the Soviet Union. Last September, Feltsman played a command performance at the White House. In November, he made his Carnegie Hall debut and within a few weeks, a recording of that event was rushed to the stores in time for Christmas shoppers.

8. Henry Kamm, "Popular Vietnamese Pianist Being Barred from the U.S.," *New York Times,* 3 May 1987.

9. Hedwig and E. H. Mueler von Asow, eds., *The Collected Correspondence and Papers of Christoph Willibald Gluck* (New York: St. Martin's Press, 1962), 46–47.

10. For dedicatory epistles by eighteenth-century musicians illustrating the same point, see Jacques Attali, *Noise: The Political Economy of Music* (Minneapolis: University of Minnesota Press, 1985), 47–49.

11. David Cairns, ed., *The Memoirs of Hector Berlioz* (New York: W.W. Norton, 1975), 393.

12. Karl Geiringer, *Brahms: His Life and Work* (Garden City: Anchor Books, 1961), 99.

13. See Walter Salmen, "Social Obligations of the Emancipated Musician in the 19th Century," in Walter Salmen, ed., *The Social Status of the Professional Musician from the Middle Ages to the 19th Century* (New York: Pendragon Press, 1983), 265–81.

14. Edward A. Gargan, "Symphonic Voice from China is Heard Again," *New York Times* 11 October 1987.

15. Theodor W. Adorno, *Introduction to the Sociology of Music* (New York: Seabury Press, 1976), 55.

16. Theodore W. Adorno, "On the Social Situation of Music," *Telos* 35 (Spring 1978): 145.

17. See the discussion of commercial *chinoiserie* in Debora Silverman, *Selling Culture: Bloomingdales, Diana Vreeland, and the New Aristocracy of Taste in Reagan's America* (New York: Pantheon, 1986).

18. Lo Chiang, "New Piano Music," *Chinese Literature* 6 (1975): 113.

19. Musicologist Robert Trotter, former dean of the University of Oregon Music School, spent several months of 1985 at the Shanghai Conservatory. Trotter had a difficult time even finding out when Chinese music would be

performed, as his cosmopolitan hosts presumed that a Westerner would not be interested in hearing it. Interview with author, Eugene, Ore., 17 September 1986.

20. See "Chang P'ing-hua's Speech to Cadres on the Cultural Front," *Issues & Studies* 14 (December 1978): 98–99.

21. See David M. Bachman, *Chen Yun and the Chinese Political System* (Berkeley: University of California Center for Chinese Studies, 1985), esp. 72–73, 87; Chen's musical writings were published in *Chen Yun Tongzhi Guanyu Pingtan De Tanhua He Tongxin* [Comrade Chen Yun's Talks and Notices about Pingtan] (Beijing: Zhongguo Quyi Chubanshe, 1983).

22. I heard the Vanguard Ensemble perform in two concerts in September 1987 as part of the Chinese Arts Festival in Beijing. Its use of massed winds produced a music that was at once harsh and majestic.

23. Bi Jizhou, "Zhongguo yinyue fazhan de xiandaihua wenti" [The Problem of Modernization in China's Musical Development], *Jing Bao* 2 (10 February 1980): 68–69.

24. Wei Liming, "Criticism: Key to Flourishing Culture," *Beijing Review* 29 (7 July 1986): 13–16.

25. "Young Troupe Keeps Shaoxing Opera Vital," *Beijing Review* 27 (5 November 1984): 32–33. The Cultural Revolution's model theatrical works are far from dead. Beijing's Central Ballet Troupe performed the first act of *The Red Detachment of Women* December 4–11, 1987, according to the program in *China Daily,* 5 December 1987. From Fuzhou, I watched China Television's New Year's broadcast on February 8, 1986, which included a selection from *The Red Lantern,* "modernized" with electric guitars and a strong beat.

26. Robert E. Fogel, "Traditional Music and the Middle Class in Argentina: Context and Currents," in Caroline Card, John Hasse, Roberta L. Singer, and Ruth M. Stone, eds., *Discourse in Ethnomusicology: Essays in Honor of George List* (Bloomington: Indian University Ethnomusicology Publications Group, 1978): 267–84.

27. Fogel, "Traditional Music and the Middle Class in Argentina, 275.

28. David Murray, "The Romantic Piano: Chopin to Ravel," in Dominic Gill, ed., *The Book of the Piano* (Ithaca: Cornell University Press, 1981), 93.

29. Bob Davis, "Hear! Hear! Addicts of High-End Hi-Fi Insist on Perfection," *Wall Street Journal,* 23 May 1986.

30. Sam Jameson, "Japanese Still Have Few Friends in Asia," *Los Angeles Times,* 18 August 1985.

31. Edwin M. Good, *Giraffes, Black Dragons, and other Pianos: A Technological History from Cristofori to the Modern Concert Grand* (Stanford: Stanford University Press, 1982), 217.

32. "His victory was every American pianist's victory. American artists

who had previously figured only in national competitions were suddenly acknowledged in the international arena. A career as a pianist was finally considered valid and important." Judith Oringer, *Passion for the Piano* (Los Angeles: Jeremy P. Tarcher, 1983), 98.

33. Oringer, 102.

34. "Shenma shi woguo jiaoxiang yishu fazhan de daolu" [What Is the Road That Our National Symphonic Art Should Develop?] *Renmin Yinyue* (June 1958): 28–29.

35. Henry Raynor, *A Social History of Music from the Middle Ages to Beethoven* (New York: Schocken Books, 1972), 36–53.

36. "Beethoven and the Central Philharmonic," *Beijing Review* 26 (26 September 1983): 29–30.

37. See Bernard Holland, "Concert: From China, Central Philharmonic," *The New York Times,* 13 October 1987; Gargan, "Symphonic Voice From China is Heard Again;" Ma Baolin, "Debut in the United States," *Beijing Review* 31 (11–17 January 1988): 31–33. I heard the Central Philharmonic in the Beijing Concert Hall on September 24, 1987, immediately before its tour. This concert featured a truly rousing performance of Dvořák's Eighth Symphony.

38. K. Robert Schwarz, "John Adams: Music of Contradictions," *New York Times,* 11 January 1987.

39. George Fencl, "Confucian Music and Its Modern Fate: Communist Provincials and Chinese Cosmopolitans," (Honors thesis, Harvard College, 1984), would add the museum of Chinese traditional music, as well.

40. Bi Jizhou, "Chen Gang Discusses Musical Composition," *Jing Bao* 1 (10 January 1982): 68.

41. Zhang Shixiang, "Teaching Violin Abroad," *Beijing Review* 31 (8–14 February 1988), 45.

42. See the article by Fang Kun, "A Discussion of Chinese National Music Traditions," originally published in *Renmin Yinyue* 178 (January 1980): 38–40, trans. with Western responses in *Asian Music* 12 (1981): 1–16.

43. Andrew Horvat, "Japan Hits Joyous Note with Beethoven," *Los Angeles Times,* 30 December 1985.

44. See Bruno Nettl, *The Western Impact on World Music: Change, Adaptation, and Survival* (New York: Schirmer Books, 1985).

45. "Intellectual and Intellectual Ideology," *Beijing Review* 29 (15 December 1986): 16–17 (originally in *Guangming Ribao).* Fang had criticized Engels for being unscientific in 1986, leading to temporarily thwarted demands for his expulsion from the Party. See Luo Bing, "Beidaihe huiyi neiqing" [Inside the Beidaihe Conference], *Zhengming* 107 (September 1986): 9. I discuss Fang more thoroughly in "The Lament of Astrophysicist Fang Lizhi: China's intellectuals in a Global Context," in Arif Dirlik and Maurice Meis-

ner, eds., *Marxism and the Chinese Experience: Issues of Socialism in a Third World Socialist Society* (Durham: Duke University Press, 1989).

46. Ni Zhengmao, "Establishing Intellectuals' Constitutional Status," *Beijing Review* 29 (15 December 1986): 19 (originally in *World Economic Herald*, 10 November 1986).

47. See Anita Chan, Stanley Rosen, and Jonathan Unger, eds., *On Socialist Democracy and the Chinese Legal System: The Li Yizhe Debates* (White Plains, N.Y.: M. E. Sharpe, 1985).

48. Lu Ming, "Li Zhengtian tan Wang Xizhe" [Li Zhengtian Discusses Wang Xizhe], *Zhengming* 82 (August 1984): 32–33; Liu Ying, "Chaunqi renwu Li Zhengtian" [The Legend of Li Zhengtian], *Zhengming* 17 (February 1979): 20–23.

49. Wang Meng, "The Wind on the Plateau," *Chinese Literature* (Autumn 1986): 3–23, esp. 8, 11, 19.

50. Zhang Xiangliang, *Mimosa* (Beijing: Panda Books, 1985), 108.

51. "Pavarotti Enthralls Chinese Audiences," *Beijing Review* 29 (14 July 1986): 31–32.

52. See Gao Ming, "Beijing yinyuejie de weiji" [The Crisis of Beijing's Musical World], *Guangjiaoiing* [Wide Angle] 161 (February 1986), 54–55.

53. Nancy L. Ross, "Imports Invade U.S. Piano Market," *Los Angeles Times,* 6 March 1987.

54. Personal visit, September 1987.

55. Gu Er, "Dianying 'Huang Tudi' guanhou gan" [Thoughts after Seeing the Film "Yellow Earth"], *Zhengming* 93 (July 1985): 50–51; Zheng Wei, "New Film Sparks Controversy and Acclaim," *Beijing Review* 29 (10 February 1986): 30–32.

56. Wang Meng, *The Butterfly and Other Stories* (Beijing: Panda Books, 1983), 41, 68.

57. "Farmers Blow Their Own Horn," *Beijing Review* 29 (24 March 1986): 24–26; Yuan Ping, "Fascination is the word for 'bumpkin' brass band," *China Daily,* 12 February 1986.

58. See Richard Curt Kraus, "Culture," in Anthony J. Kane and John Major, eds. *China Briefing 1987* (Boulder, Co.: Westview Press, 1987), 118.

59. "Rural Areas Need Musical Instruments," *Beijing Review* 27 (27 August 1984) 31.

60. "Peasants Lack Education, Culture," *Beijing Review* 28 (16 December 1985): 27.

61. E. Perry Link, Jr., *Mandarin Ducks and Butterflies: Popular Fiction in Early Twentieth-Century Chinese Cities* (Berkeley: University of California Press, 1981), 240.

62. Martin King Whyte and William L. Parish, *Urban Life in Contemporary China* (Chicago: University of Chicago Press, 1984), 177.

63. Walter Wiora, "Of Art Music and Cultural Classes," in Edmond Strainchamps and Maria Rika Manites, eds., *Music and Civilization: Essays in Honor of Paul Henry Lang* (New York: W.W. Norton, 1984), 472–77. See also Adorno, *Introduction to the Sociology of Music,* 162.

64. Malcom W. Browne, "Hindenburg is Still Aflame in Memories," *New York Times,* 6 May 1987.

65. Yang Qi, "Guanyu yinyue yishu de 'jiejixing' wenti" [On the Question of the "Class Nature" of Musical Art], *Renmin Yinyue* 192 (March 1981): 25–29.

66. Moral commitment in Chinese art flows from Russian influence as well as Confucian heritage. "The moral political commitment, without which Marxist aesthetics would not be what it is, was characteristic of Russian nineteenth-century realism, in which socialist realism had its roots, it is not characteristic of realism *per se."* Carl Dalhaus, *Realism in Nineteenth-Century Music* (Cambridge: Cambridge University Press, 1985), 5.

67. Ye Chunzhi, "Zenyang ting yinyue" [How to Listen to Music], and Zhao Jiazi, "Zenyang ting jiaoxiangyue" [How to Listen to Symphonic Music], in Zhang Zhiquo, ed., *Wenyi Xiuyang Yu Jianshang* [Cultivation and Appreciation of Literature and Art] (Shanghai: Shanghai Renmin Chubanshe; 1982), 15–39.

68. Allan Bloom, *The Closing of the American Mind* (New York: Simon & Schuster, 1987), 80.

69. Wang Xin, "Classical Music in Crescendo," *Beijing Review* 30 (16 March, 1987): 9.

70. "Li Delun tan woguo jiaoxiang yinyue shiye" [Li Delun Discusses the Task of Our Nation's Symphonic Music], *Renmin Yinyue* 187 (October 1980): 5.

71. Bo Juyi, "The Forsaken Qin," in T. C. Lai and Robert Mok, *Jade Flute: The Story of Chinese Music* (Hong Kong: Hong Kong Book Centre, 1981), 90.

Index